MAKING AVONLEA:
L.M. MONTGOMERY AND
POPULAR CULTURE

Since the publication of *Anne of Green Gables* in 1908, L.M. Montgomery and the world of Anne have burgeoned into a global cultural phenomenon, popular not only in Canada, but in countries as diverse as Japan, the United States, and Iran. *Making Avonlea*, the first study to focus on Montgomery and her characters as popular cultural icons, brings together twenty-three scholars from around the world to examine Montgomery's work, its place in our imagination, and its myriad spin-offs including musicals, films, television series, T-shirts, dolls, and a tourist industry.

Invoking theories of popular culture, film, literature, drama, and tourism, the essayists probe the emotional attachment and loyalty of many generations of mostly female readers to Montgomery's books while also scrutinizing the fierce controversies that surround these books and their author's legacy in Canada. Twenty-five illustrations of theatre and film stills, artwork, and popular cultural artifacts, as well as short pieces featuring personal reflections on Montgomery's novels, are interwoven with scholarly essays to provide a complete picture of the Montgomery cultural phenomenon. Mythopoetics, erotic romance, and visual imagination are subjects of discussion, as is the commercial success of a variety of television series and movies, musicals, and plays based on the Anne books. Scholars are also concerned with the challenges and disputes that surround the translation of Montgomery's work from print to screen and with the growth of tourist sites and websites that have moved Avonlea into new cultural landscapes. *Making Avonlea* allows the reader to travel to these sites and to consider Canada's most enduring literary figure and celebrity author in light of their status as international icons almost one hundred years after their arrival on the scene.

IRENE GAMMEL is a professor of English at the University of Prince Edward Island.

MAKING AVONLEA

L.M. Montgomery
  and
Popular Culture

Edited by Irene Gammel

UNIVERSITY OF TORONTO PRESS
Toronto Buffalo London

© University of Toronto Press Incorporated 2002
Toronto Buffalo London
Printed in Canada

ISBN 0-8020-3558-2 (cloth)
ISBN 0-8020-8433-8 (paper)

Printed on acid-free paper

National Library of Canada Cataloguing in Publication Data

Main entry under title:

Making Avonlea : L.M. Montgomery and popular culture

Includes bibliographical references.
ISBN 0-8020-3558-2 (bound)   ISBN 0-8020-8433-8 (pbk.)

1. Montgomery, L. M. (Lucy Maud), 1874–1942 – Appreciation.
2. Montgomery, L. M. (Lucy Maud), 1874–1942 – Film and video
adaptations.   3. Popular culture – Canada – History – History – 20th
century.   I. Gammel, Irene

PS8526.O55Z794 2002   C813 .52   C2002-900610-4
PR9199.3.M6Z82 2002

University of Toronto Press acknowledges the financial assistance to its
publishing program of the Canada Council for the Arts and the Ontario Arts
Council.

This book has been published with the help of a grant from the Humanities
and Social Sciences Federation of Canada, using funds provided by the
Social Sciences and Humanities Research Council of Canada.

University of Toronto Press acknowledges the financial support for its
publishing activities of the Government of Canada through the Book
Publishing Industry Development Program (BPIDP).

In memory of
Elizabeth F. Percival

Contents

II. VIEWING AVONLEA: FILM, TELEVISION, DRAMA, AND MUSICAL

III. TOURING AVONLEA: LANDSCAPE, TOURISM, AND SPIN-OFF PRODUCTS

Acknowledgments

Having edited several anthologies of essays, I have learned that contributor dedication and willingness to work within the larger thematic structure of the book are paramount in producing a collection that truly works as a book. I wish to thank the contributors, who have been exceptional in working towards this goal. I wish to thank the anonymous reviewers whose enthusiastic and detailed comments helped further sharpen the book's focus and structure. Many people have been involved in the process of shepherding the book to its final stages, but I wish to thank the following on a very personal note: Elizabeth R. Epperly, for planting the roots of Montgomery at the University of Prince Edward Island; Carole Gerson, Mary Henley Rubio, and Elizabeth Waterston, for brilliant scholarly role modelling; and J. Paul Boudreau, for inspirational counsel and generous support in procuring visual materials. I am grateful to the students in my Fall 2000 L.M. Montgomery course at the University of Prince Edward Island and to my Spring 2001 graduate students at the Friedrich-Schiller-Universität Jena and Erfurt Universität, Germany; they tested many of the ideas presented in this book and introduced me to new perspectives. I wish to thank the Canadian Association for Canadian Studies, the German Association for Canadian Studies, and the Canadian Embassy in Germany for making possible a series of guest lectures in Canada and Germany that allowed me to deepen and refine the ideas presented in this book. I am grateful to the Social Sciences and Humanities Research Council of Canada for supporting the research for and writing of this manuscript. For expert help with the manuscript, I am grateful to the dedicated staff at the University of Toronto Press: Siobhan McMenemy, who enthusiastically supported and helped shape this book; Frances Mundy, who shepherded the manuscript through its production stages; Margaret Allen, whose sharp eye helped catch errors and smooth over stylistic bumps; and the designers who created the book's attractive look.

Excerpts from *The Selected Journals of L.M. Montgomery*, volumes I, II, III, and IV © 1985, 1987, 1992, 1998 University of Guelph, edited by Mary Rubio and Elizabeth Waterston, and published by Oxford University Press Canada, are reproduced with the permission of Mary Rubio, Elizabeth Waterston, and the University of Guelph, courtesy of the L.M. Montgomery Collection, Archival and Special Collections, University of Guelph Library. Other material written by L.M. Montgomery is excerpted with the permission of Ruth Macdonald and David Macdonald, trustee, who are the heirs of L.M. Montgomery. *The Alpine Path* and *The Poetry of L.M. Montgomery* are published by Fitzhenry and Whiteside Ltd. *My Dear Mr. M.: Letters to MacMillan from L.M. Montgomery* is distributed by Fitzhenry and Whiteside Ltd. *The Green Gables Letters: From L.M. Montgomery to Ephraim Weber, 1905–1909* is published by Borealis Press. 'L.M. Montgomery,' 'The Blue Castle,' 'Emily,' 'Emily of New Moon,' and related indicia are trademarks of Heirs of L.M. Montgomery Inc. and are used with permission. All rights reserved. 'Anne of Green Gables,' 'Avonlea,' and other indicia of 'Anne' are trademarks and Canadian official marks of the Anne of Green Gables Licencing Authority Inc. of Prince Edward Island and are used with permission. In Andrea McKenzie's chapter, the author has made every effort to search for and contact the publishers and the artists' estates for any necessary permissions.

Quotations from *Anne of Green Gables: The Musical* are reproduced with the kind permission of Elaine Campbell, Norman Campbell, Don Harron, and Mavor Moore. Quotations from Paul Ledoux's stage play *Anne* are reproduced with the permission of Paul Ledoux. Quotations from the television series *Emily of New Moon* are reproduced with the permission of Salter Street/CINAR. Quotations from the television series *The Road to Avonlea, Anne of Green Gables, Anne of Green Gables: The Sequel,* and *Anne of Green Gables: The Continuing Story* are reproduced with the permission of Sullivan Entertainment.

This book is dedicated to the memory of Elizabeth F. Percival, a friend, a staunch feminist, and a long-time supporter of L.M. Montgomery studies. We miss her.

Abbreviations

AA	*Anne of Avonlea*
AAGG	*The Annotated Anne of Green Gables*
AGG	*Anne of Green Gables*
AIs	*Anne of the Island*
AHD	*Anne's House of Dreams*
AP	*The Alpine Path*
EC	*Emily Climbs*
ENM	*Emily of New Moon*
EQ	*Emily's Quest*
SJ	*The Selected Journals of L.M. Montgomery*
USB	Unpublished Scrapbooks

MAKING AVONLEA:
L.M. MONTGOMERY AND
POPULAR CULTURE

Making Avonlea: An Introduction

IRENE GAMMEL

'The freckle-faced, red-haired and verbosely romantic orphan dreamer, Anne Shirley, has become the closest any Canadian literary equivalent can get to Mickey Mouse.' So write the Canadian journalists Geoff Pevere and Greig Dymond in their 1996 book, *Mondo Canuck: A Canadian Pop Culture Odyssey* (13). Montgomery might well have turned in her grave to hear Anne Shirley compared to Walt Disney's cartoon character. Yet the backhanded compliment is apt in highlighting Anne Shirley's popular mass appeal not just in Canada but in the world. No other Canadian author has been able to create and sustain an industry that has supported an entire provincial economy for decades through tourism, consumer items, musicals, and films. No other author has had Montgomery's sustained power to export Canadian literature and culture around the world. No other author has come to be associated so forcefully and emotionally with the nation's cultural heritage. The epithet accompanying Montgomery is that of 'Canada's most beloved author.' Indeed, when it comes to defending 'Anne' in the national and popular media, it is frequently done in the name of defending an important part of Canada's heritage. As we enter the world of Avonlea, consider a few 'L.M. Montgomery and Popular Culture' snapshots.

Snapshot 1: Cavendish, Green Gables House, Guestbook Testimonials: Every year the Green Gables site is the destination for 200,000 national and international visitors, who inspect Anne's room, Matthew's room, and the surroundings. 'Today I revisited my childhood. Anne, my literary kindred spirit, is alive and well in Cavendish,' writes a woman from North Carolina (17 July 2000), her neat and energetic writing spilling over the borders of the allocated line space on the guest card:

I.1   Melissa Chapin posing with Anne braids and hat in front of Green Gables, Cavendish, 2001. Photograph by J. Paul Boudreau.

'You have managed to create the right feel. It seemed like Green Gables when I walked up to the house. The interior seemed a bit fancy for Marilla but other than that everything seems alright.' As we flip through these cards, we find testimonials of deeply felt connections. A young woman from Dorval, Quebec (August 1998), proclaims her dream in small upright letters: 'Je veux aussi être écrivaine!' – 'I too want to be a writer!' 'Canada can be proud of this restoration,' writes a male visitor from Florida (19 June 2000).[1] Many young visitors, like twelve-year-old Andrea Chapin of Oakville, Ontario, have completed school projects on Montgomery before visiting the house; Andrea's five-year-old sister, Melissa, dons the red braids and hat for a picture-perfect Anne impersonation (figure I.1).

Snapshot 2: Discussion of the 'Anne' Licence Plate at the University of Prince Edward Island, Fall 2000. In my third-year university English course devoted to 'L.M. Montgomery,' the twenty-seven students enrolled are mostly Island students, including a distant Montgomery relative. As we discuss Montgomery and popular culture, a quick debate arises about the highly visible and controversial 'Anne' licence plate (figure I.2). Living with these symbols, everybody has an opinion. The usual objections are voiced in our discussion. That the Anne plate caters too much to the tourist industry. That it looks too much like a caricature, with Anne's orange braids and Green Gables in the background. That California would not put Mickey Mouse on its licence plate, would it? That the heirs of Montgomery had not been consulted about the plate. That the plate should have said, 'Birthplace of L.M. Montgomery.' All of this was being aired when a mature student – who knew Montgomery's work inside out and whose literary credentials could not be doubted – proclaimed from her back seat: 'When I wash my car, it is the first thing I wash – I just love it.' It stopped short the discussion. Perhaps some of us were secretly delighted with this turn, having formed a quietly illicit bond with our disreputable Anne plates.

Snapshot 3: The Royal Atlantic Canadian Wax Museum, Cavendish (figure I.3). In the foreground, Anne rises tall and serious, uncannily life-like. In the background, a bespectacled Montgomery looks out from behind the Green Gables window façade. If it weren't for her extravagant hat and her name on the window-sill, we might mistake her for Marilla. The boundaries between fiction and reality disappear in this hyperreal simulacrum. And why not? Some young Islanders grow up believing that Anne really existed and are disappointed when they first learn that Anne, like Santa Claus, is fictional.

I.2   Prince Edward Island licence plate, 2001. Photograph by J. Paul Boudreau.

As these anecdotes illustrate, once situated within the domain of popular culture, Montgomery's name becomes a complex construct. No longer does it represent just the author of books; it also represents the author behind a 'pop culture' industry that includes musicals, films, tourist sites, an official provincial licence plate, dolls, postcards, t-shirts, spin-off books, and much more, as Montgomery's value spawns a multimillion dollar industry in tourism and entertainment. This value, in turn, makes her name a fiercely contested arena today. In the twenty-first century, more than five decades after her death, and more than nine decades after the publication of *Anne of Green Gables* (1908), Montgomery's name is more hotly disputed than ever. She is the only Canadian author today who commands both local and national media attention with regular, full-feature reports. Readers will recall the court case during the 1990s that pitted the Province of Prince Edward Island against the heirs of L.M. Montgomery (since then settled), and the court case that has locked the Montgomery heirs in fierce battle with Kevin Sullivan. Avonlea, far from being an idyllic and innocent pastoral space, is a highly contested and litigated arena in which passions about the appropriate representations of Montgomery's name and legacy run high.

The popularity of Montgomery brings with it crucial research questions that *Making Avonlea* addresses in a scholarly fashion:

I.3   Anne Shirley and L.M. Montgomery in the Royal Atlantic Wax Museum, Cavendish, 2001. Photograph by J. Paul Boudreau.

- How do we critically assess the emotional responses and loyalty of Montgomery's inter/national readership?
- What are the pleasures and anxieties that surround the popular Montgomery?
- What is the relationship between text and spin-off product? Who controls it?
- How do we critically assess the aesthetics of the popular?
- What roles do gender and sexuality, race and nationhood play in the popularity of Montgomery?
- What are the terms of commodification of Montgomery's name?
- What are the values that are promoted in the name of Montgomery? Nostalgia, escapism, family values, wholesomeness? Or more subversive qualities?
- How is the construct 'Montgomery' (or the construct 'Anne') read within Canada? How is it read internationally?

Earlier scholarly books and anthologies of essays on Montgomery – Elizabeth Epperly's *The Fragrance of Sweet-Grass: L.M. Montgomery's Heroines and the Pursuit of Romance* (1992), Mavis Reimer's *Such a Simple Little Tale: Critical Responses to Montgomery's 'Anne of Green Gables'* (1992), Mary Henley Rubio's *Harvesting Thistles: The Textual Garden of L.M. Montgomery* (1994), and Gammel and Epperly's *L.M. Montgomery and Canadian Culture* (1999) – focus predominantly on Montgomery's texts, as scholars claim these texts within the domain of literary studies. My own co-edited book, *L.M. Montgomery and Canadian Culture*, acknowledges in the introduction that the book does *not* deal with the films, television adaptations, musicals, dolls, and numerous other spin-off products linked to Montgomery's name, thus leaving an important gap. In a review of *L.M. Montgomery and Canadian Culture*, the British scholar Danielle Fuller praised the contributions made, but also hoped that 'a promised forthcoming volume dealing with television and other contemporary popular versions of Montgomery's *oeuvre* will ... deal critically with the emotional responses and loyalty of her international readership' (183). *Making Avonlea* hopes to do just that, providing the first critical book examining the national and international popular industry that has emerged in Montgomery's name.

Making Avonlea also hopes to advance our understanding of popular culture. Only recently have influential cultural theorists, such as Pierre Bourdieu in *Distinction: A Social Critique of the Judgement of Taste* (1984), asked for the dismantling of the 'sacred frontiers' that separate high culture from mass culture. Since the 1980s, popular culture theorists have opened a new domain of research that now allows us to study popular culture phenomena with increasingly sophisticated tools, examining the crucial influence, social significance, commodity value, and aesthetics of the popular. These studies include John Fiske, *Reading the Popular* (1991) and *Television Culture* (1989); Dominic Strinati, *An Introduction to Theories of Popular Culture* (1995); Pierre Bourdieu, *The Field of Cultural Production* (1993); Chandra Mukerji and Michael Schudson, *Rethinking Popular Culture: Contemporary Perspectives in Cultural Studies* (1991); and John Frow, *Cultural Studies and Cultural Value* (1995). Finally, the emerging scholarly theories of girl culture, including Sherrie A. Inness's *Delinquents and Debutantes: Twentieth-Century American Girls' Cultures* (1998) in the United States, Dawn H. Currie's *Girl Talk* (1999) in Canada, and Angela McRobbie's *Feminism and Youth Culture* (2000) in Britain, invite us to take seriously the study of girl culture, including dolls and teen magazines.

In Canada, the field of popular culture has just begun to be explored in scholarship, and cultural scholars have noted its vibrancy. 'Canadian popular culture exists and it is both multifarious and dynamic,' writes Lynne Van Luven, the co-editor of *Pop Can: Popular Culture in Canada* (1999). She echoes the views of *Mondo Canuck*, which begins with the acknowledgment that Canadian culture 'wasn't necessarily reflected in the icy phallic peaks of Lawren Harris, the textured verse of Earle Birney ... or the foreign policy of Lester Pearson' (n.p.). Instead, the grass roots of Canadian culture are found in movies, models, music, sports, and popular literatures. In 'Orphan Annie Green Gables, Inc,' an extensive single chapter, Pevere and Dymond write that *Anne of Green Gables* is 'the most widely read Canadian book ever written, and the basis of one of the most popular and enduring Canadian pop-cultural phenomena ever' (13). The novel's appeal is all the more remarkable, they note, if we consider the ordinariness of Anne, who lacks either the Bunyanesque superpowers of Astrid Lindgren's red-haired Pippi Longstocking or the support of a remarkable cast of characters such as those around Dorothy in L. Frank Baum's *The Wizard of Oz*. At the same time, popular culture icons are profoundly enmeshed with issues of national identity, as Priscilla Walton (the co-editor of *Pop Can*) observes, pointing to Canada's defensiveness when Canadian popular culture moves south of the border. 'Curiously,' she notes, 'it would appear that if the railroad moves north, bringing Americans to Canada, Canadians are (secretly) pleased. But if it runs

南

south, carrying Canadians to the United States, it leads to ostracism' (xi).[2] For Montgomery, too, the railroad was running south, as she published many of her novels with U.S. publishers. That trend continues today with the Sullivan Films/CBC/Disney co-production of the remarkably successful *Road to Avonlea* (see chapter 12).

As for the genesis of this volume of essays by scholars from English Canada and Quebec, the United States, Germany, and the Netherlands, it is the result of a broad, multi-year effort of researching Montgomery and popular culture. In June 2000, I co-chaired (with Deirdre Kessler) the International L.M. Montgomery and Popular Culture Symposium, hosted by the L.M. Montgomery Institute at the University of Prince Edward Island, with forty international speakers and a rigorous debate about Montgomery's investment in popular culture. The best and most original fifteen papers covering a broad spectrum of approaches and views on popular culture were selected for this volume. Nine additional papers were solicited to fill important gaps on topics such as Anne in cyberspace, the commodification of Avonlea, Anne and Emily dolls, the Emily television series, the musical version of *Anne*, Anne in Europe, and so on. In its Fall/Winter 1998 issue, the bilingual scholarly journal *CCL: Canadian Children's Literature / Littérature canadienne pour la jeunesse*, edited by Daniel Chouinard, Marie C. Davis, and Mary Rubio, presented a special issue on L.M. Montgomery and Popular Culture; two of its essays, by Christopher Gittings and Jeanette Lynes, are reprinted in this volume, as are parts of my own essays that appeared in *English Studies in Canada*. All the other essays are original works that are published here for the first time. In our one-year consolidation process for the book, contributors exchanged papers among themselves, engaging in critical readings that allowed them to incorporate cross-references to other chapters and to reflect on one another's arguments. The result has deepened the debates and dialogues as well as strengthening the book's cohesion and unity. At the same time, *Making Avonlea* does not present one unified thesis or advocate one particular approach: its richness consists in its presentation of a spectrum of debates and theoretical models that leave it up to readers to position themselves within this myriad of approaches.

The title, *Making Avonlea*, was inspired by several important references that are vital to this book. It refers to the making of the movies that arguably launched Montgomery's novels into the world as a mass culture phenomenon, along with series such as *Road to Avonlea*, often prompting viewers to pick up and read the novels. 'Avonlea,' Montgomery's name for Cavendish, is at the border of the real and the fictional, the regional and the universal. Montgomery's Avonlea has a mythopoetic quality, the name derived from a rich combination of Arthurian legend (Avalon = the enchanted Island), classical myth (*Insula Avallonis* = Isle of Apples), and Shakespearean legend (Stratford-upon-Avon), with Avon-lane suggesting our entrance into Montgomery's realm. 'Avonlea' was the name of the Japanese theme park in Hokkaido, with its fragrant lavender fields and reproduction of Green Gables, highlighting Avonlea's international portability.

This volume is divided into three parts. Part one, 'Mapping Avonlea: Cultural Value and Iconography,' gives an overview of the fluctuating value of Montgomery and of popular culture (chapter 1) and continues by examining an 'Anne debate' in the national media as the public focus on this popular icon has intensified (chapter 2). Several essays (chapters 3–5 and 7–8) investigate topics such as the enduring inter/national popularity of Montgomery's writing; the mythopoetics of Anne's red hair; Montgomery's soliciting of reader desire through aesthetic means; and the international cover images used to market her fiction. Part one also studies Montgomery's impressive visual imagination, introducing the reader to Montgomery the photographer (chapter 6). Given her expert handling of, and posing for, the camera, it comes as no surprise that her work lent itself so well to television and film.

Part two, 'Viewing Avonlea: Film, Television, Drama, and Musical' opens with a vivid debate that pits Sullivanite scholar against Montgomery fidelity critic (chapters 9–10), representing an important debate that is currently taking place in the field. Just as the heirs of Montgomery have been locked in fierce litigation with Sullivan, so Montgomery loyalists have criticized the movies, accusing Sullivan of having distorted the author's texts and spirit. While Montgomery loyalists put forth strong arguments, film studies theorists are equally persuasive when they warn us not to become locked in a static fidelity criticism, for the movies, musicals, and plays are texts in their own right, richly deserving of scholarly attention. Essays examine the aesthetics, techniques, and innovations in musical, play, and film adaptations. Essays also investigate how early-twentieth-century fiction is adapted to conform to today's vision of gender, race, and nationhood (chapters 11–16). In taking film, theatre, and musical adaptations seriously, *Making Avonlea* lays a critical foundation and invites further investigation.

What is it that has made Montgomery's landscape so universal that it can be equally popular in cultures as diverse as Canada, Japan, Germany, and Iran? Part three, 'Touring Avonlea: Landscape, Tourism, and Spin-off Products,' begins to answer this question by critically probing the portability of Montgomery across national borders (chapters 16–18). Essays investigate the Montgomery industry, the literary tourist sites, and the marketing of Montgomery as a celebrity author. To what extent is Montgomery's image enhanced or diminished through intensive marketing and commodification? With its spin-off products, 'Consumable Avonlea' is the focus of essays probing the use of Montgomery's imaginative world for business purposes (chapters 19–20). Tired of the Anne industry and oversaturated by her omnipresence as a business commodity, Islanders have reacted with whoops of delight to *Annekenstein*, the satiric parody that poked fun at her. Some liken the Anne business to the use of a Martin Luther King speech in an Internet commercial, or the use of a Bob Dylan song in a Bank of Montreal advertisement. Once again, Montgomery is a nexus for debate.

Much has been written on the Japanese attraction to Anne. This collection invites readers to visit Japan's Avonlea. We also invite readers to immerse themselves in the Japanese concept of *taishu bunka,* an experience of culture that differs radically from the West's in making no distinction between high and low art; by intimately entering Japanese culture we begin to reconfigure not only Montgomery but also our relationship with popular culture (chapters 21–22). Finally, Montgomery is about communities. In the twenty-first century, community building often takes place in cyberspace, where we encounter new formations of kindred spirits inspired by Montgomery and Anne (chapter 23). Conversely, Beate Nock's epilogue returns us from cyberspace to old-style epistolary art with a circuitous discovery of Montgomery in Altensteig, a city founded in the fourteenth century in Germany's Black Forest.

At the end of this volume, the reader will find a comprehensive bibliography listing the works referred to in the contributors' essays. For the reader's convenience, I have separated the bibliographical entries into the following categories: (i) and (ii) Montgomery's works (published and unpublished); (iii) Adaptations: Film, Television, Drama, Musical, Animation; (iv) Illustrated Book Covers and Visual Art; (v) L.M. Montgomery and Popular Culture: Secondary Sources. It is my hope that readers may find the bibliography useful for further study.

Several contributors introduce their topic through personal anecdotes, even making personal 'confessions,' that document the extent to which Montgomery solicits personal engagement. Interspersed with the scholarly essays are shorter 'snapshot' essays that provide first-hand insight into and personal experiences with the Avonlea world. Many of the essays feature visual materials, including artwork, cover illustrations, film stills, photographs of artifacts, and Montgomery's own photography, which is also featured on the cover of this book. While *Making Avonlea* is by no means exhaustive, it is my hope that it will give readers an important entry point into the debates and theoretical models examining Montgomery's popularity in a variety of arenas and national cultures. In using Canada's most important celebrity author as a case study, *Making Avonlea* hopes ultimately to contribute to the study of the complex realm of popular culture that so intimately touches the dailiness of all our lives. This book now invites readers on a journey from small-town Cavendish, Prince Edward Island, through a popular culture empire that spans the world.

Notes

1 My thanks to Doug Hainey, Christina Holloway, Patricia MacLeod, and Parks Canada for making copies of these quotations available to me.
2 See also David H. Flaherty and Frank E. Manning's edited volume of critical essays, *The Beaver Bites Back: American Popular Culture in Canada* (1993), which highlights the 'politicization of culture in Canada' (5).

Part I

Mapping Avonlea:
Cultural Value and Iconography

Chapter 1

Anne of Green Gables Goes to University: L.M. Montgomery and Academic Culture

CAROLE GERSON

In his 1995 book titled *Cultural Studies and Cultural Value*, John Frow comments that 'the modernist fantasy of self-definition through opposition to a degraded mass culture has become obsolescent, and indeed has been replaced by rather different practices of fusion of or play between high and low genres and traditions' (25). Nowhere has this change been more evident than in the development of scholarly interest in popular best sellers, especially when the authors and their audiences are women, as in ground-breaking studies of the readers and writers of the romantic fiction commonly identified with the Harlequin publishing empire.[1] David Perkins claims that 'the possible plots of narrative literary history are three: rise, decline, and rise and decline' (39). However, feminist recuperation of women writers has added a fourth pattern: decline and rise.

This chapter of *Making Avonlea* investigates the rising scholarly capital of L.M. Montgomery, who, like many popular authors, has led a multiple life with regard to her positioning in different cultural canons. For the purpose of this reception study, I would like to differentiate three strata of cultural activity. In the commercial arena of popular culture, aspects of which are analysed in part three of this collection, ample evidence of Montgomery's commodity value can be found in the extensive inventory of her titles and various spin-offs cited in *Books in Print*. The 1999–2000 edition lists sixty-three separate items under *Anne of Green Gables* alone, including the *Anne of Green Gables Birthday Book*, the *Anne of Green Gables Coloring Book*, the *Anne of Green Gables Cookbook*, the *Anne of Green Gables Diary*, the *Anne of Green Gables Journal*, and the *Anne of Green Gables Press-Out Model House*. In the academic canon, Montgomery's value can be measured by the frequency of her appearance as the subject of scholarly publications and graduate theses. Fuzzily between these two poles lies the middlebrow layer of the 'average intelligent reader' (Rubin, xix), a demarcation that emerged in the 1920s and 1930s to legitimize a category between champions of the modernist literary avant-garde and consumers of mass entertainment (Radway, *Feeling for Books* 218–23). In Canada, representations of this realm occur at the élite end of the general press, such as the *Globe and Mail*, as well as in professional periodicals such as *Quill and Quire*, a monthly magazine that addresses publishers, booksellers, and other members of the book community. While it is obvious that these three canons merge and overlap, the distinctions should assist in our understanding of differing assessments of Montgomery in Canada's varied cultural landscape.

Montgomery's popular appeal has remained consistently high ever since the birth of *Anne of Green Gables* nearly a century ago, with a discernible growth spurt in the mid-1980s, following the broadcast of the first television versions of her stories. However, her literary value, as pronounced by university professors, has altered considerably over the years. In the history of Canadian criticism, the 1920s are distinguished by an unprecedented proliferation of nationalistic studies of Canadian literature, expressing a surprising range of opinions on Montgomery. At the top end, the appreciation of Professors Logan and French of her work in the genre of the 'community' novel (299) was supported by Professor V.B. Rhodenizer's assessment of the Anne series as 'a *comédie humaine* unparalleled in Canadian fiction' (227). Qualified acclaim appeared in the condescending praise of Montgomery's former Dalhousie teacher, Archibald MacMechan, who stated that *Anne of Green Gables* 'just misses the kind of success which convinces the critic while it captivates the unreflecting general reader' (211). Most scathing was the pronouncement by the powerful Toronto journalist W.A. Deacon that 'Canadian fiction was to go no lower' (169) than *Anne of Green Gables*.[2] In subsequent decades, Montgomery was demoted by the rigorous mid-century modernists who, like Deacon, attempted to purge the Canadian canon of writing they regarded as sentimental, popular, or feminine. The year 1985 marks a discernible turning point, when the publication of the first volume of her edited journals under the respected imprint of Oxford University Press (with the second following in 1987) coincided with the first dramatizations of her fiction for television. With two subsequent volumes of journals and many more televised adaptations of her works, Montgomery's star has risen anew in two fields of cultural production, the academic and the popular, whose interaction shows how fiction remains, in the words of Pierre Bourdieu, 'the most dispersed genre in terms of its forms of consecration' (*The Field* 51).

Two recent millennial exercises in cultural evaluation, conducted at the level of middlebrow culture, illuminate Montgomery's current status with general readers. In the summer of 1999, *Quill and Quire* published a list of forty 'great works of Canadian fiction' that 'defined the country – and the century' (Smith, front cover), compiled in consultation with a selection of booksellers, authors, and professors, including myself. Here *Anne of Green Gables* ranked as number ten. In November 1999, the *Globe and Mail* published a similar selection of twenty-five 'books of the century in Canada' ('Books of the Century' D17). *Anne* not only made this list of 'classics of Canadian literature' (D16), but also merited the largest illustration – of the cover of the first edition. As well, it was one of the ten books whose first reviews were reprinted for the occasion. For Montgomery to occupy the same platform as Margaret Atwood, Pierre Berton, Robertson Davies, Margaret Laurence, Stephen Leacock, Hugh MacLennan, Marshall McLuhan, Alice Munro, and Mordecai Richler represents a level of consecration that was unimaginable fifty years earlier.

In 1949, in a comparable exercise in canon creation, a list of one hundred English-language 'Canadian Books of Special Merit' was prepared for UNESCO by an all-male committee representing the major institutions of middlebrow and élite Canadian culture. The participants were Philip Child from the Canadian Arts Council, F.C. Jennings and W.S. Wallace from the Canadian Library Association, B.K. Sandwell from the Royal Society of Canada, Watson Kirkconnell and E.K. Brown from the Humanities Research Council of Canada, and W.A. Deacon and Lorne Pierce from the Canadian Authors' Association. Their final list included many of the authors active by that date who were selected half a century later by *Quill and Quire* and the *Globe and Mail*, but not Montgomery.[3] This omission is scarcely surprising. Paul Litt's analysis of the values that informed submissions to the Royal Commission on National Development in the Arts, Letters, and Sciences of 1949–51 (known as the Massey–Lévesque Commission) indicates that, at mid-century, Canadian culture was equated with higher culture. Mass culture was disdained as morally suspect and aesthetically debilitating, even when distinctively Canadian in origin or content (170–3).

In a more academic context, the application of the same evaluative criteria by the modernist critics who shaped Canada's cultural canon from the later 1920s through to the 1970s can be seen in Professor Desmond Pacey's assessment of Montgomery. She squeaks into his influential *Creative Writing in Canada* (1952, rev. 1961), categorized as an author of the regional idyll, a genre that, in Pacey's view, is 'written predominantly in Canada at least by women, is feminine and domestic in emphasis, and treats of young love, the home and the family' (197). As the feminine, the domestic, and the sentimental were all anathema to Canadian modernists, with their preference for virile social realism, Montgomery elicited predictable scorn. Pacey stated that *Anne of Green Gables* was merely 'a children's classic and it would be silly to apply adult standards to it' (106). Its popularity, in his view, was due to its possession of 'all the features of the kind of escape literature which a materialistic and vulgar generation craved' (106). Escapist, materialistic, vulgar: harsh words indeed. Montgomery was treated with greater respect in the monumental *Literary History of Canada* (1964), which acceded to her status as a prominent author for children, with the additional comment that 'Miss Montgomery's letters reveal an intellectual depth and a speculative mind which is seldom evidenced in her fiction' (Roper, 331). However, no editor noticed that her second name was misspelled as Maude (with an 'e'), a fact that suggests her lack of status.

Looking back from the year 2000, we can see how the larger picture began to alter in the 1970s, with the rise of second-wave feminism and its challenge to traditional masculine cultural and literary canons. But with Montgomery, the situation is not as straightforward as with many women recently recuperated into their respective national literary canons, such as American writers Kate Chopin, best known for her novel *The Awakening* (1899), and Charlotte Perkins Gilman, whose story 'The Yellow Wallpaper' (1892) has received belated recognition as an American classic. When I initiated this study, I hypothesized that, in the 1980s, the appearance of Montgomery's edited journals from a reputable scholarly and literary publisher (Oxford University Press Canada) legitimated her as a subject for academic study, moving her from the relatively marginal category of 'children's author' or 'writer for girls' into the more mainstream category of 'woman writer' or 'life writer' at a time when feminist scholarship was developing a new interest in autobiography. Mary Rubio's own account of her experience of editing the journals provides additional insight into the changing temperament of Canada's scholarly community in the early 1980s ('A Dusting Off' 52–5). However, this decade also saw the first Sullivan films. Thus, Montgomery's achievement of higher legitimacy in the academic realm has been complicated by the massive renewal of interest in her from another, the realm of popular television and its myriad spin-offs and complications. Other chapters of *Making Avonlea* now expand the hitherto meagre list of scholarly articles dealing directly with Montgomery and television[4] and suggest that encounters with screen versions of Montgomery's stories may have indirectly inspired recent critics of her books. The influence of the *Journals* seems more pervasive, or at least more easily traced, as their titles appear in the 'Works Cited' lists of many scholarly studies published since 1987. However, a direct causal relationship might be difficult to argue, as in most cases the *Journals* are treated more as background to Montgomery's fiction than as topics of analysis in themselves.[5]

The 'Bosom Friends' controversy of the summer of 2000 nicely illustrates the thorny relationship between academic culture and popular culture in Canada, at least where Montgomery is concerned. As Cecily Devereux provides an extensive analysis of this episode in the following chapter, I will restrict my comments to a few general observations. In May 2000, the University of Alberta was the site of the week-long annual gathering of thousands of Canadian academics known as the 'Congress of the Humanities and Social Sciences.' However, readers of the *Edmonton Journal* – a newspaper towards the lower end of the middlebrow spectrum – were treated to a very slender sample of the range of intellectual issues presented on their local campus. The only event of 25 May acknowledged by the *Journal* was a relatively minor session titled 'Anne Lit Crit,' and the only presentation to receive any attention was Laura Robinson's paper 'Bosom Friends: Lesbian Desire in L.M. Montgomery's Anne Books.' The next day, the leader on the front page of the *Journal* proclaimed 'Analysis of Anne's loves raises ruckus.' But it didn't – at least not at the conference itself – despite the provocative, academic-bashing headline of Hanneke Brooymans' article: 'Did Our Anne of Green Gables Nurture Gay Fantasies? Or Has a Professor Had Too Many Sips of Marilla's Cordial?' While the Congress received no other coverage in that day's *Journal*, Anne did: in the entertainment section, in a column about problems concerning the licensing of Sullivan television productions. Taken together, these two Montgomery stories in the *Edmonton Journal* of 26 May 2000 illustrate the challenge of attempting to unravel the interpenetration of the academic and the popular in Montgomery studies. Such is the iconic value of 'our Anne' that the newspaper sought to create the 'ruckus' that would render professors as newsworthy as the participants in the negotiations about film rights to Montgomery's works. And indeed, as Devereux recounts, the story did briefly ricochet across the country, with middle-brow *Globe and Mail* columnists taking particular glee in exploiting the opportunity to exercise their wit at the expense of both Anne and the academy.[6]

The complexity of Montgomery's overall status in various national and international cultural canons is too large a matter to pin down in a single chapter of *Making Avonlea*. Other contributors examine the many extensions of her books into musical comedy, theatre, film, television, tourism, and the jurisdiction of Parks Canada, as well as her burgeoning appeal in Japan and Europe. However, an assessment of her growing value in the scholarly world is enabled by the ease of measuring certain manifestations of her position in the academy. Because graduate students write theses and professors publish articles in recognized scholarly venues, their titles can be collected from databases and bibliographies and analysed quantitatively. Intertwined with the following discussion of Montgomery's canonical status in academe is attention to the production of her work in formats intended for the postsecondary classroom.

To assess Montgomery's changing academic reception, we can begin by comparing academic interest in her with that in the Rev. Charles W. Gordon (pseud. Ralph Connor), prolific author of best-selling, wholesome, Protestant-Canadian novels during the first decades of the twentieth century. Specializing in formulaic, didactic accounts of the maturation of young Canadian men, Gordon can be regarded as Montgomery's male counterpart. His most popular title, *The Man from Glengarry*, appeared in 1901, just seven years before *Anne of Green Gables*, and, like *Anne*, enjoyed a tremendous appeal to youthful readers in Canada and abroad. While the two authors shared many readers and similar sales figures, the difference in their academic reputations at mid-century is evident in their contrasting publishing history. In 1960, *The Man from Glengarry* was one of the first selections (no. 14) for McClelland and Stewart's New Canadian Library (NCL), a series initiated in the late 1950s to make Canadian literature available for Canadian college classrooms; *Glengarry School Days* was added in 1975 as no. 118. Both Gordon titles reappeared in 1993 in the revised New Canadian Library. Montgomery, on the other hand, did not enter the

TABLE 1.1
Comparison of scholarly publications relating to
Charles W. Gordon and L.M. Montgomery: MLA
Database, June 2000

Year	Items on Gordon	Items on Montgomery
1965–9	2	0
1970–4	0	0
1975–9	1	2
1980–4	2	5
1985–9	2	14
1990–4	3	9
1995–9	1	38
Total	11	68

New Canadian Library until 1989, with the three *Emily* books, although McClelland and Stewart had long held copyright on most of her titles. But rather than issue them in editions prepared for the college classroom, they chose to market Montgomery in formats aimed at adolescent girls.

While the MLA Database does not cite all scholarship published on Gordon and Montgomery, it serves my purpose as a data source for a general comparison of scholarly publishing on the two authors from 1965 to 1999 (table 1.1). Gordon is represented by eleven items, spread fairly evenly across the time period. With Montgomery, however, there are no citations before 1975, and then sixty-eight publications between 1975 and 1999, with a visible increase in recent years. One simple explanation may be found in the change in gender balance in our universities during the last two decades. The majority of authors on Gordon (table 1.2) have been men: eight out of eleven, or 73 per cent. This proportion is reversed in the case of Montgomery (table 1.3), with fifty-three of the sixty-eight articles (78 per cent) written by women. It would be rash to draw large generalizations about gender patterns of Canadian popular culture and scholarly culture from this small sample; none the less, it would be interesting to learn if similar gender ratios prevail among scholarly authors on writers always deemed literary, such as the *Globe and Mail*'s other Canadian authors of the century.

Another sign of academic legitimacy is the acceptability of an author as a subject of theses and dissertations as recorded in the Dissertations

TABLE 1.2
Publishing activity on Charles W. Gordon: MLA Database,
June 2000

Year	Items by male authors	Items by female authors	Total
1965–9	1	1	2
1970–4	0	0	0
1975–9	1	0	1
1980–4	2	0	2
1985–9	2	0	2
1990–4	2	1	3
1995–9	0	1	1
Total	8	3	11

TABLE 1.3
Publishing activity on L.M. Montgomery: MLA Database,
June 2000

Year	Items by male authors	Items by female authors	Total
1965–9	0	0	0
1970–4	0	0	0
1975–9	0	2	2
1980–4	1	4	5
1985–9	2	12	14
1990–4	2	7	9
1995–9	10	28	38
Total	15	53	68

International Database, with MA theses and PhD theses combined
(table 1.4).[7] While the numbers are small, they bear out the pattern of
the scholarly articles: from 1985 to 1998, two theses were written on
Gordon, ten on Montgomery, and one (in 1997) that includes both. All
the theses on Montgomery were written by women, three of them at
American universities.

Such figures statistically confirm the well-known fact that scholarly
publication on Montgomery has vastly increased over the past twenty-
five years.[8] The quantity of this material is well documented in the
bibliography of secondary sources compiled by Heather Ludlow and

TABLE 1.4
Comparison of theses (MA and PhD) on Charles
W. Gordon and L.M. Montgomery: Dissertations
International Database, November 2000

Year	Theses on Gordon	Theses on Montgomery
1985–6	1	0
1987–8	0	1
1989–0	0	1
1991–2	0	3
1993–4	1	1
1995–6	0	2
1997–8	0.5	2.5
Total	2.5	10.5

cited in *The Bend in the Road*, the CD-ROM produced by the L.M. Montgomery Institute at the University of Prince Edward Island. Ludlow's list of scholarly and general publications runs to some 432 items, including books, book chapters, theses, scholarly articles, journalistic and newspaper articles, introductions, afterwords, entries in reference books, reviews, and audiovisual studies. The sheer numbers are indeed impressive. Especially relevant to this study of Montgomery's scholarly reception are the contexts in which these publications situate her. While the American production of two recent books – Mavis Reimer's edited collection of articles on *Anne of Green Gables* (*Such a Simple Little Tale*, 1992) and *The Annotated Anne of Green Gables* (1997) – indicates substantial American interest, the vast majority (some 80 per cent) of the journal articles (table 1.5) appeared in Canada. Given the breadth of Montgomery's appeal, as well as the difficulty of deciding whether some periodicals are indeed 'scholarly,' this table should be read for its depiction of trends rather than for its absolute figures.

Table 1.5 not only records the dates of journal articles on Montgomery but also distinguishes the frequency of their appearance in periodicals specializing in children's literature. It begins with the 1975 issue of *CCL: Canadian Children's Literature/Littérature canadienne pour la jeunesse* (dedicated to Montgomery), and includes many items omitted from the MLA database, whose citation of Canadian publications is spotty. After the surge of articles in 1975, the numbers languish until the threshold of 1985–6. The peak of ten articles in 1989–90 includes three

TABLE 1.5
Articles on L.M. Montgomery in scholarly journals

Year	Total items	Items in children's literature journals, including CCL*	Items in CCL
1975–6	9	7	7
1977–8	2	0	0
1979–80	2	1	0
1981–2	0	0	0
1983–4	3	2	0
1985–6	13	10	6
1987–8	9	4	1
1989–90	10	6	3
1991–2	8	6	6
1993–4	3	0	0
1995–6	10	4	4
1997–8	9	7	7
Total	78	47	34

*CCL: Canadian Children's Literature/Littérature canadienne de la jeunesse

written in Australia concerning the accusation that Australian writer Colleen McCullough had borrowed the plot of her novel *The Ladies of Missalonghi* from Montgomery's adult romance, *The Blue Castle*.

Table 1.5 shows that of the seventy-eight articles published on Montgomery from 1975 to 1998, forty-seven, or some 60 per cent, appeared in journals dedicated to children's literature. Of these, nearly three-quarters were published in *Canadian Children's Literature* (*CCL*). It would thus appear that academic recuperation of Montgomery has largely depended upon her identification as a children's author, and is therefore allied with the growing acceptability of children's literature as a genre worthy of scholarly attention. However, many of these articles do not treat her as an author of juvenile fiction. For example, Lorna Drew's densely argued study of the female Gothic in the Emily books never identifies their audience or their subject as youthful, despite its appearance in *CCL*. This phenomenon leads to several important questions. Are mainstream academic periodicals reluctant to publish studies of Montgomery, regardless of the scholar's approach? Or is *CCL* now so closely identified with Montgomery that it seems her natural home, even with critical articles that have little to do with children *per se*, such as the group of studies on Montgomery and popular culture published in the special issue of fall/winter 1998? It is probably impossible to ascertain whether this pattern serves to marginalize Montgomery, or, conversely, helps to pull children's literature from the margin, into the mainstream of literary study. A subsequent question concerns whether students are more likely to meet Montgomery in courses dedicated to children's literature than in courses on Canadian literature or women writers.

Both the pattern of publication presented in table 1.5 and the suggestion that scholarly attention to Montgomery strongly associates her with children's literature are diluted when we factor in two recent book-length collections of original articles. The eighteen essays in Mary Rubio's *Harvesting Thistles: The Textual Garden of L.M. Montgomery. Essays on Her Novels and Journals* (1994) and seventeen contributions to Gammel and Epperly's *L.M. Montgomery and Canadian Culture* (1999) situate her firmly in the realm of general Canadian culture, as does Elizabeth Epperly's full-length study, *The Fragrance of Sweet-Grass: L.M. Montgomery's Heroines and the Pursuit of Romance* (1992). I have quoted the full titles and subtitles of these three books to point out how resolutely they lay adult claim to Montgomery by omitting any reference to youthful readers. Publication of the two latter titles by the august University of Toronto Press further enhances Montgomery's growing scholarly capital as a writer whose significance lies in her gender and her nationality. In contrast, American essays on Montgomery published in specialized collections all affirm her categorization as a children's author, many in relation to the emerging field of 'girl culture.'[9]

Along with the contexts in which criticism appears, an author's position in the literary field is established by the physical characteristics of her books, which signal their canonical level even before the reader reaches the first page. University students are not likely to view Montgomery as worthy of serious study when presented with the pastel-coloured bindings and romantic cover illustrations of the Seal–Bantam editions of the *Anne* and *Emily* books. The same texts, repackaged in austere New Canadian Library (NCL) editions with Robert Harris paintings on the front cover and afterwords by canonical authors such as P.K. Page, Margaret Atwood, Alice Munro, and Jane Urquhart, acquire scholarly dignity by virtue of their resemblance to other books on university courses. For a dramatic demonstration of the effect of book design, we have only to examine two available editions of *Emily's*

Quest. The NCL cover, a rather formal portrait of a respectable young woman holding a thick sheaf of papers, proposes that Emily's goal is her manuscript; the Bantam cover, depicting lovers passionately embracing against the backdrop of a panoramic landscape, suggests that the object of Emily's quest is her man. Andrea McKenzie's study of international illustrations of Emily, in chapter 7 of this collection, further examines the relation of cover depictions of Montgomery's fictional young author to the position of the woman writer in different cultures.

Imprint confers value in another dimension as well: the world of collectors and bibliographers, a sphere in which middlebrow culture overlaps with academe. Consecration of Montgomery among some bibliophiles is evidenced in Ron Cohen's substantial collection of Montgomery volumes recently donated to the National Library of Canada. As well, Bernard Katz, recently retired from the University of Guelph library, is embarking on a descriptive bibliography of Montgomery's publications. However, among such specialists Montgomery still encounters disparagement from the successors of W.A. Deacon and Desmond Pacey; for example, rare-book dealer Steven Temple recently opined that 'It's a sad state of affairs when Lucy Maud Montgomery can command so much attention and important writers like Layton are increasingly ignored' (MacLeod, 10).

Academic status is further enhanced when an author becomes the focus of scholarly gatherings. While I can offer only a personal observation, it seems that the number of mainstream conferences dedicated to Montgomery, or sessions within mainstream conferences, remains somewhat sparse. The memorable, three-paper session titled 'Anne Lit Crit' in Edmonton in May 2000 was, to my knowledge, the first time that the Association of Canadian College and University Teachers of English had devoted a distinct portion of its own program to Montgomery.[10] Not long ago, the University of Ottawa attempted to arrange a Montgomery symposium in its program of 'Re-Appraisals of Canadian Authors,' an annual series dedicated to major Canadian writers or topics, initiated in 1974. Each of these conferences produces a volume of essays of high prominence in Canadian scholarship. The Montgomery conference, scheduled for 1993, would have been the eighteenth such symposium. Instead, it proved to be the only one in this series to be cancelled, due to its inability to obtain support from the Social Sciences and Humanities Research Council of Canada (SSHRC). Coincidentally, 1993 also saw the founding of the L.M. Montgomery Institute at the University of Prince Edward Island (UPEI), which subsequently enjoyed greater success with SSHRC and received funding for its first conference in 1994. In Ottawa, Montgomery experienced partial restitution when she dominated the program at the 1999 symposium on Canadian Children's Literature, co-sponsored by the University of Ottawa and the National Library of Canada. The importance of scholarly conferences lies not only in their creation of opportunities for scholars, students, and readers to gather for one glorious occasion, but also in their generation of the most commonly accepted signifier of academic value, namely, scholarly publication. It is therefore important to note the relationship between the Montgomery conferences at UPEI and books of Montgomery criticism: a selection of the papers delivered at the 1994 conference was published in *Harvesting Thistles*, edited by Mary Rubio, and many of those from the 1996 conference on Montgomery and Canadian culture appeared in the recent volume of that title, edited by Irene Gammel and Elizabeth Epperly.

The present volume, *Making Avonlea*, is thus the third collection of essays on Montgomery to arise from a conference held at the University of Prince Edward Island. It will not only enhance Montgomery studies, but will also have a substantial impact upon the underexamined field of popular culture in Canada. Given the volume of scholarly attention paid to mass culture in Britain and the United States, it is surprising to see how little analysis this field has received in Canada. Often, the popular overlaps with notions of 'folk,' a genre that tends to be constructed regionally rather than nationally.[11] In the meagre bibliography of scholarly research on Canadian popular culture, books and writers are not prominent. For example, an American and a Swede have each issued full-length scholarly studies of Harlequin's readers and authors, yet the only Canadian-authored book on our most successful publisher is a business history.[12] The few recent general studies of current Canadian popular culture treat Montgomery unevenly. While she receives sufficient attention in Geoff Pevere and Greig Dymond's *Mondo Canuck*, as well as a chapter in Lynne Van Luven and Priscilla Walton's *Pop Can*, Daniel Francis's historical study of Canadian attitudes manages to overlook Montgomery entirely. Clarence Karr's recent *Authors and Audiences: Popular Canadian Fiction in the Early Twentieth Century*, which examines Montgomery, Connor, Nellie McClung, Robert Stead, and Arthur Stringer, might signal a new academic awareness of the historical importance of Canada's contribution to national and international popular literary culture.

In direct contrast to the female, book-centred world of Montgomery's readers and critics, the one topic on which all of Canada's canons seem to converge is hockey. The subject of a dedicated course at Simon Fraser University,[13] as well as the inspiration for both a play and an opera,[14] hockey has now obtained the sanction of all levels of Canadian culture, from the ice rink to the concert hall, and was the topic of a dedicated issue of *Textual Studies in Canada* (12, 1999). Perhaps there is an unstated desire to create a Canadian counterpart to the role of baseball in the culture of the United States; perhaps the bilingual history of the sport contributes to its national mythology. We have only to recall the extensive coverage of the funeral of Maurice Richard, and the amazing popularity of Roch Carrier's story 'The Hockey Sweater,' to witness how an unspecified consensus seems to have sanctified hockey as the quintessential Canadian experience. And, despite attempts to draw attention to women's hockey, this sport (unlike curling, for example) remains a predominantly masculine domain (Gruneau and Whitson, 208–9). As Montgomery was not particularly interested in sports, and I do not recall any reference to hockey in her writing, I doubt that these two solitudes of Canadian popular culture will ever coalesce in a single site. But given the resourcefulness of Montgomery scholars, we can at least envisage her placement, alongside hockey, as one of the few elements in our culture that crosses canonical divisions, uniting cultural classes in common fascination.

Notes

1 See Radway, *Reading the Romance* (1984); Eva Hemmungs Wirten, *Global Infatuation* (1998).

2 Montgomery voiced her fury with Deacon in a letter to Ephraim Weber so damning that the editors of these letters have deleted her description of her tormentor; see *L.M. Montgomery's Ephraim Weber; Letters 1916–1941*, ed. Tiessen and Froese Tiessen, 124.

3 The final UNESCO list of 100 titles was preceded by an original list of some 350 selections, including *Anne of Green Gables*, that was published by the Canadian Authors' Association: see 'Many Called – But Few Chosen.' Earlier authors from the 1999 *Quill and Quire* list (see Smith) who did not appear on the UNESCO list were Malcolm Lowry (*Under the Volcano*, 1947), Elizabeth Smart (*By Grand Central Station I Sat Down and Wept*, 1945), and Howard O'Hagan (*Tay John*, 1939). Earlier authors from the *Globe and Mail*

list (see 'Books of the Century') omitted by UNESCO were Robert Service (*Songs of a Sourdough*, 1907), Harold Innis (*The Fur Trade in Canada*, 1930), and Elizabeth Smart. See Department of External Affairs, Information Division, Reference Papers, No. 29, Revised, May 1949. Thanks to Janet Friskney for bringing these documents to my attention.

4 See Drain, '"Too Much Love-Making"'; Frever, 'Vaguely Familiar'; Kotsopoulos, 'Our Avonlea.'

5 Among the few studies focusing primarily on the *Journals* are Buss, 'Decoding L.M. Montgomery's Journals'; Turner, '"I mean to try."'

6 See Murphy, 'Lord T'underin'; 'How Green Were Anne's Gables?'; and Laura Robinson's own account of this episode, 'ACCUTE and the Media.'

7 This source is more reliable for PhD dissertations than for MA theses. Ludlow's bibliography of secondary sources on Montgomery written from 1985 to 1999 cites thirteen theses omitted from Dissertations International including nine Canadian MA theses, three MA theses, from Italy, Finland, and Sweden, and one doctoral dissertation written in Germany. All authors are women.

8 However, this surge in scholarly publication on Montgomery does not seem to have generated a corresponding surge in her appearance on university courses. Preliminary data from Paul Martin's dissertation research, at the University of Alberta, indicates that in 1997–8, *The Man from Glengarry* was taught almost as frequently as *Anne of Green Gables*.

9 For example, Foster and Simons, '*Anne of Green Gables*'; Scott MacLeod, 'American Girlhood in the Nineteenth Century'; Poe, 'The Whole of the Moon'; Hubler, 'Can Anne Shirley Help "Revive Ophelia"?'

10 When the annual meetings of the Learned Societies were held at the University of Prince Edward Island, in May 1992, there was a session on Montgomery jointly sponsored by ACCUTE and ACQL (the Association for Canadian and Quebec Literatures).

11 See Greenhill, *True Poetry* (1989); McKay, *The Quest of the Folk* (1994).

12 In addition to Radway and Wirten, cited earlier, see Grescoe, *The Merchants of Venus* (1996).

13 'Canadian Studies 390–2, Hockey in Canadian Popular Culture,' is taught by Richard Gruneau and David Whitson, authors of *Hockey Night in Canada* (1993).

14 *Game Misconduct*, an opera with music by Leslie Uyeda and libretto by Tom Cone, premiered at the Vancouver Playhouse in August 2000. *A Town Called Hockey*, a play by Gary Jones, Liesl Lafferty, and Richard Side, premiered at the Vancouver Arts Club Theatre in February–March 2000.

Chapter 2

Anatomy of a 'National Icon': *Anne of Green Gables* and the 'Bosom Friends' Affair

CECILY DEVEREUX

Sometime in the past two decades, Anne of Green Gables has been transformed in English-Canadian culture from a popular literary figure to what is usually described as a 'national icon.' As the American literature and film scholar Theodore F. Sheckels puts it in his recent discussion of the two American Green Gables films (1921 and 1934), 'As a popular icon within the national culture, Anne Shirley ranks right up there with the moose, the beaver, the Mountie, and the Habs' (189).[1] No longer simply the heroine of a much-loved story set in rural Prince Edward Island, she has come to serve as a figure who symbolizes the 'nation' itself, as a place and as what Benedict Anderson has suggested is an 'imagined community.' She is shared by a community that collectively recognizes her and, in that process of recognition, identifies itself *as* a community. Knowing Anne of Green Gables is a mark of the 'Canadianness' that, in some way, she epitomizes.

As a 'national icon,' or a figure who has come to have a particular value within a discourse of national self-representation, Anne and what circulates about her is news. The legal conflict over the licensing of Anne goods was national front-page news, as was the more recent report of litigation pertaining to Montgomery's heirs and Sullivan Entertainment, makers of the three Anne television films. In 1999, the *National Post* carried a front-page story on fresh allegations of Montgomery's supposed plagiarism of American writer Kate Douglas Wiggin's 1905 novel, *Rebecca of Sunnybrook Farm* ('Is Anne of Green Gables Really from Sunnybrook Farm?' 10 Apr. 1999: A1). In March 2000 it was reported on the front page of the *Globe and Mail* that the Sullivans' *Road to Avonlea* series was extremely popular in Iran (York, A1, A21). In

2000, when the short-list of possible images to appear on new Canadian currency was released, Anne did not appear: her exclusion was news. What is clear in stories such as these is that Anne matters to many English Canadians as a point of national identification. What is less clear is exactly what and how she signifies in nationalist discourse. What, exactly, does she represent? What – and how – does her popularity tell us, not about 'her,' but about ourselves? These questions were recently and dramatically foregrounded in the 'Bosom Friends' affair, an event that erupted around one scholarly analysis of Montgomery's writing and revealed at least some of the ideas Canadians have about 'our Anne.'

In the summer of 2000, at Canada's annual Congress of the Social Sciences and Humanities, professor Laura Robinson presented to the Association of Canadian College and University Teachers of English (ACCUTE) a paper entitled 'Bosom Friends: Lesbian Desire in L.M. Montgomery's Anne Books.' The paper undertook to trace a line of repressed and erotic desire between women in the Anne books: it suggested that what we see in the novels is a series of exchanges between women that show them not to be engaging with a normative heterosexuality but to be covertly expressing their love for one another. Anne marries Gilbert Blythe, but she has articulated her love since age eleven for her bosom friend, Diana Barry (see figure 21.1). She marries Gilbert, but the narrative shows her (in *Anne's House of Dreams*) expressing her love for Leslie Moore. When Anne's first child is born, it is Anne and Leslie we see playing with the child. Where is Gilbert in the 'house of dreams'? He is nowhere to be seen; 'we hardly hear about him' (Spears, A3). In all the Anne books, Robinson argued, we only see *women* embracing, holding hands, kissing, and vowing undying love for each other: men are pushed to the background. What was implied in the paper was the idea that the women and girls who demonstrate affection for one another in the Anne books indicate the *existence* of what Robinson termed 'lesbian desire.' Drawing on the influential essay on 'compulsory heterosexuality' by American feminist writer Adrienne Rich, Robinson argued that the obscuring of this 'desire' in the narratives thus shows that homosexuality in the early twentieth century was culturally repressed, *and*, crucially, that Montgomery performed this repression in her novels. That is, the paper suggested, Montgomery, when she narrativized 'lesbian desire' in her fiction, drew her readers' attention to the oppressive nature of compulsory heterosexuality *and* undertook to subvert it.

The argument – or, at least, the report of it – created an immediate furor. Indeed, the furor slightly preceded the session in which the paper was actually presented: Tom Spears, a reporter at the *Ottawa Citizen*, 'broke' the story of Robinson's reading of 'lesbian desire' in *Anne of Green Gables* prior to the presentation of the paper, on the morning of the panel (25 May 2000). Spears had contacted all of the members of the panel by e-mail on 11 May, a couple of weeks before the Congress. He indicated that he was covering the conference but would not be attending; he noted that he had seen the abstracts of the papers for the session on L.M. Montgomery, which were available on the Social Sciences and Humanities Council website; he asked all the members of the panel to send him copies of their papers, suggesting at the same time that he might be interested in conducting interviews with them. There were two other presentations in the academic session devoted to Montgomery, one by University of Northern British Columbia scholar Kate Lawson on the way the figuring of the domestic in the 'Emily' books can be understood in relation to Sigmund Freud's concept of the 'uncanny' or the *Unheimlich*, and my own on the globalization of Anne as simultaneously 'national icon' and what Robert Everett-Green in the *Globe and Mail* had described as 'our biggest cult commodity export' (18 Sept. 1999: C5). But Spears's article had little to do with the ways that twenty-first-century academics are engaging with L.M. Montgomery's works (for instance, as is the focus of this study, in popular culture) and as they can be seen to reproduce the ideologies (of nation, race, gender, sexuality, 'identity') of the period in which they were written. His report, that is, was not on the session at all but on one paper to be presented in it.[2]

By the time that paper was presented, the *Ottawa Citizen* piece was already circulating in the nation's capital – and well beyond. Spears's report, which was based on a reading of the paper Robinson had sent him (see Robinson, 'ACCUTE and the Media' 37), set the tone in establishing what the paper was 'about': it was 'about' the singular discovery by an English professor that English Canada's best-loved literary heroine *was* a lesbian. The article appeared under a large photograph of Megan Follows as Anne and Schuyler Grant as Diana Barry in the 1985 Sullivan Entertainment telefilm *Anne of Green Gables*. The headline and the subheading beneath the photo's caption proclaimed, respectively: '"Outrageously Sexual" Anne Was a Lesbian, Scholar Insists'; 'Green Gables heroine's relationships full of homoerotic, sado-masochistic references, conference will hear today' (Spears, A3).

Spears's representation of the paper as something akin to the genre of tabloid celebrity 'outing' was not only a reductive treatment of the analysis itself, it also fundamentally exploited the easily anticipated response in Canada to Robinson's putative 'queering' of Anne: at a moment in Canadian history when official same-sex unions were being contested (in Alberta and in British Columbia), the existence of a rich seam of homophobia in the population could not possibly be unknown. Opposition to same-sex unions was frequent and prominent at this time in national and local newspapers.[3] One implication of the report (made evident more through responses to it than through any direct comment in the story) was that generations of children, in reading *Anne of Green Gables*, had been inculcated into unwittingly taking as a role model a figure who was *actually* a lesbian. As in all such 'reports,' the spectre of predatory sexual recruitment hovered nearby. British children's program Teletubbies had been the focus of a similar 'scandal' in 1998, when it was observed that the putatively male Tinky-Winky carried a handbag.[4] This 'exposé,' the article suggests, was far more scandalous: Anne, after all, is a Canadian 'national icon'; her 'outing' called 'national' identities into question.

The paper's 'findings' thus framed were, as Spears reports Robinson anticipated they would be, 'sensational': 'While the professor couldn't be reached for an interview,' he wrote, 'she hinted in an e-mail to the *Citizen* that she expects some reaction. She's presenting a second paper, she writes, but it is "not quite as sensational as, say, a lesbian take on *Anne of Green Gables*"' (A3). It was this comment, thus decontextualized and reported, that arguably determined the response: it suggested that the presenter was seeking 'sensation,' and it established the ideological framework within which the response to the paper would take place. 'Lesbian desire' in *Anne of Green Gables*, that is, can only be 'sensational' if homosexuality is understood to be 'perverse'; the 'revelation' of same-sex 'desire' in English Canada's best-known and most enduringly popular novel can only provoke a response of the kind Spears suggests was 'expect[ed]' if it is presented as a 'sensational' 'lesbian take,' or, in effect, as an erotic spectacle for a heterosexual audience. Robinson is here acknowledging the homophobia that she, too, could not help but know to be still a powerful element in English Canada in the year 2000, and that, at one level, her paper must be seen to be problematizing; but, in identifying her work as 'sensational,' and thus defining it in terms almost as reductive as those used in the article, she may unwittingly have helped to fuel the response, particularly as it focused on her and her work.

No one could have anticipated the scale of the response or the extent to which Robinson would be attacked and ridiculed. It is extremely rare for any scholarly work in the humanities to become front-page news; it is even more unusual for an academic presenting a paper at a conference to be publicly derided for her work. Robinson has since described the response in a short piece written for the June 2000 newsletter of the Association for Canadian College and University Teachers of English. After the appearance of the *Ottawa Citizen* article, she writes,

> CBC Newsworld contacted me, and the Southam group of papers ran the story across the country. I spoke to two reporters, on the first two days, and quickly realized that the first headline had determined the story's spin no matter what I said. Even though I did not return calls – six from radio stations, two from national magazines, and one from a national newspaper – the story continued spiraling. I had supposedly declared Anne a lesbian and must be quickly condemned from BC to Newfoundland. Add into the mix the small piece on the CNN website and the phone call from a Japanese newspaper, and the event takes on international flavour, carrying a shelf life of at least two and a half weeks. ('ACCUTE and the Media' 37)

Moreover, as the *Globe* reported, 'Anne and Diana, were they or weren't they, was the subject of fiery debate on a Maritime-wide CBC radio phone-in on Monday [29 May 2000]' (Nolen, 31 May 2000: A7). Robinson draws attention to a similar debate: 'A small rag in Halifax set up a phone-in hotline so callers could vote on whether Anne was gay or not (45 said no, two said yes)'; she herself, she notes, 'was labeled a pervert' ('ACCUTE and the Media' 37). Letters responding to the report appeared in a range of papers across the nation for the duration of this 'shelf life': many of them expressed outrage. In the *Edmonton Journal*, for instance, on 2 June 2000, the centre of the Letters page was occupied by a box headed 'Anne of Green Gables Controversy': three letters appeared beneath a photograph of Sesame Street's Bert and Ernie, and the headline (drawn from a letter's rhetorical question), 'Bert and Ernie to Be Probed Next?' (A19). The suggestion in these, as in many of the letters published in newspapers during the debate, is that the academic who had produced the paper was wasting time and public money by focusing on 'beloved Canadian literary classics' for children (A19) and that a 'jaded' academic ('I feel sorry for her narrow view of relationships,' wrote one reader from Edmonton [A19]) was destroying these classics by 'queering' them.

It is difficult not to feel sympathy for Robinson, who presents herself in her explanation to ACCUTE as 'bruised,' and who clearly did suffer a good deal of abuse in the media, much of which, as she points out, was based not on a reading of her paper but on the initial report in the *Citizen*. The day after the session at the Congress, the *Edmonton Journal* (which had sent a reporter to the session, one of the two to whom Robinson initially spoke), published an article that facetiously asked, 'Did Our Anne of Green Gables Nurture Gay Fantasies? Or Has a Professor Had Too Many Sips of Marilla's Cordial?' (Brooymans, 26 May 2000: A3). The *Globe and Mail*, which forebore to comment on the story for almost a week, finally put the story on its front page on 31 May: this longish analysis of the story and its effects (Nolen, A1, A7) treats the paper as a serious one (as the *Journal* article does not), but suggests that the real purpose of the paper may not be a politicized critique of early-twentieth-century homophobia at all. 'Prof. Robinson won't talk about it,' writes Stephanie Nolen, 'but she succeeded in creating a stir – which, one suspects, may have been her intention all along' (A7).

Although it had been slow to join the 'melee,' the *Globe* continued to foreground the story for the next week: an editorial on 3 June 'skewered' the paper by presenting a mock account of other 'hidden' meanings ('How Green Were Anne's Gables?' A14). Murray Campbell's summary of 'The Week' revisited the report under the (tediously inevitable) heading, 'Anne of Green Gay-bles' (3 June 2000: A10). 'Tertius' made reference to the impact the 'revelation' might have on the Prince Edward Island tourist industry in 'Subjects and Objects' on 2 June (R2). Rex Murphy took it up in his 'Japes of Wrath' column on 2 June ('Lord T'underin' Jaysus, Anne Dealt Crack and Voted NDP' A11) and David MacFarlane in his 'Cheap Seats' on 5 June ('Phew. Do Stockwell Day's supporters know that children are reading this kind of thing?' R2). Neither of these latter comments showed any signs of real engagement with the issue, in terms either of the paper itself, which neither writer seems to have read, or of the implications of the response. Murphy writes the paper off as a 'trendy' study that '[i]gnore[s] the words[, t]raduce[s] the author ...' and (inexplicably, given that the book is a work of prose narrative), '[s]kip[s] the poetry' (A11). 'Anyone,' he says, 'can play' (A11). MacFarlane takes a similar posture of incredulity and, like Murphy, dismisses the paper as unworthy of consideration. (He, at any rate, does not consider it.) The not-very-subtle subtext in both of these comments is a thrust aimed not at Robinson specifically but at academics in general: 'This business,' writes Murphy, 'of finding stuff in old novels that is clearly not in the old novels is very good for the mind, and a great way to spend the academic summer holidays. You get to go to Charlottetown and it's liberating, and so sensitive' (A11). MacFarlane, for his part, begins thus, with nearly the same attitude: 'A recent academic study that purported to reveal the homoerotic subtext of *Anne of Green Gables* seemed to me – glib and unencumbered with post-graduate degrees as I am – to be worth lampooning' (R2). Murphy and MacFarlane, however, are commenting on the stir, and not on the source. They are not, as they both indicate, academics: there is no reason to assume that they *should* take up Robinson's paper within the context of academic debate. But, as writers in a national newspaper, they should base their comments on at least a cursory reading of the material they 'lampoon.' Given, moreover, as at least one letter-writer pointed out, that Murphy had only a couple of weeks before written an adulatory review of Harold Bloom's recent prescriptive book on 'How to Read' (Books, 13 May), his 'lash[ing] out at a literary study' in the way he does seems particularly unfair ('Anti-academic Rant' A18).

This response – not to the paper itself, but to the reported paper – as Robinson puts it, 'snowballed' ('ACCUTE and the Media' 39), taking on a life of its own; and, as the references to 'play,' and 'fun' suggest, it *was* ludicrous. Virtually all the commentary and debate focused on the explicit question of whether or not Anne Shirley *was* a lesbian and on the implicit one of whether or not humanities scholars do anything socially and culturally worthwhile in their work. The official and national media response thus had its own perverse effect: for instance, when Murphy and MacFarlane participated, without having read the work, in the representation of the 'Bosom Friends' paper as a 'trendy' argument that could not be based on the actual books, they perhaps inadvertently lent the paper a good deal of credibility by virtue of necessitating some kind of defence. Ironically, the effect of the media hype was to shut down academic debate about the paper itself, and the polarized media frenzy did not leave much space for a rational scholarly critique of the argument presented.

In fact, however, the argument as it was presented *was* problematic, not because it read 'the novels from a queer perspective' (Robinson, 'ACCUTE and the Media' 38; *Edmonton Journal* 26 May 2000: A3), but because this perspective was not completely theorized or explained. That is, the problems with the argument, which were not noted in any commentary, were methodological: it addressed signs of 'lesbian desire' but did not situate its analysis of these signs in any kind of theoretical, historical, or even biographical groundwork that would provide a rationale and a direction for the investigation. It did not problematize the notion of 'lesbian desire' and left the term largely essentialized. Although Adrienne Rich's theory of compulsory heterosexuality obviously underpinned the argument, this theory was not given adequate attention in the paper as it was presented.

Rich draws attention to what she calls 'lesbian existence,' or, as I have already indicated, the reality of lesbianism in history, even if and when it is not represented; she also theorizes what she calls a 'lesbian continuum.' Rich's point in representing what she calls a 'lesbian continuum' is only in part to make the case that, as Hélène Cixous has interpreted it, 'we are all lesbians' ('The Laugh of the Medusa' 882): the lesbian continuum, which posits a spectrum of relationships between women that ranges from friendship to erotic love, has as its first object the construction of ways of seeing *outside* of patriarchal and heteronormative representations. In this revision of the discursive representation of relationships between women, its object is like Monique Wittig's in proposing that 'lesbian' is a liberatory term because it is not, like 'woman,' constellated in relation to 'man,' and thus can signify outside of the reductive framework of signification that has 'woman' only as 'not man.'[5]

While this conceptual framework seemed to underpin the 'Bosom Friends' argument, it was not clear how it was being used in relation to the fiction of L.M. Montgomery, or what was actually being addressed. Even Robinson's post-controversy explanation did not entirely clarify the point of the paper, which, she writes, was intended first to

question [...] our assumptions about Anne. I never said Anne was a lesbian; I did not even imply she was a repressed lesbian. Instead, if one reads the novels from a queer perspective, one can see that Anne could not be a lesbian (as the outcry will attest to!). While Anne has passionate female friendships, particularly with Leslie Moore when Anne is in her late twenties, and Montgomery's language verges on the erotic, Anne can never be a lesbian because compulsory heterosexuality always intervenes, both in terms of narrative (a wedding has to form the ending) and in terms of social constraints (as one faction of the public debate foolishly yet insightfully argues, lesbians didn't exist in 1908!). However, Montgomery's novels call attention to other possibilities that cannot be pursued and therefore highlight the extent to which heterosexuality is not a choice. ('ACCUTE and the Media' 38)

It is not clear from this account exactly what is the point of the paper, unless it is obliquely to reaffirm what Rich defined as compulsory heterosexuality and to reiterate its pervasiveness in early-twentieth-century English Canada by tracing the signs of sexual repression in popular fiction. This is, of course, not an insignificant or 'trendy' object. A crucial part of the work of queer theory is the critical dismantling of the apparatuses of sexual repression: investigating their construction is an important intervention. But the paper and its later explanation still leave some questions unanswered. Why does Montgomery frame relationships between women in erotic language? Why does Robinson call her paper 'Lesbian Desire in L.M. Montgomery's Anne Books' if she is not making a point about same-sex 'desire'? Why did she not say to the media that Anne 'could not be a lesbian'? What does the self-described 'lesbian take' on *Anne of Green Gables* actually reveal – about the text, about Montgomery, about early-twentieth-century English Canada, and about early-twenty-first-century English Canada? What 'assumptions' is her paper 'question[ing]' about Anne? Why are we not told what these 'assumptions' are, and why they are questionable?

In one sense, the 'Bosom Friends' paper is most comprehensible as an extension of the approach to *Anne of Green Gables* that Robinson has outlined in other published work: she has made the suggestion on two occasions that Anne is best understood as an 'outsider' whose integration into the community indicates a desire on Montgomery's part for a greater openness and 'tolerance' in social structures. *Anne of Green Gables*, Robinson held in 1995, is a novel that 'embrac[es] contradiction' ('"Pruned Down"' 42); it constructs 'communal identity,' she wrote in 1999, by integrating and still 'embracing' difference ('"A Born Canadian"' 20). Based on the case in the 1999 paper as it attempts to account for (what is certainly a problem in the novels) Montgomery's inscription of 'foreignness' in and around Avonlea, we might see the argument in 'Lesbian Desire in L.M. Montgomery's Anne Books,' as a comparable attempt to account for (what is also certainly a problem in the novels) the romantic language that is functionalized in exchanges between women.

Robinson is addressing real and important questions in Montgomery's writing and in early-twentieth-century English-Canadian culture, questions that have preoccupied scholars for some time. Sexuality *is* an issue, as Montgomery scholars have been quick to note.[6] The Anne books, as Robinson has argued – and, it might be added, the Emily books – *are* loaded with homoerotic language; relationships between women *are* foregrounded. Anne's relationship with her colleague Katherine Brooke in *Anne of Windy Poplars* (1936) is complicated by Katherine's positioning outside of conventional femininity; Janet Royal in *Emily's Quest* (1927) presents a comparable problem for Emily.[7] Relationships with these women are problematic for Anne and Emily because, it is implicit, there is an important element of sexual tension. It is important to read these representations in relation to gender and sexuality, and it is important to engage with them within the full spectrum of the academic debate within which Robinson's paper is situated and to which it must be seen to be contributing.

What is (perversely, perhaps) most valuable about the 'Bosom Friends' affair is the way that it has generated a news media archive of material that *does* foreground some of 'our' assumptions about Anne, about the limits of her popularity, about national identity, and about how we read and value 'national icons.' It is because readers have sought to find traces of her in Prince Edward Island that an industry has burgeoned around her image and her 'home'; it is because of this impulse to find traces of Anne that her image can be so successfully marketed. But this popular Anne is not 'invented' by readers or merchandisers; and there is not a 'real' Anne who can be exposed through judicious criticism. Rather, they are the same thing. Our Anne of Green Gables is a figure who is simultaneously a figure of individual identification (Anne, as readers often say, is 'like' them) and a figure of cultural identification. The idea of Anne that circulates in Canadian popular culture functions to perpetuate the ideas of the nation she is seen to represent. This iconic figure can be – and should be – examined precisely for what it is that makes her popular, and for the ideas and the values that she represents – as Robinson has done in her study. Those ideas and values, while they inhere in the community of readers, are not projected upon the work: they are always textually encoded. The explanation for Anne's popularity is *in* the book, and it is also *in* the 'public dispute' about the book; the 'Bosom Friends' affair is part of that debate. The paper itself may not have fundamentally changed the way the novel signifies in English Canada, but the 'ruckus,' by underlining the real importance of Montgomery's heroine in English Canada, has certainly changed the terms of the critical debate about the novel and about 'our Anne' in popular and national culture.

Notes

1 See also Jeanette Lynes's chapter in the present collection. Lynes cites an interview in 1996 in *Chatelaine* with Kathryn Gallagher Morton of Avonlea Traditions Inc.: Morton, Lynes writes, 'constructs the enduring appeal of Anne in terms of a nationalist iconography; "as long as there are Mounties and beavers," she says, "there'll be Anne."'
2 I did not send a copy of my presentation to Spears.
3 Paul Sullivan, for instance, comments on the same-sex marriage question as it was taken up in Alberta and in B.C. on 1 June 2000 in the *Globe* (Sullivan, A15). A letter about the Anne question appears on the next page (A16).
4 Like the 'Bosom Friends' affair, the Tinky-Winky crisis was played out in the press and in other media: debate raged on the Internet, and several chat-rooms and websites focused on the question of the Teletubbies' sexuality and their potential 'danger' to young children.
5 'Lesbian,' writes Wittig, 'is the only concept that I know of which is beyond the categories of sex (woman and man), because lesbian societies are not based upon woman's oppression and because the designated subject (lesbian) is *not* a woman either economically or politically or ideologically' (148).
6 There is already an important body of Montgomery scholarship devoted to issues of sexuality, eros, and girl–girl infatuation; see Campbell, 'Wedding Bells and Death Knells,' discussing Teddy Kent's androgyny and the asexuality of his relations with Emily Byrd Starr; Åhmansson, 'Textual/Sexual Space in *The Blue Castle*,' discussing sexual desire and abstinence in the life of Valancy Stirling; and Gammel's '"My Secret Garden,"' discussing Montgomery's focus on autoeroticism and girl–girl attraction in relation to the eroticized landscape of Montgomery's fiction.
7 I am grateful to Chris Gittings for his helpful discussions of Janet Royal and her relationship with Emily.

Chapter 3

Confessions of a Kindred Spirit with an Academic Bent

BRENDA R. WEBER

When I first presented the short version of this paper at the L.M. Montgomery and Popular Culture Conference in the summer of 2000, I was acutely aware of the departure it represented. I've spent the last ten years of my life disciplining my thoughts and my writing so that they might testify to my 'intellectual rigour.' A doctoral dissertation in progress, articles, and seminar papers – all make clear arguments about literary texts and cultural contexts. This paper, I felt, needed to delve more deeply into the knotty emotional core where Montgomery's books have so resonated for me. Though it is certainly possible to make sound scholarly arguments about L.M. Montgomery in particular and juvenilia more broadly, as many fine papers given at the conference demonstrated, it seemed patently false for me to journey the 1,200 miles to Montgomery's island of ruby, emerald, and sapphire, false to come to the literal and literary site that had filled so much of my girlhood imagination, false to speak and think publicly about Montgomery's Anne, who is also my Anne, false to do all of this in only intellectual terms. And so I wrote this paper in which I committed myself to laying aside the rhetorical tools I generally use so that I might talk about words on a page that changed my life.

Anne of Green Gables was not the first book to make a powerful impression on me: I had read reams of Trixie Beldens and Nancy Drews long before I discovered the freckled redhead Anne. I'd been down the westward trail with Laura Ingalls, had met lions, witches, and wardrobes, and had gone inside Eskimo igloos, fishing vessels, and airplanes with a host of other literary guides. I had already kicked *Little Women* under the bed in a furious rage, livid with Jo because she refused to marry Laurie and ended up with a stodgy old German professor instead (I am still, by the way, not completely finished with that anger). But Anne struck me in a different way. Here was a heroine both ridiculous and sublime. She could quote Tennyson while floating down the river in a high-art-induced daze, yet she didn't have enough sense to keep her boat from sinking, nor could she make a sauce without drowning a mouse in its mucky depths. She had this uncanny ability to revel in the whimsy of life and to awaken it in others, yet her own orphan story made of her a pitiable loner. I wouldn't say that Anne's isolation made me feel any more thankful for my stable life with my two loud little brothers in our nondescript house in the centre of a big hot state; indeed, I often found myself yearning for Anne's romantic loneliness that fed a ravenous imagination. I desperately wanted to bring on fancies that might convince me there were sprites and fairies in the Big Wheel–filled backyard or grumpy trolls under the green Ford station wagon parked so prosaically in the carport. Anne's was a life that seemed to me unbelievably exotic, filled with imaginative excess and Romantic splendour: my life in the suburbs of Phoenix seemed hopelessly mundane in comparison.

When I first saw the call for the L.M. Montgomery and Popular Culture Conference in 1999, my mind rushed back to those desires I felt so long ago; yet I was wholly challenged to determine how I might sustain an argument about Montgomery and popular culture. Though Montgomery is terrifically famous in Canada and has grown increasingly known in the United States since Kevin Sullivan's film adaptations came out on PBS, my relationship with Anne Shirley and Lucy Maud Montgomery has always happened against the tide of the popular current. In the desert Southwest in the 1970s when I grew up, kids were excited about video pong or the rock band Styx. And in the very Mormon town of Mesa, Arizona, where anti-intellectualism flourished, I was a lonely book-reading girl who, in taste and inclination, went against the popular grain. In many respects, I shared more similarities with Emily, Montgomery's other serialized heroine, than I did with Anne, but I didn't know that yet. In fact, I didn't even read the Emily books until three months ago, as I journeyed home from the Canadian Maritimes. I had heard of Emily, vaguely, abstractly. She was, I knew, another one of Montgomery's fictional girls, but my grandmother had sent me Anne, and out of loyalty to my grandmother, I maintained a fiercely exclusive passion for Anne.

Indeed, my presentation in June and my essay now are both inspired by my grandmother, a woman who possessed a considerable intellectual talent but not a stitch of academic curiosity. She had within her mind the largest 'scope for imagination' of anyone I've ever known, and she communicated that scope to me by plying me with books, most specifically, and most meaningfully to me, the Anne books. Through them, she nurtured in me a mind that craved textured detail encoded into words. She taught me that meaning emerges like a rainbow when you look at things from just the right angle. She made me see the multidimensionality of the worlds that can exist in the imagination. She introduced me to characters of great depth and proportion. She opened my mind to the possibility of a world that comes alive through print and desire and laughter. And she encouraged me to form intimate and lasting bonds with characters, places, ideas. In short, she gave to me what meant the most to her: a literary imagination.

She had little yellow stars pasted on the ceiling in her cubby-hole room at the top of the stairs. It was the room she moved into after my grandfather needed a special hospital bed. It was the room I slept in when we went to visit. Small, about four feet by eight feet, with twelve-foot ceilings, it was just big enough for a window and a twin mattress stacked up high, a metal cabinet, and a tiny bookshelf, stuffed with her favourite textual companions – all of the Anne books, the history of Scotland, several tales of Daniel Boone in Kentucky, and a guide to trees and birds. I remember feeling startled by the closeness of her room, but as I would lie on the tall bed, propped up high to accommodate storage underneath, I'd glance back and forth from the star-studded ceiling to the back garden where fireflies played in the summer shrubs, and it felt very calming to be there. When I would come out of that room in the morning, she'd be on the landing or already down in the kitchen, reading a book, calling me 'Kitten,' and telling me to wash my paws for breakfast.

She wore light summer dresses, with tiny flower prints in soft cotton, a handkerchief always tucked under the belt, and dark, sturdy, sensible shoes. Her hair was long, and when she combed it out, it fell in shimmering silver waves to her waist. From the time she was eight until she was eighty, she wore her hair in the same style: parted down the middle, braided into two long pigtails, and then twisted loosely around the top of her head in a crown of hair. We always saw her when it was hot outside – on summer vacations, John and Robert and I crammed into the back of the car, anxious and eager to be back in that old but unfamiliar place, this 'house where Dad grew up.' We'd go bounding up the stairs, and grandma would come laughing to meet us, several big patches of calamine lotion rubbed over her fair skin – evidence of her run-ins with poison ivy. She always had a book tucked into the pocket of her apron, or propped up behind the coffee pot on the kitchen counter, or open waiting for her on the piano stool. She'd give us what Robert and I called a 'grandma hug' – three great thumps on the back. I always remember her in summer, the sun in her eyes.

Robert and John and I would catch magical fireflies in old Mason jars she kept in the stairway on the way to the cellar. Or lie on the lumpy couch that had wooden arms in the screened-in porch, reading a book she'd refuse to let me take out of the house, no matter how much I promised I would take good care of it. When I was fourteen, my parents sent me off on a vacation by myself, a trip from Phoenix to Indianapolis to alternate nights between my maternal and paternal grandparents. My time with my mother's mother was spent shopping and looking for deals, or we'd go out for dinner at their country club, or meet her friends for golf; we stayed up late watching old movies on television and laughed about pictures in magazines while licking our fingers clean of the orange powder left from the little cheese puffs we both found irresistible.

Time with my father's family happened at a much slower pace. My grandfather was ill with Parkinson's disease, and we stayed close to home. Grandma taught me how to make tomato cages and how to bake a quiche – we did a lot of reading, searching through the house and garden for patches of sunlight to read in. One night she and I stayed up until midnight, sprawled on the floor, pasting green stamps into booklets and talking about *Anne of Green Gables*. The next day she and I and Grandpa loaded into her red Volkswagen van and drove to the Indianapolis Speedway – or rather, to the green-stamp trading centre that was in Speedway, to swap those swatches of moss-colored paper for a new iron. I was fourteen and amused and delighted by the simplicity of this adventure. My grandma in her ubiquitous sensible black shoes, her long braids wrapped around her head, driving to the site of the Indianapolis 500 – shifting gears, negotiating highways, taking her red bus where she pleased.

She had a space between the kitchen and the dining-room she called 'the Brenda wall.' She'd hang up there whatever kind of poetry or picture I made. At age six, I wrote her my first poem – an ode to my grandmother who loved words and their ability to transform what was inside into pictures. She passed that love down to me. Mine was a crude poem. The first line, as I recall was 'My grandma is so nice, and she likes to eat white rice,' but it was heartfelt and it rhymed! And she hung it on my wall with pride. When I was seventeen, I brought her a plate from Austria, wrapped meticulously in T-shirts and socks to keep it from breaking, and I watched with pride as she hung it on 'the Brenda wall.' I don't know if she had walls for the other grandkids. I think we all shared things with her, special moments, special rituals, distinct experiences inflected clearly through her. Those things now mingle for me in the scents of ivory soap and frying chicken and humidity in an old house, the vanilla scents of an old book, scents of memory. But mostly, I connect her with a love of reading that has shaped my ideas, my mind, and my career.

We grew up in Arizona. It was the desert, but it certainly wasn't a cultural wasteland, though I remember bemoaning my lot, in true Romantic eight-year-old fashion, that I lived in a place with little water and, consequently, no flowers, grass, or trees. When I turned five, my parents moved from the Air Force Base to Hill Street, and I remember thinking it the cruellest joke imaginable that our street had not a hill on it – indeed, that it was straight and narrow and uninteresting and as hot as anything else in Mesa, Arizona. Though I didn't have the language to express it then, I was startled by how little my experience conformed to my expectation. I wanted snow at Christmas and falling leaves in autumn. I wanted April showers to bring May flowers, rather than hot, dry dust storms. I wanted a Violet Vale and a bending willow to press my lips against – the mighty Saguaro cactus made a pale and painful stand-in. I wanted to buy back-to-school clothes and actually need warm shoes and long pants and sweaters in September. I used to look at my Indianapolis cousins' galoshes with unmitigated envy, and I thought their musty basement smelled absolutely heavenly.

I think my grandmother sympathized with my longings – when she'd visit, she'd look out on the immense expanse of the desert vista and mutter under her breath about all that 'dry brown stuff.' And then I'd see her close her eyes, and soon a smile would come to her face, and I knew she was imagining the rolling hills of her girlhood home in Kentucky. When I closed my eyes, I'd imagine Avonlea.

She'd send us boxes of books – always, ever since I can remember. Books were treasures to her, and she has bequeathed to many besides me a rich internal imaginary where ideas and the sheer pleasure of words can open new worlds. In a very smart family, everyone said she was the smartest. But she'd just smile when she heard us talking like that and go on reading. Once when I was visiting, she gave me a big canvas bag and her library card and directed me to the library. I was in early college by then, already a reader, though not quite as voracious as she. She was retired, getting around on a walker, looking for someone who could satisfy her reading cravings. I brought home Annie Dillard's *Pilgrim and Tinker Creek*, and she snatched it out of my hands, soaking it up with her bright blue eyes by bedtime, revelling in the kind of detail in that book, Dillard's inimitable ability to blend internal philosophy with the bugs of the field, with air bubbles in a stream, in line after line of perfectly pitched prose.

When my grandmother died last year, she left me a large cardboard box, carefully wrapped and tied with white string. On the outside of the parcel she had written, 'For Brenda, a kindred spirit.' Inside were ten clothbound books, the complete *Anne of Green Gables* series. Each had her name and a year in the frontispiece, beginning in 1908, the year after her birth. The books were familiar yet strange. When I visited my grandmother, she would let me read *Rainbow Valley* or *Rilla of Ingleside*, but I had never taken them outside of her house. I had never seen them in my grown-up hands. Holding those books now is a poignant reminder of the love of literature my grandmother and I share.

Anne has been with our family for generations, although passed not from mother to daughter, but from grandmother to granddaughter, back to mother, to cousin, to aunt, ricocheting through the family, affecting others and passing some by. It's not just anyone, I've found, who likes these books. Those who claim Anne talk in a kind of code about kindred spirits and Jonah days, and these texts by L.M. Montgomery will always stand as the gateway to my zest for reading. My grandmother first sent me *Anne of Green Gables* in paperback when I was ten, and I remember stifling laughter as I secreted a flashlight under the covers to find out how Anne would ever make her green hair red again.

Anne was a delightful childhood memory. But she stayed with me, so much so that when I was an undergraduate at the University of Arizona sitting in the Tucson Public Library and trying, really trying, to write my very intellectual honours thesis, I happened to get up and take a stroll over to the kids' section and rediscovered *Anne of Green Gables*. I devoured it, and the rest of the nine books in the series, as hungrily at twenty-one as I had done at ten. At that time I was amazed to see how much of Anne's sensibility had informed my own.

For instance, I'm embarrassed to admit that Anne influenced my sense of how to let a boy know you are interested in him until I was nearly twenty-two! Though I never broke a slate over a boy's head, I do remember, with painful clarity, bonking Scott Standage on the head with the elbow of my arm cast. I couldn't really understand why this didn't lead him to swear a lifelong allegiance to me, as Gilbert had done to Anne. I don't think I ever really believed in fairies or dryads as Anne did, but I do spend my days reading much of the same Victorian literature that peppers her speeches. And, as an educator, I share more than a little of her 'sparing the rod' philosophy about teaching. I also thrive on intellectual competition, akin to the academic race Gilbert and Anne pushed each other in. I remember my mother sitting at the foot of my bed once when I was in high school, looking at me in a very concerned way because I had brought home another report card with straight As. She assured me in her most soothing tones that both she and my father would still love me if I failed in school. She never could understand where I picked up that intellectual aggression – she'd be surprised to know I got it from Anne Shirley, the heroine of 'innocuous girls' fiction.'

Now, with several graduate degrees under my belt, I pick up Anne again, and I am impressed by how craftily Montgomery deployed her little orphan through a textual world. The Anne series is indebted to a long line of literary antecedents that employed the trope of the winsome orphan cast into the world, depending on none but herself. Yet the figure of Anne is unlike other orphans in literature, such as Edna Earl in Augusta Jane Evans's *St. Elmo* or Ellen Montgomery in Susan Warner's *The Wide, Wide World* or that very famous orphan in Charlotte Brontë's *Jane Eyre*, predominantly because the reader is encouraged to laugh at Anne even while admiring her. This is an interesting writerly device on Montgomery's part, for it pulls the reader not through common devices of sentimental fiction (for instance, tears, pious lessons, and innate goodness, though certainly the Anne books have these too), but through a shared field of humour. The result is a re-imagination of what a childhood heroine might look like. She need not be helpless and always crying like Ellen Montgomery, nor need she be perfectly pious and without flaw, like Edna Earl. She can be a girl both ardent and ridiculous, trying and talented.

Such a representation of girlhood into maturity, is subtle in its difference from hegemonic norms of literary womanhood, but it is also potent. Montgomery's imagination of Anne was in many ways a crucial form of conceptualizing independence, resilience, and imagination itself; the popularity of her books suggests there was and continues to be a willing audience to hear these kinds of messages about female potential. But again, I've slipped into the language I've trained myself to use. It would make my grandmother look at me, give a great laugh, and say, 'Oh pooh, child.' The simple fact is that for a particular kind of imaginative and brainy person (and almost always this person is a pre-adolescent girl), these books not only express but shape much of what's going on inside – the desire to belong, the intrigue of the imaginary, the delight that comes through standing your ground and letting kindred spirits magically find you. Here are few of my 'Anne moments.'

Scene One. My husband and I were in Italy in March for an academic conference. After a brilliant time wandering through Venice and exploring the lower Alps in Italy, we were tired when we flew back home. Our flight connected through Paris, and we had a long layover there. I was more exhausted than all the French *café au lait* could remedy, and I lay down on the uncomfortable bank of moulded blue plastic seating to rest. Somewhere from the back of my mind, I could hear a voice saying, 'But Marilla, you simply must let me go to the picnic. It would be a travesty of the utmost dimension if you refused.' Anne. Here? In Paris? Was this just some stored-away memory speaking to me through my sleepy stupor? I peeked up over the seats and saw a French mother and daughter, waiting to fly to the States, reading *Anne of Green Gables* in English. Both were eager and intent, and I eased back down into the chairs to listen to this mother read.

Scene Two. I was at a retirement party recently, chatting that certain kind of small talk required at such events, when I began talking to a graduate student who – quite literally – looked as if he should be a member of the Heaven's Gate cult ... bald head, white shirt, black pants, black Nike tennis shoes. He was big into sci-fi fantasy. In the course of our conversation, he asked about my plans for the summer, and I mentioned coming to the L.M. Montgomery conference. His eyes lit up! 'I love the Emily books!' he exclaimed. 'My wife and I have a policy that we each read the books that were meaningful to the other as kids. Emily and Anne were at the top of her list.' I'm not sure if he's a kindred spirit, but I'd guess his wife is.

Scene Three. I recently sang in the University of Kentucky Opera

Theatre's summer production. It's a fast and furious five weeks of rehearsal before a very demanding show. At one of the early rehearsals, we were still pounding out notes and rhythms, and I happened to glance over at the director's daughter, a ten-year-old African-American girl, all legs and eyeglasses, so intent on her book, that two hours of screeched-out wrong notes barely phased her. A few weeks later, we were staging rehearsals, and when I wasn't needed on the stage, I'd read through my Anne books – I had been reading the series again in preparation for this conference (although I brought my old paperback version of Anne. I don't think my grandmother's ghost would allow me to take her hardback first editions out of the house). Elizabeth, that reading ten-year-old, found me and shyly said, 'I looked at your book while you were up on stage, Brenda. Guess what? I've read about Anne all the way to her House of Dreams.' I had found a kindred spirit. My grandmother would have been delighted. And so too, I believe, would have been Lucy Maud Montgomery.

I recently had the occasion to experience a fourth 'Anne moment.' This semester, while I was reading the roster of students on the first day of class, one of my female students told me she preferred to be called Anne rather than Paige, as my grade sheet reflected. 'Is that Anne with an e?' I asked. I heard a sharp intake of breath from the young woman sitting immediately to my right, a chemical-engineering major from West Virginia who had long red hair. 'Are you an Anne fan?' she asked in a soft whisper. 'Absolutely,' I answered. I had found another.

So what does it mean to find a kindred spirit? Why should a professional literary scholar feel it necessary to 'confess' that she is such a thing and that she looks for others who are as well? There are long and complicated answers to these questions having to do with what count as credible knowledge and worthwhile texts, and of how one ought to be credentialized in order to legitimate discussions about these texts. Books written as juvenilia for a popular market are always a hard sell in the hallowed halls of academe, usually because their very popularity makes them accessible and so, seemingly, shallow, trite, and unworthy of serious merit. And it's not just books for children that fight such reputation battles. The classical canon is loaded with texts that fared poorly in the marketplace but have been saved by mostly male scholars as significant, difficult, and appropriate fodder for intellectual pursuits. In mid-nineteenth-century America, for example, the combined works of Melville, Crane, and Hawthorne sold fewer copies than the first printings of Fanny Fern's *Ruth Hall* or Susan Warner's *The Wide, Wide World*, yet both of the popular texts have, until recently, been considered 'too light' for scholarly attention. Popular texts by women have been so stigmatized that, as Joyce Warren says, 'no one in this century with any pretensions of intellect would be caught dead reading their work' (10). Jane Tompkins argues that sentimental and popular novels have been disparaged because modern criticism faults them as lacking 'marks of greatness' such as finely delineated characters, verisimilitude in the story line, and an intellectual/metaphysical conflict taking place separately from the plot (xii).

But this leads me back to the founding premise of my essay. Why do I feel a kind of shame about putting Anne on my academic *vita*? Is it really as simple as the classic divide between the heart and the head, that my brain recognizes and appreciates texts of complexity and ambiguity but my heart responds to what I love, and that somehow there is something lesser in bonds of emotion? I want to say no. Yet I know that no university in the country values emotional devotion over intellectual rigour. Feelings are the domain of the fan. The domain of the scholar is in intellectual assessment, making arguments, determining cultural codes of meaning. In tracing out those two camps, one can't help but see the gender and class biases encoded into them – the rigid masculinity of the entrenched patriarchy denying legitimacy to the mass of sobbing plebeians who are emotional victims rather than intellectual champions. It really doesn't matter if, as academics, we occupy a rather fortuitous position of being both intrigued by and passionate about our subjects. It's always the brain that will out.

Many of my colleagues feel that Sullivan's made-for-television renditions of the Anne tales, which first emerged in the mid-1980s and which have increasingly played fast and loose with the content and structure of Montgomery's stories, are in fact draining potential readers from the 'authentic' texts, filling the hunger for a literary imagination with the pre-packaged 'junk food' of television's empty calories. In chapter 10 of this collection, K.L. Poe argues, even more strongly, that Sullivan's films have 'anachronistically gerrymandered' Montgomery's initial story and character to such a degree that they give a feminist agenda to the story that wasn't present in the original texts. She argues that Anne's *Bildungsroman* model of character development was stretched out of recognition in the film, a move she labels as anti-feminist.

I have some sympathy for this argument. After all, when my best friend asked me what I would be speaking on at this conference, and when I said L.M. Montgomery's writing, her eyes went blank. But when I said *Anne of Green Gables*, her face showed a flash of recognition: 'Oh yes, I watched that on PBS.' Hence, she felt, she had a rightful claim to a full and total understanding of the text, a claim I found myself disputing. Yet I dispute just as strongly the notion that Montgomery's *Anne of Green Gables* is superior in all ways to Sullivan's *Anne of Green Gables*, or that somehow to fail to uphold the *Bildungsroman* formula is necessarily an anti-feminist gesture (particularly considering how fully this literary convention relies on patriarchal codes of identity for its authority). I don't think this because, as Eleanor Hersey argues also in this collection, Sullivan's Anne is an inherently more feminist text than Montgomery's or because it grabs the viewer through Anne's quest for romantic love that may or may not resemble our own. In fact, I find the relentless heterosexual logic about the possibilities for women rather depressing in both versions of Anne.

But I do think that Sullivan's films have a right to stand by themselves, with full integrity, as texts *inspired by* a set of narratives written in the early part of the twentieth century but *constructed for* a set of consumers with late-twentieth-century interests. And I think, for the most part, Sullivan has been successful in weaving a world that appeals to viewer interest – an interest in both the story he creates and the original works Montgomery wrote. Though I read the books and had my own relationship with Anne long before I saw the films, I've taught many a student who grew into reading Anne after her introduction from the films. Not incidentally, I've also had a good number of students who not only read the original Anne books after seeing the films, but also read more broadly in Victorian literature – specifically, Tennyson's poem 'The Lady of Shalott,' which is not mentioned in the books at all but plays a prominent role in the first film. These arguments, then, that pop culture dulls the masses and keeps people from authentic texts, seem more rhetorical than practical.

Additionally, if we put aside arguments about the natural mutability of narrative and the fact that many 'classic' pieces of literature have leaned heavily on earlier, and often unattributed, antecedents (for example, Goethe's *Faust* and Shakespeare's almost anything), I still feel that there are interesting canon biases worked into the logic behind the 'authentic Anne' argument. There seemed to be a prevailing sense at the 2000 conference that the way Montgomery imagined the story was the way it must always remain, a form of literary fundamentalism that

I found astounding. When I visited the Green Gables home in Cavendish, I immediately knew which of the rooms had been Marilla's and which Anne's, and no, it wasn't the group of sobbing Japanese fans that gave it away. Marilla's room had an amethyst brooch on the dresser; Anne's had a brown-silk dress with puffy sleeves hanging on the wardrobe. These were details lifted from the books, 'authentic' details that gave the totally constructed site some ring of verisimilitude. (Though let's be clear what we're talking about here: fans flocking to a site they believe to be the 'real' home of a fictional girl they've grown to love, an author's imaginary becoming so strong and seemingly real that a National Park is established on the site of where events never took place but were said to have. Montgomery could have given Baudrillard a run for his money in simulacra speculation.) I've never been fond of brown, and when Matthew goes to all the trouble to buy fabric and conspire with Mrs Lynde to make Anne the fabled puffy-sleeve dress, I had to overrule Montgomery and make Anne's dress a lovely shade of pale green in my mind. So, I can't say that I was the least bit bothered when Megan Follows wore a sky-blue dress rather than a brown one.

Now, the colour of Anne's dress may seem a trivial thing indeed, but my point here is, I hope, a bit more sophisticated. And that is that readers have always claimed the right of idiosyncratic reading – of imagining different endings, of failing to make it to the ending at all, of imagining that characters live free of the page or that readers themselves can occupy the literary landscape. Under these terms, it is as possible for me to drink a glass of wine in Auerbach's cellar with Faust and Mephistopheles as it is for me to stroll along the Lake of Shining Waters with Anne. The imagination does not need to obey high-art–low-art boundaries; it only needs to be fascinated. Yet still, we become snagged by that perplexing cultural capital dilemma that esteems one group of élite texts while casting the rest into a veritable dustbin.

But I'm beginning to wonder if that's changing. If more and more academics begin not only to trace love's trail in domestic novels but also publicly to acknowledge their own love for a text, perhaps we can turn the stigma. Can personal fondness justify a new canon? Yes and no. If fan response constitutes a viable criterion for canon formation, then certainly Kevin Sullivan has as much right to legitimation as Montgomery. Yet when Harold Bloom talks about his love for Shakespeare, he does little to open up the possibility for new voices. And when Oprah Winfrey constructs a de facto canon of her own, choosing texts that appeal to her and millions of viewers for primarily emotional reasons, she may be raising public awareness, but she does little towards toppling a pervading sense of important books that should be read. Irene Gammel noted in her opening remarks to the conference that Pierre Bourdieu's demand to dismantle the 'sacred frontier' that separates high culture from pop culture applies to what is happening in Montgomery studies. Indeed, I'm beginning to think that the only way to make any difference in the long-held institutional bias for high culture over pop culture is deliberately to cross, complicate, and confuse canonical divisions so that separations between high and low become less intelligible. We do that not through high-profile testimonials but in the figurative trenches: the classroom, academic conferences, and publications such as these.

Why do I think this is true? Because I've become increasingly convinced that the subject matter we read is less important than the manner in which we read it. And this engaged way of reading, I would argue, is precisely what constitutes the meaning of a 'kindred spirit.' Let's take Montgomery's two most famous heroines as models for the kind of engaged reading I refer to. Anne is a fiercely autonomous reader who carefully interprets the world for meaning. Optimistic against all better evidence, she is glad to be alive, even in her abject poverty, because there is so much to learn. Anne's natural and Romantic sensibility recoils against the mundanity of quotidian life: she takes narratological control, renaming the unevocative sites in Avonlea so that their language better suggests their transcendent value. The avenue, the woods, and the pond become the White Way of Delight, Lovers' Lane, and the Lake of Shining Waters. Throughout the initial book, Anne promises to reform and conform, to be a good girl, to stop getting into scrapes. But by novel's end, it is really Marilla (and, one would suggest, the reader) who alters, who is better able to perceive a kind of scintillating energy present in all things. Montgomery gives Anne a special kind of good looks – pale and big eyed (*AGG* 268), but she also gives Anne a razor-sharp brain that hungrily engages with all manner of texts, be they words on paper or leaves on the trees.

Emily also stands as a model of engaged readership, delving into both the natural and the textual worlds with a kind of voracious determination that borders on obsession. But Emily's characterization is different from Anne's; it is darker. She is a character who sometimes makes bad decisions, who can be too stubborn for her own good. On her path to professional authorship, Emily must learn to discipline her

Romantic sensibilities, to weed out, to sweat over, to discipline the text, which often means to burn or otherwise torture it. This internally con- flicted Emily – driven by her passions and ambition, feeling erotic desire, even experiencing psychic phenomena – is a character who rewrites the code of the heroine even as she writes her stories. When Emily avows, 'I'm not beautiful ... but I'm very interesting' (*EQ* 73), Montgomery has clearly turned the tables on what counts in a text of this sort, suggesting that the degree of engagement in one's com- mitment surmounts outward cultural status generally denoted on a woman's body by beauty.

These two characters, I would suggest, offer the reader models quite comparable to the models my grandmother offered me. Anne and Emily are interested, eager, questioning – the very qualities we try to instil in our students in literature courses. And further, they participate in the very process that academics esteem most highly, the kind of lit- erary alchemy that transforms black symbols on a white page into something that allows the imagination to create a rich internal land- scape.

Significantly, too, these characters speak to a theme dominant in 'classic' literature, the sense of where we fit in. Both Anne and Emily must reconcile how to conform to the world so as to have a place in it. Anne's dilemma is resolved through the Romantic transcendent: her loneliness marks her singularity and eventually brings her a safe nar- rative closure in a husband and children. Emily's dilemma, however, is more wrenching, for her loneliness is one of alienation, of an existen- tial separation from all around her. For Emily, her existential cry is answered by the page itself. Words become her conduit to '*Something Else*' (*EC* 17), but that path to the transcendent is rocky and arduous, and in many ways it sets Emily even more intrinsically apart from the people around her at New Moon.

Though I grew up on Anne's stories, it is really Emily who voices my sense of separation from the world, a separation that increases with each year I pass in academia. Like Emily, the specialized discourse I've trained myself to speak in many ways furthers my separation from a non-academic world, and I feel that same desire to be known and understood without first being oversimplified.

After I presented this paper, my family clamoured to read it. They knew I was talking about my childhood reading experiences and about my grandmother, and I know they all felt, though they didn't say it, that they might finally be able to understand what it is that I do. But of course, they didn't really understand it. They chided me for exaggerating details, for telling a version of family history that didn't quite 'get it right' to their way of thinking. My dad stopped reading at the intellectual parts, and my mom felt intimidated by words such as 'hegemonic' and 'patriarchal.' My Aunt Betty corrected my recollection of the books my grandmother had on her shelves, and my brothers argued that they were never all that interested in catching fireflies. I even felt my connection to my grandmother slipping away when I sat down with my Aunt Ann (spelled without an e!), arguably the biggest Anne fan in the family. 'I'm an Anne purist, you know. I just felt that the first book was the best and that none of Montgomery's other books were even in the same league as the Anne books. It's ridiculous. And don't even get me started on those fool movies,' she sighed in exasperation. By this point, I had decided to surrender, to put aside my intellectual ideas, to try to suppress the gnawing feeling that all of the thinking I do about this stuff makes me a kind of freak. 'I'm sure Grandma would have been upset about getting away from Anne too,' I said, silently tucking away my ideas about alienated Emily.

'Oh, I don't know,' said Aunt Ann. 'Your grandmother, for some odd reason, always seemed to like Emily best.'

Chapter 4

Taking Control: Hair Red, Black, Gold, and Nut-Brown

JULIET McMASTER

'It can't be denied your hair is terrible red,' Rachel Lynde tells Anne Shirley (*AAGG* 10:123).[1] If we remember nothing else about *Anne of Green Gables,* we remember that this garrulous orphan girl has red hair, that the red hair troubles her sorely, and that it also gets her into trouble. Anne's flaming red hair is her visible and identifying sign: it is what gives her her mythopoetic power and makes the helpless orphan denizen of a small Canadian island a heroine for all seasons and all climes, 'popular' in the widest sense. Her red hair is her Achilles' heel, her Waterloo, her fatal flaw, her touch of nature that 'makes the whole world kin.' We all know what it is like to think we have a 'defective' body part. Anne of Green Gables focuses that anxiety for us and articulates the uneasy relation between the body and culture.

Anne's intense sensitivity about her hair and its colour is part of her developed awareness of the multitudinous social codes and taboos, popular and otherwise, with which her culture surrounds her. What she reads and is taught, what people say and imply, the whole apparatus of social approval that is distinct from moral and religious systems though coexisting with them: all this Anne absorbs and reflects with a vividness beyond the reach of more prosaic souls like Marilla and Diana. And her accessibility to influence from her surrounding society realizes it for us, and moreover feeds back into the culture of which she has become a beloved icon.

Hair, like fingernails, eyebrows, and the outer layer of skin, is dead tissue that is still attached to the body, and growing out of it. At the growing end, it is physiological and deeply personal. At its extremities, it is available for many kinds of social structuring – cutting, trimming, dyeing, curling, straightening. Hair is the body substance that mediates between the individual and the culture. No wonder it is a site of intense conflict: external authorities – parents, church, peer groups, schools, gangs, fashion gurus – seek to impose their conventions on the individual, while the individual may want her hair to declare allegiance to a different authority altogether. In the long history of women's war to win control over their bodies, the subject of hair would deserve a substantial chapter. And in that putative chapter, *Anne of Green Gables* and *Emily of New Moon* could furnish eloquent examples.

In the oral version of this paper, I asked for a show of hands from those who could recall an incident from their own childhood when they made an unsanctioned intervention in their hair – by cutting, curling, or dyeing. Many hands went up, almost all of them female. Subsequent autobiographical anecdotes made it clear that the subject of hair and what we or others do to it touches us where we live. On my own behalf I confess that, yes, when I was about four I cut my own hair, and was punished for it. And my daughter did the same thing. Adjusting our hair is a female declaration of independence.

Anne Shirley is alert and dedicated to the conventions of popular culture of her day, both oral and literary. And to demonstrate her allegiance to the literary, I begin my study of *Anne of Green Gables* by a consideration of the story Anne writes for her Story Club, with its intertexts. 'It's a sad, sweet story,' Anne tells Diana of her own composition:

> It's about two beautiful maidens called Cordelia Montmorency and Geraldine Seymour who lived in the same village and were devotedly attached to each other. Cordelia was a regal brunette with a coronet of midnight hair and duskly flashing eyes. Geraldine was a queenly blonde with hair like spun gold and velvety purple eyes. (26.280)

Anne's usual artistic mode is oral rather than literary; her best creations, like the flowery, fictional 'confession' about taking the amethyst brooch, come in speech; and even here, where the subject is a written story, we hear of it as described to Diana. But written or spoken, Anne's compositions show a developed awareness of literary precedent. When she invents her blonde and brunette heroines, she has the authority of Walter Scott and Tennyson and James Fenimore Cooper behind her, as well as many other writers, popular and otherwise.

On this important matter of hair colour, many of her precedents are familiar, not to say clichéd. The fair–dark contrast goes back at least as far as Shakespeare's 'Two loves ... of comfort and despair' (sonnet 144), the fair Mr W.H. and the Dark Lady of the sonnets – and probably much farther. John Caspar Lavater, in his immensely influential *Essays on Physiognomy* of the late eighteenth century, also lurks behind Scott, because he claimed some scientific authority for moral judgments based on physical appearance. He associated tenderness and weakness with flaxen hair, the opposite with dark (Lavater 299).

Most famous for the contrast of blonde and brunette, of course, is Scott, for whom it is virtually a trademark. In *Waverley* (1814) the hero is placed between Rose Bradwardine, who has 'a profusion of hair of paley gold, and a skin like the snow of her own [Scottish] mountains in whiteness' (10.70), and Flora Mac-Ivor with 'dark eyes' and hair that 'fell in jetty ringlets on her neck' (21.146). Together, we hear, they 'would have afforded an artist two admirable subjects for the gay and the melancholy muse' (21.148). *The Pirate* (1821) presents the Troil sisters, Minna of the 'raven locks,' and Brenda, whose hair 'receives from the passing sunbeam a tinge of gold' (3.148). And perhaps most famously, in *Ivanhoe* (1819) we have the Anglo-Saxon Rowena, with 'clear blue eyes' and 'profuse hair, of a colour betwixt brown and flaxen' (4.54), over against the Jewess Rebecca with her 'profusion of sable tresses' (7.86). By the time of James Fenimore Cooper's *The Last of the Mohicans* (1826) the contrast is routine. Again we have sisters, Alice the fair, with 'golden hair,' and Cora the dark, with tresses 'shining and black, like the plumage of the raven' (1.10). And again the fate of the blonde is happy, that of the dark beauty tragic. 'Profuse ... dark ... raven'; 'clear ... bright ... golden': the terms recur with the persistence of ritual.

The Victorians often reacted from this set of stereotypes. Thackeray, for instance, though he also presents contrasting women, tends to reverse the Scott pattern: he makes *his* Rebecca, named after Scott's, a blonde, while milky Amelia is the brunette. And George Eliot's Maggie Tulliver, unapproved for her shaggy dark hair, refuses to finish reading *The Pirate* (Eliot 5.1.401) and *Corinne* because she's tired of books, she says, 'where the blond-haired women carry away all the happiness ... I want to avenge Rebecca and Flora Mac-Ivor, and Minna and all the rest of the dark unhappy ones' (5.4.433). But Scott's paradigm asserts itself none the less, and Maggie goes to the bottom of the river, like Anne's heroine. The story Anne writes, then, would not be one that Maggie would rejoice in, because Anne, too, still thoroughly conventional, awards the guy to 'the fair Geraldine' rather than to the raven-haired Cordelia (26.281).[2]

The novel *about* Anne, though, carries on the reaction to the stereotypes. Replacing the tall, dark, tragic beauties, we have plump, imperturbable Diana Barry, with 'black hair and eyes and rosy cheeks' (8.106), a habit of laughing before she talks (12.138), and a tendency to be 'just a dumpling' (33.349). And instead of the stately golden-haired beauty, we have Anne Shirley, with hair not blonde, not golden, but 'red as carrots,' in Rachel Lynde's words (10.123).

In fashion, different conventions obtain for hair colour. When Jo of *Little Women* sells her 'chestnut' locks, she gets only twenty-five dollars because her hair 'wasn't the fashionable color.' 'One black tail' in the hairdresser's window, though not as thick as hers, is priced at forty dollars (Alcott 5.163); so unless the mark-up on hair is considerable, it seems that for that time and place *black* hair is the fashionable colour. Somewhat later, though, in the rural England of Hardy's *The Woodlanders*, Marty South's profuse locks, of 'a rare and beautiful approximation to chestnut,' are considered highly desirable (Hardy 48).

Anne identifies with both her blonde and her dark heroines, Geraldine and Cordelia – both names she covets for herself. But she most likes to imagine that her hair 'is a glorious black – black as the raven's wing' (2.57). More realistically, she hopes for her hair to turn 'auburn,' the more fashionable variation on red. Auburn is the *de rigueur* colour for Jane Austen's personnel in her youthful parody *Love and Freindship* [*sic*]: From the fact that a certain young man's hair 'bore not the least resemblance to Auburn,' the narrator instantly concludes that he can have 'no soul' (Austen ltr 12.19). A triumphant moment from late in *Anne of Green Gables* arrives when Anne is called the girl 'with the splendid Titian hair' (33.355–6). 'Being interpreted, ["Titian"] means just plain red, I guess,' she laughs (356). Now it's all in a word. But when she was eleven, her red hair was no laughing matter.

The popular associations of red hair that she inherits are unpropitious both aesthetically and morally. Early in the novel, Anne puts the question to Matthew: 'Which would you rather be if you had the choice – divinely beautiful or dazzlingly clever or angelically good?' (2.58). Not surprisingly, the question is puzzling to shy old male Matthew. But girls have to ponder such things. They are forever bombarded with such maxims as 'Be good, sweet maid, and let who will be clever.' The three categories of brains, beauty, and morality are recalled in the forfeit of party games, which requires the boy to 'Bow to the wittiest, kneel to the prettiest, and kiss the one you love best.' And by the end, Matthew echoes these categories when he rejoices, 'She's smart and pretty, and loving, too, which is better than all the rest' (34.360).

For the young Anne, however, the priorities are different. Her first prayer goes 'Please let me stay at Green Gables; and please let me be good-looking when I grow up' (7.99). Diana tries to convince Anne that she is 'the smartest girl in school. That's better than being good-looking.' But Anne, 'feminine to the core,' firmly responds, 'No, it isn't … I'd rather be pretty than clever' (15.164).

In the world-view she inherits from the popular culture of her own day, 'pretty' is incompatible with having red hair. For Rachel Lynde, the oracle of Avonlea, being skinny and freckled and red-haired is the same as being 'homely' (9.114). Indeed, in certain contexts in the nineteenth century, 'red hair' was virtually synonymous with 'ugly,' as 'dark' was for Shakespeare. When the hero of Thackeray's *The Rose and the Ring* awakens from his magically induced love for the Princess Angelica, he instantly recognizes she is ugly – that is, marked by smallpox, squinting, and red-haired (Thackeray 7.255–6).

If literary precedent suggests that you can't be beautiful with red hair, it also determines that you can't be good. Long tradition declares that the devil and Judas both have red hair. Novels provide a string of red-haired villains: Dickens's Fagin, Samson Brass, Sally Brass, and Uriah Heep, and the devilish Peter Quint in James's *The Turn of the Screw*. No wonder Anne laments, 'You'd find it easier to be bad than good if you had red hair' (7.98). Her hot temper is another attribute linked to her red hair. Her most furious outbursts – verbally attacking Rachel Lynde and physically attacking Gilbert Blythe – are both immediate responses to their drawing attention to her carroty hair. 'Her temper matches her hair, I guess,' says Rachel Lynde sagely (9.116). Even as far back as Elizabethan times, red hair was associated with the choleric temperament.

What Anne overlooks, in her agony over her red hair as ugly, is its association with that other attribute of doubtful value in a female, intelligence. After her prompt and effective action with the colicky baby, the doctor says, 'That little red-headed girl they have over at Cuthbert's is as smart as they make 'em' (18.206). But Anne's maxim continues to be 'Be pretty, sweet maid, and let who will be smart.'

For Anne – and for thousands of readers since – her hair colour is almost as closely bound up with her identity as her gender. Although she tries to, she *'cannot* imagine that red hair away' (2.57). She knows she is a reject from Green Gables for being a girl rather than a boy. She also wistfully wonders, 'If I was very beautiful and had nut-brown hair, would you keep me?' (3.69). In fact, her red hair connects her deeply with the island of her adoption. 'What *does* make the roads red?' she asks Matthew on that first journey to Green Gables, as well as drawing attention to the colour of her 'glowing braids' (2.55, 56). We are meant to recognize a propitious kinship between Anne's red braids and Prince Edward Island's red roads. (Better to match the roads than the gables, she learns later.) As other critics have noted, Anne's body is indeed mythologized, though not always in the ways she supposes. 'Her hair is a sign that she belongs to her tribe – she just bears its standard more vividly than others do' (Doody 29). Her hair colour connects her not only with the earth but with blood, passion, and creativity.

The nineteenth century fetishized hair: because it is a body part relatively easy to detach and preserve, it regularly served as a relic to be mounted in jewellery, and a synecdoche for the whole person. One can't read far in nineteenth-century novels, for instance, without coming across a ring with Lucy Steele's hair in it, or a locket in which Cathy's hair is braided with Edgar's and Heathcliff's. Anne, too, is steeped in this culture. She covets Marilla's amethyst brooch with the hair in it; and when she is parted from her bosom friend, she begs poetically, 'Diana, wilt thou give me a lock of thy jet-black tresses in parting to treasure forever more?' (17.192).

When Jo March of *Little Women* saw her 'dear old hair laid out on the table,' she explains, 'It almost seemed as though I'd an arm or a leg off' (Alcott 15.163). Likewise, Anne's hair is irreducibly a part of her self; and one she must come to terms with. In a sense, Anne is already healthily at home in her body. There is a moment when she renounces her fantasy identity of Lady Cordelia Fitzgerald and reminds herself, as she looks in the mirror,

> 'You're only Anne of Green Gables,' she said earnestly ... 'But it's a million times nicer to be Anne of Green Gables than Anne of nowhere in particular, isn't it?'
> She bent forward, [and] kissed her reflection affectionately. (8.109)

This genuine and innate self-satisfaction vanity but as part of Anne's value, and Cuthberts and so many of the rest of us

[handwritten note: this quote useful about belonging]

world and its beauties and pleasures, and in her own place among them. Her problem is her cultural inheritance, and the dour moral, religious, and social influences that teach her to want to renounce her red hair.

Deprived of love as she has been for the first eleven years of her 'lonely, starved' childhood (*AA* 26.215), Anne desperately craves approval. Like the battered wife who is cowed into believing *she* must be the one at fault, Anne instinctively seeks a reason for the world's rejection, and locates it in her hair colour. The books she reads and the people around her give her sufficient reason to believe this stigma of hers marks her out as an inferior brand of humanity. In real life, her orphan's experience of alternating exploitation and rejection would be apt to produce a child crushed, withdrawn, resentful. But it is part of Anne's generous spirit that she doesn't blame people for her painful lot in life. They can be *expected* to disapprove of her for her red hair, as she does herself. Blaming God for purposely visiting her red hair on her is as far as she ever goes in resentment, and even that is a temporary attitude.

If thy hand offend thee, cut it off. And likewise, if thy hair colour offend thee, dye it. Anne can hardly be blamed for the radical action she takes, at least not by us readers. But nineteenth-century culture was another matter.

In a long and fascinating article, 'The Power of Women's Hair in the Victorian Imagination,' Elisabeth Gitter argues that the Victorians provided a climax in a long tradition of mythologizing and fetishizing women's hair: 'The powerful woman mythologized in Victorian literature and art achieved her vitality partly through her hair, which both contributed to and expressed her magic power. She used her hair to spin her discourse and to spin her plots, to strangle her lovers and to shelter them, to build deadly snares and webs and to proclaim her own divinity and glory' (Gitter, abstract, 857). Gitter explores the deep ambivalence in the Victorian obsession with hair as both supremely beautiful and supremely dangerous. The woman's golden hair could indicate her approved tractability or her fatal power. It was a valuable endowment, hers to keep but not to barter: Hardy's Marty South, for instance, comes to no good: Her act of cutting off her gorgeous chestnut hair for two sovereigns sets off a string of unfortunate events. (Mind you, in Hardy everything does!) Dickens's golden-haired Lucie Manette and Jenny Wrenn have a redemptive power that plucks their heroes back from death to life. But the *femme fatale*, typified in the mythic figure of the paralysing Medusa with her serpentine hair, is the terrifying castrating woman of Freudian nightmare.

In the fairy tales endlessly retold throughout the nineteenth century, 'golden hair tumbles ... in impossible quantities' (Warner 365). Pre-Raphaelite paintings feature woman's hair as profuse, beautiful, threatening, meandering, labyrinthine: a sign both of her daunting power and her appealing victimization. Millais's *Ophelia* with her floating hair matches Tennyson's pathetic Elaine, whom Anne so memorably personates. Lizzie Siddal was also the model for D.G. Rossetti's martyred *Beata Beatrix*, painted after her death, whose hair even emits a halo. But the profuse hair of other female figures is more like a weapon: John Waterhouse's *La Belle Dame Sans Merci* (1893) shows a dangerous seductress who winds her hair around the throat of the enthralled knight-at-arms. And often the flowing hair is merely a decorative attribute of a series of languid beauties.

It sometimes seems, though, that for all the power implicit in these women's tresses, the women themselves are not all that powerful. The power seems to work *through* the hair, rather than by the agency of the woman. Although Gitter documents her article with dozens of examples of representations of women's hair by men, she seems to be rather short of representations by women. For instance, Hardy's transgressive Marty South is there, but not George Eliot's Maggie or Alcott's Jo, both of whom are significant forebears for Anne in her radical action of intervening in the natural growth and colour of her hair. And a visual representation that seems to me to be significant is by a woman Pre-Raphaelite: Eleanor Brickdale's *The Little Foot Page* of 1907 shows the heroine taking the scissors to her own hair before following the man she loves into battle, disguised as a boy. The painting inspired women art students of the day to take to the 'Pageboy' haircut (Marsh and Nunn, frontispiece, 153).

It seems that the principal function of the gorgeously coroneted heroines of Scott, Cooper, Tennyson, and the male Pre-Raphaelite painters is to *be*; whereas what Maggie and Jo and Anne and the Little Foot Page most want is to *do*. Hence their radical action with the scissors and the dye.

As abundant hair is a sign of abundant sexuality, so the shearing of hair is a kind of castration: hence the biblical Samson, and Dickens's Patriarchal Casby. For women, in representations by men, cutting off hair is commonly a desecration, and cognate with rape, as with Belinda's lock. Marty South, cropped, can't bear to face her 'deflowered visage' in the mirror (Hardy 58). In *Dombey and Son*, when the witchlike Mrs Brown whips out 'a large pair of scissors' and proceeds to ruffle little Florence's luxuriant hair 'with a furious pleasure,' we can hardly bear to contemplate the threatened violation; and in fact Dickens can't bear it either, and he spares Florence's hair (6.130).

But it matters, after all, who wields the scissors. Will it be Delilah, the Baron in *The Rape of the Lock*, the witch in 'Rapunzel'? – or will it be the girl with the locks herself? When Maggie Tulliver takes the law and the scissors into her own hands, there is a keen sense of exhilaration. And here I can't resist a substantial extract:

> Tom followed Maggie upstairs into her mother's room, and saw her at once go to a drawer from which she took out a large pair of scissors.
>
> 'What are they for, Maggie?' said Tom, feeling his curiosity awakened.
>
> Maggie answered by seizing her front locks and cutting them straight across the middle of her forehead.
>
> 'O, my buttons, Maggie – you'll catch it!' exclaimed Tom ...
>
> Snip! went the great scissors again while Tom was speaking, and he couldn't help feeling it was rather good fun ...
>
> 'Here, Tom, cut it behind for me,' said Maggie, excited by her own daring, and anxious to finish the deed ...
>
> The black locks were so thick – nothing could be more tempting to a lad who had already tasted the forbidden pleasure of cutting the pony's mane ... One delicious grinding snip, and then another and another, and the hinder locks fell heavily on the floor, and Maggie stood cropped in a jagged, uneven manner, but with a sense of clearness and freedom, as if she had emerged from a wood into the open plain. (Eliot 1.7.120)

True, that temporary sensation of 'clearness and freedom' is swiftly replaced by a 'bitter sense of the irrevocable,' and Maggie is made to suffer for her transgression. But every reader sides with Maggie and her rash act of rebellion, and not with Tom and his instinct for socially approved behaviour. Similarly, when Jo March sells her hair to help the family finances in a crisis, even though she grieves for the part of her body that has been lopped off, she bravely asserts, 'a crop is so comfortable I don't think I shall ever have a mane again' (Alcott 15.163). 'I only sold what's my own,' she insists reasonably (161); whereas the male fetishizers are apt to regard a woman's hair not as her own property but rather as a sacred trust, hers to preserve but not to sacrifice or modify.

These are the precedents that Anne has before her when she takes her bold resolution to choose her own hair colour and buys the package 'warranted to dye any hair a beautiful raven black' (27.290). The historical placement of *Anne of Green Gables* is significant here. Set in about 1890,[3] but published in 1908, the narrative allows Montgomery to endow Anne and surrounding personnel with Victorian attitudes, while herself bringing twentieth-century views to bear on them.

Marilla is scandalized by Anne's action: 'Dyed it! Dyed your hair! Anne Shirley, didn't you know it was a wicked thing to do?' (27.288). Anne's response is in a different register altogether: it belongs to a new generation and a meliorated world view. 'Yes, I knew it was a little wicked,' she admits. 'But I thought it was worth while to be a little wicked to get rid of red hair. I counted the cost, Marilla. Besides, I meant to be extra good in other ways to make up for it' (288). Anne is practical and pragmatic. Where for Marilla wickedness is generic and monolithic, for Anne it is subject to qualification: there are degrees of wickedness, and one can choose among them. Unlike those Pre-Raphaelite beauties who sit around *being*, she takes steps and *does* – though not without counting the cost. Her hair is her own, like Jo's, and she takes responsibility not just for having it but for doing something about it. The moral and existential issues are not so portentous for her as for Marilla.

The fact that her hair turns green instead of the beautiful raven black she aspired to is for her a failure in technology rather than morality. But for Marilla, the green affords a heaven-sent opportunity to moralize: 'Well, I hope you'll repent to good purpose,' she says severely, 'and that you've got your eyes opened to where your vanity has led you' (27.290). But the lesson Anne actually does learn is somewhat different. On seeing her cropped hair in the mirror, she resolves: 'I won't try to imagine [my hair] away, either. I never thought I was vain about my hair, of all things, but now I know I was, in spite of its being red, because it was long and thick and curly.' (27.292) In *doing* something about her hair, even though the act was not an immediate success, she has learned to claim her own appearance and her own identity, and to be proud of both. It won't be long until she is ready to kiss her own reflection again.

Emily of New Moon actually *has* the raven locks that Anne longs for. Montgomery, too, plays the game of the contrasted heroines, the gay and melancholy muses, but across two series, and with the 'gold' alloyed with a rich copper. And as Anne's red hair is associated with her joyful, unmediated expressiveness, her gift for the spontaneous spoken word, so Emily's black hair goes with her talent for writing, her more thoughtful and nuanced creativity that leaves a recoverable record. As the Pre-Raphaelite painters associated women's hair with weaving yarns and spinning tales, so Montgomery locates power and creativity in Anne's and Emily's hair, which is 'profuse' and flowing like their words.[4] But to the surrounding authorities, Marilla and Aunt Elizabeth, both oral and written expression need to be curbed and controlled. 'You talk entirely too much for a little girl,' Marilla tells Anne (4.78). And Aunt Elizabeth seeks to censor Emily's writing.

It's about control, as the tyrants know. 'Why that abundance?' demands Mr Brocklehurst at Lowood School, of a girl's richly curling hair (Brontë 7.73). 'All those top-knots must be cut off,' he decrees, to a group of terrorized pupils. 'My mission here is to mortify in these girls the lusts of the flesh' (7.74). 'I think the gell has too much hair,' says Maggie Tulliver's aunt Pullet, before the fateful episode with the scissors. 'I'd have it thinned and cut shorter, sister, if I was you: it isn't good for her health. It's that as makes her skin so brown, I shouldn't wonder' (Eliot 1.7.118). Emily and Maggie both have dark hair and powers of expression altogether too profuse for approval.

Unlike Maggie and Anne, Emily doesn't feel like dyeing or curtailing her abundant locks; but others do. As in *Jane Eyre* and *The Mill on the Floss*, the puritanical moralist goes to war with the sensuality and expressiveness traditionally implied by hair. Aunt Elizabeth 'come[s] to the conclusion that Emily's heavy masses of hair "took from her strength," and that she would be much stronger and better if it were cut off' (*ENM* 10.116). Females, apparently, are the opposite of Samson in this respect. Here cutting hair is a kind of physical euphemism for quenching creativity, a species of intellectual lobotomy. Montgomery makes the connection clear through the imagery. Later, in relation to Emily's writing, we hear, 'No Murray of New Moon had ever been guilty of writing "stories" ... It was an alien growth that must be pruned off ruthlessly. Aunt Elizabeth applied the pruning shears' (321). But to return to her literal application of shears:

> With Aunt Elizabeth to decide was to act. One morning she coolly informed Emily that her hair was to be 'shingled.'
>
> Emily could not believe her ears.
>
> 'You don't mean that you are going to cut off my hair, Aunt Elizabeth,' she exclaimed.

'Yes, I mean exactly that,' said Aunt Elizabeth firmly. 'You have entirely too much hair ... Now, I don't want any crying.' (10.116)

It is a fraught moment, such as we encounter in Victorian novels. Girls are not allowed to question such decrees. Rapunzel must give in to the witch, Florence Dombey is meekly submissive: 'She offered no resistance or entreaty, and merely raised her mild eyes towards [Mrs Brown's] face' (Dickens 6.131). The already disempowered girl is to be chastened even further.

Emily is initially like them: 'Emily waited – quite hopelessly. She must lose her lovely hair – the hair her father had been so proud of' (10.117). But presently a new kind of magic is activated.

Aunt Elizabeth returned with the scissors; they clicked suggestively as she opened them; that click, as if by magic, seemed to loosen something – some strange formidable power in Emily's soul. She turned deliberately around and faced her aunt. She felt her brows drawing together in an unaccustomed way – she felt an uprush as from unknown depths of some irresistible surge of energy.

'Aunt Elizabeth,' she said, looking straight at the lady with the scissors, '*my hair is not going to be cut off*. Let me hear no more of this.'

An amazing thing happened to Aunt Elizabeth. She turned pale – she laid the scissors down – ... and then for the first time in her life Elizabeth Murray turned tail and fled. (10.117)

Hooray! It is one of those sudden reversals of power, when the underdog triumphs, that make us want to stand up and cheer: Elizabeth Bennet defeating the bullying Lady Catherine De Bourgh, or Nicholas Nickleby taking the birch to Squeers, or Jane Eyre getting the better of Mr Brocklehurst (Brontë 4.34). In a crisis, in defence of her hair and her creativity, Emily is miraculously invested with a patriarchal authority that enables her to leap the generations and defeat the illegitimate power. Emily is still under discipline. But like Anne, she discovers that the moment of taking control of the management of that significant bodily tissue, hair, is a crucial stride in her development of subjectivity and agency.

Emily, like Maggie, later takes the scissors into her own hands and cuts her own bangs. 'Snip – snip – went the scissors. Glistening locks fell at her feet.' Her initial triumph at the provocative effect swiftly gives way to guilt: 'It was wicked to cut a bang when Aunt Elizabeth had forbidden it' (25.235). And in panic she cuts the bangs right down to the hairline, in a penitential tonsure.

Again the incident is bound up with her identity. Although her own reflection, 'little Emily-in-the-glass' (1.13), had been her best friend in her father's house, at New Moon, where Aunt Elizabeth's mirror is hung too high for her, she is alienated from her own image. But the cutting of the bangs, notwithstanding the associated guilt, helps her first to Old Kelly's gift of the little pocket mirror (22.250) and ultimately to 'a room of her own' (27.298) – with all the intellectual freedom this implies – where the mirror hangs at the right height for her.[5] In taking control of the management of her hair, she has recovered her self.

'The Victorian vision of magic hair did not survive long into the twentieth century,' Elisabeth Gitter notes; and she cites Hélène Cixous on the laugh of the Medusa and stories such as O. Henry's 'The Gift of the Magi' and F. Scott Fitzgerald's 'Bernice Bobs her Hair,' where the severing of ladies' hair is treated lightly, with humour and irony (953). But women had been representing this move towards control for a long time previously, and heroines such as Maggie and Jo, and later the 'Little Foot Page,' Anne, and Emily, had taken bold though unapproved steps in adjusting those long, golden, raven, red, and nut-brown locks.

An interesting semantic change in the verb 'to grow' is a significant indicator. The word goes back to Old English, but only in its intransitive senses: grass grows, trees grow, children grow. The transitive sense that takes an object – I grow tomatoes, he's growing a beard – is a relatively recent development, according to the *OED*, dating only from the late eighteenth century. For those grandly coroneted Pre-Raphelite ladies, it is their *hair* that grows, God-given, and that is similarly valued and fetishized. But the modern woman can say, '*I* am growing my hair,' and so claim agency in the process, and full possession of her own body part. Likewise, she can stop growing it, stop others from cutting it, and curl and colour it according to her choice. As the lyric in the musical *Hair* triumphantly proclaims: 'Yes! Blow it! Show it! Long as I can grow it – *my* hair!'

Notes

1 I use *The Annotated Anne of Green Gables* and supply chapter and page number for the cited edition, so that it may be traced in other editions.

2 The Scott heroine who does lurk behind Anne of Green Gables, I think, is Anne of Geierstein, in the 1829 novel of that name. It's not only that Montgomery's title echoes Scott's, but Scott's Anne is also a child of nature, spiritual and ethereal. When she emerges out of the mists of her native Swiss mountains, she shows 'rather the undefined lineaments of a spirit than a mortal maiden,' as Montgomery's Anne seems a creature of 'rainbow and moonshine' (AAGG 20.227). Anne Shirley makes her conventional heroine Geraldine passive: the hero Bertram De Vere saves her life and she faints in his arms (26.281). But Anne herself is more unconventional and more active, like Scott's Anne, who actually rescues the hero instead of being rescued *by* him. And Scott's hero, like Anne's, is called De Vere.

3 The datable historical event of the visit of the Canadian 'Premier' (AAGG 18.199) with the notable nose – evidently Sir John A. Macdonald (207n) – brings the action to about 1890 (199n).

4 The root meaning of 'profuse' is pouring forth, and its application to hair as well as to language suggests generous abundance. Anne's stated preference for spontaneous speech ('Something just flashes into your mind, so exciting, and you must out with it. If you stop to think it over you spoil it all' [220]) connects her with Shelley's symbol of the poet, the skylark, which pours out its heart 'In profuse strains of unpremeditated art' ('To a Skylark,' 1820).

5 The connection between Emily's cutting of the bangs and the recovery of her reflection is carefully marked. 'The bang was just about at its best' (ENM 21.239) when Aunt Nancy's invitation arrives; on the journey there her prettiness leads to Old Kelly's gift of the pocket mirror (22.250); and Emily's growth towards maturity ('taller and older, in soul if not in body' [27.397]) qualifies her for her mother's room with the accessible mirror.

Chapter 5

'This has been a day in hell': Montgomery, Popular Literature, Life Writing

MARGARET STEFFLER

'When I feel that I have come to "the end of my rope" I write it here – and find at the close of writing that the rope has lengthened a little and I can go on' (*SJ* 3: 170). So L.M. Montgomery noted in her journal on 16 March 1924, articulating a balance of pain and relief, a tension that engages the journal reader. Within a few sentences, Maud can move from describing 'the strange exquisite pleasure' inspired by 'a fiery autumnal sunset, with sorrowful dark cedar spires against it' to complaining of the exhaustion of feeling 'cold and tired all the time' (*SJ* 4: 310). This tension may explain why in her reading of Montgomery's journals, Pulitzer prize-winning author Carol Shields encountered a much more attractive voice than the 'romantic effusions' and the 'fey self-cherishing' of the character of Anne in *Anne of Green Gables*. Shields marvels at the strength and power of what she terms this 'wholly other voice' ('Loving Lucy' D18). Having long resisted the 'contrived' character of Anne, beloved by both her mother and daughters, Shields was surprised to find herself so strongly drawn to Montgomery's persona and voice in the journals. Even those who were not girlhood 'kindred spirits' with Anne can become very close to Anne's creator through their responses to the vitality, honesty, and humour in Montgomery's life writing.

For those of us who read Anne in the 1960s and then waited expectantly for the publication of the first volume of the journals in 1985, our reading has been enriched and layered by our response to the voice and persona of L.M. Montgomery in the journals. As our reading of Anne and Emily helped us to construct our girlhood identity, so our reading of L.M. Montgomery in the journals has played a role in confirming our places as women; and few of us have been disappointed in the role that she has played. The reading of the novels and the journals, when viewed as a continuous process, connects girlhood and womanhood in a remarkable manner, accounting to a certain extent for the popularity and attraction of the journals and of the persona of L.M. Montgomery as a woman as well as a writer. It is a connection that we welcome and crave, as our reading of Maud, developing out of our earlier reading of her characters, continues to be an active process that often recognizes and validates our needs, choices, and decisions as Canadian women at the beginning of the twenty-first century.[1]

Like her fiction, Montgomery's journals, I contend, sustain a popular appeal. The American film critic John Fiske, writing about the popular text in *Understanding Popular Culture,* maintains that 'popular meanings are constructed out of the relevances between the text and everyday life' (126). Fiske emphasizes the reader's participation in this construction, arguing that 'popular pleasures derive from the production of these meanings by the people, from the *power* to produce them' (126). Montgomery's novels and journals, I argue, inserted into our everyday lives and culture, succeed in producing popular meaning and pleasure because the reader has been involved in 'the power and process of making meanings' (127). Our girlhood reading of Anne and Emily in the novels and our adult reading of 'Maud' in L.M. Montgomery's journals can be viewed as a connected and continuous process. Reading the journals as a continuation and completion of reading the novels is certainly a different process from simply reading the journals as a resource to provide background for the novels. Considering the reading of the novels and the journals as a continuous and active process performed by the same readers addresses some of the concerns about 'confession' expressed by Brenda Weber in chapter 3.

Carol Shields's extensive interest in biography and autobiography perhaps explains to some extent her fascination with Montgomery's journals and 'the depth of pleasure' she derives from knowing 'what the inside of another woman's head looks like' ('Loving Lucy' D18). After all, Shields has invited her own readers inside the head of Daisy Goodwill Flett, the main character in *The Stone Diaries,* and thus it is not surprising that she values as 'priceless' the 'excavation into the mind of a woman' (D18) provided so admirably by the journals.[2] Shields does concede that Anne Shirley and L.M. Montgomery start out as 'equals, both of them young girls eager for the wholeness of life' (D18). However, the difference between the novels and the journals, noted by Shields, is significant. If L.M. Montgomery is as different from Anne and Emily as she appears to be, then the reading of the journals on one level is a way to measure and celebrate our own difference from the girls we once were. Examining the relationship between the reader born in the middle of the twentieth century and the journal persona, it is obvious that the journal reader, devouring each volume as it is published, is shedding the 'eager[ness] for the wholeness of life' displayed by the character of Anne and by the young Maud. It is in this loss of youth and eagerness that we can begin to examine the significance of the reading of the journals as it follows the reading of the novels.

As readers of Anne in our girlhood, we grew with her even as she grew away from us. She became a woman, married, and had children while we were still at the Avonlea stage of life. The journals fill a void and pick up where we left off – where we lost Anne as a powerful presence in our lives. The publication dates of the journals (1985, 1987, 1992, 1998), for those of us born in the mid-twentieth century, have corresponded with the stages of our own womanhood in an amazing manner, reinforcing and validating many of our feelings about marriage, motherhood, work, domesticity, leisure, and society in much the same way that the eager young Anne duplicated our enthusiastic dreams of girlhood and Emily reflected our artistic ambitions. The comfort of the journals is that we are close to Montgomery's voice and thoughts and are invited to establish an intimate relationship with the writer.

The discoveries made in the journals confirm vague feelings and shadowy suspicions of empowerment that were present in the reading of the novels but were never solidified or articulated when we were girls. The basis of this empowerment is concentrated in those moments of the novels during which oppression is subverted by Montgomery's female characters in conjunction with the reader. In reading the journals, we contribute to a more direct challenge and subversion of an oppressive patriarchal structure (seen for example in Maud's legal battle with the Page Company) that corroborates our earlier reading of the fiction. The tension we sensed in the novels but could never actually explain or understand was really there. Moreover, the interplay between light and dark, romance and disappointment, is laid out for us once again, and much more directly, in the journals. The possibility that darkness and disappointment may dominate light and romance is borne out in the journals, which, unlike the novels, valiantly expose the often complex depths beneath the surface as being too murky to be 'solved' or too complicated to be mitigated by clarity and resolution. As women at the beginning of the twenty-first century, as opposed to girls in the middle of the twentieth, we are relieved to participate in the recognition of the presence and the value of darkness, depression, boredom, and exhaustion. The acknowledgment of the darkness speaks to the gap of years between the reading of Anne and Emily and the reading of Maud, allowing us to transfer the current text of the journals to lives that, like Montgomery's, contain darkness and boredom in varying degrees at various times.

If popular culture is based, as Fiske argues in *Reading the Popular*, on the 'struggle to make social meanings that are in the interests of the subordinate and that are not those preferred by the dominant ideology' (2), then the basis of Montgomery's work lies not only in the reader's identification with the child character or developing woman but also in the construction of 'social meanings' for those subordinate groups to which the reader belongs. As active participants in that construction, we allow the text to be fluid, the 'activation of the meaning potential of a text [occurring] only in the social and cultural relationships into which it enters' (Fiske, *Reading* 3). The reader's response to Montgomery's fictional characters may, on one level, be similar to the response of the Harlequin reader to heroines who make her feel that 'it's a lovely world, people are good, one can face anything and we are lucky to be alive' (Radway, *Reading the Romance* 6). Readers of Montgomery's work, however, are far from 'passive, purely receptive individuals who can only consume the meanings embodied within cultural texts' (ibid.). The active reader uses the text in a responsive manner. Montgomery's fiction provides the relevance demanded by the subordinated and disempowered reader, achieving its popularity through the provision of an opportunity for the reader to participate in the empowerment of the marginalized group to which she belongs.

Our enthusiastic reception of the journals is based on our ability to maintain a 'sense of social difference that is also a difference of interest' against 'attempts to control, structure, and minimize social differences' (Fiske, *Reading* 8). We indulge in our difference as women, but specifically as women who are allowed to be disillusioned, weary, and worried. The empowerment lies in the strength of the confession, which attempts to displace and devalue the shame and secrecy of admitting such feelings and conditions.[3] Maud's recognition of the source of her 'blackness' as the feeling that she is compelled, both internally and externally, to ensure that 'all must be hidden from the world' (*SJ* 4: 337) highlights this position of tension, which drives her to 'hide [miseries] and carry on, with false smiles and forced calm' (*SJ* 4: 337). This is not a position that is eventually broken or relieved by a 'solution' or conclusion, as in the case of the fictional characters; it is a chronic condition that does subside from time to time, but is stable in its permanence. The personal disclosure of darkness and depression, in tandem with the public denial of such emotions and conditions, sets up a situation of tension and balance that empowers by providing the recognition and articulation of an internal opposition to society's expectations of women.

In our identification with 'the other,' our reading of 'Maud' duplicates and continues our reading of Anne and Emily, blurring the border between child and adult. Neil Postman, in *The Disappearance of Childhood*, maintains that 'differences between adults and children are disappearing' (98). He goes on to argue that 'the adult-child may be defined as a grown-up whose intellectual and emotional capacities are unrealized and, in particular, not significantly different from those associated with children' (99). According to Postman, we are living in a culture that encourages the breaking down of this distinction between child and adult, and thus 'the two stages of life merge into one' (99). Our re-enactment of our girlhood reading reinforces and fulfils our desire to cross over or break down this barrier that society is encouraging us to challenge. As participants in the blurring of that boundary, we confirm the continuation of the popularity of girl culture into the years of womanhood. Although Postman's thesis concentrates on many of the negative effects of forcing children into adulthood and adults into childhood, the discovery of the connections between the two stages or states of girlhood and womanhood can be both strengthening and enlightening. For the reader of Montgomery's novels and autobiographical writings, the connection is the recognition of a tension, a recognition that results in a degree of control over those dominant structures of society that attempt to impose power.

What holds our attention in both the novels and the journals is tension. Fiske outlines for us the 'tension between forces of closure (or domination) and openness (or popularity)' (*Reading* 5). For the reader of Montgomery's journals and novels, the tension in the text – specifically, the tension between the girl/woman on the one hand and a stifling society on the other – is the substance and the producer of meaning that is applied to the social and cultural experience and identity of the reader. Once the tension or conflict disappears from the text, the popular appeal vanishes. For example, the 'difference' readers respond to is threatened and compromised by the stable state of marriage or 'love fulfilled' in the case of Anne. Thus, in *Anne's House of Dreams*, the attention turns from Anne's marriage to characters such as Leslie Moore and Captain Jim, who are experiencing the tension, darkness, and shadow of moments before and after marriage or love. If popular culture depends on the interplay between the textual and the social, then that interplay ceases to exist if the tension is not present in the text and applied to everyday life. Of course, it is that tension itself that invites the application of the literature to the life and culture of the reader. The moments of conflict constitute the opportunity for empowerment on the part of the reader, and the open indulgence in tension, as presented in the journals, is a confessional confirmation of the shadow and darkness that constitute and result from the state of being in conflict. The reader, like the writer, indulges in an extensive and continuous canvas of darkness working alongside light rather than being submerged or compromised by it.

The tone of the journals matches the most intense moments of the novels and breaks the practice or convention which dictates that the young woman must become mature and stable, relinquishing the struggles and contradictions she was free to experience and give voice to in girlhood. The tension of the journals takes us back to those moments in Anne and Emily when we responded with a resounding 'Yes'; and those were the moments when discontent was acknowledged and oppression was challenged, not the moments when darkness was subsumed or compromised by the status quo. It is no mistake that we remember the slate over Gilbert's head more vividly than the conversation between Anne and Gilbert at the conclusion of *Anne of Green Gables*. We respond to the tension that precedes the conventional love relationship and are bothered by the unrealistic dissipation of that tension when love and marriage are applied. Even as young readers, we knew we were questioning and subverting the successful love relationships that compromised Anne and Emily for us. We read and reread in order to apply to our daily lives the tension rather than the harmonious and romantic 'solutions.'

The journals plunge us back into those moments of tension that we now realize drew us into the worlds of Anne and Emily. Our reading of Maud corroborates our own feelings about our reading of Anne, a reading we were perhaps not willing to admit until we were given this express permission by L.M. Montgomery herself. In the journals, Montgomery tells us that writing *Anne of the Island* in order to please demanding readers and publishers was like 'marrying a man to get rid of him' (*SJ* 2: 133). She maintains that the grown-up Anne cannot 'be made as interesting as when a child' because her 'forte is in writing humor,' and 'young women in the bloom of youth and romance should be sacred from humor' (*SJ* 2, 133). This observation within the text of the journals begs for comment. Although as readers of Anne we appreciate Montgomery's humour, we see her strength not in the humour itself but in the ability to explore and delineate the tension between her vibrant young female characters and the very limited world in which they live. This insular and repressive world is supposedly limited by the men who have established and control it, but it is obviously challenged and subverted by the women who seem to hold much of the power. Although the challenge and subversion are often treated in a humorous manner, the source and substance of the repression of the child and the female are not humorous.

In the 'real life' depicted in the journals, we see something close to the marrying of a man to get rid of him,[4] while we see very little of the gentle and idealistic bloom of youth and romance in Maud, or in any other young woman for that matter. The difficulty for Montgomery in the writing of *Anne of the Island* does not seem to lie in the sacredness of romance or the lack of scope for humour, but in a reluctance to compromise Anne by positioning her with Gilbert: 'I must at least engage Anne for I'll never be given any rest until I do. So it's rather a hopeless prospect and I feel as if I were going to waste all the time I shall put on the book. I might be doing something so much more worthwhile' (*SJ* 2: 133). As readers of Maud, after being steeped for years in the role of readers of Anne, we find a great deal to consider in this comment. The gap between Anne and Maud obviously deepens as Anne's own world and experience begin to contrast with, rather than reflect, Maud's. However, even before we were privy to Maud's personal thoughts about Anne, we read Anne's engagement as an ending rather than a beginning. The interest goes and the identification and sympathy wane once the tension disappears. It is not a matter of the child being more interesting than the adult; it is a matter of the child being allowed the complex and contradictory feelings that are denied to the adult.

We feel disappointed and betrayed when the woman is not allowed to indulge in the tension and despair that are acceptable for the girl at odds with her environment and society. What a relief to meet in the journals not only an acceptance of that tension in womanhood but an acceptance of the darkness and depression that are playfully and humorously dealt with in the young girl, acceptable only because the child is allowed to be viewed as overly dramatic and sensitive. In the novels, the young girl 'outgrows' this darkness and conflict. We are strangely relieved to meet such darkness and conflict once again in the journals. The girlhood *angst* of Anne, the tension that delights and validates us, continues into womanhood in the journals, bridging the gap between girlhood and womanhood in a much more positive manner than that outlined by Postman. The discovery of similarities continues the difference of girlhood into womanhood, providing relief for the reader, who now sees that crossing the border between childhood and adulthood does not magically cause tensions and contradictions to vanish or supply a new brand of more mature dilemmas. This connection between girlhood and womanhood accentuates difference by permitting the woman to accept and indulge in the contradictions and tensions that began in girlhood. The popular appeal lies in the validation of girlhood feelings and questions that can continue into womanhood without being relinquished or changed. No longer obligated to suppress or solve these conflicts through romance, or to exchange them for something new, the reader of the journals can live with them and even celebrate them as enriching and necessary.

Even as readers of Anne, we were unable and unwilling to submerge the tensions of girlhood. We read the continuation of tension in Anne even as it was supposedly released, this continuation of tension occurring in the transfer of the text to our own social and cultural positions. As readers of Maud, any hesitation that we may have had to read the novels in this way is gone. The journals act as the completion and the commentary on what we sensed was already there in the novels; our positions as readers of Maud open up and confirm our positions as readers of Anne. The tension, conflict, and contradictions accentuate difference, and position us as a disempowered group challenging the structures of power. In reading Anne, we are excited by our participation as readers in the challenge of the status quo; in reading Maud, we are rewarded with moments of triumph in the opposition to conventional power structures, moments which reinforce our feeling that the tension, albeit difficult to live with, results in change and empowerment. As we transfer both the tension and the action of Maud to our own lives and situations, we re-enact and confirm the earlier transfer of Anne to our girlhood selves. It is a familiar reader–text relationship, as is the sensation of empowerment that results.

What we clearly realize as journal readers is that without the tension, there is no empowerment. It is precisely because Maud refuses to submerge her discontent, frustration, and anger as an adult that she is able to challenge her position. We sense that no matter whom Maud married and no matter what her circumstances were, she would maintain the contradictions of girlhood into womanhood. The idea that romance can smooth over tension, so that the woman outgrows the complexities and questions of girlhood, is disempowering. Hence, the concentration on the child characters in the novels and the feeling of 'coming home' when we meet the same characteristics and temperament in the adult Maud. We are drawn to the moments, characters, and situations that inspire us to transfer the tension of the text to our own lives. We can all think of those moments in Anne and Emily; and as the journals become familiar texts (despite the fact that we have less reading time now than we had as girls), we begin as active readers to assimilate those journal moments into our own lives. It is the transfer of that text to our own positions and situations that accounts for its popularity. Maud embodies our difference just as Anne once did. That difference provides the substance of the tension that results in the power that comes with challenging a world that tends to stereotype and limit us.

Maud's panicky reaction, which comes over her like a wave after the marriage ceremony with Ewan, is intense, but temporary. The 'sudden horrid inrush of *rebellion* and *despair*' (*SJ* 2: 68) is preceded by having felt 'contented all the morning' and is followed by feeling 'again [her] contented self' (*SJ* 2: 68) by four o'clock. The amazing aspect of the experience is not the intensity itself but the way in which a reaction of such intensity can engulf and then leave her so quickly and easily. Montgomery's assertion that she 'was as unhappy as [she] had ever been in [her] life' (*SJ* 2: 68) appears to be offered without exaggeration, which renders the simplicity of the comment 'the mood passed' (*SJ* 2: 68) all the more surprising. The return the following evening of this mood, in which she reached a 'depth of despair and futile rebellion,' is defeated by Montgomery's own will: 'I conquered it – thrust it down – smothered it – buried it' (*SJ* 2: 68). Although Maud may have succeeded in rendering the 'wild and free and untamed' (*SJ* 2: 68) part of herself 'dead or quiescent' (*SJ* 2: 68), she continues to be the recipient of such waves, which rise up in her and then subside, constituting the tension and conflict that resemble 'a black cloud of wretchedness'(*SJ* 2: 68) but also empower through their refusal to submit to the conventions of her time.

The language used by Montgomery in the journals begins to establish a regular ebb and flow of the darkness and depression that refuse to leave her and yet do not succeed in overpowering her. The use of the word 'again' becomes familiar to the reader, as it signals the repetition of the familiar emotions that will eventually pass. When referring to the loss of Frede, for example, Maud writes: 'Again I have been depressed and heartsick' (*SJ* 2: 315). In her comment about Ewan's illness – 'I have again almost given up hope' (*SJ* 2: 343) – the words 'again' and 'almost' are accentuated, as the retrospective viewpoint of the journal genre allows the reader and writer the knowledge that this near hopelessness obviously passed as well. Similarly, references to time emphasize the temporary nature of these overwhelming emotions. Montgomery writes that 'Tonight I feel that life is *too hard* – that I cannot endure it any longer' (*SJ* 1: 368). Although the words 'too hard' are italicized, the emphasis in the sentence also falls on 'tonight.' Of Chester's marriage, Montgomery writes: 'This has been a day in hell' (*SJ* 4: 242) and of the events leading up to the marriage: 'The past two weeks have been dark and cold' (*SJ* 4: 212). An acknowledgment of the role and bias of her own perspective – 'Never had life looked blacker and more hopeless to my tired eyes' (*SJ* 4: 337) – also serves to suggest that less tired eyes would temper the hopelessness and cause the blackness to become somewhat lighter, thus relieving the intensity in a manner similar to the passing of time.

The tone used to describe these low moments ranges from fairly matter-of-fact and detached statements, such as 'I am cold and tired and worn-out' (*SJ* 1: 195) in reference to Maud's relationship with Edwin Simpson, to much more dramatic and extreme treatments: '"That which I have feared" has come upon me – I have had a month of nervous prostration – an utter breakdown of body, soul and spirit ... I wanted to die and escape life' (*SJ* 1: 392). This range of tone in the expression of these moments seems to reflect a range, balance, tension, or contrast in the actual substance of these emotions themselves. Maud's comment when Ewan is diagnosed is a telling one. She claims that 'religious melancholia' is 'good news' compared with the 'manic depressive insanity' that she feared (*SJ* 2: 334), and that 'everything is measured by contrast in this world' (*SJ* 2: 334). Indeed it is contrast and opposition that provide the tension that empowers Maud and the reader of Maud, as the feelings of darkness are both the result of, and in reaction to, the oppressive forces of society that limit reader and writer.

Carol Shields's observation that Maud's voice differs from Anne's is perceptive and correct. However, for those of us who read Maud after years of being immersed in Anne and Emily, there are important similarities that account for the popularity of Maud as the journal writer and persona, and the popularity of the reading of the journals as an extension and completion of the reading of the novels. The transfer of the text to our own social and cultural positions as girls and women means that we continue to concentrate on the tension between ourselves and the world around us. As we blur the border between girlhood and womanhood through the way we read, we feel more comfortable assuming the daring positions of reader-as-Anne and reader-as-Maud because the journals affirm the connection between text and reader just as they confirm the link between girl and woman. Although at certain points we would like to believe, like Anne, that 'God's in his heaven, all's right with the world,' we are relieved to be able to balance such a viewpoint with the admission that, like Maud, we are 'horribly afraid of life' (*SJ* 4: 159). Maud is closer to the women we now are, but Anne is closer to the girls we once were. The organic intertwining of the two, created in texts written at the same time by the same woman, both still existing through our reading and our living, allows us to continue to derive power from the transfer of the literature to our own marginalized positions, as we insert Maud into our everyday culture. Through her posthumously published journals, L.M. Montgomery takes an active role in connecting our girlhood in the mid-twentieth century with our womanhood at the beginning of the twenty-first century.

Notes

1 I am using the group of readers with which I identify myself to emphasize the ways in which I and this particular group have been affected by our reading of Montgomery. Our positions as women and as Canadians are integral to the intensity of our responses. Of course, the responses of readers of the other gender and other nationalities may be just as intense.
2 Shields's description of Maud, as she knows her through the journals, is similar in tone and style to the descriptions of Daisy Goodwill Flett provided by the narrative voice in *The Stone Diaries*. In both cases, the reader takes the

many fragments offered, fills in the gaps, and establishes a relationship with Daisy and Maud that has the potential to spill over into the reader's everyday life.

3 In the introduction to her edited volume of essays, *Confessional Politics: Women's Sexual Self-Representations in Life Writing and Popular Media* (1999), Irene Gammel discusses the creative ways in which women shape and manipulate 'confessional modalities' when they tell their sexual life stories. This approach applies to Montgomery's relationship with Herman Leard, but there are other levels and degrees of disclosure in the journals that require examination along the 'confessional modalities' theorized by Gammel (7–10).

4 I am referring here to Montgomery's relationship with Edwin Simpson (*SJ* 1: *passim*).

Chapter 6

The Visual Imagination of L.M. Montgomery

ELIZABETH R. EPPERLY

Your photography is a record of your living, for anyone who really sees.
– Paul Strand (in Susan Sontag, *On Photography* 200)

There are few things I regret more than the fact that kodaks were unknown in my schooldays.
– L.M. Montgomery (*Selected Journals* 4: 47)

L.M. Montgomery had a powerful visual imagination. She was able to create descriptions of places so convincingly in her novels that millions of tourists have travelled to Prince Edward Island to see for themselves if the rich colours, shapes, and atmosphere they have read about can really be found on a modern-day island. For at least forty years of her life, Maud Montgomery was an avid amateur photographer, taking pictures on Prince Edward Island, in Ontario, and on her travels. She first mentioned photography only casually in her journal in the late 1890s as one of her hobbies, but she used photographs in her personal scrapbooks and in her recopied journals, and she collected pictures of her favourite people and places all her adult life. Montgomery's photographic collection, owned by the University of Guelph, offers us an opportunity to reconsider a number of ways she made use of her visual skills. In all her novels, her characters are vividly rendered for the eye, and scenes depend on her ability to make readers see. Her Romantic written descriptions make readers 'see into the life of things,' and her photographs show us her intelligent seeing in another way. Guiding us through their frames, pointing us towards keyholes of light and around curves and inviting bends and through textured shadows and bright spots of time, Montgomery tells us wordlessly what mattered most to her and what patterns she sought to create and to preserve in her prose and poetry.

Romantic 'Memory Pictures'

Long before she discovered photography, Montgomery saw in pictures. She strove to capture these pictures in words as vivid as the colours and shapes she half created as she perceived them. Describing her childhood memories in her journals, Montgomery says that her first six years were 'hazy' with few 'connections' but that 'here and there a picture-like scene stands out in vivid colours' (SJ 1: 369). Recalling the earringed sailors in the yard and piles of gold in the Macneill parlour the summer when the great ship the *Marco Polo* was wrecked off the coast of Cavendish when she was eight, she notes, 'The whole summer was a series of "pictures" to me' (SJ 1: 354).

L.M. Montgomery's way of seeing was thoroughly Romantic (Epperly, *Fragrance, passim*). She, like William Wordsworth, believed that the poet/writer is inspired by the 'mighty world / Of eye and ear – both what they half create, / And what perceive' ('Lines: Composed a Few Miles above Tintern Abbey' ll 106–7). Like the Romantic-inspired writers she loved most – Robert Burns, Wordsworth, Sir Walter Scott, Alfred Tennyson, Charles Dickens, Ralph Waldo Emerson, and both Elizabeth Barrett Browning and Robert Browning – she lived with nature and was transported by it. She focused on nature as a way to understand and to illustrate the human heart and as a way to commune with those who also were inspired by natural beauty. No orthodox Christian in her private letters and journals, Montgomery, like the young Wordsworth, was pantheistic in her written descriptions. Wordsworth's poem 'Tintern Abbey' describes the poet's enraptured response to nature and also talks about the poet's obligation to 'see into the life of things' (l. 49), to uplift himself and others from the 'still, sad music of humanity' (l. 91) when the 'burden of the mystery' (l. 38) can be lightened. Though she made no grand claims for herself or her writing in these terms, I contend that Montgomery subscribed to this view of the world and spent her career trying to 'see into the life of things' and trying to capture some of the inspiriting joy she herself experienced when she communed with nature and worked to understand the human spirit and what encompassed it. She captured her efforts in writing and in the medium of photography.

Writing of Wordsworth's command of these mental pictures and their connection with his philosophy, Ernest Tuveson says 'Since ideas are images, since even complex ideas are multiple pictures, and since understanding itself is a form of perception, the visual and the intellectual would tend to become amalgamated' (quoted in Lindenberger, 95–6). In Montgomery's poetic fiction, the vivid word pictures may tell us how to interpret character as well as atmosphere. In the descriptions, Montgomery uses colours, careful directions, personification, and strong images to help us to see places, people, and scenes. Colour is a passion; the effects of sunlight and sunset are lifelong fascinations. Even in the young Montgomery's journals, we find descriptions filled with colour and its effects. At fifteen, crossing Canada by train with her grandfather, she notes in New Brunswick: 'The road went through high wooded hills. Here and there they would sweep around to disclose a beautiful lake or river curve, like a mirror set in an emerald frame' (*SJ* 1: 26). Her first glimpse of Manitoba is captured thus: 'Acres of ground are covered with sunflowers as with sheets of light' (*SJ* 1: 28). *Anne of Green Gables* has eleven sunset descriptions – most of them with dazzling colours and all of them connected with pivotal moments in Anne's story (Epperly, *Fragrance* 32).

Anne's House of Dreams (1917), the most consciously poetic of Montgomery's novels, is filled with descriptions of sea and sunsets and landscapes and affords excellent examples of the ways Montgomery encouraged readers to see. She is intent on making readers imagine and experience the colours and textures of Four Winds life. She even uses colour to guide the eye and to connect the themes and characters of the story. The picture of Lesley Moore's house caught in sunset red becomes an emblem of Lesley's personality and encourages an early reading of passion confined. Montgomery expertly directs the eye:

> The red light flamed on the white sails of a vessel gliding down the channel, bound to a Southern port in a land of palms. Beyond her, it smote upon and incarnadined the shining, white, grassless faces of the sand dunes. To the right, it fell on the old house among the willows up the brook, and gave it for a fleeting space casements more splendid than those of an old cathedral. They glowed out of its quiet and grayness like the throbbing, blood-red thoughts of a vivid soul imprisoned in a dull husk of environment. (*AHD* 52–3)

The careful positioning of the image ('beyond,' 'to the right') helps to link the other uses of red in the novel back to this vividly red, personified place. There are hundreds of such passages in the fiction.

Montgomery shows the greatest preoccupation with the power of the visual imagination in the Emily series, a *Künstlerroman*, where seeing is creating (see also Epperly, *Fragrance* 145–207). In the first few pages of *Emily of New Moon* (1923), when Emily Byrd Starr is only eleven, Montgomery describes Emily's 'flash,' a glimpse of perfect beauty when the veil of this world flutters for a moment aside. In this supernal (and Romantic, Neoplatonic) moment, Emily experiences 'inexpressible delight' (7) and is immediately desperate to fix in words what she has seen. Emily rushes home from her walk so she can write down what she has seen and felt before 'the memory picture of what she had seen grew a little blurred' (8). This 'memory picture' is perhaps the best illustration of how Montgomery herself saw, remembered, and recaptured. Montgomery makes it clear that Emily's 'flash' is a gift, but it is a gift that Emily half creates because she is able to experience it. This 'gift' to Emily's senses is matched on one level by visitations of second sight and on another by the inspiration for her poems and stories. In the instances of the 'flash,' second sight, and inspiration, Emily 'sees' something Montgomery is determined to have the reader see.

It is significant that Montgomery admired the American first edition cover of *Emily of New Moon*; there the viewer sees Emily inspired by the 'flash' and gazing at her imagined Wind Woman, as Andrea McKenzie documents in the next chapter of this volume. The cover shows Emily as actively creative, and viewers are encouraged to identify with Emily's energy and abilities. M.L. Kirk is faithful to Montgomery's intention of featuring Emily as artist/creator, whereas the cover illustrations of the Dutch and the Swedish translations of the first Emily novel do not entirely capture Emily's creative seeing powers. Evidently, many illustrators and publishers have, in ignorance or consciously, tried to wrap Emily's power in pretty, pastoral, harmless packages, as K.L. Poe points out (chapter 10) in describing Sullivan's slick packaging of Anne for mass-marketability.

'The Kodak Girl'

We do not know exactly when Montgomery began to take pictures, nor do we know how closely she studied the photographs or lithographs in the dozens of magazines that passed through her hands in the post office in the Macneill kitchen. We do not know what make of camera she first owned.[1] We do not know where she purchased this first camera, whether it was through mail order from a place such as Eaton's, where the photographic equipment is listed in pages at the turn of the century, or whether one of the professional studios in Charlottetown or Summerside carried equipment or helped her to select it. We do know she used a tripod for many family and landscape shots, and we know from various references that over time she took pictures by taking off a lens cap, pulling a string, squeezing a bulb, and pressing a button. We know that in 1911 she bought a 'dandy new' Kodak, 'said to be the best made,' so that she could use film cartridges and get snapshots of her honeymoon trip in Britain (*My Dear Mr. M.* 58).

There is an enormous amount that we do not know about Montgomery and photography, however, and there is considerable scope for further study. Montgomery took such delight in her own travel across the country by rail with her grandfather in 1890 that it would be surprising if she never encountered the photographic work that celebrated Canada's emerging nationhood, such as William Notman's Maple Box Portfolio of scenes prepared for the Prince of Wales after his 1860 visit to Canada (see Skidmore).[2] Did she know of Lady Aberdeen's 1891 cross-Canada trip recorded in *Through Canada with a Kodak* (Greenhill and Birrell, 126)? Did she know of the Romantic photography of a contemporary professional such as Edith Watson (1861–1943), who was drawn from New England to photograph Canada's east and west coasts, and especially the islands, and who published extensively (under her own name) in such places as the *Canadian Magazine*, where Montgomery also published (see Rooney)? Did she know the photographic criticism of Sadakichi Hartmann, who also just happened to publish four books of art criticism (1901, 1902, 1903, 1910) with the L.C. Page Company of Boston (Hartmann, 2), the publishers of *Anne of Green Gables*?

As with her writing, so it is with photography: Montgomery comments very little in her journals or letters about the processes, much less about the creativity involved. What we have learned about Montgomery's way of writing (apart from the Emily series) we have largely deduced from the manuscripts of the novels, treating them as archaeological sites where changes and complexities in subject matter are often registered as disturbances in the pattern of revision on the pages (Epperly, 'Approaching'). With the photographs we can at least look at a wide variety over the years to see what patterns there are in the subjects captured and what we can learn from these about Montgomery's preferences for framing, shaping, composing, and seeing generally.

In photographs, Montgomery could not capture colour or the full glory of sunsets; she could not tell us where to look; she could not show us sight itself; she could not tell us a complete story or help us to witness the mystery of second sight. And yet she could suggest many of these things in the way she captured an angle or textures or shape, in the way she used costume, in the way she framed a moment or used the contrasts of light and shadow. Perhaps Montgomery understood the language Susan Sontag suggests when she says, 'Photographs, which cannot themselves explain anything, are inexhaustible invitations to deduction, speculation, and fantasy' (23).

Considering Montgomery's own long fascination with photography, there are surprisingly few photographers in her fiction. There are some painters, such as the young man in 'The Waking of Helen' (a 1901 story republished in *Along the Shore*) or the young woman in 'Jane Lavinia' (a 1906 story republished in *Akin to Anne*). In only one episode (132–47) in *Anne of Windy Poplars* (1936), where she reworked an early short story, does photography play a prominent part.[3] Still, Montgomery did make good use of photographs and photography in some important published and private documents. Combing through the early scrapbooks of Montgomery's published pieces, when she was experimenting most freely with picture taking and processing, we find some significant details. One early story, 'Detected by the Camera: The True Story of an Unexpected Development,' published in June 1897 in the *Philadelphia Times* and republished in *Among the Shadows*, begins: 'One summer I was attacked by the craze for amateur photography. It became chronic afterward, and I and my camera have never since been parted' (57). In taking a picture of a house and not paying attention to the shot itself when she took the cap off and put it back on, Amy accidentally took a picture of a thief exiting the house and pocketing a large wallet full of cash. One wonders what kinds of adventures Montgomery's camera did lead her into – there cannot have been an abundance of people in Cavendish in the 1890s and early 1900s who would be willing to take family and group pictures at weddings, picnics, and clan gatherings. (The scrapbooks do have cyanotypes of some now-unidentifiable people at such gatherings.)

'The Second-Hand Travel Club,' a story published in the 12 April 1902 issue of *Forward and Wellspring* (USB, CM 67.5.14), uses three photographs to illustrate Montgomery's story about Persis, an orphan who lives with a kindly widowed aunt and works in an office. Persis decides to relieve some of the boredom of her fellow women employees by creating a second-hand travel club, where she will show them photographs she has taken and curios she has picked up on her many travels with her aunt and her late sea-captain uncle. In the first meeting of the club, Persis chooses the theme of Japan and dresses in Japanese costume. Two of the three photographs illustrating the story show a Western woman in Japanese costume. Could these be Montgomery's own photographs, now lost? We do not know if Montgomery had a kimono, but we do know of her interest in Japan and things Japanese.

Perhaps of even more interest are the pieces that are illustrated with Montgomery's own photographs. The story 'Ethel's Victory,' published in *Illustrated Youth and Age* (*ca* 1900), uses three photographs (USB, CM 67.5.18). One is meant to be an academy for girls called 'Rowan Villa' and is Montgomery's photograph of her Uncle Sutherland's house, Melrose Cottage, in Sea View close to Park Corner, Prince Edward Island, a picture now owned by the University of Guelph Archives. The second photograph is of a young girl, in a long dress and flat hat, walking along a country lane that has trees on one side and an open field on the other. This is not a picture that is now in the Montgomery collection at Guelph, but it looks like Montgomery's style, with a curve in the lane and the diminishing point of light centred behind the girl, who stands just to the right of the centre of the photograph. The third photograph, entitled 'The Moonlit Gloom of Her Room,' is actually the bookcase corner of Montgomery's own bedroom in Cavendish, a familiar view featured with others in Laura Higgins's helpful article on Montgomery's 'Dear Den.'

Several of the published poems in the scrapbooks are illustrated with Montgomery's own photographs (USB, CM 67.5.18). In the late 1890s (she did not always identify the periodical or the exact date), Montgomery published at least three poems using her own unsigned Cavendish photographs to illustrate them: the poem 'In Twilight Fields' shows the brook field below the Macneill farm; 'The Trysting Spring' shows the spring Montgomery later called Dryad's Bubble in the woods along Lovers' Lane below the Green Gables house; and 'At New-Moon Time' shows a daytime fence and field from the Webb farm and a clear sky into which the ingenious Montgomery has placed a slender new moon in the processing stage, just as she described it in her 1902 Halifax *Daily Echo* article on photography.[4] One long Montgomery serial, 'The Way of the Brick Oven,' published in the Toronto periodical *East and West* from 3 October 1908 to 14 November 1908 (USB, CM 67.5.24), uses a separate photograph to illustrate each of the seven episodes. While I cannot identify the people or the exact places in the photographs, they are clearly pictures taken expressly for the story, and could easily have been staged on the spruce lanes and in the lace-curtained interiors of Cavendish or Park Corner.

We do not know if the early original journals were illustrated, but in 1919 when she began to recopy the journals into the ten uniform-sized ledgers now owned by the University of Guelph Archives, Montgomery illustrated them liberally. There are hundreds of pictures, most but not all of which are also preserved in the separate photographic collection. Interestingly, the photographs in the journal do not always illustrate so much as they offer a visual marker or relief on the page. In the early volumes, some photographs of places are used repeatedly, sometimes six times within pages of each other, and one wonders if Montgomery had some private reason for wanting thus to break the text.

The illustrations in the early journals may seem perfunctory at times, but the illustrations in the early personal scrapbooks, in particular, are so wonderfully and densely arranged as to form mixed-media collages. In the scrapbooks before 1911, owned by the L.M. Montgomery Birthplace on Prince Edward Island and housed at the Confederation Centre Art Gallery and Museum, Montgomery uses cyanotypes of many of her photographs, cutting them to suit a page already crowded with clippings, swatches of fabric, clusters of pressed flowers, greeting cards, twists of favourite cats' fur, calendars with circled dates, and magazine advertisements and illustrations. Images of people and places find a rich setting in these sadly disintegrating volumes of mostly happy memorabilia. In the scrapbooks at Guelph, particularly the volume 1911–13, we find a concentrated arrangement of photographs, postcards, clippings, pressed flowers, and snippets of cloth. The mixed-media collage and cyanotypes have disappeared, but the crowded chronicle shows such things as a swatch of fabric from each of her trousseau dresses pasted lovingly beside a photograph of herself in each of the dresses, or a full page of pressed flowers from her grandmother's birthplace in England beside a photograph of the old Woolner place itself in Dunwich. Here and there a comic news piece punctuates these early photographs as surely as the later scrapbooks show fewer photographs and more disturbing and tragic clippings. The scrapbooks suggest through the quality and diversity of photographs what the journals capture in written descriptions. How different Maud of Cavendish was from the Maud of 'Journey's End,' yet how similarly determined each was to see and to re-create.

Composing in Photographs

Among the two thousand images owned by the University of Guelph Library, the viewer can see the patterns that most attracted Montgomery's eye, the images that compelled and challenged her. By examining the photographs together, one can learn a great deal about Montgomery's sense of perspective, quality of framing, depth of composition, attraction for textures and patterns, use of foregrounding, and choice of subject. Again and again, in hundreds of these pictures, one finds her fascination with curves and bends in roads[5] and rivers – her love for an arc of beach or a twisting line of trees; one will also find a love for archways and bridges and fences. She used preferred shapes to frame central images. And in many of her photographs one finds her delighted focus on a distant keyhole of light: a favourite technique was to capture a curving tunnel made by arching branches. Lovers' Lane in Cavendish is the subject of a dozen photographs in various seasons. One example of this keyhole of light Montgomery loved to capture is found above the S-curve of Lovers' Lane (figure 6.1), with the bend in the road, the enveloping trees, and the distant circle of light. Montgomery captures this light in her fiction, too. In her fiction, the nature descriptions are full of directions (look to the right, look to the left) and colour, as in the quotation above from *Anne's House of Dreams*. In black-and-white photographs, she directs the viewer's eyes with a light that beckons. Consider figure 6.1 in the context of Anne Shirley's enraptured response to the White Way of Delight on her first buggy ride home after Matthew picks her up at Bright River. Anne has just been struck dumb by the sight of the white apple blossoms in a snowy canopy over the red lane they travel, and the narrator says,

> The 'Avenue,' so called by the Newbridge people, was a stretch of road four or five hundred yards long, completely arched over with huge, wide-spreading apple-trees, planted years ago by an eccentric old farmer. Overhead was one long canopy of snowy fragrant bloom. Below the boughs the air was full of a purple twilight and far ahead a glimpse of painted sunset sky shone like a great rose window at the end of a cathedral aisle. (24–5)

From this description, the reader can easily picture the arch and the rose-and-gold window or keyhole of light at the end. Montgomery's glorying in colour in the prose and the poetry finds its outlet in shapes in the photographs.

6.1   Lovers' Lane. Photograph by L.M. Montgomery. Courtesy of L.M. Montgomery Collection, Archival and Special Collections, University of Guelph Library.

6.2   Chester Macdonald with cat, 1913. Photograph by L.M. Montgomery. Courtesy of L.M. Montgomery Collection, Archival and Special Collections, University of Guelph Library.

Montgomery was always a storyteller – whether she was writing her journals and recounting her life or filling her scrapbooks with cyanotypes of her own photographs along with swatches of material of her favourite clothes. In a single picture of her first-born son, Chester, in 1913 (figure 6.2), she tells a story of contentment. Chester is all curves and plump self-absorption. He is perfectly at ease and secure. The cat, normally all curves, is almost angular in its attention to Chester – the viewer can imagine the cat speaking to the small boy and the strength of each creature in its separate agency. Montgomery loved cats and must have laughed with delight at this close encounter of two creatures she adored.

Ten years later, around 1923, when Chester was eleven and Stuart, his brother, eight, Montgomery, standing behind them on a P.E.I. shore, captured the spirit of each boy – as life later proved each to be (figure

6.3   Chester and Stuart Macdonald, *ca* 1923. Photograph by L.M. Montgomery. Courtesy of L.M. Montgomery Collection, Archival and Special Collections, University of Guelph Library.

6.3). Chester, on the left, sits somewhat inert, with rounded softer body and stooping shoulders; he waits for the waves to come to him. And beside him, with an animated glee one can imagine hearing, the young Stuart thrusts his angular, finely muscled arms out in front of him as though he is greeting the waves with a shout, his hair almost standing on end with electric life. You know Montgomery's sharp and loving eye did not miss a detail or an implication in this double portrait.

Finally, consider a photograph Montgomery did not herself take but for which she posed very deliberately, and provocatively, considering the times (figure 6.4). Montgomery and the Cavendish school teacher Nora Lefurgey struck up an immediate friendship in 1902–3. Nora boarded at the Macneill place and the two took pictures together and swam together. On Nora's last trip to Cavendish in 1904, before she left the Island, she and Maud took daring shots of each other in their com-

6.4   L.M. Montgomery posing as a sea nymph, *ca* 1904. Photograph by Nora Lefurgey. Courtesy of L.M. Montgomery Collection, Archival and Special Collections, University of Guelph Library.

bination bathing costumes. Montgomery described her scanty costume more than twenty years later in her journals (*SJ* 4: 145–6) when she came across the picture she knew would have scandalized her grandmother if she had ever found it. What is important about this photograph is the opportunity it affords to emphasize Montgomery's dramatic sense of self.[6] She usually posed very carefully for a camera, avoiding a close, full profile, for example, since she did not like the hump in her nose. She always dressed meticulously and prided herself on the image she created for the public, whether she was the famous author or the minister's helpful wife. And even here in the pre-Anne days, Montgomery is telling a story with her pose – of an ocean nymph just risen from the waves and gazing out to sea. One imagines that, aware of the romance of the image and the power of implied story, she encouraged Nora to match curve of rock with curve of body.

Montgomery's Romantic nature descriptions in the fiction often make rural Prince Edward Island sound exquisite, almost exotic. Early evening beaches or fields are orchestrations of colour and metaphor. To millions of readers all over the world, Montgomery's pictures of Prince Edward Island *are* Prince Edward Island. Her ability to create word pictures makes her capturing of photographic images all the more interesting. How did she see? The willing observer might see a grey farmhouse, close to sand dunes, in a willow wood, struck by sunset light. She saw and captured in words a 'dull husk' suddenly 'incarnadined' and suggesting the 'blood-red thoughts' of the inmate (*AHD* 52–3). Her sensitive eye behind the lens could suggest hidden drama by using a keyhole of light or mysterious shadows or powerfully framing branches. She could show in photographs the glimmerings of what her eye could absorb; looking at her photographs, the viewer observes her looking. Montgomery as photographer invites viewers to consider how images reflect and demand creativity.

Montgomery took photographs for her own pleasure and to chronicle the events in her own and her children's lives. She may have begun taking pictures as a hobby and then thought that they could help her to sell the occasional story or poem. There is no way to know how many hundreds of photographs she destroyed in the last years of her life or how many she gave away. But of the more than two thousand remaining images, we have an ample record of an active and observant eye, determined to catch the shapes of things and to suggest their stories. The creative labour involved in her photography is intense. The black-and-white photographs and the colourful, Romantic 'memory pictures' of the novels together suggest how ceaselessly and how hard a passionate and disciplined observer can work to make others imagine and see.

Notes

My thanks to the Confederation Centre Art Gallery and Museum for encouragement to publish this essay, a much-different version of which was prepared for a proposed 1999 exhibition catalogue; to the L.M. Montgomery Collection, Archival and Special Collections, University of Guelph Library, for permission to use the four photographs; to the L.M. Montgomery Institute at the University of Prince Edward Island and to the Social Sciences and Humanities Research Council for research funds; to Emilie Adams, Anne-Louise Brookes, Irene Gammel, Ellen Morrison, and Kevin Rice for invaluable personal assistance.

1 It is worth noting that there are no cyanotypes (blue prints) or personal prints in the first volume of the personal scrapbooks (USB, CM 67.5.15) covering 1893 to 1896 (but sometimes including pressed flowers, cats' fur, and souvenirs from as early as 1887). In the second album (USB, CM 67.5.12), beginning in 1902 but also including bits of the 1890s, we find close to the opening several of Montgomery's cyanotypes. Amid these pages, we also find a glamorous advertisement drawing of a beautiful woman carrying a parasol and cradling a flat, rectangular Kodak. The caption reads: 'The Kodak Girl.' Could Montgomery have said she got a 'dandy *new*' Kodak in 1911 because she had owned one before?

2 The 1893–6 scrapbook (USB, CM 67.5.15) does contain three photographs, probably Notman ones, of railway scenes from the West: 'Kamloops, B.C.,' 'Hell's Gate on the Thompson River,' and 'At Messiter, B.C.' They have on them 'Courtesy of the Nat'l Rys.'

3 For the episode in *Anne of Windy Poplars*, Montgomery reworks the short story 'The Little Fellow's Photograph' from the 8 September 1906 *The Classmate: A Paper for Young People*. Her copy of the story is tucked into the back cover of scrapbook CM 67.5.11. The drawings illustrating the story show a dry-plate camera with tripod, development pans, and a dark lantern.

4 Published under the pen-name 'Cynthia,' the chatty *Echo* articles offer some wonderful insights into Montgomery's interests and the interests she believed her readers held. The article on photography is especially illuminating for the developing techniques she describes, among them, this inserting of false moons: 'A pretty effect may sometimes be obtained in a landscape picture by cutting out of white paper a tiny new moon and pasting it properly on the glass side of the negative. The result is a "summer moonlight scene"' (McCabe and Heilbron, 167).

5 The exhibition *The Visual Imagination of Lucy Maud Montgomery* and video clips showing Montgomery's scrapbooks and manuscripts are available for viewing on the CD-ROM *The Bend in the Road: An Invitation to the World and Work of L.M. Montgomery.*

6 For a detailed discussion of this photograph, see Irene Gammel, 'The Visual and Performative Diaries of L.M. Montgomery, the Baroness Elsa, and Elvira Bach.'

Chapter 7

Writing in Pictures: International Images of Emily

ANDREA McKENZIE

The little girl really does look as I imagined 'Emily' looked. Although there is one weird mistake. The moon in the picture is an old *moon, not a new one!*
— L.M. Montgomery on M.L Kirk's cover (*Selected Journals* 3: 147)

Cover images lure, attract, and often linger, dancing on the edge of our gaze. In the realm of literary scholarship, the connections between illustrations and texts have just begun to attract the attention of literary scholars. In their study *Reading Images* (1990), Gunther Kress and Theo van Leeuwen make an argument for 'visual literacy.' Their method of analysing visual images is to examine both the social relations within the picture, as formed by the relationship of objects towards one another in the picture, and the social relations established with the viewer, who is outside the picture. As a result, we examine not only composition, planes, and vectors within the picture, but also the viewer's position (above, below, or level with the picture), any obliqueness in the viewer's and painter's relation to the picture, and whether the viewer's gaze meets the eyes of the person depicted. All of these relationships denote aspects of social power, either demanding social interaction or distancing the viewer. And book illustrations, which are commissioned by publishers to market a given text, often embed the dominant, mostly hidden, value and power structures that inhabit a given culture at a particular time in its history.

In this chapter, I use Kress and van Leeuwen's 'grammar' of visual rhetoric as a frame of reference to explore images of Emily across time (from the mid-1920s to the late 1950s) and in different countries (the Netherlands, Sweden, the United States, and Canada) to determine to what extent writing is presented as empowerment for young girls and women in the respective cultures and periods. L.M. Montgomery's Emily trilogy (1923, 1925, 1927) focuses on a writer's struggle for a voice against cultural and social domination and depicts writing as embedded in power relationships. By examining the illustrations with which these texts are packaged and promoted, I attempt to determine the cultural value embedded in the texts. The Emily novels are profoundly autobiographical, documenting the complexity of life for the Canadian woman writer in the early twentieth century. As Montgomery scholars have documented in a plethora of studies, the lack of support for women's writing (Epperly, *Fragrance* 149–207), the struggle of the developing female writer (Campbell, 'Wedding Bells'), as well as the female drive to write (Gammel, 'My Secret Garden') are all embodied in Emily Byrd Starr. As Epperly notes, 'Montgomery's novels suggest how radically life scripts must change if the female is to read herself as heroine': her aunts are 'not supportive' of Emily's writing, and 'the underlying and encoded messages about woman's place in the male literary establishment eventually make their quality of support suspect' (*Fragrance* 152–3). Not surprisingly, those who support Emily's ambitions – Ilse, Teddy, Cousin Jimmy, Mr Carpenter – stand on the margins of society.

How, then, do the different national versions visualize their portrait of the young woman as an artist in the respective cover images? How is Emily visually translated as she travels across cultural borders into Europe? By examining composition, planes, participant perspectives, presence, and exclusions, I propose to uncover whether the images work with or against Montgomery's text, arguing that these images of Emily become a subtle means of educating 'readers' in the attitudes towards women writers that were considered appropriate for the time and culture. How, ultimately, did national boundaries transform the image of the writer and the social messages communicated? What effects would they have on the reader at the time of publication, and could the reader 'read' herself into the image? Finally, what are some of the tensions between Montgomery's textual script and the cover image?

Emily of New Moon

The original 1923 American cover of *Emily of New Moon* by the illustrator M.L. Kirk is the cover that Montgomery called, on 29 August 1923, 'the prettiest one on any of my books' (*SJ* 3: 147) (figure 7.1).[1] In Kirk's visual interpretation, a romanticized, pastoral landscape in pastel colours is set off by the stronger colours of the frame. The trees in the background are very detailed and realistically depicted. The young Emily herself, however, is slightly abstract, not as realistically portrayed; even the ground she stands on is blurred. Our eye is drawn from Emily to the trees and sunset on the left of the picture, the traditional site of the given. Emily's hands are clasped in a typical spiritual pose, and she is gazing, presumably at the landscape beyond our view, connected to it by the colours of her clothing and face, which are repeated in the sunset and trees.

The faint figure behind her, with the gauze of her garment connecting Emily with the romanticized scene, reinforces Emily's connection with the imaginative and the inspired. Emily is placed at the right of the picture, in the space traditionally devoted to the new as opposed to the given; the Wind Woman, the product of her imagination, looks down, not at Emily, but at the scenery behind her. The Wind Woman's figure extends beyond the right side of the frame, and she is actually stepping into the frame – the only action depicted in this illustration. The positions of these two figures in the landscape, then, suggest that nature is the given and real upon which Emily gazes, and from which she creates the new or the imaginative, as symbolized by the Wind Woman. The picture epitomizes Holly Pike's claim that 'Montgomery presents Emily as a particular type of Canadian writer, focusing on pastoral life, tied to the landscape, and dwelling on its beauty and significance' ('(Re)Producing Canadian Literature' 74).

If we apply the theories of Kress and van Leeuwen, the long shot of Emily – the full-length figure – should suggest distance from us, as should the frame. Yet the flowered frame, with the title at the top and Montgomery's name linked to the picture, suggests a mirror frame as well as a picture frame. Emily, the Wind Woman, and the landscape are all beautiful objects that offer themselves up to our contemplation. Emily does not demand a relation with us by a direct gaze: she's intent on her vision. Yet the suggestion of a mirror frame offers the viewer the idea that, by reading this book, the reader can also create beautiful visions like Emily's – can, in fact, become Emily. This idea is reinforced by the placement of the viewer of this picture: we stand below Emily, looking up at her: the trees and the Wind Woman form two downward vectors, towards Emily but also towards the viewer; as a result, we aspire to her vision, and she is the focus of power.

7.1   Maria Louise Kirk, *Emily of New Moon* cover illustration, 1923. Courtesy of
L.M. Montgomery Collection, Archival and Special Collections, University of
Guelph Library, McClelland and Stewart, and the heirs of L.M. Montgomery.

Contrast this original North American version with the cover of the Dutch translation, published as *Emily van de Nieuwe Maan* in 1924, a year after the original. Here, we must ask if the woman depicted is actually to represent Emily, or the anticipated reader. This woman, luxuriously attired in flowing robes, her dress cut low at the back, her hair piled around her head, and with one foot, slipper-clad, peeping out from her gown, is comfortably seated in front of a blazing fire with a cat on a cushion by her side. She does not demand social interaction with the viewer but offers herself to our gaze. The woman herself is the focal point of the picture, with the flower pattern of the chair emphasizing the romanticism implicit in the full, beruffled sleeves of her gown and subtly reinforcing the pattern of her hair style. The details of the surroundings – the overly large fireplace that suggests a spacious room, the artistic lamp, the low vase with flowers, the supply of wood piled close by, the bow on the cat – all of these suggest a comfortable style of living and a sensually rich reading experience. It is, in contrast to the North American version, a very domestic image, suggestive of a lady of leisure who can afford to spend an evening reading by the fire. Creativity does not flash in this picture; the pages of the book are blank, open to reading, but no pen is in sight, and the fireside setting suggests the reader not the writer.

Kress and van Leeuwen state that the degree of modality of a picture – its assumption of reality – determines the degree to which the reader can 'enter' the picture. In this vision, the woman is somewhat realistically depicted, but the details are not etched. Her face is simply drawn, without detail, as is the rest of the room. As such, the image allows the reader to envision herself as entering the picture, in place of the woman. By buying the book, the purchaser will possess this lovely, peaceful, romantic image, and will become the woman seated in comfort before her own fireplace, enjoying a book. The very obliqueness of the woman's stance, with only her profile depicted, suggests the intensity of her interest.

In essence, Emily the writer and Emily the child have disappeared from this image to be replaced by a woman whose age could be anywhere from seventeen to thirty, and one who lives in such well-to-do circumstances that she has the leisure to immerse herself in a book. These changes – both the erasure of Emily's complex life as a writer, and the revision of her circumstances to a luxurious standard of living complete with electricity – refocus the promise of the work. Emily of New Moon has been trivialized, in this image, to a potential evening of beruffled, cosy, distinctly feminine pleasure for the buyer of the book.

A third cover of the young Emily of New Moon, the 1956 Swedish translation, *Emily och hennes vänner*, returns the viewer to the child. The difference between this picture and that of Kirk, however, is in the direction of Emily's gaze. Here, she creates demand by looking directly at the viewer; she stands in a medium shot, with her face turned to the viewer but her body turned towards the house at the right of the picture. Clearly, she invites us to join her in going to the house and entering it. The decontextualized background of hills sloping into the distance suggests space, while the kitten cuddled in Emily's arms repeats the home-like qualities of the sketched-in house. Emily herself is the most detailed object in the picture, connected both to the house and to the hills by her positioning; she is poised on a hill, inhabiting it, and establishing her ownership of the house, which is below her. Yet she also 'owns' the hills in the distance, for her image cuts across them. This Emily belongs both outdoors and indoors. At the same time, however, because of the picture's perspective and the angle of Emily's gaze, the viewer stands slightly above Emily, looking down on her and the hills from a position of power; by buying the book, we will possess this vision.

Creativity, however, is erased from this picture just as it was from the Swedish version. Emily has become *any* girl, albeit in a distinctly Swedish landscape, but clad in a typical dress and shown in a typical girlish action as cuddling a kitten. The girl in this portrait lacks the distinctive edge of Kirk's creative vision; she is earthbound, tying herself firmly to her vision of the reader, instead of to her vision of herself as a creative force. At the same time, the starkness of this version – the angles of house and hills, the sharp angles formed by Emily's dress and white collar – lacks the seductive femininity of the Dutch image. The kitten and the bow on Emily's sash provide the only softening of the Swedish image.

These three versions of Emily as a young girl demonstrate widely differing 'workings' of the text: Kirk's American cover offers the lure of imagination and creativity, with Emily holding power and promise over the reader, just as Montgomery's text depicts the power and promise of writing as a creative force. The Dutch cover, with its feminine image, and the Swedish cover, with its 'anygirl,' empower the reader to possess the image, and through it, the text. The erasure of Emily's writing in the latter two diminishes her creative force, thus working against Montgomery's text. Both the American and the Dutch covers target a 1920s female audience, with the Dutch audience seemingly older than the American one. The Swedish cover, from the 1950s, lacks both the American promise of creativity and the Dutch artist's evocation of sophistication; the Swedish artist has demoted Montgomery's work, in fact, to just another girl's book. Montgomery's work, in Kirk's American cover, holds the power to transform, albeit without the darker complexities of the text, but loses that power in both European versions.

Emily Climbs: Anygirl?

In the American version of *Emily Climbs*, Kirk's teenage Emily is again placed in a pastoral landscape, but this time with books scattered around her. The landscape slopes back towards the sunset, thus having the viewer gaze down at Emily; compared with the earlier Kirk representation, the position of power has been reversed. The landscape offers no hidden objects of imaginative beauty; Emily's hands are unclasped, holding a book. Though she still gazes into the distance in thoughtful contemplation – for all we know, before reading *Emily Climbs* – she could very well be thinking about what she has read instead of about what she is going to write, because the pen is absent from the picture. Emily, here, has become a typical schoolgirl, with her imaginative powers dimmed and diminished. The landscape is again romantic, soft, pastoral, and framed, but the books scattered around are in brighter colours and draw more attention than the flowers, connecting her character with the realm of literature. The style of clothing, the books, and the hair ribbon all suggest a mode of life with which the putative teenage girl reader would be familiar: school.

Contrast Kirk's teenaged Emily with Eva Laurell's 1957 cover of the Swedish translation, *Emily på egna vägar* (figure 7.2). Emily is climbing a hill towards us, away from the building behind her, as though she is about to step out of the frame. She is in the act of closing a gate that leads to the building – possibly a school – and gazes towards the unknown to the left. The gate is still ajar, suggesting her connection to the building, an impression reinforced by the colour of her hat and dress, which are reflected in the colours of the windows. Though part of the building, she still leaves it behind. Note the book under her arm: unlike the North American version, where the pages of the book are blank, thus allowing the viewer to write on the pages, Laurell's Swedish version has a label on the front, with the last few letters of Emily's

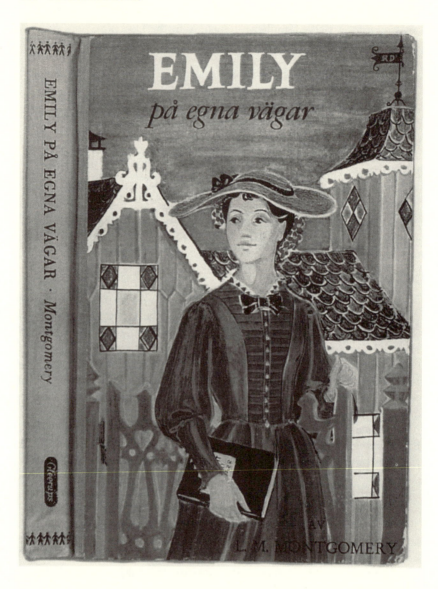

7.2   Eva Laurell, *Emily på egna vägar* (*Emily Climbs*) cover illustration, Swedish edition, Lund: Gleerup, 1957. Courtesy of L.M. Montgomery Collection, Archival and Special Collections, University of Guelph Library, the heirs of L.M. Montgomery, and Ingegard Björn and Sigfrid Laurell.

first and last name visible: Emily is an author, firmly holding her book (possibly a diary) against her, thus taking ownership of her writing. Her status is thus clearly delineated as a writer, especially to readers of *Emily of New Moon*: this is her writing.

The school, rather than Emily, denotes a local Swedish setting. The architecture, including the rounded shingles, stained-glass windows, and tower with a small sign at the top, resembles that of a Swedish building rather than an American one. Yet the lack of specific realism in the building and in Emily allows the reader to place herself imaginatively 'in the picture.' The pastoral is gone: the only symbol of nature is the bunch of flowers on Emily's hat. Her gaze is firm and determined, like her hold on the book, but it places no demand on the viewer. A medium shot, this illustration is closer to us than the last one, permitting us to come socially nearer to Emily. Although there is no demand in this picture, Emily's movement towards us is an invitation to enter the picture and take a further step up with her, the writer. Compared with the earlier Swedish cover depicting Emily as a child, this cover is more elaborate, reflecting her new status as she moves into young adulthood: the hat, the hair up instead of in a braid, the darker, more elaborate clothing, with its intricate sleeves and with lace replacing the plain white collar, and the book replacing the cat all contribute to this picture of young-ladyhood.

With this Swedish 1957 *Emily på egna vägar* cover image in mind, let us now take a step back in time to 1939 to view the cover design by the Canadian illustrator and painter Stanley Francis Turner (1883–1953) on a Cavendish Library edition of *Emily Climbs* (figure 7.3). Turner renders the adolescent Emily as a grown woman with a late-1930s hairstyle and scarf. This is a fashion-inspired illustration, with the plucked, well-defined eyebrows, the curls over the forehead, the lipstick, and the wide-shouldered coat. It could, in fact, be any young woman on the cover of almost any novel (or in any film of the time), although the snow may give it a distinctly Canadian flavour. Emily is outdoors, and stars twinkle above her; the landscape, with the exception of the tree beside her, is distanced and blurred, with the stars becoming the most distinctive aspect. Most importantly, all allusions to writing or books have disappeared.

Where, however, is this 1939 Canadian Emily gazing? If we trace the angle of her gaze, she does not appear to be looking at the stars for inspiration. She gazes intently at something slightly above her and has her back turned to the landscape. What her gaze suggests, given its

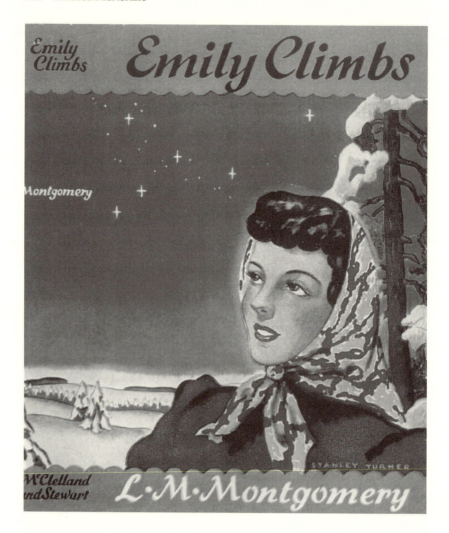

7.3   Stanley Francis Turner, *Emily Climbs* Cavendish Library cover illustration, 1939. Courtesy of L.M. Montgomery Collection, Archival and Special Collections, University of Guelph Library, McClelland and Stewart, and the heirs of L.M. Montgomery.

angle and height, is that the object outside our vision, but within hers, is, in fact, a young man. The landscape, with its twinkling stars, becomes a background, not for creative inspiration, but for romance. In the Canada of 1939, Emily has become a beautiful young woman with romantic possibilities; the writer has vanished completely. Whereas Laurell's 1957 Swedish version of Emily places her in distinct possession of her writing, the earlier American and Canadian versions do not: Kirk reduces her to a schoolgirl, while Turner portrays a lipsticked young woman ripe for romance. Creativity is diminished, though the pastoral landscape remains.

Emily's Quest: **International Portraits of a Writer?**

In *Emily's Quest* (1927), the last volume of the trilogy, Montgomery intensifies the struggle between writer and woman, with the wedding bells of marriage announcing the death knells of the author, as some scholars have argued (see Campbell, 'Wedding Bells'). In Kirk's American cover, the colours have darkened and the mood is more dramatic. Emily reads from a book by the combined light of the full moon and the candle, with books strewn around. She is enclosed by the room, no longer in a pastoral setting. The darkness outside is framed, with the moon the only clear-cut object and the candle balancing the moon's natural illumination with candlelight. The trees outside form another wall. At the same time, the cover also exudes a sense of subversion: Emily is reading/writing when she obviously should be asleep. As though caught between the natural (moonlight) and human-made (candlelight) world, she kneels on the floor by the window. This adult woman is trapped between walls, those of the room and those of the trees outside, as though growing up was causing the walls to close in upon her.

Kirk's darkly romantic illustration, then, dramatically contrasts with the startling modernity of the 1928 Dutch translation of *Emily's Quest*, *Emily's Eerzucht* (figure 7.4), as the (anonymous) Dutch illustrator effectively rendered Montgomery's black-haired Emily as a bobbed blonde vamp. By her side is her husband-to-be, Teddy Kent, a modern Heathcliff, judging by his anguished look – an equally dramatic shift. The only cover depicting a person other than Emily, it is also the only one that includes a pen. This cover addresses itself to modern adults, with a flavour of the sexual politics of the roaring twenties. Although Teddy is positioned above his bride, a placement that would denote power

7.4 *Emily's Eerzucht* (*Emily's Quest*) cover, Dutch edition, Haarlem: Tjeenk Willink, 1928. Courtesy of L.M. Montgomery Collection, Archival and Special Collections, University of Guelph Library, and the heirs of L.M. Montgomery. Illustrator unknown.

over her, she is looking off into the distance, unheeding of his gaze, and thus negating that power. The inkpot and quill pen loom larger than the persons, but are painted the same colour as the background. Emily, centred, is balanced between Teddy and the pen and ink; her head inclines on both, giving her ownership of both. The vertical line of the pen emphasizes the connection between Teddy and Emily; the horizontal line of the inkpot is imposed on top of Teddy but behind Emily, creating a barrier between the two. It also, however, points to the flower in Emily's hand: blue, with a pink centre, it reflects the joining of the two romantically through the colour of their clothing. There is an implicit question posed by the picture: will Emily choose the pen, the man, or both? All of these possibilities are contained in the illustration, given the placement of the figures, the pen and ink, and the flower.

The open sexuality of the 1928 Dutch picture comes as a shock after the virginal 1927 American version. Certainly, the change in Emily's hair colour from black to blonde and her fashionable flapper dress appeal to the contemporary audience. Seductive, sophisticated, and poised between romance and writing, this Dutch Emily is much more unsettling than her American counterpart, who is safely contained in the picture, framed by flowers, ultimately non-threatening. But how is this cover related to Montgomery's 1927 text? Montgomery, positioned in the North American market as an author of children's and young-adolescent books, could not openly depict the sexuality of her characters, although she did depict sexuality subversively (Munro, 'Afterword' 357–61; Gammel, 'My Secret Garden' 39–65). On the Dutch cover, Montgomery's subversive eros explodes into sexually charged modernity.

In the third volume of the novel, Montgomery documents the contradictory demands of artistry and marriage for a post-Victorian, modern woman. She leaves her reader with an ending that has caused much debate, when Emily, the successful author, becomes engaged to Teddy, the successful artist. Emily and Teddy's '"late" joining is not merely a sop to romantic convention ... nor a denial of feminist principles, nor a pandering to audience taste,' argues Epperly, and continues: 'Montgomery does not let Teddy and Emily wed in their first youth perhaps because both still have so much to learn about their respective gifts' (*Fragrance* 190). Epperly's perspective builds on that of Judith Miller, who suggests that Montgomery's vision shows 'that it is possible to have both [family and success in writing], but not without pain, honesty, and the proper management of pride and propriety, through an almost superhuman strength' (317). Other scholars, including T.D. MacLulich ('L.M. Montgomery's Portraits' 459–73), Marie Campbell ('Wedding Bells' 137–45), and Ian Menzies ('The Moral of the Rose' 48–61), are more negative in their assessment, Menzies claiming that 'Emily is first damaged by Dean, then subsequently leashed by Teddy' (60).

These covers, then, reflect this continuing controversy about Emily's status: will she continue to write, or will she allow marriage to consume and subsume her creative force? The covers depicting the adult Emily show a wide range of perspectives and interpretations revealing distinctly different cultural values. Kirk embeds the ambivalence of a writer enclosed in domesticity in her picture, but one who disrupts domestic conventions; the Dutch artist (see Figure 7.4) balances Emily between romance and a career. Still, in all illustrations, it is as though the struggle of a female writer, for the most part, is erased from the illustrations; even the Dutch cover shows Emily seductively reclining, with a flower in her hand.

What is, then, perhaps most disturbing about the full range of covers, created across three decades, and spanning four different countries, is their consistent demotion or denial of the female author and of the complexities of Emily's life as a young writer. Kirk's original vision of Emily (see figure 7.1) denotes her creativity; Laurell's cover for the Swedish translation of *Emily Climbs* (see figure 7.3) gives her ownership of her writing; the Dutch version of *Emily's Quest* (see figure 7.4) envisions her caught between a romantically drawn quill pen and Teddy. Yet the rest of the collection depicts Emily either as generic – the anygirl, the school girl – or as reactive, as a reader at best, instead of as a writer. This consistency across decades and national boundaries demonstrates the socially encoded nature of the role of 'woman' colliding with that of 'writer'; backgrounds and hair colours may be localized, but the portrait of a female artist continually deprives her of a pen.

In chapters 1 and 17 of *Making Avonlea*, Carole Gerson and Holly Pike, respectively, briefly discuss the cover illustrations of Montgomery's work within a context of marketing, raising astute questions about promotional strategies in reaching the widest possible readerships. Marketing generally demands the creation of images that have the potential to captivate a broad readership, yet do so within safe parameters that do not disturb or unsettle prospective buyers.

This analysis covers only a small fraction of available illustrations, but suggests a possible framework of questions for future explorations, about the power of the illustrator to affect our readings, past, present, and future, of Montgomery's works. Given the power of illustrations to define a work as within or outside a particular cultural canon, how did covers target audiences and affect the placement and reviews of Montgomery's works? How do these covers position the female reading audience and the values they are expected to accept? In the larger context, what power structures govern the positioning of Montgomery and her audiences in other cultures through the illustrations of her works? Through illustrations, we can examine the shifting depictions of Montgomery and her characters in different places and times; we can also question our own cultural expectations of Montgomery and the place of the female writer by tracing the encoded values in the covers produced in other cultures.

Note

1 According to *Who's Who in American Art*, Maria Louise Kirk (born in 1860 in Philadelphia, PA) attended the Philadelphia School of Design for Women and the Philadelphia Academy of Fine Arts. She exhibited work at the Philadelphia Academy of Fine Arts and the Art Institute of Chicago in the 1890s and early 1900s, winning an award in Philadelphia in 1894. Kirk illustrated more than fifty books for children, including George MacDonald's *The Princess and the Goblin*, Longfellow's *Hiawatha*, and Frances Hodgson Burnett's *The Secret Garden*.

Chapter 8

Safe Pleasures for Girls: L.M. Montgomery's Erotic Landscapes

IRENE GAMMEL

This evening I spent in Lover's Lane. How beautiful it was – green and alluring and beckoning!

– L.M. Montgomery, August 1909 (*Selected Journals* 1: 357)

In my home office, overlooking the tidal flats of the Hillsborough River and the Island scenery beyond, I have two cherished works of art that encapsulate two different ways of looking at the Island landscape. One is a reproduction of Alex Colville's *To Prince Edward Island* (1965), a painting figuring in its foreground an almost life-sized female viewer with shoulder-length, sun-bleached hair. Resting her arms on the bench of a ferry boat, she is looking through large binoculars directly at the viewer, aggressively intruding into the viewer's field. Dominating the viewer, the young woman in the painting literally possesses the (traditionally) male gaze of Western art. Given that the woman is looking 'To Prince Edward Island,' the painting is, perhaps, an apt metaphor for the many female travellers and tourists who have intruded into the field of Prince Edward Island, profoundly reshaping the island through the powerful tourist gaze, as explored in the essays in part three of this volume.

The second painting in my office, an original watercolour by Island artist Erica Rutherford, entitled *L.M. Montgomery* (1994) (figure 8.1), speaks more directly to my chapter. Most remarkable about this painting is the striking sensuality of the colours: different shades of rich green in the fields are interspersed with the red contours of winding pathways that are suggestive of the red earth itself, the landscape, rolling and undulating until it meets a brilliantly turquoise and

8.1   Erica Rutherford, *L.M. Montgomery*, 1994. Watercolour painting. 10 in.
24 in. Charlottetown, Private collection.

blue sky. In the lower right corner sits Montgomery, the rightful pro-
prietor of Avonlea, overlooking this landscape, which spans a wide
canvas suggestive of the Island's east-west expanse. In its centre is an
ordinary Island farm, its green roofs and red contours a nod to Green
Gables.

Whereas Colville distanced the viewer, Rutherford solicits the
viewer's desire with an invitation to enter Montgomery's imaginative
landscape. Absorbed in intense contemplation of the landscape, Montgomery has turned her back to the viewer; her arms are flung out, and
the book in her hand has dropped on the ground. Rutherford has captured the author in the midst of the 'flash,' her dramatic connection
with nature that Montgomery described in her journals, as in this entry
of 23 July 1925: 'I looked over to Mr Leask's hayfield on my left. Wave
after wave of sinuous, glistening, wind-shadows were going over it. I
have not seen just that exact effect in years. A flood of ecstasy washed
through my soul. The mystic curtain fluttered and I caught the glimpse
of Eternal and Infinite beauty which Emily called "her flash"' (*SJ* 3:
241). In the painting, this evocation of the flash is the only movement
in what is otherwise a still life, further highlighting the profoundly
sensual and quasi-orgasmic experience that connects Montgomery

with the land. Looking over Montgomery's shoulder, the viewer is compelled to enter a sensually charged relationship with her world. The landscape beckons and we follow.

Originally commissioned for *An Island Alphabet* (1994), a children's alphabet book, with each artwork illustrating a different aspect of Island life in alphabetical order to teach the letters (a = Abegweit, b = Belfast Church, c = Ceilidh, and so on), the painting directs itself to both youths and adults, very much as Montgomery's works do, and invites different levels of reading and decoding. Rutherford captures Montgomery's profound opening of the senses, but is also careful to desexualize the experience. Montgomery's entire body is covered in a long-sleeved dark brown dress (a colour that connects her with the earth); only her white hands and the tips of her shoes peek out from underneath the covering. On the right, a tall tree rises, the only vertical configuration in the painting, with its fleshy and glistening stem evoking the traditional phallic and patriarchal symbol. Yet the tree, too, is desexualized; as the stem gently curves up above her, its bouquet of leaves filling out the upper right, the tree is transformed from potentially sexual symbol into innocent shade. The sensuality and sexual deflations are appropriate, given the target audience for this painting.

Rutherford's painting is emblematic for Montgomery's writing of eros. In her journals, Montgomery uses the tantalizing phrase 'my "secret garden"' to describe her creative realm of imagination and fantasy (*SJ* 3: 331). Montgomery's imaginary world in her journals is one in which orchards become feminized erotic spaces; trees become responsive lovers; girls are allowed to have passionate love affairs; and cats provide a safe space for sensual caressing. 'I myself don't know of many nicer things than to waken up in the night and put out a hand to feel a soft, warm, velvety purring little flank in the darkness,' she writes of her cats in her journal (*SJ* 3: 135), while in another scene erotically anthropomorphizing a tree she has known since her childhood: 'There it was smothered amid that intruding growth. I wonder if it felt my kiss on its gnarled trunk and if its aged sap coursed with a momentary quickening at the step of its lover' (*SJ* 3: 347). Nature provides her with frissons and delights, with thrills and flashes.

Here, in the erotic charges projected into the landscape, I propose, lies the key to Montgomery's popularity across different time periods, cultures, and nationalities. For the pleasures articulated in the journals powerfully spill into Montgomery's fiction. Lovers' Lane, the White

Way of Delight, the Lake of Shining Waters, White Sands, Violet Vale – this mythopoetic world of Avonlea's *Anne of Green Gables* is charged with visual, oral, haptic, and olfactory sensuality that solicits the reader's desire and draws her into the sensual world of Avonlea. Appropriately, the Avonlea theme park in Hokkaido, Japan, reproduced this atmosphere with the intensely sweet perfume of large fields of lavender. In *Anne of Green Gables*, Anne Shirley 'opened the gates of her soul' to the 'honey-sweet fields of clover,' 'the mingled hues' of the sea, and its 'unceasing murmur' (*AGG* 327). In addition to being expert readers and writers of literary texts, Montgomery's characters are emotionally and sensually literate. The Montgomery heroine always opens her senses – and compels the reader to do the same.

In *Reading the Romance* (1984), her landmark ethnographic study on popular romances, the American feminist scholar Janice Radway has detailed through interviews with American readers of popular romances that for overworked working women, romances present highly charged experiences, combining rare moments of private time with sexual pleasures (the stuff of romance reading). In a provocatively titled study, 'Mass Market Romance: Pornography for Women Is Different' (1983), the American Women's Studies scholar Ann Barr Snitow examines the Harlequin romance (the cornerstone genre of a publishing empire founded by Canadian Richard Bonnycastle in 1949). Snitow traces 'the Harlequin's' formula for success in sexually charged descriptions of clothing and food, and in scenes in which 'sex is bathed in romance, diffused, always implied rather than enacted at all. This pornography is the Harlequin romance' (257). As 'pornography' for women, the formula Harlequin multiplies moments of erotic pleasure for women: 'Clearly, getting romantic tension, domestic security, and sexual excitement together in the same fantasy in the right proportions is a delicate balancing act. Harlequins lack excellence by other measure, but they are masterly in this one respect' (259). Pleasure, though, is typically designed to arouse male desires, as Snitow argues (252); the Harlequin is a genre in which women are taught to love and endure that which subjugates them.[1]

While also multiplying moments of pleasure for girls and women, Montgomery puts the romance to a very different use, however, as she applies erotically charged language to the act of literary creation and to concepts of female autonomy. In contrast to the Harlequin heroine, Montgomery's romance heroine, I propose, takes charge of her own pleasure and sidesteps the traditional model of male dominance and female submission.[2] Her girl heroines grow into young women who generate their pleasure through creative work and professional careers, and who delay marriage and child-bearing, a plot all too familiar to many twentieth- and twenty-first-century career women who love the work they do and often identify themselves through it. Montgomery's girls are profoundly modern in that they do not wait for pleasures to materialize in heterosexual romance. Montgomery empowers her girls to be agents in their erotic universe, to indulge in sensualized pleasure without feelings of guilt; indeed, to cultivate and map their erotic imaginary. In 'Cultivating One's Understanding: The Female Romantic Garden,' the British literary scholar Jacqueline Labbe writes that women authors are culturally accustomed to being enclosed and therefore 'can actually find more freedom within the garden. Indeed, confinement – whether by garden, parlour, or boudoir walls – is so expected it might prove to be the most open avenue for women to subvert cultural expectations of feminine submission and decorum' (39). In just this way, the fictional island garden emerging from Montgomery's pen is a space for girls' and adolescents' emotions and desires, giving expression to girls' raptures, ecstasies, infatuations, longings, and satisfaction, while also detailing the pains arising from the pressures and prohibitions of a repressive society. Montgomery encourages her girls to take control of their pleasure and puts them in touch with their bodies and their surroundings. In presenting girl readers with a rich arena of erotic alternatives, her writing changes the fabric of social relations from the bottom up.

Let us briefly trace, then, Montgomery's erotic imaginary in the Emily trilogy (1923, 1925, 1927), her most autobiographical fiction, written during a period when she was recopying her childhood journals (see Turner, 'I mean to try' 93–100). This trilogy powerfully dramatizes Montgomery's youthful drive to be a writer, as well as giving voice to her profoundly subversive demands for female pleasure. Emily does not escape the heterosexual logic of her society but sidesteps and subverts it, as *Emily of New Moon* presents eroticized girl crushes with great complexity and realistic detail, critically expanding Montgomery's template for powerfully emotional female attachments such as Anne and Diana's bosom friendship in *Anne of Green Gables*. Emily's crush on the pretty Rhoda Stewart has the emotional intensity of any adult infatuation: 'Rhoda says I mustn't have any chum but her or she will cry her eyes out. Rhoda loves me as much as I love her. We are both going to pray that we may live together all our lives and die the same day' (*ENM* 106).

As the crush on the teasing Rhoda burns itself out in pain, the novel is propelled forward by the deepening bond between Emily and Ilse Burnley, and even though boys and beaus figure in their friendship, they are secondary in the bond connecting the two girls. Having escaped from the spare room, where she had been locked up for punishment, Emily spots 'Ilse Burnley huddled up on the top of a fence panel, her pale-gold head making a spot of brilliance against the dark young firs that crowded around her' (123). The ensuing thunderstorm promptly forces the two girls to hide, the classical love plot of Dido and Aeneas that serves as backdrop for the new friendship: 'I want you for *my* chum,' says Ilse (124), declaring her desire, while Emily discloses her most cherished secret: that she wants to be a 'poetess' (125). The pleasure of this bond, in part, is mediated through their bodies, as in the scene when Emily reawakens to Ilse's physical attractiveness after a period of separation: 'Emily discovered she had forgotten how vivid Ilse was – how brilliant her amber eyes, how golden her mane of spun-silk hair, looking more golden than ever under the bright blue silk tam' (294).

Montgomery's focus on girl–girl attraction is woven through the tapestry of erotic fantasies projected into the island landscape, most notably that of the Wind Woman, a figure to whom the novels return with refrain-like regularity. The Wind Woman is Emily's imaginary friend, a fantasy figure composed of Emily's idealized dead mother, mythologized nature goddess, and figure of female Eros. To Emily she is physical and mythological, 'tall and misty, with thin, grey, silky clothes blowing all about her – and wings like a bat's – only you can see through them – and shining eyes like stars looking through her long, loose hair' (13). The gale-force winds are a well-known feature of the Canadian Maritimes, and Emily's imagining of nature's strength as benevolently female presents an important feminist element in this novel – a female landscape mythology, with the Wind Woman, 'a giantess' and protean shape-shifter, providing the heartbeat of this universe. Embedded in action verbs and kinetic energy, the Wind Woman is an active force, 'ruffling' the grass, 'tossing the big boughs,' 'teasing' the pine, and 'whispering' (13), an element that is brilliantly visualized in Maria Louise Kirk's cover illustration of the first edition (see figure 7.1). When forced to share a bed with her tyrannical Aunt Elizabeth, Emily resorts to fantasizing her bond with the Wind Woman:

> Her soul suddenly escaped from the bondage of Aunt Elizabeth's stuffy feather-bed and gloomy canopy and sealed windows. She was out in the open with the Wind Woman and the other gipsies of the night – the fire-flies, the moths, the brooks, the clouds. Far and wide she wandered in enchanted reverie until she coasted the shore of dreams and fell soundly asleep on the fat, hard pillow, while the Wind Woman sang softly and lur-ingly in the vines that clustered over New Moon. (70)

This fantasy is all the more powerful as the 'long and stiff and bony' body of Aunt Elizabeth beside Emily's powerfully signifies the deter-rence of physical contact (66), ensuring that the child does not indulge in forbidden pleasures – including the tactile pleasures of her cats that Emily longs for.

Many of the conflicts in the novel relate to Emily's claim of being *an agent* of her body pleasure: after walking barefoot, she is punished by being locked up in the Gothic room; after enjoying the uncannily human touch of the cats at her ankles, she has to give up one of her cats; in cutting her bangs, she punishes herself. But there are also some dra-matic scenes in which she resists the claims adults make on her body: she refuses to be kissed by Uncle Wallace, refuses to have her hair cut by Aunt Elizabeth (as Juliet McMaster detailed in chapter 4), and refuses to yield to Dean Priest's offer of seductive bondage. The novel is about who is allowed to control Emily's body and body pleasure.

Yet it is Emily's drive for writing and creative expression that is most consistently eroticized, while also becoming the most intense focus for conflict. This may explain why Emily Starr – more so than Anne Shir-ley – has won a special place in the lives of today's Canadian women writers, editors, academics, and journalists, including Margaret At-wood, Lillian Nattel, Jane Urquhart, Kit Pearson, Arlene Perly Rae, Elizabeth Epperly, Ann Shortell, and Val Ross (Gwyn, 72).[3] While the rigid world of New Moon condemns writing, Emily is in secret com-munion with Montgomery and the reader when she relishes, savours, and reclaims writing as her sweet, autoerotic secret that has to be hid-den from the world of her guardians: 'Then she stepped softly across to an old, worn-out sofa in a far corner and knelt down, stowing away her letter and her "letter-bills" snugly on a little shelf formed by a board nailed across it underneath. Emily had discovered this one day when playing in the garret and had noted it as a lovely hiding-place for secret documents' (103). Claiming the space of covert pleasure *not* for a tryst with Teddy Kent, but for writing (103), Montgomery strategically eroticizes the writing process itself, embedding it in a cluster of words – 'breathlessly,' 'feverishly,' 'heedlessly,' 'intently,' 'the delightful throes of literary composition' – that are generally associated with romance and the sexual tension of courtship. Montgomery's 'flash,' as described in her journals, is so overt in its physical mimicking of female orgasm ('Wave after wave of sinuous, glistening, wind-shadows were going over it' [*SJ* 3: 241]) that she takes pains in her fiction to mask its physicality under the guise of pantheistic ecstasy, as a glimpse into the transcendent world beyond. Critics have focused on the flash's religious dimensions, but have glossed over the profound sensuality of the experience. But Emily's flash is pagan and it is physical: 'This moment came rarely – went swiftly, leaving her breathless with the inexpressible delight of it' (*ENM* 15).

The flash is also linked to writing. Scores of women writers have worried in their private diaries about becoming ugly and unattractive through the lonely activity of writing. Montgomery's message to her girl and women readers is the opposite: writing, far from de-eroticizing the woman, truly puts her in touch with her sensual powers, makes her attractive to herself and to others. Indeed, when we meet Emily as a young adult in *Emily's Quest*, the 'violet shadows [under her eyes] always seemed darker and more alluring after Emily had sat up to some unholy and un-Elizabethan hour completing a story' (*EQ* 10). Similarly, in *Emily Climbs*, the adolescent Emily forgets about being in love with Teddy Kent in the rush of writing a story about being in love, the writing superseding the real experience in intensity: 'Her cheeks burned, her heart beat, she tingled from head to foot with the keen rapture of creation – a joy that sprang fountain-like from the depths of being and seemed independent of all earthly things' (*EC* 275). The putative sexual lover becomes muse, the erotic battery that charges the writing process. In Montgomery's realm, manuscripts are not sexual *ersatz*, as Freudian sublimation theory suggests: they are the true sexual rivals in erotic triangles, as when Emily is engaged to be married to Dean Priest. 'I hated the book. You were more interested in it than in me,' he says about her writing (*EQ* 103), as Emily remains true to her motto, 'I shall be *wedded to my art*' (*EC* 13).[4] Much to the disappointment of Alice Munro, who sees in Dean Priest Montgomery's most plausible flesh-and-blood lover (in *Emily Climbs*, he even slips the heroine a presumably pornographic novel! [*EC* 36]), Montgomery excises him from Emily's life and from the novel.

Montgomery's romance puts on hold and indefinitely delays sexual consummation, while providing powerful forms of female satisfaction in the recurring raptures of writing, the ecstasy of the flash, the cooing murmur of the wind, and the delight of spun-silk hair. The lavish multiplying of such moments, the deliberate lack of 'restraint and economy' in describing moments of pleasure and joy, are Montgomery's trademark and the key to her popularity. Completing *Emily Climbs* in January of 1924, she complained in her journals that 'the public and the publisher won't allow me to write of a young girl as she really is [...] you have to depict a sweet, insipid young thing – really a child grown older – to whom the basic realities of life and reactions to them are quite unknown. *Love* must scarcely be hinted at – yet young girls in their early teens often have some very vivid love affairs. A girl of "Emily's" type would' (*SJ* 3: 157). Yet Montgomery did know how to write subversively and how to address herself to both girls and adults. And she made sure her readers would have it both ways. She always returned to conventional reading pleasures to close her novels, as the reader anticipates the inevitable coming together of Teddy and Emily, of Gilbert and Anne, in the marriage plot. Yet these conventional reading pleasures pale in comparison with the transgressive pleasure provided in feminized nature descriptions, pleasures that leave the female in control and often place the male in a feminized waiting position.

In contrast to *Anne of Green Gables, Emily of New Moon* is at its core a complex female-initiation story whose bodily subject matter daringly pushes the boundaries of girls' fiction as Montgomery gives voice to an important tabooed topic by using a complex code of literary and mythological allusions. In the Wyther Grange episodes, the moon of her novel's title assumes the meaning Anaïs Nin describes in her erotic diaries as the 'moonstorm' (145, 161, 174, 202, etc.), that is, menstruation, perhaps the ultimate taboo in girls' fiction. As always, the landscape announces and prepares the event: when Emily journeys to 'Priest Pond,' the name signals a sacred ritual. With the nail as her talisman in her pocket, a good luck charm given to her by the coach driver, Old Kelly, she enters the strangely pagan, subterranean, underworld space of Wyther Grange. The omnipresence of water – the Gulf Shore, 'fringed rivers and inlets,' 'three blue lakelets,' and finally 'Priest Pond' – announce the fluidity of Emily's menstruation in the landscape's imagery. 'The air seemed to be filled with opal dust over the great pond and the bowery summer homesteads around it. A western sky of smoky red was arched over a big Malvern Bay beyond. Little grey sails were drifting along by the fir-fringed shores. A sequestered side road, fringed thickly with young maples and birches, led down to Wyther Grange' (252). With the water turning red against the sky's smoky red arch, Montgomery sets the stage for Emily's initiation. In this ancient pagan ritual, she is welcomed by two crones, 'Caroline Priest,' a witch, as Old Kelly says, and Nancy Murray, equally witch-like, with her shrivelled yellow skin and long, gold-tasselled earrings. The two women have special sexual knowledge and promptly initiate the young heroine into the world of womanhood with their tales of sex, seduction, and adultery. The adults also conspire to sexualize her body: She has 'come-hither eyes,' says Old Kelly (249), who weaves Emily into a tapestry of marriage plots, while Aunt Nancy scrutinizes her ankles for their erogenous potential in luring men (257).

Sequestered in her own room, the 'Pink room,' in the 'Deals with Ghosts' chapter, Emily's initiation is dressed in the language and codes of female Gothic romance – an ordeal – as Emily is kept awake at night by mysterious noises in the chimney. What has been read as a simple case of nervous hysteria, or as the result of Emily's overactive imagination after having consumed too many Gothic romances, the discerning reader of Montgomery's journals will be able to decode as Montgomery's complex literary cryptogram for menstrual symptoms, depicted in Emily's striking bodily responses: cold perspiration, anxiety, terror, horror, panic, and a none-too-subtle Gothic vision of a 'bleeding nun' (259–61).[5] Unable to sleep, Emily stares at the high, white ceilings and then through the open window that connects her with the outside world: 'Through it Emily could see summer fields lying in the magic of a rising yellow moon. But the room was big and ghostly. She felt horribly far away from everybody.' Wyther Grange signals the young heroine's entrance into fertility, the age of reproduction, encoded in the landscape and settings: 'Grange' (= grain) evokes the ancient fertility rites, as do the summer fields she sees in the moonlight; the moon, of course, is the classical symbol for both menstrual and agricultural cycles. 'The crescent moon ruled the sexuality of women,' writes Barbara Walker in *The Woman's Encyclopedia of Myths and Secrets* (673), which explains Montgomery's dismay at M.L. Kirk's cover mistake showing a *decreasing* rather than a crescent moon (see the epigraph in chapter 7). 'The moon was supposed to be the receptacle of menstrual blood by which each mother formed the life of her child' (Walker 672). Emily wakes up the next morning with black-ringed eyes, and learns from Nancy Murray and Caroline Priest that there is an ordinary explanation for her terrifying experience: the haunting noises in the chimney were produced by swallows, migratory birds that, like her own cycle, will return with predicable regularity. Emily's initiation is promptly followed by a letter from New Moon with the news that her cat Saucy Sal has given birth to kittens. This haunting underworld of initiation creates a connection with the reality of a woman's life, propelling her from the safety of eros into the dangers of sexuality.

Indeed, Emily has barely been initiated as sexual being when the real-life demon lover appears. Readers are bound to remember the disturbing appearance of the thirty-six-year-old Dean (Jarback) Priest as quasi-lover for the thirteen-year-old heroine in *New Moon*, an appearance so disturbing 'that the author, after a while, hardly seems to know what to do with him' (Munro, 358). Attracted by his 'magnetic green eyes,' his 'musical and caressing' voice, and 'his ironic tongue' (*ENM* 282, 281, 280), Emily is seduced and unsettled, as are the author and the reader. Accustomed to news-media disclosures of child sexual abuse, today's reader finds herself startled by this twist into a Lolita plot; Jarback Priest is a wounded and exiled Humbert Humbert figure whose desires for and Egyptian fantasies about Emily are keenly sexual, although like all of Montgomery's fictional lovers, he is willing to wait. Heightened sensitivity in a mainstream audience prompted the makers of the *Emily of New Moon* CBC television series to swiftly rejuvenate Dean Priest by at least ten years, presenting him in his twenties when he meets Emily on the television screen.[6] So what is Montgomery's point in exposing her heroine to such dangers? The danger is not gratuitous, for Montgomery's point is to show that Emily, schooled as she is in her erotic sensibilities, also knows when and how to set boundaries in the real world. She literally puts her foot down, destroying the aster that symbolizes Dean Priest's hold over her. She plays with fire but knows exactly when to say no (when her guardians apparently do not).

Like Emily, Montgomery the fiction writer sets firm boundaries. Throughout her writing career she remained loyal to the contract she had with her girl reader. Rape, abuse, and violence – these were issues that she kept away from her girl readers, preserving a space of safety in her fiction by relegating these issues to the margins and gaps of her text. While courageously subverting the genre and pushing it to its very edges, Montgomery carefully refrained from collapsing the genre's boundaries; after all, the romance genre provided her and her readers with the pleasure of female-controlled eros and identity. The girl-series were the ultimate safe space, the last bastion of wholesomeness and well-being in an increasingly troubled postwar world. It has to be remembered, too, that her genre was under siege. She published her trilogy among a flourishing of landmark texts of modernism (*Ulysses, Women in Love, Lady Chatterly's Lover, The Sun Also Rises*), works presenting a sexually liberated New Woman: 'Some "sex" novels are interesting and stimulating,' Montgomery conceded in a 30 December 1928 journal entry (*SJ 3:* 387), although she generally dismissed "the arid, sex-obsessed, novels of today" (*SJ* 3: 71), including Morley Callaghan's *Strange Fugitives,* 'the deadliest dull thing I ever tried to read' (*SJ* 3: 387). Swept by a wave of modernist experimentations intent on lifting the veil of Victorian reticence in sexual matters, Montgomery staunchly defended Victorian values through her heroine in *Emily's Quest:* 'The whole world to-day seems to be steeped in a scorn for things Victorian. Do they know what they're talking of? But I like sane, decent things – if *that* is Victorian.' And Ilse agrees: 'After all, the Victorians were right in covering lots of things up. Ugly things should be hidden' (*EQ* 212, 213).

Throughout her life Montgomery did just that. Only in her journals, as Margaret Steffler has reported in chapter 5, did she present that 'wholly other voice,' disclosing her wrestling with the complexities of sexuality. She startled her readers posthumously with disclosures of intensely sexual experiences with Herman Leard that had taken place in the spring of 1898 (*SJ* 1: 204–28). She took pleasure in detailing her many infatuations and flirtations, presenting herself as a quintessential (cock)tease. She scandalously disclosed that she never loved her husband. She soberly reported on her premenstrual depression and masochistic strain (*SJ* 3: 205). Yet if sexuality was a complex and treacherous domain that required careful negotiation in both life and writing, eros was her safety zone, the arena she mastered and controlled to perfection and with abandon as both woman and writer. 'It was a labor of love,' she wrote about *Anne of Green Gables.* 'Nothing I have ever written gave me so much pleasure to write' (*SJ* 1: 331); the realization of the book was 'sweet – almost as sweet as a dream!' (*SJ* 1: 331). By mapping her universe of pleasure in fictional writing, she escaped from her own worries and anxieties, indulging in the unadulterated pleasure of writing: 'I found solace and escape – I was free from my bonds and torments and roamed in an ideal world – coming back to reality at the end of my three hour's "stint" with renewed courage and "grit"' (23 March 1924, *SJ* 3: 191). It is a refrain she repeats with each novel. The domain of eros was her forte and her legacy, as she created a shelter from the rough storms of the new sex novels and sexual practices – a fictional space supremely controlled by the woman writer and her girl reader. It was also the space through which she shamelessly solicited reader desire, making us always come back for more.

Notes

My thanks to *English Studies in Canada* for permission to reprint parts of my essay '"My Secret Garden": Dis/Pleasure in Montgomery and Grove,' *ESC* (March 1999): 39–66.

1 See also Dawn Currie's recent sociological study, *Girl Talk: Adolescent Magazines and Their Readers* (1999), an ethnographic study of girl readers in Canada, examining their responses to issues of beauty, fashion, and body-image in girls' magazines.

2 In *Fragrance* (*passim*), as well as in her chapter in this volume, Elizabeth Epperly traces the influence of British Romantic poets on Montgomery; Ann Howey (chapter 11) documents Montgomery's use of Tennyson, as well as exploring Sullivan's translation of these elements in the *Anne* movies. In distinction from these important arguments, my focus here is not on the Romantic tradition, but on the *erotic* and the *sensual* qualities that solicit desire and that may be found in formula romance writing.

3 See, for instance, the title of Epperly's academic study of Montgomery's novels, *The Fragrance of Sweet-Grass*, a citation drawn from *Anne's House of Dreams*. The title invites the reader to enter the landscape and experience its sensual delights, an invitation reinforced visually with a cover painting of a Prince Edward Island landscape: a wide red clay road that summons the viewer on a walk towards the reddish-blue sea.

Conversely, a brilliantly satiric writer like Atwood was influenced by Montgomery's flair for social satire, a dimension explored by Mary Rubio, who explained in the introduction to her aptly titled edited collection of essays *Harvesting Thistles* (1994): 'To many readers, the thistles were all but obscured by the fragrance of her roses of romance, lilies of sentiment, and marigolds of wholesome child-life' (2); for an exploration of Montgomery's satire, see also Rubio, 'Subverting the Trite'; and 'Scottish-Presbyterian Agency.'

4 Epperly discusses the problematic influence of Father Cassidy, Mr Carpen-

ter, and Dean Priest as they 'test' Emily in her development as a writer (152–6); Marie Campbell argues that marriage is tantamount to death for Emily the artist ('Wedding Bells and Death Knells'); and Rubio notes that Montgomery's husband 'manifested a deep underlying hostility to her success as a writer' ('Introduction,' *Harvesting Thistles* 8).

5 In her journals Montgomery discusses the Brontë sisters within the context of menstruation, implying that the writing of Gothic pain is prompted by menstrual symptoms. Noting that Charlotte Brontë delighted in 'tormenting' her characters in 'a sort of spiritual, vicarious self-flagellation,' Montgomery continues by disclosing that 'all through the years of my sex life there was always one day or two every month when I became very nervous and somewhat depressed. During this time a mental masochistic tendency made its appearance in me and I heaped all sorts of misfortunes on myself in imagination – and enjoyed it' (*SJ* 3: 205). Her own 'self-flagellation' sparked her literary encoding of Emily's menses by using the classical intertexts of Gothic pain. See also the phonetic similarity between 'Wyther Grange' and Emily Brontë's *Wuthering Heights* (1848).

6 The scriptwriter for the *Emily* television series, Marlene Matthews, in a lecture at the University of Prince Edward Island, Charlottetown, February 1997.

Part II

Viewing Avonlea:
Film, Television, Drama, and Musical

'It's all mine': The Modern Woman as Writer in Sullivan's *Anne of Green Gables* Films

ELEANOR HERSEY

In 1985, Kevin Sullivan's television film adaptation of L.M. Montgomery's *Anne of Green Gables*, with Megan Follows as Anne and Colleen Dewhurst as Marilla, attracted nearly six million Canadian viewers, making it the most popular drama ever shown on CBC (Canadian Broadcasting Corporation) television. In the United States, too, the film quickly became a household name, reaching fans from New England to California. Sullivan responded to the demands of audiences for more films with *Anne of Green Gables: The Sequel* (1987) and, most recently, with *Anne of Green Gables: The Continuing Story* (2000). He also chose to depart from the novels with a new storyline in which Anne Shirley becomes a professional writer. This important and, for some Montgomery readers, controversial change will be the focus of my chapter. *The Sequel* dramatizes Anne Shirley's transition from adolescence to adulthood, through which she grows into a professional writer who recognizes the value of her environment and the significance of ordinary women's lives. In *The Continuing Story*, Anne conquers the prejudice of the male-dominated New York publishing industry with her book *Kindred Spirits*. By making Anne more like L.M. Montgomery and less like the character in the novels, Sullivan created a powerful narrative of women's struggle to balance professional work and domestic life that reflects the central concerns of many late-twentieth-century viewers.

Literary critics, including Susan Drain in Canada ('Too Much Lovemaking' 63–72) and Gabriella Åhmansson in Sweden (*A Life and Its Mirrors*, 71–3), have argued that the films are inferior to Montgomery's novels, since they focus on Anne's romance with Gilbert Blythe rather than the other aspects of her development. K.L. Poe will join these critics (see chapter 10), claiming that Sullivan's attempt to transform Anne into a 'modern' heroine disguises a profoundly anti-feminist representation of her as a superficial and subservient character who is guided by men in everything she does. Poe condemns Sullivan for attempting to gain power and wealth by manipulating the devotion of unsuspecting female viewers and challenges readers to resist this attempt and to reclaim the novels for themselves. Yet the popularity of these films among many of Montgomery's most devoted readers suggests that the image of Anne as a professional writer contains a genuine appeal for contemporary women. The publication of Montgomery's *Selected Journals* and the literary criticism of her fiction necessitated critical rereading of the novels and renewed intellectual engagement with them, and Sullivan's films demand a similar effort. With their focus on the difficulty of being both woman and writer, the films form a unique contribution to late-twentieth-century popular culture and provide a new perspective on Montgomery's life and work.

Kevin Sullivan and the Making of the *Anne* Films

From the beginning of his work on *Anne of Green Gables*, Sullivan approached his film adaptations as independent works of art that are inspired by the source novels yet are distinct from them in their technical aspects and appeal to audiences. Sullivan describes this approach as follows: 'You study the books, you understand the characters, you learn the environment, and then you have to really put them aside and then say okay, I'm going to create a new story here.'[1] The overwhelmingly positive response of viewers to *Anne of Green Gables* inspired Sullivan to create *The Sequel*: 'I had absolutely no intention of making the second film when I started the first film ... but I responded to a keen audience and broadcaster interest from all around the world. I mean, keen is probably an understatement – obsessive is more like it.' The response of audiences to *The Sequel* was equally dramatic, compelling Sullivan to create *The Continuing Story*, despite his earlier decision not to make another *Anne* film: 'People kept writing and saying "What happened to Anne and Gilbert after we saw them on the bridge?"' Sullivan compares the pressure he felt to create more films to the pressure Montgomery felt to create sequels to the novel *Anne of Green Gables*: 'I found myself in a similar experience, because we were involved with Disney and CBC and PBS and ... the international audience around the world wanted to see more of who those characters were that we had interpreted and then kind of recreated.'

Sullivan's approach may horrify fans who are deeply loyal to Montgomery's novels, yet many film theorists agree that the best adaptations function as acts of criticism rather than as faithful illustrations of their sources. As early as 1952, Béla Balázs noted in his book *Theory of the Film* that there is 'an old – one could almost say classic – aesthetic viewpoint which rejects on principle all adaptations on the grounds that they are necessarily inartistic.' As Balázs reminds us, however, 'The history of literature is full of classic masterpieces which are adaptations of other works' (258–9). In *Filming Literature: The Art of Screen Adaptation* (1986), Neil Sinyard argues that the truly great screen adaptations are 'the ones that go for the spirit rather than the letter of the text; or exploit a unique affinity between the personalities of the original writer and the present film-maker; or use the camera to interpret and not simply illustrate the tale' (x). In a more recent study, *Novel to Film: An Introduction to the Theory of Adaptation* (1996), Brian McFarlane also warns us of the shortcomings of the fidelity approach: 'Fidelity criticism depends on a notion of the text as having and rendering up to the (intelligent) reader a single, correct "meaning" which the film-maker has either adhered to or in some sense violated or tampered with' (8). In *Adaptations as Imitations: Films from Novels*, James Griffith argues that we should evaluate adaptations based on the filmmakers' intentions: 'When filmmakers do make deliberate changes, they presumably are trying to improve upon the original or take it in a different direction ... Even a good novel, adapted by a perceptive and imaginative filmmaker, may yield further or different pleasures the novelist did not consider' (73–4).[2] These film-adaptation theorists encourage us to investigate critically Sullivan's artistic construction of Anne Shirley in film and to probe the reasons behind his popularity, rather than denouncing him for his infidelity to the novels.

Making Anne into a professional writer, I propose, was a creative and innovative way for Sullivan to allow her character to mature and develop in ways that Montgomery may have resisted because they were too close to her own experiences. In *Anne of the Island* (1915), Anne Shirley earnestly attempts to publish her early stories, revising them according to the demands of Canadian and American editors and weeping when they are rejected. Yet after she is married, Montgomery's character decides that she would rather spend her time with her family than write for publication. Sullivan based his representation of

Anne as a writer on the earlier novels and on Montgomery's own life: 'I certainly didn't go out of my way to say "Oh, I must update this character like she's from the twentieth century." My intention was simply from a character point of view and from a dramatic point of view and from an emotional point of view.' Although Sullivan does not think of himself as a feminist writer any more than Montgomery did, his portrayal of Anne as a character who 'learns to write simply and honestly about the things that are real to her' is empowering to contemporary women who value professional development as much as domestic life.

Anne of Green Gables: The Sequel

The opening scenes of *Anne of Green Gables: The Sequel* focus on Anne's creation of the sensational story 'Averil's Atonement' and its publication as a baking-powder advertisement, following the hilarious intervention of Anne's best friend, Diana Barry, who believes that she is doing her friend a favour by submitting the manuscript. These scenes are adapted from the novel *Anne of the Island*, in which Montgomery makes fun of her own sensational writing of the 1890s. (In Montgomery's 1898 story 'The Red Room,' for example, the dazzlingly beautiful Alicia Montressor stabs her husband with a jewel-encrusted dagger in order to elope with her foreign lover: 'He fell heavily, yet held her even in death, so that she had to wrench herself free, with a shriek that rings yet in my ears on a night when the wind wails over the rainy moors' [*Among the Shadows* 197–8].) In *Anne of the Island*, Anne never fully recovers from the humiliation of seeing her story published as an advertisement, nor does she take the opportunity to change her writing style dramatically. In *The Sequel*, in contrast, the writing and publication of 'Averil's Atonement' introduce the tensions between private life and public writing, marriage and career, feminine desire and masculine economic control that pose challenges to Anne's eventual literary success.

Sullivan's *Anne of Green Gables* begins with her recitation of Alfred Tennyson's 'The Lady of Shalott' in the woods, a motif to be discussed in detail by Ann Howey (see chapter 11), and *The Sequel* begins with Anne's recitation of 'Averil's Atonement' on the beach. Anne's first words in the film reveal her literary style: '"Where is sleep?" "Over the mountains of the moon, down the valley of the shadow, 'neath the waves of the deep, gulf stream," replied the handsome duke, in dark, languid tones.' With these lines, viewers of *The Sequel* are assured that Anne has lost neither her romantic sensibilities nor her passion for the written word, and that she continues to conflate her desire for an ideal romantic hero with her love of sensational stories. When Anne sits and opens her notebook, the credit 'Produced, Written, and Directed by Kevin Sullivan' appears, establishing this film as a rewriting of the novels that will focus on Anne's literary career.

Sullivan's introduction of the character Morgan Harris, the handsome stranger who seems to embody Anne's romantic ideals, reveals the connections between Anne's development as a writer and her search for romantic love throughout this film. When Anne becomes absorbed in her story, the wind begins to blow the pages of her manuscript across the beach, a moment reminiscent of Sullivan's opening of *Anne of Green Gables* when Anne's recitation of 'The Lady of Shalott' is interrupted by the appearance of Mrs Hammond. Whereas Mrs Hammond burned Anne's book of poetry, Morgan approaches to help rescue her manuscript and compels her to assert her uncertain professional identity:

MORGAN: Are you ... a journalist?
ANNE: No, a teacher. No, I'm a writer. Actually, I write books.

Unlike his prototype (the handsome Royal Gardner with whom Anne falls in love in college), Sullivan's Morgan Harris will inspire Anne to confront and ultimately to reject her youthful vision of romance while she develops her identity as a writer.

The publication of Anne's story as an advertisement reflects the popular association of women's writing with mass audiences and mass markets, both in the late nineteenth century and in the 1980s. In the film, she walks into a general store to find a crowd of people gathered to take copies of the story, to get her autograph, and to purchase Rollings Reliable Baking Powder (a scene much more private in the novel). The copies of the story are free, but the storekeeper's plea that the crowd purchase 'this remarkable product' reflects the commodification of the story itself. Diana's role as editor of the story also reflects two enduring stereotypes about women writers: that their work is easy and spontaneous and that it is motivated by greed rather than artistic integrity. When Anne claims that there is not a word about baking powder in the story, Diana explains: 'Oh, *I* put that in, [...]. It was easy as a wink. [...] You know the scene where Averil makes the cake? Well, I just stated that she used Rollings Reliable in it, and that was why it turned out so well' (*AIs* 113). Anne learns an important lesson from the Rollings Reliable episode: she writes the next book in secret and shows it to her guardian, Marilla Cuthbert, and to Gilbert only after its publication.

Montgomery's Anne in *Anne of the Island* is still invested in false romantic fiction, as seen when she meets Royal Gardner: 'Anne looked up. Tall and handsome and distinguished-looking – dark, melancholy, inscrutable eyes – melting, musical, sympathetic voice – yes, the very hero of her dreams stood before her in the flesh' (*AIs* 163). Sullivan, in contrast, focuses on the shock that forces Anne to mature: Gilbert, whom she has always taken for granted, breaks the news that he is engaged to someone else. This shock inspires Anne to give up her youthful romantic fantasies and to write a book about her own life. Whereas Gilbert made fun of 'Averil's Atonement' in earlier scenes of the film, he now encourages Anne not to give up on her writing:

> GILBERT: You know, I always thought you should write a book about Avonlea – change the name of course, or Rachel Lynde would think she was the heroine.
>
> ANNE: Avonlea is the dearest place in the world, but I don't think it's an interesting enough setting for a story.

The details of this dialogue represent Gilbert's faith in Anne's writing, despite his earlier criticism. Gilbert uses the word 'book,' which signifies a material object with a relatively high commercial value, while Anne uses the word 'story,' which signifies a minor, cheap text or an oral narrative. Yet the fact that Anne will soon begin work on *Avonlea Vignettes* suggests that Gilbert's words do inspire confidence. This dialogue also reveals Anne's changing views about fiction: in the novel, Anne claims that Avonlea is not a 'romantic' enough setting, while in the film she worries that it is not 'interesting' enough. This detail of the film reveals her growing recognition that fiction should reflect the lives and interests of the people whom she knows, including the outspoken community leader Rachel Lynde, rather than provide an escape to exotic times and places.

The film scene in which Anne begins to write *Avonlea Vignettes* represents her transition from sensational, melodramatic stories to fiction based on her own experience. Less than one minute long, it is one of the few scenes in the film that contains no dialogue. With a slow, slightly melancholy version of the film's major musical motif in the background, Anne enters her room at the college, looks at the photographs of Green Gables, Marilla, and Matthew Cuthbert on the wall, and sits at the desk. She takes the manuscript of her latest sensational story, 'Rosamund's Revenge,' out of the drawer and throws it away, takes out clean sheets of paper, and dips her pen into the inkpot to begin a new text. In contrast to the public beach where Anne composed 'Averil's Atonement,' this room of her own suggests that she has attained the quiet, private, traditionally masculine writing space necessary for the creation of an important literary work, while the pictures on the wall reflect the community about and to which she is finally writing. Yet this scene contains no images of writing: the scene ends with an image of Anne holding the pen over the paper, imagining how she will begin the story. The text of *Avonlea Vignettes* remains invisible to us, suggesting that its realism is both illegible within and identical to the film in which it appears.

These scenes are not based on Montgomery's novels but are inspired by Montgomery's life. Anne's decision to write a book about her own experiences parallels Montgomery's decision to move beyond melodramatic magazine fiction and to publish novels such as *Anne of Green Gables*. By making Anne the author of *Avonlea Vignettes*, Sullivan situates her within the school of nineteenth-century women's local-colour writing. Josephine Donovan has noted that female local-colour writers described the people and places that they knew intimately, creating 'a counter world of their own, a rural realm that existed on the margins of patriarchal society, a world that nourished strong, free women' (3). As part of this tradition, Montgomery's *Anne of Green Gables* novels depict a matriarchal world that has been celebrated by feminist literary critics. Carol Gay has documented that the novels 'revolve around a steady pattern of breakfast, dinner, and supper, and the intricate relationships between neighbors, mothers and sons, mothers and daughters, and the problems of growing up and raising children' (11). Elizabeth Epperly argues that as Anne grows up in Avonlea, she learns to appreciate this rural, domestic space more than the romantic settings of novels and poems: 'Anne grows to value the beauty around her and understands better than Diana why Avonlea is preferable to Charlottetown, or why an artificial romance is inferior to consciousness of belonging to a world of solid values and lasting but humble pleasures' (*Fragrance* 27). With its plain prose style, rural setting, episodic structure, and autobiographical nature, *Avonlea Vignettes* represents this important genre of women's writing and the maturity that Anne has achieved since she wrote 'Averil's Atonement.'

As soon as Anne learns that *Avonlea Vignettes* has been accepted for publication, Morgan approaches and follows her down the street, just as Gilbert did earlier in the film:

> MORGAN: What's nagging you, Miss Shirley? You're behaving rather like a spinsterly old schoolmarm, don't you think?
>
> ANNE: Perhaps that's because I am one.
>
> MORGAN: I say that with admiration; it is a compliment. I am a great proponent of independent thinking. Moreover, I've always held that early marriage is a sure indication of second-rate goods that had to be sold in a hurry. Wouldn't you agree?
>
> ANNE: Well, you can be sure I am of the first-rate kind, Morgan Harris. And I certainly have far greater ambition than marriage, if that is what you are insinuating is nagging me. I am about to have a short work of fiction published. I'm afraid it has me completely preoccupied.

This conversation suggests how much confidence Anne has gained since the early scenes of the film. Earlier, Anne joked to Diana that she would 'die an old maid' if she never met her romantic ideal; here she claims to have 'far greater ambition than marriage' now that her book has been accepted.

Sullivan emphasizes the close relationships between Anne's personal and professional development and her romance with her future husband, Gilbert Blythe (figure 9.1). On the same day that Marilla brings her the copies of her book, Anne learns that Gilbert is dying. Anne's devastating fear of loss is thus combined with her joyful sense of achievement in a moving and realistic representation of a woman's negotiation of love and work. Anne's dedication of *Avonlea Vignettes* to 'Marilla and Matthew Cuthbert, for their unfailing love and support, and to Gilbert, who inspired me with the idea in the first place' proves that she feels as indebted to her guardians as to her future husband. Although Poe will claim that Sullivan fails to represent Anne as an individual apart from Gilbert, Anne's conversation with Marilla in this scene proves that Anne realizes her profound feelings for Gilbert in her *own* time, after she has developed a sound individual and professional basis in his absence. At the end of the film, Anne accepts Gilbert's mar-

9.1   Anne Shirley and Gilbert Blythe in *Anne of Green Gables: The Sequel* © 2001
Sullivan Films.

riage proposal *after* she has joyfully announced that the publishers are
planning a second edition of her book.

Sullivan's artistic intervention – an important one – consists in
incorporating a vital moment from Montgomery's journals into the
dialogue of this film scene. Sullivan's Anne claims that her book is
'not a classic, or a romance, or anything important. It's just a humorous book of stories I did about Avonlea in my spare time last fall.
But it's mine. It's all mine.' Sullivan adapted this statement from
Montgomery's intensely proud description of her feelings when she
received her advance copy of *Anne of Green Gables* in her home at Cavendish on Saturday, 20 June 1908: 'Not a great book at all – but *mine,
mine, mine,* – something to which *I* had given birth – something which,
but for me, would never have existed' (*SJ* 1: 335). Sullivan dramatizes
the tension between a woman writer's pride in her literary possession,
'something to which *I* had given birth,' and her recognition that she is
indebted to her loved ones for her accomplishments. His careful reading of Montgomery's journals also demonstrates his serious intellectual interest in her life and work, suggesting that artistically he does

much more than merely manipulate the unsuspecting viewer, as Poe will argue.

The film builds on the final chapters of *Anne of the Island* to make a more powerful statement about Anne's right to pursue her literary ambitions. When Montgomery's Anne learns that Gilbert is dying, she compares his loss to the severing of her right hand, a symbol of her identity as a writer: 'She knew that she could no more cast him out of her life without agony than she could have cut off her right hand and cast it from her' (*AIs* 236). Even after Gilbert recovers, Montgomery's Anne feels that her life will never be complete without his romantic love: 'She could do good, if not noble, work as a teacher; and the success her little sketches were beginning to meet with in certain editorial sanctums augured well for her budding literary dreams. But – but – ' (*AIs* 240). As these passages suggest, Montgomery's Anne is not only profoundly in love with Gilbert, but feels that he is more important than anything else in her life. Sullivan's intervention is therefore not to exaggerate Anne's romantic desires but to represent them as equal to and compatible with her identity as a writer. Rather than trying to console herself for the loss of Gilbert with thoughts of her 'little sketches,' Sullivan's Anne takes her published book to his bedside and actively encourages him to recover his health.

In the final scene of *The Sequel*, Anne tells Gilbert that the success of her book has inspired her to stay at Green Gables and write rather than teach: 'It has been a long lesson to learn, but you were right.' This image of Anne continuing to write following her engagement reflects the values of 1980s feminism: both partners will receive professional training, Gilbert as a doctor and Anne as a writer. Anne's words also reflect her struggle to write from her own knowledge about her local community: 'It's just that I went looking for my ideals outside of myself, and discovered that it's not what the world holds for you, it's what you bring to it.' While this statement does not appear in the corresponding scene in *Anne of the Island*, Montgomery expressed a darker version of this sentiment in a 1904 letter: 'But there is a certain discontent which I believe does ennoble because it impels us to try to improve our surroundings – to measure our happiness by what we can *put into* our environment, not by what we can *get out*' (*My Dear Mr. M.* 7). Like Montgomery, Sullivan's Anne fights against a great deal of condescension and prejudice in order to fulfil her identity as a woman writer, and finally learns that she can change the world through her literary work.

The Continuing Story

In *Anne of Green Gables: The Continuing Story* (2000), Anne faces a new challenge to her professional identity as she moves from Prince Edward Island to New York City and attempts to find a publisher for her second book. With this film, Sullivan significantly departs from the chronology of Montgomery's novels, in which Anne and Gilbert are married in the last decades of the nineteenth century, and transforms Anne into a young married woman during the First World War. Sullivan claims that this change allowed him to take Anne's character to another level and into a different world: 'She learns ... that the security that she thought she had in Green Gables and in the world of Avonlea is truly gone, it's evaporated. Matthew and Marilla are gone. The world has changed.' The setting of *The Continuing Story* thereby challenges viewers to move beyond their nostalgia for the Victorian era and to confront the political complexities of the time period in which Montgomery struggled to defend her rights as a female author in a male-dominated publishing industry.

Anne's confrontations with New York publishers in *The Continuing Story* allow the filmmakers to develop her professional identity in a more competitive setting and to critique the prejudices that surrounded women's writing in the early twentieth century. Sitting under the stuffed and mounted animal heads that decorate the office walls, Mr Winfield and Mr Owen represent the reactionary side of a publishing industry that has learned to see women as potential consumers of fiction but not as artists shaping the field with a new vision. Owen reminds Anne: 'We've never published stories for young women. Our speciality is adventure, detective novels, and all manner of books for a man's man ... We have never published a female author. Ever.' When Anne determines to change their minds with her romantic novel *Forever into Eternity*, the popular novelist Jack Garrison criticizes her efforts. Jack advises her to 'Aim much higher creatively, if you want my opinion, Miss Shirley,' echoing Gilbert's critique of 'Averil's Atonement' in the previous film: 'If you want my opinion, Miss Shirley, I'd write about places I knew ... instead of these silly school-girl romances.' Anne initially makes the mistake of revising the novel according to Jack's demands and nearly allowing him to steal the credit for her work. Yet she remembers the lessons that she learned when writing *Avonlea Vignettes* and goes on to write another book that is true to her own experiences.

When Anne throws away her draft of *Forever into Eternity* and begins to write *Kindred Spirits*, director Stefan Scaini creates visual echoes to the scene in the previous film in which Anne throws away 'Rosamund's Revenge' and begins *Avonlea Vignettes*. Standing alone in her New York apartment, Anne looks at the manuscript of the romantic novel and tosses it out the window into the street. The next shot focuses on Anne's hands and face as she sits at her typewriter, completely absorbed in her work, and pans over to a novel by Jack Garrison entitled *Toward a Distant Peak*. The fact that we see Anne steadily typing away at the manuscript rather than merely hesitating over the page as in *The Sequel* suggests that Anne is now a disciplined professional rather than an amateur. The image of *Toward a Distant Peak* landing in the wastebasket further symbolizes Anne's decision not to emulate a male writer, but to develop her own literary voice.

We learn that Anne has overcome the prejudices of Winfield and Owen and published a book under her own name when she sits at her typewriter at Green Gables later in the film, surrounded by a stack of novels entitled *Kindred Spirits*. In this brief scene, the images of red-haired women on the book covers link Anne once again to L.M. Montgomery, as does Anne's decision to publish under her maiden name rather than that of her new husband. With this final image of Anne as a novelist and the later images of her as a journalist and public speaker in London, viewers are assured that *Avonlea Vignettes* and *Kindred Spirits* represent the beginning of a serious professional literary career that will never be sacrificed to the demands of marriage and family. Like Montgomery, Sullivan's Anne will continue to write after she leaves her childhood home to create a new life with her husband. Unlike the character of the novels, she will remain Anne Shirley professionally long after she becomes Mrs Blythe in her domestic life. When Sullivan's Anne holds a copy of her published book and exults that 'It's all mine,' she lays claim to a professional identity that makes her character more empowering for contemporary viewers than the largely silent 'Mrs Blythe' of the later novels in the series. Numerous Montgomery scholars, from Åhmansson to Elizabeth Epperly, have bemoaned the fact that Montgomery's Anne becomes static and uninteresting in the sequels. Sullivan's Anne, in contrast, continues to maintain her spark.

Reviews of the *Anne of Green Gables* films in popular newspapers and magazines prove that viewers are rarely as unsuspecting as Poe claims but often discriminate among the films in the trilogy, and between the films and the novels, to engage with them on an intellectual level. Reviewers focus in particular on the sequels' demands on viewers, their increasingly complex subject matter in relation to the original film. In 1985, *Maclean's* reviewer Gillian Mackay praised Sullivan's *Anne of Green Gables* for its 'fairy-tale charm.' Yet the *Maclean's* cover story devoted to *Anne of Green Gables: The Sequel* provides an in-depth analysis, including a series of interviews with the filmmakers and actors, an examination of Montgomery's journals, and an analysis of Anne's appeal to fans around the world (see Brian D. Johnson et al.). In the United States, the *Chicago Tribune* and *Washington Post* presented pairs of reviews that debated the appeal of Anne's maturity and seriousness in *The Sequel* with titles such as '"Anne" Sequel Charms but Shows Its Age, Too' and 'Megan Follows Grows Up with "Anne" Role' (see Terry, Brogan, Brennan, and Shales). The same debate took place in reviews of *The Continuing Story*: while Julie Salamon of the *New York Times* expresses regret that the heroine has 'lost much of her childhood poetry,' interviews with Follows in the *Christian Science Monitor* and the *Los Angeles Times* focus on the way in which Anne's innocence is transformed into a mature strength (see Mason and King).

Beginning with the film version of *Anne of Green Gables*, Sullivan has drawn audiences around the world to the character of Anne Shirley and to Montgomery's novels. With *The Sequel*, Sullivan represents Anne's development from a romantic teenager to a mature adult who is ready to face the challenges of marriage and career. With *The Continuing Story*, Sullivan departs from the Victorian setting of the first two films and focuses on the struggles of twentieth-century women living and working in societies that denied them fundamental rights. The popularity of these films may make literary critics nervous, as we struggle to disseminate an image of Montgomery as a serious writer who is worthy of academic study. Yet by condemning these films and urging viewers to resist their powerful appeal, we risk supporting the idea that popular texts inevitably send conservative political messages to the masses. We also risk plunging into a form of literary fundamentalism, as Brenda Weber warned us earlier (see chapter 3). Just as we have worked hard to claim recognition for the academic seriousness and the artistic complexity of Montgomery's popular novels, so we should show the same respect to Sullivan's popular films.

Notes

1 I interviewed Kevin Sullivan by telephone on 23 November 2000. This and all subsequent quotations by Sullivan are taken from this interview.
2 For further studies on film adaptations, see George Bluestone, *Novels into Film* (1957); Geoffrey Wagner, *The Novel and the Cinema* (1975); Joy Gould Boyum, *Double Exposure: Fiction into Film* (1985).

Chapter 10

Who's Got the Power? Montgomery, Sullivan, and the Unsuspecting Viewer

K.L. POE

In her 1993 book, *Literature and Feminism: An Introduction,* Pam Morris raises many questions about the ways in which literature and, more particularly, literature by women, is analysed through the lens of feminism. 'What perception of reality do the great books of our language offer us?' asks Morris in the introduction. 'What sorts of images of womanhood are constructed for us in their work?' (8) As more and more critical scrutiny is turned on children's literature, and especially on literature for young girls, new respect and value are being given to the work of authors such as L.M. Montgomery. With this increased interest, however, has come another area of concern for both the scholar and the reader as this literature takes on a new mutation on screen. Adaptation of young adult literature for film and television is, to say the least, a booming business. From *A Little Princess* to *Little Women,* classic girls' books, and particularly girls' series fiction, have found a new lease on life through adaptation. The lure of these adaptations is twofold: for the reader who loved and cherished these books in her youth, it is a chance to live through those beloved books once again;[1] for the young reader of today, it is a way to learn about strong female characters in classic stories of the past. Mothers want their daughters to read the books they themselves loved, and, quite possibly, to show their daughters a strong female character as a role model. All is safe and good, empowering the young women of today for a better tomorrow.

But is this actually true? Do these adaptations really serve the needs of their viewers as they purport to, by 'empowering' them through the viewing of an 'empowering' film about an 'empowered' female character? Do they present strong female role models of a bygone era, or are they merely imposing modern sensibilities and jargon on characters from the past? By taking the characters away from their original stories and placing them in an adaptation that has been anachronistically gerrymandered to fit an agenda that was in no way suggested by the novelist, these films, I argue, may in fact erode the subversive feminism of the original text.

Is the adherence to the original text a function of the infamous clinging of readers to a beloved text? Do readers of young adult fiction, especially that for girls, hold these books closer to their collective bosom, resentful at the slightest deviation from the sacred text? In their desire to protect the books they love, do readers reject literary and artistic licence with these stories out of hand? Do they, as was mentioned by several at the Fourth Biennial International Conference, L.M. Montgomery and Popular Culture, take these things 'too seriously'?[2] Or, as suggested by Eleanor Hersey (chapter 9), are adaptations akin to academic criticisms and perhaps improvements to the original works?

Certainly, if the adaptations provided at the very least the essence of the classic text, it would not be necessary to adhere exactly to that original text; likewise, the role model of a strong female character (which exists in all of the texts adapted in recent years) would be a welcome creature. The sad fact is, however, that in many adaptations of a classic text with a female protagonist, the original story, that of personal development (in the traditional sense of a *Bildungsroman*), is either completely put aside or watered down to the point of insignificance. Most often, the female protagonist in the film ends up even more subservient to the traditional patriarchal order than the original character ever was.[3] Whose perception, indeed? I would hold that through these adaptations, the perceptions not only of the stories from which they are drawn but also of authorial intent are easily mistaken, or forsaken, by the desire of filmmakers to appeal more to the (supposed) desires and interests of a modern audience.

A leader in this trend has been Kevin Sullivan, whose adaptations of the works of L.M. Montgomery have been extremely successful and well received in both Canada and the United States. The first of these, *Anne of Green Gables* (1985), was lushly photographed and featured the solid work of actors Colleen Dewhurst and Richard Farnsworth. The sets were detailed, the musical score lovely. Yet there was none of the connecting narrative, just a series of adventures that seem to serve as textual touchstones for the reader/viewer. In approaching the text in this manner, Sullivan and his co-writer, Joe Wiesenfeld, took the first step in removing Anne Shirley from her own story; and with each successive instalment of Sullivan's Anne movies, we see less and less of Montgomery's Anne, and more and more of Sullivan's Anne. In the case of the films in Sullivan's Anne trilogy, more is most definitely *less*.

The heart of Montgomery's story of Anne is a traditional *Bildungsroman*, or novel of development. As the series progresses, so we see Anne progress from a hopeful orphan to a loving (and eventually griefstricken) mother during the First World War. Her experiences mould her, but her true nature is what shines throughout.[4] Readers can love Anne because, if anything, she remains true to herself; her sense of personal honour and devotion to duty guides her throughout her life. I do not wish to go into a lengthy discussion of the *Bildungsroman* here, but I do want to make a few particular points about the genre as it applies to the narrative process and Montgomery's work.

The German essayist Wilhelm Dilthey, who in 1904 was among the first to bring the *Bildungsroman* into critical focus, delineated the narrative process of the genre as follows: 'A regulated development within the life of the individual is observed, each of its stages has its own intrinsic value, and is at the same time the basis for a higher stage. The dissonances and conflicts of life appear as the necessary growth points through which the individual must pass on his way to maturity and harmony' (394). More simply, Jerome Hamilton Buckley, in *Seasons of Youth: The Bildungsroman from Dickens to Golding*, describes a 'typical *Bildungsroman* plot' as starting with 'a child of sensibility' growing up in the country. The child comes into contact with others who are hostile to his imaginative growth, and, as a result, he 'leaves the repressive atmosphere of home ... to make his way independently in the city. ... There his real education begins.' This *Bildungsroman* concludes with the hero's accommodation to society, a resolution achieved after 'painful soul searching' and signalling the completed passage to maturity (12).

Also crucial to the narrative structure of the *Bildungsroman* is its setting, and in more ways than just the movement from country to city, as Buckley suggests. In the *Bildungsroman*, the setting is practically a character itself, so strong is its presence. In Montgomery's writings, Prince Edward Island is so lovingly and clearly described that, when one actually sees the island, it is like meeting an old friend. Elizabeth Epperly points out in her essay in chapter 6 of this collection that Montgomery was able to create descriptions of places so convincingly in her novels that millions of tourists have travelled to Prince Edward Island to see 'Anne's world' for themselves. The protagonist of a *Bildungsroman*, no matter how alienated from the home base, still carries that place with him, if only as a resentment. In the case of a female *Bildungsroman*, the 'life journey' is often one of confinement within the home sphere, and the heroine must reconcile her feelings of resentment towards her confinement with her love of home and hearth. Further, in the early Germanic *Bildungsroman*, the setting (as well as the emotional and spiritual growth of the hero) was crucial to the building of a strong sense of nationalism; the protagonist was developing not into mere manhood, but into a *German* manhood.

As isolated as the protagonist might appear, the narration of the *Bildungsroman* shows that the protagonist is inextricably linked to a community, for better or worse. In some cases, the narration gives the reader a sense of the other lives that orbit around the protagonist, and this, in turn, helps the reader to see the protagonist through other eyes. Thus, although the definition of the *Bildungsroman* would suggest a solitary journey, the varying delineation of *Bildungsroman*, especially in terms of female protagonists, indicates quite the opposite: in spite of the existence of a solitary journey, the protagonist of a *Bildungsroman* is nevertheless a part of a larger community that ultimately shapes his, or in the case of Anne Shirley, *her* destiny.

So how does this apply to Anne's story, and how was this shown in Sullivan's films? In the books, we follow Anne's development from the inside out. Throughout the series, she seeks to define herself as a worthy member of the household at Green Gables and in the larger community of Avonlea. Over time, her concerns about belonging shift from her personal appearance to her spiritual, moral, and emotional presence. She is not told that she should be grateful; she *is* grateful, and shows it in every way she can. Given her position in society, that always-suspect identity as an orphan girl, Anne goes out of her way to prove her worthiness in spite of her humble beginnings. Further, she is surrounded by an almost completely matriarchal society that operates within a patriarchal world.[5] The esteemed ladies of Avonlea set the standards for proper behaviour, and Anne, always watchful, does her best (leavened by her sense of humour) to live up to that standard.

On an emotional level, Anne is guided in the first novel by the almost maternal presence of Matthew, who nurtures and encourages her inner spirit. Under his loving guidance, Anne learns what it means to be truly loved, and she strives to live up to his love for her. Marilla, on the other hand, deals more with the external aspects of Anne's development.

In the first instalment of Sullivan's Anne trilogy, there is no 'internal': the development of the young heroine is all surface, no depth. Missing are the finer points of Montgomery's narrative, in which she gradually unfolds the development of Anne the orphan into Anne of Green Gables, someone who belongs. In the film, Anne's adventures flip by like flashcards, and although the viewer, especially one who has read the novel, can manage to fill in the blanks to some extent, the result is certainly less than satisfying. Anne of the trilogy pays some lip service to belonging, but not much more; the emphasis remains on the action, not the personal development.

Further, although Anne Shirley has been lauded as a quintessential Canadian heroine (Robinson, '"A Born Canadian"' 19–30), there is little sense of Canada in any of the Anne movies. Yes, there are some beautiful shots of the lovely Prince Edward Island landscape in the first, fewer in the second, and barely any in the third and most recent instalment, but is Anne any different from any other American girl heroine? The books are imbued with a subtle sense of nationalism, often with less than kind words for the neighbours to the south.[6] Why, then, is Canada so vaguely represented in this 'great Canadian story' once it is projected onto the screen? By diminishing the role of Canada, and particularly of Prince Edward Island, a main character is virtually absent from Sullivan's trilogy.

As has often been noted, the focus of Sullivan's initial Anne adaptation shifted from Anne's story, as written by Montgomery, to a rather typical eighties' romance. The romance between Anne and Gilbert Blythe was an important *aspect* of Anne's story as written by Montgomery, but it was not the central story; even when Anne and Gilbert are newlyweds in *Anne's House of Dreams*, the focus of the story is almost entirely on the members of the community, especially Leslie Moore's friendship with Anne, and not on the lovebirds. Had Montgomery wanted to have the romance be the focus of her series, she most likely would have called it *Anne and Gilbert*, not *Anne of Green Gables*, *Anne of Avonlea*, and so on. In fact, as Marah Gubar points out, it is not the heterosexual unions in the Anne series that form the basis of the narrative, but rather the 'passionate relationships between women that prove far more romantic than traditional marriages' (47). She further argues that 'the real romance in this series develops between young people and grown-ups who are not their parents' (65). The slighting of these non-heterosexual, non-sexual relationships in Sullivan's trilogy leaves a void that Sullivan's privileging of Anne's alleged writing career and her romances with Gilbert, Morgan Harris, and Jack Garrison cannot fill; because Montgomery's narrative focus (that of a young girl's development, and of her wanting to belong and eventually belonging to a community, friendship, etc.) is not the focus of Sullivan's films, the latter seem less an adaptation of a storyline than of a group of character names and a few choice plot points and phrases. Ann F. Howey's depiction, in chapter 11 in this collection, of this as 'shorthand in characterization' is apt, but the shorthand used by Sullivan becomes less and less decipherable as his trilogy continues.

The second instalment of Sullivan's Anne trilogy, entitled either *Anne of Green Gables: The Sequel* (on public television in the United States) or *Anne of Avonlea* (on Canadian television or on video), released in 1986, takes the viewer even farther from the original texts, bringing in a U.S. context in the form of a rival for Anne's affections. What Anne is personally and professionally (in terms of her teaching) at that point in her life takes a back seat to her romantic life and her 'writing career.' (As a teacher, I find it troubling that this Anne is so neglectful of her duty; even her teaching is based on what she is writing and what she likes to read, rather than on real lessons.) In the texts from which the storyline is apparently drawn, *Anne of Avonlea* and *Anne of Windy Poplars*, Gilbert is but a shadow, appearing occasionally in the former, and barely at all in the latter (except as the recipient of Anne's letters); here, Gilbert and his editorial instructions (and half-hearted wooing), are featured prominently. There are touchstones to *Anne of the Island* as well in this Sullivan instalment, but configured in such a way that they point strongly away from the text and towards Sullivan's own plot points. The viewer who has read the books will easily recognize phrases from Montgomery's texts sprinkled here and there, but the appearance of these phrases out of context makes the film's narrative seem jumpier than it might actually be in reality.[7]

The seedlings of another Sullivan invention start to bear fruit in this second film instalment: Anne the Author. While this is a commonly held misconception among many who have read Montgomery's Anne books, perhaps because there is that unfortunate habit some readers (and critics) have of conflating female authors with their creations, Sullivan takes this misconception to heart and will not let go of it; it forms the basis for a major plot point of the third – and least successful – instalment of his trilogy. To put it simply, Anne Shirley was not a professional writer and had no serious aspirations to be one. A born story-teller, Anne liked weaving tales, but she acknowledges on more than one occasion that serious professional writing is beyond her skills, though she does have some short pieces published. In contrast to Emily Starr, whose life was consumed with writing and professional aspirations along those lines, Anne's writing always took a secondary place to her real mission in life: to belong.

In the preceding chapter in this volume, Eleanor Hersey indicates that it was Sullivan's intention in his Anne trilogy to depict the struggles of a female author during that time period. Yet the Edwardian period depicted in Sullivan's films does not exactly match (and, in the third instalment of his trilogy, is abandoned completely) the time frame set by Montgomery. As shown by Carolyn Strom Collins and Christina Wyss Eriksson, Montgomery's Anne would have been born in 1866, making most of the action in the series clearly in the era of Victoria (16).[8] Still, Hersey's assertion begs the question: if Sullivan indeed intended to depict the struggles of a female author during the early part of the twentieth century, why did he not just write a story about such a person, or make a film autobiography of Montgomery herself, rather than trying to force the character of Anne Shirley into a mode that is not suggested by Montgomery's texts?[9] Supporters of Sullivan's films cite the 'sentimental' or 'Victorian' nature of Montgomery's series as the reason Sullivan was 'forced' to 'update' them, but the ways in which the texts are ignored has less to do with the structural problems or supposed dated nature of the texts themselves than with the attempt to attach modern ideas and sensibilities to a story that can in no way support them.

Sullivan's Anne is forced to remain perpetually adolescent, still living fantasies rather than reality, frequently humiliated or embarrassed publicly. Montgomery's adult Anne still daydreams, still entertains fancies, but her main focus is the duties of adulthood, as a student, as a teacher, as a friend, and as a wife and mother; she is respected and admired by others in Avonlea, Kingsport, and Glen St Mary. The manner in which Sullivan's Anne selfishly puts her own fancies and desires first is not indicative of any sort of development.[10]

It might be argued that Sullivan's Anne offers the best of both worlds: the Anne of the books, with the added 'dash' of modernity that provides the new audience with an Anne that 'has it all': love *and* career. Yet must we only have heroines who combine shades of the past with modern sensibilities? Can we not enjoy and gain inspiration from a character whose life does not mirror our modern viewpoints? Is it essential to make Anne a historical anachronism just so modern audiences will 'get' her? Montgomery's Anne did not live in our time. She cannot be expected to hold any views beyond those of the times in which she lived. Montgomery lived in her time and wrote a heroine of that time; modern readers are not so ignorant that they must have everything they read relativized to 'match' what they are living now.

In her essay 'The Present Reshaping the Past Reshaping the Present: Film Versions of *Little Women*,' Robyn McCallum points out some of the problems with anachronism as it applies to the adaptation of the classic work of another famous female author: 'To expect *Little Women* to conform to twentieth-century feminist values and narrative patterns is to impose anachronistic ideological and generic paradigms, and such expectations create for filmmakers, and for critics, the problem of trying to negotiate the clash between the pastness of the past and the presence of contemporary cultural values and evaluations' (84).

This 'problem' is at the heart of most modern adaptations of classic works for girls. But what is the value of books written in the past if we perpetually modernize them? First, if we insist on wiping away any contextual traces under the misconception that modern audiences won't 'get' what is going on, we risk pushing the past farther and farther out of sight. Second, if we continually privilege the present over the past, there is little way that we can educate 'unsuspecting' younger generations, and girls in particular, about how far people (especially women) have come in the intervening years. The homogenizing effect creates a world in which no one is able to understand that others live(d) and believe(d) differently than they do; it emphasizes not the internal elements that can bridge the gaps of ages but rather the superficial aspects that are ultimately meaningless without the contextual situation. The extreme devotion of the Japanese to Montgomery's Anne should be evidence enough that a work must not reproduce its readers' world exactly to be loved and respected.[11]

But if Montgomery's Anne was not about Anne the Author, or Anne the Romantic Interest, or Anne the Pseudo-American, how is she connected to Sullivan's film 'franchise'? Seeing the strong attachment so many readers, chiefly women, have to Montgomery's writings (and, in addition, to the writings of Lovelace, Weber, Wilder, etc.), the moneymaking opportunity remains ripe for the picking, as women viewers are lured in with the recognizable, beloved object. As Julaine Gillispie remarks regarding the trend to create film versions of beloved classics: 'It is logical that their texts are currently experiencing a cinematic rebirth: Hollywood seems to recognize that working women that have children do spend money on family films, and American society appears ready for movies that provide reparation for young women tired of reading about dead white men in school and dismayed by seeing so few good female role models in films' (146).

Still, while it is possible that Sullivan's real mission was to make wholesome, empowering movies for girls, the many ways in which Montgomery's writing is ignored in favour of plots that simply do not follow the development set forth by Montgomery would indicate something else. By ignoring Montgomery's development of Anne as a character, and her story as a series, Sullivan seems to be saying that Anne's story, the 'simple little tale' about a girl, a regular girl, growing up on a beautiful little island, is just not good enough.

While on Prince Edward Island this past summer, I found *The Anne of Green Gables Storybook*, 'based on the Kevin Sullivan Film of Lucy Maud Montgomery's classic novel' and adapted by Fiona McHugh.[12] This adaptation of an adaptation, though recognizing its original source, points only towards Sullivan's film, right down to its misspelling of the surname of Anne's beloved teacher (that's Miss *Stacy*, not *Stacey*) and the elimination of poor Moody Spurgeon MacPherson's surname. There would not be anything particularly wrong with this storybook if the adaptation were not from a perfectly acceptable classic work of fiction; it leaves the impression that Montgomery's books are not worth looking at except through Sullivan's lens.

If anything, Montgomery's works (and the Anne series in particular) have a place in what Deborah Stevenson calls 'the sentimental canon': 'The sentimental canon [...] is formed largely on custom: it favors books that comfort over books that challenge, books that reinforce the status quo over books that attempt to change it; it renders all books safe by their very inclusion therein' (115). Certainly, Montgomery's works, and particularly the Anne series, would fall into this category, as would many classic works of children's literature. It is perhaps that situation within this canon, that connection with generations beyond its original readership, that causes this need to adapt, literally and figuratively, books like Montgomery's. Stevenson continues:

The primary effect is extremely important – the version one encounters first, be it parodic or filmic, is the real version, and the real version is the one to be transmitted. Attention-catchers such as films may temporarily increase a response to a print text, but increased availability does not necessarily imply canonicity. Nor does a resurgence of popularity, even of a canonical book, necessarily extend to an author's work in toto [...]. Canonicity does not translate between film and literary versions. While a watchable version of a text can affect a book's standing and popularity, it has yet to demonstrate an ability to restore a forgotten text to the sentimental canon. (124)

Putting aside the connection to Montgomery's Anne, the first two films of Sullivan's trilogy are typical eighties' romances whose heartwarming quality has had popular appeal with a wide audience. The costumes and sets are pleasant to look at, and the performances of Dewhurst and Farnsworth are compelling. Howey (chapter 11) demonstrates effectively how Sullivan's use of Tennyson's 'The Lady of Shalott' to make connections between Anne's character and those 'kindred spirits' she encounters in the script, and to underscore his Anne's development as an author, is woven throughout the first two films.[13] But by the third instalment of the trilogy, where the connection to Montgomery is so faint that there is no mention of her in the credits, Sullivan's 'empowered' Anne is mostly just rushing around looking frantic. While many women on the home front were frantic with worry, such worry is diminished when Sullivan's Anne takes off to Europe to 'find Gilbert': this Anne is rarely seen doing anything but activities related to her own interests.

Rather than draw from Montgomery's own *Rilla of Ingleside*, in which Anne and Gilbert's youngest daughter grows into womanhood while the world is at war, this film instead forwards a storyline that jerks from P.E.I. to New York to P.E.I. to Europe to P.E.I., apparently involving Anne in some sort of wartime intrigue. This is extremely unfortunate, for *Rilla* is considered by many to be what Marie C. Campbell calls 'a valuable fictional account of the Canadian experience on the World War I homefront' ('Lucy Maud Montgomery' 466). Again, it is the negating of the importance of two key aspects of Montgomery's works: home and nation. Would it not be of greater value to the viewing audience, especially younger viewers, to get a glimpse of what life was for the 'homefolks' during the war, rather than to have Anne, as seen in the third film, rushing around in a nun's habit with diamonds sewn into its folds – the scene an entire fabrication for the sake of slapstick humour. This instalment was so far from Montgomery's Anne that the contrast to Montgomery's 'simple little tale' has created an uncomfortable stir even among staunch fans of the earlier films of the series, as seen in the many online discussions of various electronic Montgomery- and Sullivan-related discussion groups.

Some may argue that Sullivan's films have a strong female protagonist who could even function as a modern feminist role model. On careful viewing, however, it can be seen that Sullivan's Anne is not so strong as Montgomery's Anne; she is shrieky, silly, often rude, and consistently described as being 'ridiculously impulsive' and 'going off unpredictably,' having 'harebrained schemes,' et cetera (and these phrases come from the latest instalment of the trilogy, featuring Anne as an *adult*).[14] She is often humiliated publicly, as in the scene in the second instalment of the trilogy that has her falling into a muddy field while chasing a cow with Diana (who should happen by but Gilbert and his father?) and, later, falling through the roof of the campus storage shed. In Montgomery's text, however, these scenes are smaller, less slapstick, and certainly less public. Sullivan's Anne has 'scrapes' long after Montgomery's Anne has grown out of them, and Anne's filmic scrapes are always much more public and humiliating, usually in front of Gilbert or some other authority figure.

As with many modern adaptations of classic girls' books, Anne is almost always directed by a man in everything she does, the rare exception being Matthew; but even there, Sullivan's Matthew has a lot more to say than Montgomery's Matthew ever did. And even though Diana gives Anne literary advice in the second film, as Hersey observes in this collection, it is mostly to impart her belief that Anne would be more likely to find a man if she were to be a published author. In the latest instalment of the trilogy, Anne is enjoined not to 'rewrite the past,' and is told by Gilbert, 'believe in your own ability.' Further, Gilbert counsels, 'No one can tell *you* how to write. Don't sell yourself short!'[15] Anne's involvement with the hack writer Jack Garrison, and his harsh criticism of her writing, drives her to rewrite her novel to satisfy Garrison's expectations, not her own. Of course, Sullivan's Anne, in 1915, is living in a world where the state of women authors is more like it was back in Alcott's day, rather than an era in which women authors were not only accepted but did well critically and financially.[16] And, as with many aspects of this latest instalment of the trilogy, Anne's New York adventures seem eerily reminiscent of another film; in this case, Jo March's New York experiences in the most recent film version of *Little Women*.[17]

What I keep coming back to, therefore, is this idea that somehow the simple story of a girl's development is not 'good enough,' not 'interesting enough.' If adaptations are meant to be empowering for girls, how can they ignore and diminish the real lives that very real girls live every day? How are girls ever to learn to be happy with themselves, happy in their own environments, and, consequently, to learn to work to make their own, albeit normal, way in the world?

In adaptations besides those of Sullivan, we see movies that are promoted as being empowering stories for girls, but that, in reality, merely have girls doing 'guy stuff' or being guided by some male creature (such as the jive-talking dragon in *Mulan*). Deborah Thacker, in her discussion of stories that 'switch around gender roles,' notes that '[...] in most cases, these texts merely switch roles around but retain the stereotyped features of male and female characterization, so that strength, activity, and triumph are still opposed to passivity, beauty, and gentleness. In this way, books that attempt to act as a corrective only impose another way of thinking and reading conventionally, rather than challenging readers with a new way of approaching gender or inviting them to question the imposition of socially constructed modes of behavior' (4). Exchange 'books' for 'films' and you have a good description of how these modern 'empowerment' movies do not really empower girls at all. This reinscription of the patriarchal code, under the guise of empowerment for females, is not exactly the backlash Susan Faludi wrote about in her groundbreaking 1991 book. Instead, it seems somehow more problematic in that it sublimates the strength of women while at the same time claiming to be an empowering force.

I hope I may be allowed to end on a polemical note. I do not want to imply that there can be no good adaptations of girls' fiction. It can be done, and it has been done, most notably with Sally Benson's *Meet Me in St. Louis* and the British versions of Edith Nesbit's *The Railway Children*, which have portrayed the lives of normal girls who lead normal lives.[18] But until we, the readers who hold close to our hearts wellwritten stories about regular girls, the adults who want to help regular girls find their own path in this world, make the effort to force those beyond our sphere at the very least to respect such stories (and, consequently, the simple lives that inspired them), rather than swallow anything and everything with the slightest connection to beloved books, we have no one to blame but ourselves when such bad adaptations are made. This is not about holding texts so dear that we decry any interpretation as besmirching their essence, but rather about bringing more critical and scholarly focus to the original texts in order to reclaim the power stolen from us by those who seek to make their fortunes from our 'devotion' while we, unsuspecting, are looking in another direction. Who's got the power? We do. Let us use it wisely.

Notes

I wish to thank Betsy Jones and Siobhan Wee for their encouragement and 'advices.'

1 For a discussion of sequels and their commodification, see Richard Flynn's 'Imitation Oz: The Sequel as Commodity.'
2 My presentation of this essay at the L.M. Montgomery and Popular Culture conference 2000 was part of a session that generated much lively discussion, including the dismissal of the argument of this essay by session chair Richard E. Sherwin of Bar-Ilan University (Israel) on the grounds that Sullivan's adaptations are like *Classic Comix*. I beg to differ.
3 In the 1995 version of *A Little Princess*, for example, Sara Crewe is guided by her father's opinion of her to an almost Electra-like degree, to the point of cowing headmistress Miss Minchin with the cutting question: 'Didn't your father ever tell you you were a princess?' (as if that would explain Miss Minchin's heartless cruelty: she didn't listen to daddy). In the second instalment of Sullivan's Anne trilogy, his heroine is repeatedly told what to do by both Gilbert and Morgan Harris, and in the third instalment, she is directed by Gilbert (even in his absence) and Jack Garrison. And in the 1998 Disney film *Mulan*, the title character is guided by a jive-talking (male) dragon (with the voice of Eddie Murphy).
4 In her essay 'Revisiting Anne,' Margaret Atwood notes that 'the inner Anne – her moral essence – remains much what it has always been' throughout the series (225).
5 For more on this aspect of Montgomery's Anne, see my essay 'The Whole of the Moon: L.M. Montgomery's *Anne of Green Gables* Series.'
6 See also Epperly's discussion about the anti-American sentiment in *Rilla of Ingleside* (*Fragrance* 120). Owen Dudley Edwards also discusses this sentiment in *Rilla* in 'L.M. Montgomery's *Rilla of Ingleside*' (133).
7 Thus, a person viewing this film and the previous instalment might not

notice the textual inconsistencies as the reader of Montgomery's texts most certainly would.

8 Strom Collins and Wyss Eriksson set a general timeline based on information from *Rilla of Ingleside* and clues from other books in the series. They deduced that Anne was born in 1866, and Gilbert in 1864 (16). It might be wondered why it is that I do not find Strom Collins and Wyss Eriksson's *Anne of Green Gables Treasury* an affront to Montgomery's texts; the difference in this case is that Strom Collins and Wyss Eriksson's book is solidly based on textual foundations, not on so-called artistic licence.

9 This question could also be asked of the screenwriters of the animated *Anastasia* (1997) and *Mulan*.

10 See Eleanor Hersey's essay on how Anne stammers over her introduction to Morgan Harris in the second film; she seems unsure as to whether she is a teacher or a writer, but then says that she is a writer, though at that point in the film, she is most definitely an author only in her own mind. Later in that film, Anne has her students on her first day at Kingsport Ladies College read one of her favourite works (Ann F. Howey discusses this in chapter 11), and later has them listen to her reading of her own writing. In the third instalment of the trilogy, Anne volunteers for the Red Cross only to get over to Europe to find her husband (which is no doubt what many women did in those days).

11 See the very interesting essays by Yoshiko Akamatsu and Calvin Trillin in *L.M. Montgomery and Canadian Culture* for more on this topic.

12 This book is reminiscent of the one put out as a companion to the Steven Spielberg film *Amistad* (1997); the book purported to be a history lesson but included the fictional characters and subplots created for the film.

13 I find Howey's dissection of these insertions very interesting and effective, though I have subsequently wondered if Sullivan means to indicate that this is the only way one can know a 'kindred spirit.'

14 Cf PAX-TV's *Little Men*, created by Carl Binder and Meyer Shwarzstein, and 'inspired by the writings of Louisa May Alcott.' Loosely inspired, it would seem. Again, the names and settings have been hijacked from Alcott's text into an adaptation that is anachronistic and derivative to the point of (apparently unintentional) parody and that uses every opportunity to portray the now-adult March sisters as immature ninnies guided by the Jesus/Michael Landon/handyman/moral compass Nick Riley (portrayed by Spencer Rochfort).

15 Gilbert seems to have forgotten that he told Anne how to write in the previous film.

16 A quick perusal of Ellen Moers's classic *Literary Women* gives ample evi-

dence to prove this point. See also Carole Gerson's essay, '"Dragged at Anne's Chariot Wheels": The Triangle of Author, Publisher, and Fictional Character.'

17 I have tested this theory by describing scenes from the third Sullivan film and having people guess what movie it is from; *Gone with the Wind* is echoed in at least two scenes.

18 Even though Benson's book was transformed into a musical, the film still manages to capture the essence of the Smith family, especially in the depiction of the girls.

Chapter 11

'She look'd down to Camelot': Anne Shirley, Sullivan, and the Lady of Shalott

ANN F. HOWEY

In 'An Unfortunate Lily Maid,' one of the most memorable and hilarious episodes in *Anne of Green Gables,* Anne Shirley, assisted by Ruby Gillis, Diana Barry, and Jane Andrews, enacts the final boat ride of Alfred, Lord Tennyson's tragic Elaine. Although Anne protests that 'a red-haired person cannot be a lily maid' (*AGG* 238), the impersonation suits her sense of romance, and soon she is floating down the river, dramatizing Elaine's post-mortem journey to Camelot. Tennyson's poem 'Lancelot and Elaine' (1859) appeals to Anne and her friends, first, because it tells a story about an emotion so strong it literally kills – as Anne remarks, 'it's so much more romantic to end a story up with a funeral than a wedding' (*AGG* 227) – and also because Anne is 'devoured by secret regret that she had not been born in Camelot' (239–40). No ordinary love, this is a grand and legendary passion: the young Elaine dies when Lancelot, the most famous and accomplished knight of King Arthur's court, cannot love her because of 'The great and guilty love he bare the Queen,' King Arthur's wife ('Lancelot and Elaine' l. 244). Elaine arranges for her body to be taken down the river to Camelot, with a letter explaining her love and tragic fate clasped in her hand.

What makes this episode so memorable is the contrast between Tennyson's tragic story and Montgomery's ingenious parody of it. The romantic scene Anne is trying to recreate dissolves as the fair maid suddenly realizes that she is dripping wet; the boat (weighted down, perhaps, by too many romantic aspirations) is sinking. The prosaic reason is that a submerged stake 'had torn off the strip of batting nailed on the flat' when the boat was pushed off from shore (*AGG* 241). Irony, not tragedy, becomes paramount, and the contrast between Anne and Elaine is clearly marked.

Rea Wilmshurst, who has catalogued the many literary quotations in the Anne novels, notes that Montgomery's use of quotations and allusions helps her to create character, while also reflecting 'Montgomery's own voracious reading' (15). Tennyson was her favourite poet; the number of Tennyson quotations in the Anne series is exceeded only by quotations from the Bible and from Shakespeare.[1] Montgomery's choice of Tennyson's poem as an intertext for this episode was hardly accidental, given its focus on romance. The nineteenth century witnessed a revival of interest in the medieval Arthurian legend, with its focus on courtly love, as seen in the publication of four different editions of the medieval text *Le Morte Darthur* by Sir Thomas Malory.[2] In addition, the nineteenth century saw the publication of numerous original Arthurian works, including Thomas Love Peacock's novel *The Misfortunes of Elphin* (1829), William Morris's collection *The Defence of Guenevere and Other Poems* (1858), which contains six Arthurian poems, Matthew Arnold's poem *Tristram and Isolde* (1882), Algernon Charles Swinburne's poem *Tristram of Lyonesse* (1882), and Mark Twain's novel *A Connecticut Yankee in King Arthur's Court* (1889).

Tennyson, however, is perhaps the most notable author of the Arthurian revival, since he produced numerous short poems on Arthurian subjects, including the intensely popular 'The Lady of Shalott' (1832, revised 1842), as well as *Idylls of the King*, a twelve-book epic poem published in various stages from the 1850s to the 1880s. That Tennyson's Arthurian vision was one of the most popular is reflected in the number of Tennyson-inspired artworks, including William Waterhouse's *The Lady of Shalott* (1888) and William Holman Hunt's paintings (1886–1905) as well as in the number of parodies of the *Idylls*.[3] As the Arthurian scholar David Staines notes, 'Tennyson ... turned to the Arthurian world throughout his poetic career,' and the sporadic publication of 'individual Idylls or groups of Idylls as they were completed ... created a large reading public' (287). By the time Montgomery wrote her Anne novels, therefore, the Arthurian legend – especially Tennyson's version of it – was circulating in various media and had become an integral part of British popular culture.

When writer, producer, and director Kevin Sullivan translated Montgomery's novels to the screen in his first two *Anne* films, *Anne of Green Gables* (1985) and *Anne of Green Gables: The Sequel* (1987), he, too, was drawn to Tennyson.[4] In contrast to Montgomery, however, who was inspired by 'Lancelot and Elaine,' Sullivan prominently foregrounded 'The Lady of Shalott' in the film adaptations, a significant departure from the novel, since Montgomery, although likely familiar with 'The Lady of Shalott,' never refers to this poem in the novel, except possibly for Anne's allusion to 'towered Camelot' (227).[5] As a result of Sullivan's use of 'The Lady of Shalott,' I contend, there is an important thematic (not to say ideological) shift: the Anne of Sullivan's films is much more obviously an artist-figure, as Sullivan emphasizes late-twentieth-century ideals of women's roles. That he accomplished this emphasis through the use of a nineteenth-century text is ironic; it also problematizes criticism that suggests that in the first two films he imposes anachronistic ideals onto Montgomery and her heroine. Ultimately, it was a popular choice, given the overwhelmingly positive reviews and responses of viewers.[6]

Translating a novel into a movie inevitably constitutes an act of transformation. Because of the difference between the two media, a movie based on a literary text, as described by the film studies scholar Louis Gianetti, may fall into three categories: a 'loose adaptation' that picks up only a few elements of the original (370–1); a 'faithful' adaptation that tries to capture 'the spirit of the original' (371); or a 'literal' adaptation – usually a translation of a play into film (371–2). Sullivan's first two *Anne* pictures fall between Gianetti's first two categories, with the first movie more of a faithful adaptation and the second movie more of a loose adaptation (Frever, 'Vaguely Familiar' 36–7).

The most notable and frequent changes created in the translation of a novel into a film are the compression of action and the shift from the inner world of characters' thoughts to the outward appearances of their actions and speeches. In her pioneering article on the *Anne* movies, the Canadian literary scholar Susan Drain comments that 'however sympathetic the camera, its eye settles on exteriors' (63), keeping viewers outside, too (64). Film-makers thus tend to use shorthand in characterization: they use key scenes, fragments of dialogue, striking images, or recurring music to manifest the inner world of the character for the viewer. Sullivan's first two *Anne* films employ as one such device 'The Lady of Shalott.' Quotations from and allusions to this poem occur four times in the two films and are situated at strategic moments to suggest Anne's character and to help mark the 'kindred spirits' that surround her.

Sullivan's *Anne of Green Gables* opens with a female voice whispering

'Willows whiten, aspens quiver' as the picture appears. Sullivan uses a long shot for this opening, so that from a distance we see Anne, played by the Canadian actress Megan Follows, wandering through the trees of an unidentified location. Although burdened down by a basket and a pail, she is completely absorbed in a book; as the titles roll, she continues to walk and to read aloud in that expressive, reverent whisper:

> Little breezes dusk and shiver
> Through the wave that runs for ever
> By the island in the river
> Flowing down to Camelot.
> Four grey walls, and four grey towers,
> Overlook a space of flowers,
> And the silent isle imbowers
> The Lady of Shalott.

Thus the first words spoken in the movie are recited from Tennyson's poem (ll 10–18). The regular rhythm and rhyme scheme identify the words immediately as poetry; furthermore, the recitation pauses at the end of the stanza, right after a line that identifies not only the heroine of the poem but also its title. The pause in the recitation is accompanied by a swell of music and Anne's running downhill from the woods into brighter sunlight. Shortly after, during another quotation from the poem, a loud voice screeches from somewhere out of view, 'Anne!' – thus identifying the film's heroine. The voice belongs to Anne's employer, Mrs Hammond (played by Jayne Eastwood); when she burns the book a few minutes later, she is clearly *not* a kindred spirit.

The film's opening scene, in part because of these quotations, teaches viewers how to 'read' Anne. She has literary tastes, since she reads poetry (and the work of a poet laureate, at that!) – something late-twentieth-century audiences would equate with 'literature' and 'high culture.' However, she also delights in the fantastic and romantic; we hear enough to know (or to be reminded) that the poem is about a cursed lady and her love. Anne is imaginative and sensitive, reacting to the words with dramatic sighs. Moreover, her situation contrasts the Lady's, in that Anne's life, unlike the Lady's, is full of mundane cares and duties such as fetching water and changing diapers.[7]

Tennyson's poem effectively becomes the touchstone that helps the viewer to identify kindred spirits, including Matthew Cuthbert (Richard Farnsworth), Emmeline Harris (Genevieve Appleton), Diana Barry

(Schuyler Grant), Jane Andrews (Trish Nettleton), and Ruby Gillis (Jennifer Inch). When Anne arrives at the Bright River train station and Matthew Cuthbert meets her for the first time, she refers to her worn-out carpetbag by saying: 'Not at all the sort of luggage I imagine the Lady of Shalott would travel with, but of course hers would be suited to a horse-drawn pavilion and not a train.' Matthew accepts this speech, among many others, without criticism. Anne is convinced at once that he is a kindred spirit, and so is the viewer. In both films, Sullivan interweaves the Lady's story into Anne's, even though such references are not always logical or accurate, as in Anne's reference to the Lady's luggage. Tennyson's poem emphasizes the Lady's confinement in the tower; she travels by boat only after the 'curse [has] come upon [her]' (l. 116), and since she travels to her death, she takes no luggage. The playful and imaginative nature of Anne in this scene, however, somewhat justifies the liberties taken with the events of 'The Lady of Shalott.'[8]

Even more liberties are taken in *The Sequel*, when Anne, now a schoolteacher in Kingsport, teaches 'The Lady of Shalott' to her English class. One of Anne Shirley's students, Emmeline Harris, reads the poem in class, and her sensitive reading contributes to the viewer's recognition of her as 'kindred spirit.' As the class scene begins, Anne says that they will read the first four verses of 'The Lady of Shalott,' but the lines that Emmeline recites, in fact, begin with the second stanza, the same one read by Anne in the opening scene of the first film that describes the Lady's island (although Emmeline's reading leaves out the third line). Next Emmeline reads, 'There she kept her vigil only / Waiting in her chamber lonely / And looked down to Camelot,' lines which are not in either the 1832 or the 1842 versions of Tennyson's poem.[9] Whereas the first film's scene at the train station presents the description of the Lady's luggage as obviously the product of Anne's imagination, making misrepresentations understandable as part of her characterization, this classroom scene in *The Sequel* presents the altered lines as a recitation of the poem.

After a scene between Emmeline's father, Morgan Harris (Frank Converse), and Anne's superior at the school (Rosemary Dunsmore), the viewer is taken back to the class; Emmeline is reading the (unaltered) fifth stanza, which Anne also recited in the first film's opening:

There she weaves by night and day
A magic web with colours gay

She has heard a whisper say,
A curse is on her if she stay
To look down to Camelot. (ll 37–41)

The repetition of such references throughout Sullivan's first movie and into the second, I argue, creates a sense of unity in the films, giving Tennyson's poem great emphasis and importance. The references contribute to the historical setting, since the memorization of poetry for pleasure or for school is a pedagogical technique more favoured early in the twentieth century than later. More significantly, however, the references act as a leitmotif; for viewers, their reoccurrence continually places Anne in relationship to the Lady, and to the Lady's defining characteristics of isolation and artistry.

When Anne floats down the river in the boat, both Montgomery's novel and Sullivan's film make it clear that Anne is acting out the end of Tennyson's 'Lancelot and Elaine.' None the less, in the film Anne quotes lines from 'The Lady of Shalott,' a poem much better known to late-twentieth-century viewers than 'Lancelot and Elaine,' as it is routinely featured in introductory English literature courses at universities, while reproductions of Waterhouse's *The Lady of Shalott* (1888) remain perennial bestsellers at poster sales. Recently, the Canadian singer Loreena McKennitt has further popularized this poem with her musical adaptation. Yet perhaps even more important than the audience's familiarity with 'The Lady,' Sullivan's use of the 'Lady of Shalott' presents an artistic choice: it develops the film's vision of Anne as an artist figure who works in isolation.

Briefly consider the contrasts between 'The Lady of Shalott' and 'Lancelot and Elaine.' Like Elaine's, the Lady's story is about overwhelming passion, since Lancelot's appearance, described by Tennyson in four detail-filled stanzas, makes the Lady risk all just for a closer look. Both the Lady and Elaine arrive in Camelot in barges, dead, to the consternation of the populace. However, Tennyson's source for 'The Lady' is not Malory's story of Elaine of Astolat but 'an Italian novelette, *Donna di Scalotta*' (Ricks 1: 387).[10] As J.M. Gray reports, 'late in life Tennyson said that "The Lady of Shalott is evidently the Elaine of the *Morte d'Arthur* [and thus of 'Lancelot and Elaine'] but I do not think that I ever heard of the latter when I wrote the former"' (210). Consequently, the two women differ in their type and degree of isolation, their ability to choose, and their artistic vocation.

First, although both women are isolated, they differ in the extent of the isolation that they endure. Elaine lives with her family, and although she separates herself from them to brood over Lancelot, her isolation is her own choice and it is temporary. Although 'day by day, / Leaving her household and good father, [Elaine] climb'd / That eastern tower, and entering barr'd her door' (ll 13–15), she appears to spend evenings with her family, so that household companionship remains intact. In arguing that Elaine is a 'Tennysonian artist' (343), Arthur L. Simpson, Jr, emphasizes Elaine's isolation; none the less, he acknowledges that it is 'self-imposed and intermittent' (343). However, the fact that Elaine chooses to isolate herself makes her significantly different from the Lady, who must lead a solitary existence in a tower, unseen by any, because of a curse.[11] Tennyson's rhetorical questions, 'But who hath seen her wave her hand? / Or at the casement seen her stand?' (ll 24–5), imply that no one sees her, and although some 'reapers, reaping early' (28) hear her, even they suspect that she is not real but a 'fairy' (l. 35). Magic, in the form of the unexplained curse, imposes isolation upon the Lady; when she is finally seen in Camelot, she is dead. Unlike Elaine, the Lady is never part of a community.

Second, Elaine chooses her fate as well as her isolation; the Lady cannot choose either. Lancelot gives Elaine several reasonable alternatives to that of pining away for him, such as waiting for a lover her own age, or being endowed by Lancelot with 'broad land and territory' (l. 952). Elaine's reply emphasizes her choice: she says, 'Of all this *will* I nothing' (l. 961, emphasis added). Likewise, when she plans her death barge, she says, 'Now shall I have my will' (l. 1040). Elaine's determination to choose death has led critics such as Simpson to describe Elaine's primary characteristic as 'willful egocentricity' (358). Such characteristics are not given to the Lady of Shalott. Because the curse can only be accepted by the reader as a given – magical, unalterable by the Lady, and rather unfair – her decision to risk the curse to experience the world and not just shadows seems neither wilful nor unreasonable but heroic, unlike Elaine's.[12]

Third, the two women differ in the degree to which they are depicted as artist figures. Elaine reproduces Lancelot's shield's design in needlework and therefore is, to a certain degree, an artist figure.[13] However, all of 'The Lady of Shalott' emphasizes the Lady's creative, artistic activities – the only activities she is allowed. She weaves 'by night and day' (l. 37), reproducing the outer world in an artistic form; she sings, another form of artistic expression which, at both the beginning and the end of the poem, is heard but not understood by the public; near the end, she writes her name on the boat, arranging herself to be perceived by the viewing public and expressing her identity. These details have led many critics to read the poem as Tennyson's exploration of the role of the artist and the conflicting demands of the world and of private inspiration and poetic expression.[14]

The most important of these qualities to Sullivan's films are the Lady's isolation and her identification as an artist. Anne, as we find out shortly after the first film sequence where she quotes 'The Lady of Shalott,' is also very alone. She is an orphan, surrounded by those who do not want or understand her. In *The Sequel*, when Anne begins teaching in Kingsport, she is once again isolated, away from Green Gables and people who love her, at a school where Miss Brooke and all the Pringles resent her intrusion. Emmeline Harris, the only other character to read extensively from the poem, is also isolated; although she has relatives, they do not seem to care much about her or give her much affection. While Emmeline reads from 'The Lady,' her father and Miss Brooke are having a discussion that will result in greater isolation for both Anne (who will lose her favourite pupil for a while) and Emmeline (who will lose the school community). The altered lines that Emmeline reads in the classroom scene end with 'only' and 'lonely,' a rhyme emphasizing the Lady's isolation, and thus Anne's and Emmeline's as well.

Moreover, Anne is, like the Lady, an artist. A major plot thread in the second film, as Eleanor Hersey has shown (chapter 9), is Anne's development into a professional writer, a clear departure from Montgomery's novels, where Anne's literary accomplishments are much less grand. Significantly, the lines of the poem most often quoted in Sullivan's films depict the Lady's artistic vocation: 'There she weaves by night and day / A magic web with colours gay' (ll 37–8). In the first film, Anne recites these in the initial scene and in the Elaine scene; in *The Sequel*, Emmeline reads these in the classroom scene. I would propose, therefore, that the incorporation of references to the Lady of Shalott and her artistic ability is one of the many ways that Sullivan's films emphasize Anne's role as writer, as Sullivan translates this figure for a modern viewership by (ironically) using a nineteenth-century female icon.

To argue that Sullivan's films emphasize Anne as literary producer is not to argue that they downplay Anne as heroine of a romance-defined-as-love-story, however. The added emphasis given to the love story of Gilbert and Anne in the movies has been noted by several scholars. Temma Berg says that the romance is 'intensified' (127); Drain argues that, in Sullivan's first film, 'the scriptwriters take increasing liberties with the text in order to make the romance prominent' (69), an observation that applies to Sullivan's second film as well. Allusions to Tennyson also play a role in the romance, particularly in the romantic conflict caused by Anne's refusal of Gilbert's proposal early in *The Sequel*. At Diana's wedding, Gilbert tells Anne, 'You'll marry all right. Some fool who'll sit and read Tennyson by firelight no doubt.' Such allusions ironically further the romance plot of the movie while attempting to criticize Anne's exaggerated romantic notions of love and courtship.

In depicting Anne as a writer, Sullivan draws on two popular (and romantic) conceptions of the artist figure: the artist creating in seclusion, withdrawing from the world to produce art; and the artist creating without effort, the vehicle for a gift that mainly requires opportunity.[15] In Sullivan's second film, with the exception of 'Averil's Atonement,' we see little of Anne's literary activities, and then her book is published. Gilbert meets her in Kingsport and repeats his belief, 'I always thought you should write a book about Avonlea.' After he leaves town, Anne retreats to her room (which, although not in a tower, is at least upstairs in the forbidding, grey, stone school); she gazes at a picture of Green Gables, stares off into the distance, seizes pen and paper, and begins to write. The next we hear of this endeavour, Anne announces to Morgan that her book is being published. Even the successful Montgomery did not find writing and publication this effortless, describing her career as an 'Alpine Path.'[16]

Why emphasize Anne the writer if Anne the potential wife is still the crucial aspect of her character? In chapter 9, Hersey documents that Sullivan injects L.M. Montgomery's own life writing into the Anne films. Another intertext available to Sullivan was Montgomery's Emily series, a portrait of the young woman as female artist.[17] When Montgomery first wrote the Anne series, few people would have questioned the convention that led to Anne's 'writing living epistles,' as she calls her children in *Anne of Ingleside* (268), rather than publishing literary works. Late-twentieth-century audiences, however, may want to see Anne as *equally* Gilbert's love and a successful writer. Today's viewers, perhaps, expect these roles to be combined. Thus, one important key to Sullivan's popularity with his viewership is that the film satisfies popular taste for fantasies depicting women (of whatever era) as people capable of successfully pursuing both interesting careers and romance.

Ultimately, then, the translation from the novels of Anne to these films demonstrates the interaction of popular genre and viewer expectation. Montgomery's Anne novels have influenced generations of girls, but the social conditions of women's lives and changing ideas about women's roles influence the way Anne is interpreted and re-presented to the world. In adapting Montgomery's stories for a different medium and in targeting those adaptations for a broad popular audience,[18] Sullivan effectively updated Montgomery's Anne to make her more consistent with contemporary, Western ideas about women's roles after several waves of feminism.

Still, not everybody welcomes these changes to Montgomery's novels. 'Why Did They Have to Differ So Radically from L.M.M.'s Work?' asks one (anonymous) reviewer of *Anne of Green Gables: The Sequel*, a sentiment shared in this collection by K.L. Poe, who rejects Sullivan's Anne the Author because, she argues, it imposes late-twentieth-century ideas onto Montgomery's heroine. Still, there are hints in the Anne novels that writing is an important part of Anne's life,[19] there is Emily's determination to be a writer in that series, and there is Montgomery's life and career. The first two films may be transforming aspects of Anne's identity but are not imposing modern ideals that are completely *foreign* to Montgomery's context.[20] In particular, Sullivan's addition of 'The Lady of Shalott' as an intertext in the story of Anne helps him avoid such dangers. Allusions to Tennyson abound in Montgomery's novel; Sullivan is adapting Montgomery's technique in this respect. And the use of this intertext in the film underscores the movement away from isolation that occurs in both films as well as in the Anne novels. Sullivan's Anne, like Montgomery's, escapes the fate of Tennyson's Elaine and the Lady. At the end of *The Sequel*, Anne has become part of the community and the recorder of its life.

Sullivan's Anne movies have been an enormous Canadian success story. The movies have been seen in 150 countries (St Germain). *Anne of Green Gables* won an Emmy award in the United States for best children's program (Bawden, 'Women Cop Top Emmys' D1) and nine Gemini awards in Canada in 1986 (Boone D1), but the viewership figures suggest that the film's appeal extends beyond children and beyond national boundaries. At the 1986 Gemini awards ceremony, '*Anne* also won a special award from TV Guide as the most popular program in a poll of the magazine's readers' (Boone D1). Also, reviews of the first two Sullivan movies were impressively positive.[21] Many fans recognize that these are films in their own right, independent entities that may be watched without any previous knowledge of their sources (Montgomery's novels) or their intertexts (such as Tennyson); even viewers who know these sources may choose to accept the films as texts to be enjoyed in their own right rather than as replacements of the novels. Inevitably, however, the films will also be watched by viewers who know (and love) the source texts; in this sense they are translations and will be judged for their ability to adapt those sources to a different medium. As translations, they are part of a growing trend in film to market canonical authors and their texts to an increasingly audio-visual, rather than textual, society.[22] Sullivan's films depend less on faithfulness to source texts and more on the sheer recognition of name: Montgomery and Tennyson become points of recognition, cultural icons, in films that refashion their stories and then create an association between their names and the filmic image of those stories.

Ultimately, Sullivan accentuates Anne's role as an artist figure while maintaining her role as romantic heroine. Whether Sullivan was right to make these changes (among others) to Montgomery's story is debatable and is ultimately up to the choice of individual viewers. And choose we always do, to paraphrase John Fiske in *Reading the Popular.* In making such choices, we also re-create Anne for the twenty-first century, building in our own imaginations an Anne who is not just Montgomery's or Sullivan's but our own. And that we choose to debate the permutations of this character ultimately marks Montgomery's success in creating an enduring popular heroine.

Notes

1 I derived this statistic from Wilmshurst's helpful index of authors (39–43).

2 These editions appeared in 1816, 1817, 1868, and 1889–91; Malory's text had last been printed in 1634. For further details of Malory's text and its publishing history, see Eugene Vinaver's edition, *The Works of Sir Thomas Malory.*

3 David Staines, who surveys Victorian prose fiction devoted to Arthurian themes, concludes, 'it is Tennyson's Arthurian world rather than a medieval version which stands directly behind these writings' (287). More direct parodies also appeared, such as Oscar Fay Adams's *Post Laureate Idylls* (1886).

4 Sullivan and Joe Wiesenfeld wrote the script for *Anne of Green Gables;* Sullivan wrote the script for *The Sequel.* Since there are no references to Tennyson in Sullivan's third movie, it will not be discussed in this paper.

Scholars have been critical of Sullivan's changes: see Susan Drain, '"Too Much Love-Making"'; Temma Berg, '*Anne of Green Gables*: A Girl's Reading'; Joyce Nelson, 'Kevin Sullivan's *Anne of Green Gables*'; and K.L. Poe's chapter 10 in this collection. More neutrally, Trinna Frever's 'Vaguely Familiar' discusses the role of film intertexts such as *Little Women* (1933), *The Sound of Music* (1965), and *My Brilliant Career* (1981) in Sullivan's *Anne of Green Gables: The Sequel*.

5 Tennyson describes Camelot's many towers throughout *Idylls of the King*, but 'The Lady of Shalott' speaks specifically of 'towered Camelot' (l. 32).

6 For reviews of *Anne*, see Bill Musselwhite, 'CBC's Version of *Anne* Would Please the Author'; Doreen Martens, 'With Superb Cast, *Anne*'s a Joy'; Rick Groen, '*Anne*'s a Winner of Hearts'; and Basil Deakin, '*Anne* "Quite Irresistible."' For reviews of *The Sequel*, see John Haslett Cuff, 'Slick *Anne* Sequel Takes No Chances with Success'; Jim Bawden, '*Anne of Green Gables: The Sequel*'; Robert Fulford, '*Anne*'s Secret Quality Keeps Her Coming Back,' and Bob Blakey, 'P.E.I.'s Spirited Redhead Returns.' An article in the *Montreal Gazette*, 'US Critics Rave over *Anne of Green Gables* Sequel,' surveys American responses to the second film.

7 While the Lady is occupied by a traditionally domestic task, weaving, the artistry involved in this task is much more 'romantic' than anything Anne is required to do by Mrs Hammond.

8 This scene occurs before we see Anne as scholar.

9 The Tennyson scholar Christopher Ricks (1: 387–95) discusses the various editions of the poem.

10 This novelette is Novella LXXXI from the *Cento Novelle Antiche* (Ricks 1: 387). For more information on Tennyson's sources, see Ricks's annotations to the poem. D.L. Chambers, another Tennyson scholar, also discusses sources.

11 Constance W. Hassett and James Richardson point out that revisions to the 1832 poem mean that the Lady is practically unseen even by the reader of the poem, as Tennyson eliminated lines that described the Lady's clothing and actions (295).

12 Since Lancelot rides by the tower unaware of the Lady's existence or of his effect upon her, she is not responding to rejection as much as to the desire to see more.

13 For contrasting views of Elaine as artist, see Hassett and Richardson, who argue that Elaine is an 'infantilized' version of the Lady (301), versus Simpson, who argues that Elaine is a 'Tennysonian artist,' albeit a negative one (343).

14 For examples, see Arthur Simpson, 'Elaine the Unfair'; Linda M. Shires,

'Rereading Tennyson's Gender Politics'; and Gerard Joseph, *Tennysonian Love* (1969).

15 The Lady of Shalott exemplifies the first of these conceptions of the artist. The second view of artistic production is perhaps best expressed ironically in *Strong Poison*, a novel by the famous scholar and detective novelist Dorothy L. Sayers; she has one of her characters say, 'I gather that sitting down is all that is necessary for producing master-pieces' (63).

16 See Montgomery, *The Alpine Path*. Also, scholars note that Montgomery had 'eight years of growing success in writing for periodicals' before she wrote *Anne of Green Gables*, which was rejected by four or five publishers before being accepted by L.C. Page Company (Wiggins 19).

17 See T.D. MacLulich's 'L.M. Montgomery's Portraits of the Artist,' which begins its discussion by arguing that '*Emily of New Moon* and, to some extent, *Anne of Green Gables* are worthy anticipations of the portraits of young female artists that are given in the works of later writers such as Margaret Laurence and Alice Munro' (459). Gittings, in chapter 13 in this collection, also emphasizes that 'the act of writing is central' to the Emily novels.

18 The films were first presented to audiences as television miniseries. The first film drew 'more than 5 million viewers when it appeared in December 1985 [on CBC], and a repeat ... [in December 1986] drew about 2.8 million viewers' ('Sequel to *Anne*' H7). The second film also had over 5 million viewers; it was 'the most-watched Canadian mini-series ever' (St Germain).

19 In *Anne of the Island*, Anne is described as 'transfigured' (210) when a magazine accepts 'a little sketch' (210) of hers. In the same book, before Gilbert's final proposal and Anne's acceptance, Anne tries to 'reconcile herself to a future where work and ambition must take the place of love' (240) (see Hersey, chapter 9).

20 This argument does not hold for *The Continuing Story* (1999). See Poe, chapter 10.

21 Reviews generally applaud the quality of the acting and of Sullivan's direction. Reviews of the *Anne of Green Gables* film tend to be overwhelmingly complimentary: Musselwhite suggests that only with Sullivan's film 'has *Anne of Green Gables* really been done properly' (F1); Deakin believes that 'this version ... seems ... to be entirely in the spirit of the work and of the time at which it was written' (44); Martens refers to the film as a 'superb adaptation' (18). Reviews of *The Sequel* had a few more reservations. Although Blakey believes it 'is everything the spirited redhead's millions of fans expect: a fairy tale with a romantic start, a happy ending and adventure in between' (D1), Cuff refers to it as a 'superficial production' (C5), and

Bawden acknowledges that 'the pacing at times is positively lethargic' ('*Anne of Green Gables: The Sequel*' F12); all critics, however, praise the performances and production values of the second film.

22 Authors such as William Shakespeare, Jane Austen, and Mary Shelley, in addition to L.M. Montgomery, come to mind in this regard. Publishers often use film stills to sell either reprints of these authors' texts or novelizations of the films that were based on these texts. For discussion of this trend, particularly with regard to Montgomery, see film critic Joyce Nelson's 'When Books Become Grist for the Media Mill' and Montgomery scholar Roderick McGillis's '*Anne*: The Book from the Film.'

Chapter 12

Road to Avonlea: A Co-production of the Disney Corporation

BENJAMIN LEFEBVRE

A well-known adage in Canada's television and film industry is that 'co-production means compromise,' as W. Paterson Ferns explains in his contribution to *Making It: The Business of Film and Television Production in Canada*. Co-production is a 'dirty word,' with consequential creative compromises that are 'often a threat to quality' (253). At the same time, Canada has sometimes lacked the financial resources and the viewership to create high-quality films and television series uniquely for Canadian consumption. As a result, until recently many Canadian series have been dependent on U.S. or other foreign funding or on pre-production foreign sales.[1] What happens, then, when two very different partners vie for creative control of a commercially and critically successful product? For *Road to Avonlea* (1990–6), a television series from Sullivan Entertainment co-produced by and for the Canadian Broadcasting Corporation (CBC) and the (U.S.) Disney Channel,[2] the name and the work of L.M. Montgomery have been adapted and reformulated for the era of episodic television into a product sold and re-sold to nearly every country with broadcasting capabilities. For seven years, the producers at Sullivan Entertainment negotiated between two very different networks – Canada's public broadcaster on the one hand and a premium cable network (similar to Pay-TV in Canada) on the other[3] – to create a series whose appeal, they claim, is intergenerational, cross-cultural, multinational, timeless, and enduring.

As an episodic series, *Road to Avonlea*'s initial challenge was to replicate the appeal and spectacular success of Kevin Sullivan's miniseries *Anne of Green Gables* (1985) and *Anne of Green Gables: The Sequel* (1987).[4] Although it never achieved the same following as its source films, conceptually and thematically the series is very much an *Anne* spin-off. Citing audience response as a motivating factor, Sullivan adapted unrelated Montgomery texts – her novels *The Story Girl* (1911) and *The Golden Road* (1913), with additional material excerpted from her collections of short stories *Chronicles of Avonlea* (1912) and *Further Chronicles of Avonlea* (1920) – for a filmic environment that had already drawn unprecedented responses from both CBC and Disney Channel audiences. Aspasia Kotsopoulos suggests that *Road to Avonlea*'s success and popularity are largely due to the very nature of the period drama, which she defines as 'an imagined distant past born out of contemporary desires' (101). Applying Andrew Higson's term 'modern past' (13) to the series, she calls it 'a pastiche of present-day anxieties and olden-day artifacts' (98). Still, as Kotsopoulos also notes, the revisionist proto-feminist narrative is often more progressive in its depictions of women than most 'contemporary' films and television series (99–100). I would add to Kotsopoulos's discussion of *Road to Avonlea*'s nostalgic rewriting of the past the suggestion that the series reinforces late-twentieth-century popular understandings of Victorian and Edwardian time and space. In other words, I would argue that *Road to Avonlea* attracts a large viewership in part because it confirms the desires of an audience that expects the historical moment to be uniformly conservative, sexually repressive, and morally monolithic. Within such a revisionist space, then, *Road to Avonlea* emphasizes themes that are absent from the specific source texts from which it is derived but that have already proven appealing to viewers of the *Anne* films. For instance, while *The Story Girl* and *The Golden Road* offer an ideal depiction of childhood, the *Road to Avonlea* scripts focus on the resolution of intergenerational conflict; the outsider's success at creating a community and an alternative family; the legitimization of possibilities for women outside marriage; the widening of supposedly static gender-appropriate boundaries for both women and men; and, particularly in its last years, the conflict for women between the desire for a career and the social pressures to rely on traditional roles within patriarchal relationships.

In addition to consistently maintaining a high quality of script, direction, aesthetic design, and performance, *Road to Avonlea* filled a significant void in the larger scheme of 1990s mainstream television and proved enormously successful and popular, in spite of the disappointment of the many Montgomery readers who would prefer a more literal translation of Montgomery's fiction to the screen, and in spite of the occasional critique in popular and academic circles that the series is sometimes excessively sentimental.[5] In 1990, the *Montreal Gazette* called *Road to Avonlea* '[t]he most successful series in the history of Canadian television' (Nicholls, F1) only seven weeks after its CBC premiere. During its seven-year run, the series achieved unprecedented and still-unsurpassed ratings for a Canadian dramatic series in English, reaching at peak 2.6 million viewers during its first season and rarely missing the 1-million mark for the duration of its ninety-one episodes, even for prime-time rebroadcasts. According to a press release from Sullivan Entertainment, a 1994 Angus Reid poll found that *Road to Avonlea* had the highest awareness level of any Canadian television production, easily recognized by 82 per cent of the Canadians surveyed ('*Road to Avonlea* Returns' n. pag). For its excellence in television, the series earned four Emmy Awards (out of sixteen nominations), five Cable Ace Awards (out of twenty-eight nominations), seventeen Gemini Awards (out of sixty-six nominations), and numerous other prizes and accolades. Finally, in 1999, *Road to Avonlea* neared the top of the all-time Ten Best Canadian TV Series entry in *The Great Canadian Book of Lists*, second only to the 1964–6 news program *This Hour Has Seven Days* (Kearney and Ray, 24).

Despite the series' enormous response and appeal in Canada, most CBC viewers appear unaware of the Disney Corporation's involvement in it. As several sources have indicated, however, Disney Channel executives outlined a substantial number of creative requirements in the series to protect Disney's investment of 60 per cent of the total budget of $110 million. In addition to pushing for the frequent inclusion of prominent American guest stars, Disney executives encouraged what Knowlton Nash calls 'an old-fashioned, sentimental, almost syrupy, innocence in the series' (298).[6] In March 1996, as *Road to Avonlea* ended its seven-year run on the CBC, Martin Knelman's *Financial Post Magazine* article 'Mickey on the Road to Avonlea' suggested that the implications of seeking the financial and creative investment of the Disney Corporation, an American conglomerate known for its subtle patterns of cultural domination, in a 'Canadian' popular culture phenomenon needed critical exploration. For this reason, instead of debating the extent to which *Road to Avonlea* is a responsible adaptation of Montgomery texts or an accurate reproduction of Edwardian Canadian time and space, this chapter proposes to analyse *Road to Avonlea*'s lures and pleasures through the lens of American cultural theories that have explored the Disney phenomenon. More specifically, I argue that the appeal and the international portability of the *Road to Avonlea* series, which Kotsopoulos refers to as a fantasy that 'suppresses differences and history in its effort to create a utopian vision of the past' (100), works in tandem with Disney patterns of 'innocence' that result in a highly complex and problematically constructed space. As cultural theorist Henry A. Giroux notes, 'the Disney Company has become synonymous with a notion of innocence that aggressively rewrites the historical and collective identity of the *American* past. Behind the ideological appeal to nostalgia, wholesome times, and a land that is "the happiest place on earth," there is the institutional and ideological power of a $4.7 billion multinational conglomerate that wields enormous influence pedagogically and politically in a variety of public spheres' (45; emphasis added). Although ideally the series could function simultaneously as 'the prodigal child of Canadian television' (Shaw, F1) *and* as an embodiment of this Disney hegemony, I posit that Knelman's question – 'Who would have guessed the shadow of Walt Disney lived behind the "sunny" veneer of Lucy Maud Montgomery's Canada?' (22) – is entirely appropriate.

'Exclusively on the Disney Channel'

Road to Avonlea appeared for the first time on 7 January 1990 as part of the umbrella series 'CBC Family Hour' with high expectations even before it first aired. When the CBC's broadcast of the first season of thirteen episodes was shortened because of budget cuts, the national media did little to mask the public's outrage: though – and perhaps because – the remaining four episodes were postponed to the following television season, within two months of its appearance *Road to Avonlea* was declared a national treasure. On 5 March 1990, two months after its CBC debut, the series (re)premiered on the American Disney Channel as *Avonlea*. At first glance, the decision of the Disney executives to alter the title of the episodic series could be simply to maximize its viewers' association with the film *Anne of Green Gables: The Sequel*, which the Disney Channel had co-produced with Sullivan Films and aired as *Anne of Avonlea: The Continuing Story of Anne of Green Gables*. However, the cover of the March–April 1990 issue of *The Disney Channel Magazine* – with its headlines 'Prime Time Series Premiere!' and 'From the creator of the acclaimed miniseries *Anne of Green Gables*' – is indicative of a more complex control dynamic. Though Holly Macfee's feature article includes cast lists, interviews, and detailed background information about Sullivan Films, it never mentions the Canadian Broadcasting Corporation as co-producer or initial broadcaster. Instead, *Avonlea* becomes 'An Original / Disney Channel Series / Created and co-produced by Kevin Sullivan' (22). Thus, in different ways, and to different ends, both the CBC and the Disney Channel take advantage of their mutually exclusive broadcasting territories to minimize viewers' awareness of the other's participation in the series. Though identical episodes had already aired on the CBC, Disney could truthfully claim to offer the 'world premiere' and hold the exclusive broadcast rights to *Avonlea* simply because it was the only venue in the world to employ that title. In turn, this confusion complicates *Road to Avonlea*'s status as the epitome of Canadian popular television: as Betsy Hearne warns, 'the sheer sophistication and international dominance of the Disney commercial machine guarantee that a Disney version of a fairy tale or classic will be THE authorized version for millions and millions of young viewers all over the world' (140; emphasis in original).

This 'shadow' of Walt Disney over a Canadian popular culture phenomenon extends to some of *Road to Avonlea*'s choices of character and plot introduced in the first episode of the series, 'The Journey Begins.' A wealthy Montreal businessman is framed for embezzlement; to shield his spoiled daughter from possible scandal, he sends her to her late mother's Prince Edward Island relatives, unknown to her, on the assumption that 'she'd be away from scrutiny there' ('The Journey Begins'). Immediately, Prince Edward Island is constructed – both to Canadian viewers and to American viewers whose knowledge of Canadian geography may be uneven – as a microcosmic safe space that can protect an innocent child from 'real-life' problems she cannot understand. But if the Island acts as insulator against these 'outside' problems, then Sara Stanley (Sarah Polley) becomes very much an object of scrutiny *within* the insulated space: her aunts, her cousins, and the other children and adults of the school and village all seek to identify the outsider as other. This trope of negotiating and making an unfamiliar space familiar, absent in *The Story Girl* and *The Golden Road*, dominates thematically throughout *Road to Avonlea*.

As well, the series introduces new concerns about the definition of family not present in these source texts and not common for American family drama, whether period or not, where most families tend to be nuclear (or recreated to mimic a nuclear structure). In order to reassure her father that she will make the best of this situation, Sara speculates about the advantages of having 'a real family – I mean a big one, with aunts and uncles and everything' ('The Journey Begins'), indicating a suspicion that something may be lacking in her own alternative family unit, where a widowed father, though caring, is too preoccupied with the business world to be a fully active parent. Sara Stanley and Nanny Louisa (Frances Hyland) travel to Prince Edward Island to be embraced within the nuclear family of Aunt Janet (Lally Cadeau) and Uncle Alec King (Cedric Smith), whose three children – bossy Felicity (Gema Zamprogna), troublemaker Felix (Zachary Bennett), and angelic Cecily (Harmony Cramp) – round out a cast of archetypes who simultaneously conflict with and complement each other. As a result of space constraints, however, caused by another visiting cousin, bookish Andrew King (Joel Blake), Sara and Nanny Louisa are sent instead to live with Sara's spinster aunts, the dominant, inflexible, independent Hetty King (Jackie Burroughs) and the meek, more feminine Olivia King (Mag Ruffman).

In this way, and likely prompted by late-twentieth-century sensibilities, *Road to Avonlea* widens the boundaries of the family nucleus by legitimizing alternative family constructions. Literally, there is no room for Sara within the nuclear family; instead, Sara's relationship with Hetty and Olivia, central to the series, necessitates a revision of the traditional family structure. In episode 25, 'A Mother's Love,' Sara decides to enter Aunt Hetty in an essay contest for Mother of the Year in order to legitimize their relationship to the larger community. Felicity and her friends taunt Sara with her anomalous family status, while Janet insists to Hetty that the natural blood bond between mother and child supersedes all other possible ties. As revenge, Sara writes a letter that convinces Felicity – and, subsequently, everyone else – that Felicity was switched at birth with a schoolgirl who is portrayed as lower class. This news momentarily threatens Felicity's middle-class security and proves to all – children, adults, and viewers alike – that the circumstances of childbirth are secondary to the quality of family relationships. If period dramas are more a reflection of contemporary concerns than an attempt at historical re-enactment, then *Road to Avonlea* creates a space for alternative families of the 1990s while resisting a direct critique of nuclear normativity: the traditional family is available next door, but the emphasis of this series is on an orphan girl and her two spinster aunts. While such lessons are shrouded in a fantastic, innocent world where reconfigurations are presented as timeless, these 'innocent' values are potentially problematic if the microcosmic community of Avonlea is to be seen as a utopia. As Giroux remarks, '[i]nnocence in Disney's world becomes the ideological vehicle through which history is both rewritten and purged of its seamy side' (46), thereby producing 'a series of identifications that relentlessly define America as white and middle class' (47). Giroux's critique can be applied to *Road to Avonlea* in several ways. From the beginning of the series, Sara the 'poor little rich girl' is aggressively pressured to shed her privileged position and be retailored for middle-class domesticity. Under the guises of 'fitting in' and 'learning responsibility,' Sara must discard her elaborate lace dresses for gingham aprons and then learn to cook, clean, and sew in order to belong within a space whose inhabitants are *almost without exception* white, middle class, and Presbyterian. Although Disney films tend to eschew specific religious worship in favour of a generalized Protestant moral ethic, *Road to Avonlea* does not constrain itself to this boundary: instead of replicating Montgomery's use of religious satire or updating her problematic emphasis on Protestants and her stereotyping of French and Irish Catholics (Rubio, 'Scottish-Presbyterian Agency' 89–105), *Road to Avonlea* strives to eliminate any religious or cultural tension. The result is a monolithic community in which difference is erased. While church figures prominently in only a dozen or so episodes, every social activity in Avonlea – from concerts to Sunday School picnics to the Avonlea Sewing Circle – is church-related.

In episode four of *Road to Avonlea*, 'The Materializing of Duncan,' Colleen Dewhurst reprises her *Anne of Green Gables* role as Marilla Cuthbert. At a meeting of the Avonlea Sewing Circle where old beaux are discussed by the town gossips, Sara – there to practise her sewing – breaks social decorum by speaking without having been spoken to and asks Marilla if she ever had a beau. Marilla, tired of being pronounced a social failure because she never received a marriage proposal, invents an old beau from her youth in order to legitimize her decision to remain unmarried. Pressed for details, Marilla explains the relationship was 'impossible' because of 'differences': they quarrelled because '[h]e was a Methodist.' Rachel Lynde (Patricia Hamilton), unsettled by this sudden revelation, quickly regains composure: 'A Methodist! Well – no wonder you never mentioned him. You can move heaven and earth, but Providence knows you can't bring a Methodist and a Presbyterian together.' In a later scene, Sara discusses the incident with her cousins and mourns the fact that interfaith tension came in the way of 'true love':

SARA: Sometimes I think religion's more trouble than it's worth.

CECILY: Sara Stanley, you can't mean that!

SARA: I do mean it. Tell me – what is the difference between a Presbyterian and a Methodist?

FELICITY: There's a good deal of difference. Everyone knows that.

FELIX: Methodists say 'Amen' a whole lot more than Presbyterians do ...

SARA: That's still not reason enough not to marry one of them.

As an outsider to the community, Sara initially resists the sanctity of the monolith and challenges its norms and values; her three cousins, too well socialized into the community, are unable to pinpoint Methodist difference, and the discussion stalemates ('The Materializing of Duncan').[7]

Sara's resistance, however, is only temporary: three episodes later, Sara is inspired by a visiting missionary who thrills the congregation with tales of danger and suspense from his career of 'converting the heathen.' After she decides she 'can be a missionary right here in Avonlea' because 'there are lots of people who don't come to church,' her efforts to lure hired boy Peter Craig (Miklos Perlus) into the Presbyterian community are met with opposition by both Felicity, who vows she will not sit in the same pew as 'that heathen Peter Craig,' and Aunt Hetty, who demonstrates no interest in Peter's spiritual development and leaves the decision to come to church entirely in his hands. The storyline of this episode, titled 'Conversions,' is key to the discussion of *Road to Avonlea* as monolithic utopia: Peter feels like an outsider ('I'm not like the rest of the people in this town') as a result of his father's prison sentence and his mother's work as a washerwoman in a neighbouring village; because his parents are still alive and because they play social roles not seen as respectable, Peter sees the dissolution of his familial nucleus as a source of shame. Though well-intentioned, Sara capitalizes on Peter's insecurity to coerce him to join the congregation. Contradicting her earlier claim, she states: 'Church is where everyone meets in Avonlea. Don't you ever want to come with us?' Felicity, on the other hand, is extremely unsympathetic to Peter's right to choose a religious community when he is older and expresses her outrage at Peter's 'hankering' to be a Methodist: 'A Methodist! ... I know one thing – I'd rather be dead than be a Methodist.' In her mimicry of Rachel Lynde, Felicity has internalized and now replicates the values of the previous generation and reinforces the ideal of religious heritage. Though she appears to have inherited a similar religious tradition, Sara initially approves of Peter's right to choose his own religious community but later insists there is no difference between the two faiths and reminds Peter that Avonlea has no Methodist church. No third option is ever introduced. Peter's eventual decision to come to church – and enter fully into the Avonlea community – is presented as entirely his choice; but with no alternative, it is his only choice ('Conversions').[8]

If *Road to Avonlea* perpetuates a fantasy of Anglo-Saxon Presbyterianism as cultural monolith within Canada and the United States, then I wonder how this monolith is understood when broadcast outside this territory. On 4 March 2000, an article on the front page of the *Globe and Mail* announced *Road to Avonlea*'s success as the highest-rated television drama in the history of Iran. That the series has managed to appear on Middle Eastern television is not entirely surprising given its general success in the foreign market. What proves significant in light of the present discussion is the way *Road to Avonlea* generalizes and renders exotic Canadian time and space for Middle Eastern consumption. As Geoffrey York reports, 'most Iranians seem convinced that Canada is a paradise of happy families whose lives are marred only by the occasional broken romance or lost animal' (A21). Thus, by allowing essentialist icons such as *Anne of Green Gables* and the Mountie to overgeneralize Canadian multiculturalism, in this case Disney fantasy is understood as Canadian reality. Certainly, in presenting a bucolic paradise from which a didactic message can be extracted, *Road to Avonlea* can fill an important function for the audience of a television network controlled by a state monopoly that for censorship reasons allows very little American programming to air. However, in this article that praises 'Canadian' television, the Disney Channel's involvement in the series is noticeably censored from the discussion, even in the interview with Kevin Sullivan. This implies that *Road to Avonlea*'s status as either Canadian or American (Disney) is interchangeable and that a Disney co-production can infiltrate the Iranian market that otherwise systematically eliminates American content and manage to do so undetected.

So far in this paper I have argued that *Road to Avonlea* both embraces and resists the Disney paradigm: instead of reinforcing the nuclear family's monopoly on 'wholesome family values,' the series undercuts this master narrative by allowing such values to be included within alternative families constructed for a time and space presented as 'universal.' This universality is achieved partly as a result of the absence of a historically specific time line. In addition, because *Road to Avonlea* was filmed almost entirely in southern Ontario (Davidson, 9–10), the physical reality of Prince Edward Island is substantially reduced, in different ways, for Canadian, American, and non–North American audiences. With history and geography constructed by viewer subjectivity through the guise of nostalgia, *Road to Avonlea*'s euphemism 'the Island' creates a fantastic, microcosmic bubble into which real time and space never intrude. As early director Dick Benner explains, 'What they're delivering is such an idyllic look at the past; these children are so perfect and so sweet. The biggest crisis is that somebody stole the pie-tasting tin. That will appeal to a whole lot of people as so-called "family, escapist" – pretty, nostalgic stuff' (Fisher, 17).

This systematic lack of historical grounding contributes greatly to the international portability of the series. At the same time, however, the producers remove the right from the casual viewer to question the plausibility of character motivation and choice of subject matter, relying on generalization and archetype rather than attempting to re-create specific historical moments. Such an emphasis on stock character and artificial time–space construction limits options of critique by minimalizing an appropriate lexicon of film criticism. The editors of *From Mouse to Mermaid: The Politics of Film, Gender, and Culture* lament this reduction in their overview of how the Disney phenomenon has traditionally been (mis)read: 'Not unlike certain relatives forcing their feet into Cinderella's shoe, Disney film is the ugly stepsister unfit for the glass slipper of high theory. With no conventional system or vocabulary for approaching Disney film, film theory ultimately protects and preserves the inviolability of the Disney canon and its status as American metonym. In this case, "American" Disney is below artistic and cultural worth' (Bell, Haas, and Sells, 3).

In 1996, Kevin Sullivan remarked that 'if Disney had had their way "Avonlea" would have been a very different show ... [b]ut the fact is the show just would not have happened without Disney' (quoted in Knelman, 28). Though economically necessary, the reliance on Disney in the project of adapting Montgomery's novels for CBC, Disney Channel, and non–North American audiences, to whom complex constructions of gender, race, class, and nation are continually being reformed, transforms Montgomery's Avonlea – as paradigm, as metonym, as hegemony – into very much a Disney/land.

On 31 March 1996, the CBC aired the final episode of *Road to Avonlea*.

The day marked the end of a unique Canadian popular culture phe-nomenon, as well as the end of Sullivan's partnership with the Disney Corporation. Since then, the CBC 'Family Hour' time slot has been home to two new series, *Wind at My Back* (Sullivan Entertainment: sixty-five episodes, 1996–2001) and *Emily of New Moon* (Salter Street Films/CINAR Corporation: forty-six episodes, 1998–   ), the latter also based on Montgomery's novels and discussed by Christopher Gittings (in chapter 13). Though both series purport to belong to the 'family drama' genre, they both openly and realistically explore such themes as illegitimacy, drug addiction, child abuse, and the effects of extreme Protestant repression. As such, they are both the antithesis to *Road to Avonlea*. Though financed entirely in Canada, neither series has come close to replicating *Road to Avonlea*'s impact on Canadian popular cul-ture. Likewise, Sullivan Entertainment's other two follow-up projects, the *Road to Avonlea* reunion movie *Happy Christmas, Miss King* (1998) and the miniseries *Anne of Green Gables: The Continuing Story* (2000), have been less successful.

Such is the paradox of Canadian television: whereas most series financed and produced solely in Canada receive only lukewarm responses from Canadian viewers, the one 'Canadian' popular culture phenomenon is the series that Mike Boone aptly called 'family viewing in the finest tradition of Disney' (F2).

Notes

This chapter was written thanks to years of detailed discussion with fellow *Road to Avonlea* viewers, especially Maryam Haddad, Vikas Duggal, and Aspa-sia Kotsopoulos. At the University of Guelph, I thank Gordon Lester and Linda Rodenburg for their discussion and feedback.

1 This has begun to change since the mid-1990s, thanks to the creation of more government funding agencies and tax credit programs.
2 The Toronto-based production company was founded in 1979 by Kevin Sul-livan and Trudy Grant as Sullivan Films; the name changed to Sullivan Entertainment in 1994. Telefilm Canada and, in later years, the Ontario Film Investment Program and the Cable Production Fund also invested in the series, but it is not clear to what extent they offered and/or demanded cre-ative input.
3 Since 1996, when *Avonlea* ended on the Disney Channel, the network has become part of most basic cable packages in the United States.

4 *Anne of Green Gables* was co-produced by CBC, PBS (U.S.), City-TV (Canada), and ZDF (West Germany); for *Anne of Green Gables: The Sequel*, CBC, PBS (U.S.), Channel 4 (U.K.), and the Disney Channel acted as co-producers.

5 In 1990, Antonia Zerbisias compared *Road to Avonlea* to 'slurping up mounds of country fresh buttermilk, flapjacks oozing with sunny, yellow butter[,] and dark maple syrup with whipped cream and a cherry on top' (C1). By the show's end, Alex Strachan described the series as 'gentle-natured, harmless family entertainment, a character-building fable for children, not too maudlin or sentimental for parents' (B11).

6 See Knelman; Shaw; Atherton. The list of guest stars well known to U.S. audiences includes Faye Dunaway, Stockard Channing, Madeline Kahn, Dianne Wiest, Meg Tilly, Peter Coyote, Michael York, Kate Nelligan, Christopher Reeve, and Christopher Lloyd. By fall 1996, the Disney Corporation's *Avonlea* Web page (no longer on-line) included the tag 'Produced by Sullivan Entertainment in association with THE DISNEY CHANNEL' (emphasis theirs). In addition to changing the title of the series, Disney changed the titles of eight episodes. As well, in 1993–4, Walt Disney Home Video repackaged several early episodes of *Avonlea* into four videocassettes under the title *Tales from Avonlea*; they include the tag 'Disney Presents' as well as a trailer for the two initial *Anne* films that reappropriates them into 'the grand Disney tradition.'

7 Andrew, the other outsider, remains noticeably silent during this exchange. In the rest of the episode, a stranger named Duncan McTavish (Tom Peacock) arrives in town and discovers that Marilla's invention has preceded him. Before Marilla's reputation for honesty can be tarnished, however, the two decide, for the benefit of the town gossips, to pretend that their 'quarrel' (religious difference) had been made up. McTavish assures her, 'I'm not a Methodist, so our way is clear.' Even in farce, religious propriety is central within this microcosm.

8 To the best of my knowledge, there is only one mention of a religious denomination, Protestant or otherwise, in any other episode of the series: in the sixth season, Sara wants to attend a women's college in France but is convinced of Aunt Hetty's disapproval because it is 'a Roman Catholic institution' ('Comings and Goings').

Chapter 13

Melodrama for the Nation: *Emily of New Moon*

CHRISTOPHER GITTINGS

Move over, Anne, Emily has arrived. While images of the eponymous character of L.M. Montgomery's *Anne of Green Gables* are impressed upon Prince Edward Island licence plates, and while Anne is described by Canadian pop culture gurus Geoff Pevere and Greig Dymond as a Canadian 'Mickey Mouse' at the nexus of a multimillion-dollar tourist trade (Pevere and Dymond, 13), over the past years Emily Byrd Starr has also received increased media attention. The reason for this interest is the $13-million, thirteen-episode, Salter Street/CINAR co-production of the 1925 novel *Emily of New Moon* broadcast on CBC from January to April of 1998. Anne herself has been the subject of two American-made feature films (1919, 1934) and, in 1985, a four-hour CBC television adaptation viewed by just under six million Canadians. The success of Prince Edward Island as an international tourist destination is due largely to the attractions of Anne Shirley and Montgomery's global readership. Japanese travel agencies alone book ten thousand trips to the island annually. Given the economic importance of Montgomery's characters to the province, it is not surprising that the provincial government invested $1.9 million in the production of *Emily of New Moon*. Drawing an average audience of 843,000 viewers per episode, *Emily of New Moon* was the only one of ten new CBC shows to capture an average audience of more than 500,000 (see Atherton, 'CBC, CTV' A1, A3). With this kind of success, and a second season of Emily, it comes as no surprise that Emily dolls are now stocked alongside Anne dolls in the tourist shops of Charlottetown (see chapter 21).

However, the series was not a success for devoted Montgomery readers who have a strong identification with the *Emily* books, as an excerpt from disgruntled viewer Barbara Lord's letter to the *Globe and Mail* indicates: 'Are there others who share my outrage at the travesty the writers have made of the memorable characters created by Lucy Maud? New ones have been introduced and old ones completely altered. Goodness knows what nonsense is to come' (D7). Lord touches on the crux of my present analysis, the problematic of adaptation, the translation of a literary source text into a visual medium, the political re-visioning of a melodramatic novel into a national televisual melodrama. National cultures are dependent upon the circulation of national icons such as Montgomery; however, Montgomery's caricatures of Irish difference in the *Emily* books and her absenting of Micmacs from the social terrain of the trilogy conflict with contemporary imaginings of a racially diversified nation. Therefore, producers of a contemporary national culture – Salter Street / CINAR – work to rehabilitate the national icon so that it is compatible with late-twentieth-century Canadian imaginings of nation. Hence the alterations that outrage Lord.

Lord is not alone. The informal response of Montgomery scholars to the series has not been overwhelmingly positive. Privately, some complain about the televised version's lack of subtlety, and its indulgence in melodramatic excesses, 'melodramatic' here being used not as a critical term but as a pejorative marking 'an exaggerated rise-and-fall pattern in human actions and emotional responses, a from-the-sublime-to-the-ridiculous movement' (Elsaesser, 521).[1]

I discussed the challenge of adaptation with the supervising producer and main writer of the series, Marlene Matthews, as she was shooting the second series and months before the first series went to air. Matthews is negotiating at least two dynamics: translation from the written word to the televisual sign, and her desire to re-vision Montgomery's late-nineteenth-century story for a late-twentieth-century Canadian audience.[2] In response to my questions about adaptation and difference from the source text, Matthews outlines one of the practical problems she encountered: 'There's never enough in a novel to sustain thirteen hours of television, and so far we've done twenty-six hours; so you do have to take certain liberties, and the key is to be true to the spirit of the author' (Gittings, telephone interview with Marlene Matthews).

What is striking about Matthews's comments is the desire to provide authenticity for the viewer, something Lord feels is missing from the production. Borrowing from Walter Benjamin's argument for linguistic translation, I would suggest that the act of bridging a gap between two seemingly incommensurable systems, whether linguistic or visual, necessarily creates a new text (73). Benjamin says of the translation: 'For in its afterlife – which could not be called that if it were not a transformation and a renewal of something living – the original undergoes a change' (73). Now, in translating across the linguistic screen of conceptual apprehension to the direct perception of the moving image, in exchanging the linguistic trope for the televisual sign, Matthews effects shifts in plot and inventions of character in the name of historical authenticity.[3] In an effort to map the processes of adaptation at work here, I would like to begin by examining the technical and artistic challenge of translating a written narrative about the development of a writer into a visual and spoken narrative for television. The second part of my discussion will take up Matthews's attempts to re-vision the books as a national televisual family melodrama.

The novels' dominant trope signifying Emily's intense and visionary relationship to the spiritual and imaginative realms is the 'flash.' As Montgomery constructs it, the flash permits Emily in her waking hours fleeting access to 'a world of wonderful beauty,' 'an enchanting realm beyond' (7). To communicate this concept, Matthews cannot draw solely on linguistic tropes, as Montgomery does: 'Between [the world of wonderful beauty] and herself hung only a thin curtain; she could never draw the curtain aside – but sometimes, just for a moment, a wind fluttered it and then it was as if she caught a glimpse of the enchanting realm beyond – only a glimpse – and heard a note of unearthly music' (*ENM* 7). Instead, from the source material, Matthews must create a televisual code that transmits a sense of this experience to the viewer. Matthews sets about this task by collapsing the closely related, but separate, second-sight episodes Emily experiences while sleeping or during illness into the 'flash' experiences. All second-sight and flash episodes in the television series are colour-coded. As Matthews explains, 'the flash takes form in Emily's visions and what we've done there is that when she sees, when she has this moment of inspiration, and sees something that others don't see, we will see it on the screen as a vision of hers and we differentiate it from real life by showing these visions in primary colours so that they're a hyped reality.' This exemplifies what I have been referring to as a televisual code. Matthews's sustained use of the flash code increases the probability that it will be decoded similarly by different receivers (Fiske and Hartley, 63).

In addition to technical televisual codes, such as the flash code, televisual representation is also dependent upon the transmission of cultural codes such as dress, language, and economics that establish the norms and conventions of a given society. Our perception of reality is, as John Fiske and John Hartley postulate, 'always mediated through the codes with which our culture organizes it, categorizes its significant elements or semes into paradigms' (65–6). For example, the pregnancy of a single woman in white, North-American invader–settler culture has been coded historically as a spectre of shame, through the linguistic marker of 'fallen woman' and through the economic deprivation and social marginalization of such women. Matthews elects to communicate this historical and gendered reality in the story of Maida Flynn, a character and scenario absent from Montgomery's books. In the television episode entitled 'Falling Angels,' Maida is shunned by polite society, abandoned by her lover, fired from her job, and expelled from her father's home because of her pregnancy.

The television series must also communicate the writing process, an activity coded historically as a vocation for men and, as the influential work of Sandra Gilbert and Susan Gubar (1979) indicates, a pathology for women. While Montgomery inserts excerpts from Emily's writing into the novels, complete with spelling errors, purple prose, and trial-and-error searches for the right turn of phrase, Matthews is dependent on the codes of television to signify the metamorphoses of Emily's innermost thoughts into the written word. A medium shot of Emily writing cuts to a close-up of the pen inscribing letters onto paper and is accompanied by a voice-over track of what is being transferred to the page; in the CBC series, this becomes the televisual code for literary production. At the beginning and end of every episode, Emily is seen and heard 'writing' in her journal (figure 13.1). This device marks another 'liberty' taken with the novels or another translation from the novels to the small screen. In the novels, although Emily writes letters to her deceased father, she does not start keeping a diary until the end of *Emily of New Moon*. In the series, however, Matthews sustains the device of Emily writing to her father 'on the road to heaven' for a very long time as 'a way for the audience to know [Emily's] inner thoughts.' The act of writing is central to both the novels and the television series; writing facilitates Emily's self-expression and empowerment. Initially, it is a covert practice that must be hidden from Elizabeth Murray, who seeks to withhold the pen from Emily as a means of socializing her charge. A single woman in a man's world, Elizabeth has internalized

13.1   Emily Starr (Martha MacIsaac) writing in her journal. Salter Street /
CINAR.

patriarchal values, the dominant phallocentric Presbyterian codes of what it means to be a socially acceptable girl/woman in nineteenth-century Prince Edward Island. Withholding the pen from woman is tantamount to denying woman access to knowledge and communication; it is an action perpetuating inequity. Elizabeth acts as an agent of the patriarchy to ensure that Emily is contained within the status quo, to ensure that Emily becomes a 'lady' who will not 'waste' her time on any activity that is not utilitarian and that might mark her difference from mainstream society. However, when she sees that Emily can earn money through her work, Elizabeth softens. Although three men – Douglas Starr, Jimmy Murray, and Mr Carpenter – are instrumental in inspiring and supporting Emily's literary endeavours, Starr and Carpenter are both progressives, perceived as socially unacceptable to the Murrays, while Jimmy is regarded by the community at large as a mental defective. These men exist outside the Presbyterian patriarchy as Wallace Murray represents it in the novels and the series. As the foregoing illustrates, representations of life in the novel and television are indeed mediated through cultural codes – in these cases, the cultural value assigned to gender and other formations of social difference by a dominant social group. The television series and the novel may be read profitably through the genre of the family melodrama, of which gender, generational, and cultural conflict are but three characteristics (Gledhill, 'Melodramatic Field' 9, 37).

Montgomery's *Emily* novels are written in the melodramatic tradition of the late nineteenth century. Melodrama is a large and unwieldy category; its roots in Greek tragedy, the bourgeois sentimental novel, Italian opera, and Victorian stage melodrama contribute to what Christine Gledhill describes as the confusion surrounding its generic definition (Gledhill, 'Melodrama' 73). Traditionally, melodramatic plots revolve around the powerless and their victimization by a corrupt social system as this is represented through family relationships (Elsaesser, 514–15). In Thomas Elsaesser's conceptualization of melodrama, Charles Dickens's *Oliver Twist* and Victor Hugo's *Les Misérables* are paradigmatic texts. The story of orphaned Emily's life reflects this paradigm to a limited degree; however, the *realpolitik* of earlier melodramas by Dickens and Hugo is diluted in Montgomery, replaced by the struggles of an orphan against a repressive family and community regime. Martha Vicinus's characterization of the melodrama as a genre that 'always sides with the powerless' (quoted in Gledhill, 'Melodrama' 14) needs to be qualified with reference to Emily. Emily's position, as a white, female orphan under the rule of New Moon, is one of powerlessness; however, a position of powerlessness is mitigated by the social standing of her Murray family as part of a land-holding Presbyterian élite. Emily's powerlessness is relative to the socio-economic positions of Perry Miller, in the novels and television series, and Little Fox, the Micmac boy invented for the television series. However, Montgomery's and Matthews's figuring of Emily as an outsider to the Blair Water community by virtue of her artistic sensibility, writing, and orphan status grants her access to, and community with, other outsiders such as Ilse, Perry, and Lofty John in the novel and Father Ducharme, Maida Flynn, and Little Fox in the television series.

A central cultural paradigm of the nineteenth century (Gledhill, 'Melodrama' 5), the melodrama contributed to what Gledhill refers to as the 'institutional and aesthetic formation of "the popular"' (36), and thus was a logical choice for Montgomery, whose nostalgic representations of the late nineteenth century became synonymous with middlebrow popular culture. Part of this aesthetic formation was the family melodrama, which was coded through the home, family relations, moral values, romance, and fantasy, all essential ingredients in Montgomery's trilogy.[4] As Susan Hayward notes, in melodrama the family becomes the site of patriarchy and capital and therefore reproduces them (200). I have already discussed how the matriarchal Aunt Elizabeth reproduces patriarchy in the reconstituted family structure formed by herself, Laura, Jimmy, and Emily. The bourgeois ideology of the Murrays is pronounced in Elizabeth's interactions with the working classes of Stovepipe Town, as represented by Perry Miller, and the economics of Emily's welfare. Elizabeth, Ruth, and Wallace Murray ensure that Emily is aware of the cost of maintaining her from the very beginning of the first novel. In the television series, the best example of reproducing patriarchy and capital in the family is the Maida Flynn episode I referred to earlier, where patriarchy and capital work together to forge mutually agreeable constructions of woman and woman as labour. When her pregnancy contravenes their image of woman, Wallace Murray, the father of Maida's lover, and the owner of the fishery where she works, fires her, and her own father expels her from his house. Importantly, all of these elements place the novels and the television series squarely in the domain of the popular melodrama, an aesthetic that 'facilitates conflict and negotiation between cultural identities' (Gledhill, 'Melodrama' 37).

This conflict and negotiation between cultural identities is, of course, present in the novel in Murray and Blair Water society's interactions with working-class Perry Miller and Irish Roman Catholic Lofty John. However, Matthews's re-visioning of Montgomery focuses on this element of melodrama as a coordinate for transforming Montgomery's source text into a more diverse and inclusive narrative of Canadian nation. For as Gledhill argues, 'melodrama only has power on the premise of a recognizable, socially constructed world. As the terms of this world shift so must the recognition of its changing audiences be re-solicited. As melodrama leaves the nineteenth century behind, whose moral outlook it materialised, these two levels diverge, and it becomes a site of struggle between atavistic symbols and the discourses that reclaim them for new constructions of reality' ('Melodrama' 37).

Resoliciting the audience with a recognizable social world is precisely what Matthews is attempting. She rewrites the cultural differences Montgomery inscribed in the 1925 source text in a script that engages the atavistic symbols of Roman Catholic, Irish, French-Canadian, and Micmac cultures as these conflict with the normative category of white, Anglo-Celtic, Protestant cultural hegemony. This conflict is structured by a camera eye that would re-vision it through a politics of difference and national pluralism framing the cultural moment of the series' production in 1996. Like all historical novels or films, the CBC series reformulates the past – specifically, Montgomery's representation of a Canadian past – based on present concerns about the injustices suffered by groups read by the dominant as other to the nation.[5] The television adaptation constitutes a melodramatic narration of nation as a family, an ideological allegory that would sew into the cultural fabric of the nation those who have been excluded from a historically white, Protestant, fictive ethnicity that came to signify Canada in the nineteenth and twentieth centuries.[6] In his conceptualization of melodrama, Elsaesser explores this allegorical aspect of the genre that involves tailoring 'ideological conflicts into emotionally charged family situations' (516).

Fiske's and Hartley's work on the relationship between the communicator of television's communicated message and the audience is useful in understanding the national inflection of the televisual *Emily*. Drawing on Umberto Eco's concept of aberrant decoding in mass media – that is, the slim possibility that professional encoders such as Matthews and her team of writers will be decoded as intended by an undifferentiated mass audience – Fiske and Hartley argue that 'this very characteristic of the television communication imposes a discipline on the encoders which ensures that their messages are in touch with the central meaning systems of the culture, and that the codes in which the message is transmitted are widely available' (81).

Matthews taps into the central meaning systems of the culture by referencing the very debates about differences from a national identity – French-Canadian nationalism and Native land claims – that have become the dominant codes for Canadian nation, as these contemporary debates are figured, abstractly, in the characters of French-Canadian Father Ducharme and Micmac Little Fox. Moreover, the significance of the CBC's position as both national broadcaster of the series and ideological state apparatus should not be underestimated. The CBC has a long history of representing Canada to Canadians and, as Richard Collins notes, 'since 1968 television drama has been defined as the strategic position on which the future of Canada's nationhood turns' (42).[7] Despite the problematic claim of such a sweeping statement, the nationalist thrust of the 1968 Broadcasting Act and subsequent debates over Canadian content indicate that Canadian nation has, in part, been staked on the ability to represent the nation to the nation.[8] As a broadcasting institution that communicates the message of a television drama such as *Emily*, the CBC is a transmitter of Canadian culture, or of what Raymond Williams would call 'the *signifying system* through which a social order is communicated, reproduced, experienced and explored' (*Culture* 13).

I would like to focus on the processes of adaptation that render the television series an overt attempt to narrate the nation. In her representation of Irish-Catholic difference, Montgomery is attempting to reproduce and explore a Canadian social order for her readers to experience. Irish Roman Catholics Lofty John Sullivan and Father Cassidy mark an ethnic and cultural difference from and a conflict with the hegemony of Anglo-Celtic Presbyterian society in the novel *Emily of New Moon*. The source text creates a fifty-year feud between the Scots-Presbyterian Murrays and the Irish-Catholic Sullivans over land purchased legally from Archibald Murray by Mike Sullivan, Lofty John's father. Because of a falling out between the two patriarchs, the families are not on friendly terms; Elizabeth Murray attempts to buy back the land, and Lofty John Sullivan refuses to sell it 'for spite' (66). Emily describes Lofty John as 'an enemy to my family' (130). The enmity between both families reaches a crisis point when Lofty John plays a cruel joke on Emily; he tells her that an apple she stole from him and ate was poisoned. In response to Elizabeth's disciplining of him for this incident,

Lofty John vows to cut down every tree on his tract of land that borders New Moon. Knowing that Sullivan is a devout Catholic, Emily visits the local Irish priest, Father Cassidy, and asks him to intercede. Despite her culturally constructed anxieties about Catholicism and priests, Emily has a successful meeting with Cassidy, who agrees to assist her. In the process she learns that no 'mysterious ceremonies' are required for a meeting with a priest, nor is there anything 'alarming or uncanny' about his abode or person (193). As much as Montgomery appears to be demystifying the spectre of Irish Roman Catholicism as it is constructed by its other, Scots-Presbyterianism, her chapter title, 'A Daughter of Eve,' contextualizes Lofty John as the evil Irish-Catholic serpent who tempts the innocent Protestant Eve/Emily, and in this way reinscribes a prejudicial representation of Irish Catholics. Similarly, Montgomery's Father Cassidy is a figure of fun, a walking, talking stereotype or stage Irishman who blathers on about leprechauns and fairies to the delight of Emily (197). While this representation of Cassidy assists Montgomery in establishing an instant and magical rapport between the priest and the romantic Emily, it is a signification dependent upon a flattening out of Irishness into a cliché.

Although what Homi Bhabha refers to as the 'ambivalent, and vacillating representation' of the nation's ethnography is visible in Montgomery's *Emily* books, Matthews's adaptation of Montgomery attempts to reveal 'the possibility of other narratives of the people and their difference' (300). Exploiting the codes of melodrama, Jeremy Hole, a writer working under Matthews's supervision, makes a radical and significant departure from the source text. In episode five, entitled 'Paradise Lost,' the dispute between Lofty John and the Murrays is translated from interfamily rivalry to intrafamily rivalry; it is about legitimacy and contested membership in the family. Whereas Montgomery's source text figures the Sullivans and the Murrays as two discrete entities, genetically and culturally, Hole's script rewrites Lofty John as the illegitimate progeny of an adulterous affair between Lally Malloy and Alexander Murray. Here, Lofty John is given five acres of land by the Murrays to silence the story of his, in their view, scandalous relationship to their family. In Hole's and Matthews's hands, the narrative shifts to become a story about difference in and expulsion from the family, remedied by a healing acceptance of difference and movement towards an inclusion in the family and community. Hole's script underlines the pejorative construction of Irish-Catholic difference that is at work in the Murray family and in the larger community of Blair Water. Laura Murray describes Lofty John as a 'crazy old papist' who 'worships false Gods and graven images' and, as Emily reports, schoolchildren say that he is 'Old Nick, the Devil himself' ('Paradise Lost' CBC). As in Montgomery's novel, Matthews and Hole represent the anxieties about and prejudices towards Catholicism in Emily's approach to the church and her visit with the priest. However, Hole and Matthews must translate the linguistic signs of Emily's prejudice into televisual signs.

Significantly, this translation process shifts the message communicated in the book to a message in the CBC series that reveals how a young and imaginative mind internalizes and further exaggerates distorted social constructions of otherness and how these phantasies are shattered. Subjective camera shots of her approach to and entry into the Catholic church grant the viewer agency to Emily's perspective. The exterior of the church is shown from a low-angled long shot, giving the impression of it as looming up before the small figure of Emily. A soundtrack of sinister string music, tolling bells, and Latin chants accompanies a cut from the exterior to a subjective camera shot of what Emily sees when she enters the building. Catholic difference, as Emily has internalized it, is transmitted to the viewer through the televisual *mise en scène* of lighting, costumes, and props. Emily's introjection of the nineteenth-century Gothic is projected onto Catholicism. Through the subjective camera we see a darkened church, lit only by candles. The centre aisle is lined with hooded Franciscans waving incense burners, and as Emily travels down the aisle she collides with a statue of Mary that cries a tear of blood. Emily's phantasy is shattered by the voice of the priest, whom she first perceives as one of the hooded Franciscans. The disruption of Emily's phantasy of difference is signalled by a cut from the image of the bleeding Virgin in the candle-lit church to a low-angled long shot of Emily and the priest in a light-filled white interior of the same building, *sans* incense-burning Franciscans, bleeding icons, and threatening sound track. In the television adaptation, Roman Catholicism is demystified by the priest's explanation of his religion in terms comprehensible to Emily: 'The Pope is God's vicar on earth, and I am God's vicar in Blair Water' ('Paradise Lost'). Furthermore, the adaptation avoids the reinscription of Irish stereotypes present in the novel by substituting a French-Canadian priest, Father Ducharme, for the novel's Irish Father Cassidy. In avoiding the Irish stereotypes of the novel by inserting a French-Canadian priest, the adaptation elides the Irish prejudice of the source text and thus performs the political work of making Montgomery more consumable as a national icon compatible with the nation's late-twentieth-century diversity and official policy of multiculturalism.

This substitution is central to the narrating of nation that I am arguing is taken up through the processes of adaptation to the televisual medium. By representing a non-Anglo-Celtic element of Canadian cultural identity as part of the community, the CBC series 'opens up the possibility of other narratives of the people and their difference' (Bhabha 300). Ducharme becomes more of a presence in the television version than Cassidy is in the source text. Not only does Ducharme attempt to talk to Lofty John, this French Canadian becomes a mediator between the warring factions of the Anglo-Celtic family, paying a visit to New Moon and lobbying Elizabeth for the 'protection of Lofty John's interests' ('Paradise Lost' 5). The Lofty John of the adaptation is going blind and accidentally sets fire to his barn. The entire New Moon household, alerted by Emily, rushes out into the night to save Lofty John from the fire. Following the fire, Father Ducharme negotiates a deal with Elizabeth whereby the Murrays will farm Lofty John's land and donate the revenue earned to his care in a Roman Catholic hospital. Ducharme mediates another crisis of illegitimacy in the Murray clan when Emily's cousin Oliver refuses to take responsibility for the pregnancy of Maida Flynn. Although Ducharme's intervention comes too late to integrate the 'fallen' Maida back into the community, he ensures that Oliver accepts the baby into the Murray family as his own ('Falling Angels'). Despite the adaptation's attempts to integrate otherness into the national family, the role of mediator for different factions of an Anglo-Celtic family maintains Father Ducharme and, allegorically, French Canada, as an outsider to the national family.

Perhaps the most striking evidence of Matthews's present re-visioning of a national past and transformation of the novel's negotiation of difference is the presence of the colonized other in the television program. The first episode, 'Eye of Heaven,' written by Marlene Matthews, introduces the Micmac character Little Fox into the adaptation, a character absent from the source text. Commenting on this aspect of the adaptation Matthews explains: 'I felt that was important because the Micmacs were such an integral part of the fabric of the island and there was no mention of them in the novel, and then it occurred to me that if Douglas Starr was a teacher, Emily would have many of the same notions that he did about quality in the schools. And how Natives were treated in that period is a fact of life.'

When Little Fox attempts to join classes at the local schoolhouse, he is beaten by the teacher, Mr Morrison, who denigrates him as a dirty, nit-ridden 'mangy little fox,' projecting a white cultural construction of indigeneity onto the Aboriginal subject. He teaches his students that Aboriginal difference is synonymous with abjection and should be met with violence. Emily disrupts this lesson in colonial oppression by physically attacking the teacher, who then turns his violence on her. Here we have contested membership to a larger national family, and an expulsion of First Nations from that community by the authoritarian sign of the teacher standing in for the state. Following this incident, Little Fox and Emily become fast friends; she teaches him how to read and he teaches her the sweet-grass ceremony. This cultural exchange could be read as assimilationist, with Emily acting as an agent for an education that would displace Micmac language and values. However, the narrative pre-empts such an interpretation by having Little Fox depart to continue his education with his people. Emily's adaptation of the sweet-grass ceremony to assist her father's recovery and later to beckon spirits to escort her father to heaven can be read as a healing acceptance of difference or, alternatively, as a white appropriation of Native culture diegetically by Emily and extra-diegetically by Matthews.

Although the addition of Little Fox to the televisual narrative is somewhat unstable, as it risks exoticizing the Aboriginal subject, it does attempt to facilitate a resoliciting of a changing audience and the shifting demographics of nation by including other formations of difference outside of western-European culture that are integral to any identification of a Canadian national narrative. However, non–Anglo-Celtic Canadians are being invited to identify as outsiders to the nation, as the others in the series are never part of the 'family.' Matthews's insertion of Little Fox also elides Montgomery's decision to absent the Micmacs – 'an integral part of the fabric of the island' – from the *Emily* books. Moreover, the 1996 reformulation of the national past, while acknowledging the increasing autonomy of Aboriginal peoples in Little Fox's return to his culture, also works to repress the horrors of residential schools that Little Fox is spared when he goes to learn from his people. With the insertion of Little Fox, the rehabilitation of Montgomery as a consumable national icon embracing French-Canadian and First Nations' differences is complete.

Matthews's re-visioning of national televisual melodrama transmits an imagined community to a national television audience. Part of Matthews's work in adapting the novel for television is restoring what she perceives Montgomery removed from the social terrain – Micmacs, for example, and also the social conditions of women as these are referenced in the series by Maida Flynn's pregnancy and Laura Murray's addiction to laudanum. Speaking about the insertion of laudanum addiction into the adaptation, Matthews makes some telling comments about the influence pre-production research of the historical period had on the revisionist writing of the script: 'there are certain things we discovered in our research that would have to have been reflected if we're going to tell an honest story about what life is like at the time, and how women were treated medically was a very important factor.'

The desire expressed by Matthews for a historical authenticity acknowledging elements of the past that Montgomery chose not to negotiate is in direct conflict with the desire of Barbara Lord and Montgomery devotees for a textual authenticity. Through her reworking of the melodramatic form and Montgomery's text, Matthews tells a story that is self-consciously 'national' in its inclusion of the two 'founding nations' – the French and Anglo Canadas – and the First Nations of Canada. This 'national' story is also suffused with the ideological content of federal policy on national identity. Although not always successful, and despite a tendency to elide some historical truths in the process, the insertions of Little Fox and Father Ducharme reflect the 1988 Multiculturalism Act, which recognizes and promotes 'the understanding that multiculturalism is a fundamental characteristic of Canadian heritage and identity' (quoted in Hutcheon and Richmond). Matthews works in the melodramatic tradition sketched out by Elsaesser where 'ideological conflicts,' manifest here in the layers of colonialism underpinned by French-Canadian and Native differences to Anglo-Celtic hegemony (the conflict of the colonized and the colonizers), are tailored 'into emotionally charged family situations' (516).[9]

Notes

It would not have been possible to research and write this paper without the generous cooperation of Marlene Matthews and Linda Jackson, who both agreed to speak with me about their work on the television series. Thanks are also due to Mary Rubio for suggesting that I write on the television series and for encouraging me during the writing process. I would also like to thank CBC research officer Laura Craig, who made me aware of Tony Atherton's article. I am grateful to Mark Simpson and Teresa Zackodnik for their helpful comments on an early draft of this paper. I am grateful to *CCL: Canadian Children's Literature / Littérature canadienne pour la jeunesse* for permission to reprint 'Revisioning *Emily of New Moon*: Family Melodrama for the Nation,' which originally appeared in *CCL* 91/92. 24.3/4 (Fall/Winter 1998): 22–36.

1 As Christine Gledhill explains, melodrama has been conceived in 'predominantly pejorative terms' from the turn of the century to the 1960s ('The Melodramatic Field' 5).
2 Unfortunately, because of time constraints and CBC restrictions on accessing viewer mail, it was not possible to do a full-scale reception study of *Emily of New Moon*.
3 I am indebted to George Bluestone's discussion of the trope in language and the limits of the novel and the film (20).
4 For a more detailed discussion of the family and melodrama see Gledhill, 'The Melodramatic Field' (12) and Hayward, 'Melodrama' (200).
5 See Hayden White on historical pluralism and pan-textualism (485).
6 The term 'fictive ethnicity' is Etienne Balibar's. Balibar argues that a nation does not possess an ethnic base naturally (96). On race, ethnicity, and identity in Canada see Berger and McLaren.
7 Collins interrogates the validity of this commonly held belief, arguing that political institutions play a greater role than a national culture does in holding Canada together.
8 For a discussion of the 1968 Broadcasting Act and its ramifications see Collins, 66–104.
9 While these shifts in plot and inventions of character contribute to an ideological narrating of nation, they are also motivated by economics. If the series did not include a French Canadian in a recurring role, would French-language CBC (Radio Canada) have been as quick to purchase the first thirteen episodes? Moreover, with sales of the series to more than twenty international markets ranging from Denmark to Brunei, the production has to communicate Canada to a global audience through codes – such as the historically recognizable coordinates of French, Anglo, and Native as markers of Canadian nation – that are mutually agreed upon as constituting Canada.

Chapter 14

Paul Ledoux's *Anne*: A Journey from Page to Stage

GEORGE BELLIVEAU

'Mrs. Lynde says that all play-acting is abominably wicked.'[1]
— L.M. Montgomery, *Anne of Green Gables*

Since the publication of *Anne of Green Gables* in 1908, L.M. Montgomery's story of the red-headed orphan – as the following list shows – has been adapted and transformed into numerous media, including radio, stage, television, and feature-film production, both in Canada and beyond (see Table 14.1).

TABLE 14.1
Selected film, stage, and television adaptations of *Anne of Green Gables*

Title	Medium	Year
Anne of Green Gables	silent film	1919
Anne of Green Gables	Hollywood film	1934
Anne of Green Gables	CBC television musical version	1956
Anne of Green Gables	Polish stage play	1963
Anne of Green Gables	stage musical (Charlottetown)	1965
Anne of Green Gables	film for television	1985
Anne	stage play for youths	1998

Little has been recorded about the 1919 silent film except that it had an American flag flying above the Avonlea school and that, according to Montgomery, the 1934 film by Mintz and Nicholls 'was a thousand-fold better than the silent film' (*SJ* 4: 326). However, also on the subject of the 1934 film, Montgomery notes in a letter how 'she liked the first two-thirds of it reasonably well but the last third I did not care for' (*Road to Yesterday* 11),[2] and Theodore F. Sheckels states in his essay 'Anne in Hollywood: The Americanization of a Canadian Icon' that '[t]he critical elements that made the novel a distinctly Canadian and feminist work were sacrificed' (191) in the thirties' film. Mary Rubio comments on how the stage version of *Anne of Green Gables* by Andrzej Konic 'has been extremely popular in Poland, achieving several thousand performances since its premiere in 1963' (24). The same popularity has attended the 1965 Don Harron–Norman Campbell stage musical,[3] which grew out of their ninety-minute CBC-TV version from 1956. Furthermore, television versions of *Anne of Green Gables* have appeared in France (1957), Poland (1958), and England (1972), and the 1985 Kevin Sullivan film, made for television and starring Megan Follows, broke all Canadian television ratings records, winning numerous awards and making Anne of Green Gables into a household name in Canada.

The primary focus of this chapter, and (to my knowledge) the most recent dramatic version of *Anne of Green Gables*, is the last item on the list, Paul Ledoux's 1998 stage play, simply entitled *Anne* (figure 14.1).[4] *Anne* premiered in April 1998 at Toronto's Young People's Theatre, where it had a successful six-week run.[5] 'Trust the Young People's Theatre to get it just right with *Anne*,' wrote theatre critic Kate Taylor in the *Globe and Mail*, praising the 'strong script from Paul Ledoux' (C3). 'If you are going to adapt the ubiquitous *Anne of Green Gables*, you had better do it well,' she noted. Published in 1999 by Playwrights Canada Press, Ledoux's adaptation breathes new life into Montgomery's story. It begins with a mature Anne arriving home from teacher's college, then flashes back to earlier events before moving forward again. Instead of depicting the traditional hero's journey from innocence to experience, therefore, Ledoux's structure takes Anne on a journey from experience to innocence and back to experience. The challenges of adapting a well-known story are many. *Anne of Green Gables* has been influenced by the passage of time, the publication of Montgomery's journals and letters having led to new interpretations. Added to that, the development of feminist and postcolonial thinking, shifts in aesthetic fashion, and the application of new techniques to stagecraft, film, and text all alter the scope of what can be said and seen and influence what an artist wants to say or show.

Whereas Christopher Gittings's analysis of the *Emily* adaptation in

14.1 On stage at the Blyth Festival: Anne Shirley (Samantha Reynolds) waits at the train station for Matthew to take her to Green Gables. Courtesy of Off Broadway photo, London, Ontario.

chapter 13 focused on the political and ideological implications of adaptations, I investigate Ledoux's structural innovations, as the playwright adapts the story to the stage and to a late-1990s youth audience. I begin by examining Ledoux's use of the *memory play* in his retelling of the classic story and document how this dramatic device suits his intended audience. Ledoux has been working extensively in television over the last few years, experience that has likely influenced his stage writing. Ultimately, I argue that Ledoux's *Anne* propels Canada's iconographic redhead into new creative territory, making her come alive on stage with the strategies of a televisual age.

The Memory Play

Ledoux's two-hour stage play keeps the majority of memorable events, as *Anne of Green Gables: The Musical* also did. Ledoux's creative innovations are structural, as he turns *Anne* into a televisual memory-play structure. He first shifts Montgomery's omniscient narrative voice over to two narrators: Rachel Lynde and Ruby Gillis. Representing the adult and adolescent voices, they guide the audience by recollecting events from Anne Shirley's past. Ledoux's most daring strategy consists in fragmenting and disrupting Montgomery's linear story by incorporating flashbacks and memories, 'zapping' the audience back and forth in the chronology of the story. In *Television Culture* (1987), John Fiske defines zapping not only as 'flicking through channels watching snatches of each,' but also as the ability to 'watch two programs simultaneously by zapping back and forth between them' (104–5). Just so Ledoux's structure reflects today's 'discontinuous, interrupted, and segmented' (105) television text, and results in a story that is 'episodic – although not disjointed,' according to theatre critic Vit Wagner (C2).

There are a surprising number of contemporary plays that incorporate the memory structure,[6] yet scholarly research in the field of the memory play has only begun to emerge.[7] In *Flashbacks in Film: Memory and History* (1989), Maureen Turim credits the Russian formalists, who privileged form over content, as a significant influence on early filmmakers using the flashback device. According to Turim, the formalists introduced 'the notion of "device," a construct within form that complicates the formal patterning of the textual object, providing form with variations' (5). As film structure became more sophisticated, artists tried to justify their use of the flashback device, and Turim suggests that flashbacks in modern drama and film began to hide their formal function by being presented as memories, dreams, or confessions (6). Literary works made use of memory, dreams, and confessions within their narratives long before moving pictures, although precisely what influenced the increase of the memory structure in plays is a difficult question. Nevertheless, the popularity and sophisticated development of flashbacks in films (and later in television) has likely had a large impact on the development of memory plays during the second half of the twentieth century.[8]

Arguably, Tennessee Williams's *The Glass Menagerie* (1945) was the first work from the modernist canon to be categorized as a memory play. His contemporary drama is a narrated flashback framed by the rememberer (Tom Wingfield), who turns back time. As he explains in his opening frame monologue: 'The play is memory. Being a memory play, it is dimly lighted, it is sentimental, it is not realistic' (Williams, 2–3). Williams's play was soon followed by Arthur Miller's landmark play *Death of a Salesman* (1949), which also makes use of the memory structure. The success of these two memory plays sparked the beginning of a distinct genre that has grown rapidly in the second half of the twentieth century, and one that several Canadians embrace, including Ledoux in *Anne*.

Rather than using a first-person narrator, such as Tom in *The Glass Menagerie*, Ledoux opted to have two third-person narrators in Rachel Lynde and Ruby Gillis. In this way, his play structurally resembles Thornton Wilder's classic *Our Town* (1938), which has the Stage Manager retelling the story of Grover's Corners from a third-person perspective. The protagonist in Ledoux is undoubtedly Anne, but Rachel and Ruby guide the audience in the memory process, much as does Wilder's Stage Manager, whose various roles in the town contribute to the action without its being his story. In choosing Rachel, Avonlea's community spokesperson, and Ruby, a young Rachel in the making,[9] Ledoux is able to recollect the majority of significant events in Anne's life from an adult and adolescent perspective. Also, the two third-person perspectives generate the sense of a community constructing myths and suggest comparisons with conventions of traditional Maritime story telling.[10]

Community recollections, including gossip, also become integral in depicting particular events within the play, for even when neither Rachel nor Ruby witnessed certain private episodes in Anne's life, they have the uncanny ability to share them. For instance, act two, scene four has a group of Avonlea women sitting in the parlour at Green Gables recalling the time when Anne dyed her hair green:

RACHEL: She [Anne] told Marilla, 'I'll never, never look at myself again until my hair grows.' Then she said,

RACHEL/DIANA/RUBY: 'Yes, I will, too!'

RACHEL: 'I'll do penance for being wicked that way. I'll look at myself every day and see how ugly I am. And I won't try to imagine it away, either.'

RUBY: And Marilla had to let her stay at home until it grew in! (64–5)

Without a narrator guiding, or directing, the action, Ledoux must rely on dramatic conventions to recollect Anne's adventures; consequently, he includes a quasi-chorus through the town gossipers. This chorus-like device supports the memory structure, because most often the townspeople in *Anne* are retelling past events, as the above quotation demonstrates.

Links can be traced between Ledoux's play and *Anne of Green Gables: The Musical*, which contains classic gossip numbers from the town busybodies, such as, 'Where Is Matthew Going?,' 'Where'd Marilla Come From?,' and 'Did You Hear?' Another structural connection between both dramatic interpretations appears in the opening verse of the musical's title number, 'Anne of Green Gables' (quoted in the epigraph of chapter 15). These lyrics suggest that the townspeople of Avonlea know Anne before she actually arrives in Bright River; therefore, the musical, too, could be categorized as a memory play.

Montgomery's novel provides its reader with a few remembered events (Anne recollects her life in Nova Scotia in chapter five, and Marilla and Matthew reminisce about Anne in chapter thirty-one), but the narrative structure is predominantly linear in chronology. Nevertheless, in places the narrative voice appears to be a step ahead of the action, giving the impression of retelling a known story. For example, chapter one closes with Rachel expressing her pity to the wild rose bush, while the narrative voice intercedes with irony: 'but if she could have seen the child who was waiting patiently at the Bright River station' (15). This prepares the reader for the surprise awaiting Matthew at the station. Montgomery's play with time in the narrative voice creates irony, whereas Ledoux's temporal shifts reflect his desire both to emphasize memories (to be discussed shortly) and to appeal to a contemporary theatre audience.

The target audience for *Anne* at Young People's Theatre consists of youths eight and up, largely from urban Toronto and its environs. The majority of these young people have grown up with television and the

Internet. A juxtaposed and fragmented structure, therefore, is easily accessible to them. As Wagner suggests in his review, '(t)he story's flips back and forth in time are fluid enough to keep the target audience in the game' (C2). The shift between present and past becomes an effective means to sustain the attention and interest of the 1990s school-aged audience. Television programs usually have at least two stories developing simultaneously with frequent flips back and forth and, as John Fiske states, 'a televisually literate viewer (and many younger viewers are particularly literate) can watch two programs simultaneously by zapping back and forth between them, using his or her televisual literacy to fill in the enlarged syntagmatic gaps' (*Television Culture* 105). The non-linear memory structure becomes a means of engaging the young theatre audience, who are easily able to bridge the gaps in time and make meaning from the dispersed events presented.

Canadian playwright Sharon Pollock, who writes predominantly memory plays, mentions in an interview that 'if you don't find the form that matches the content appropriately, you have a leak in your show' (Dufort, 4). The memory structure in *Anne* complements its content, for Anne's dark memories of being bounced from family to family, constantly surrounded by death, are emphasized in the recent adaptation. Unlike the musical, which presents Anne as imaginatively and playfully remembering being born in a Viennese Palace in the song 'The Facts,' Ledoux's act one, scene six has the orphan vividly recollect her painful past in Nova Scotia, describing first her parents' death, then looking after the four Thomas kids while dealing with their drunken father (until he eventually dies), and finally caring for the three sets of Hammond twins and having to leave when their mother dies. When asked if the families were good to her, she responds, '(o)-o-o-h ... Oh, they meant to be – I know they meant to be just as good and kind as possible' (Ledoux, 26). As Anne recalls her horrible childhood past, Marilla detects 'the mute misery on [Anne's] face' (Ledoux, 28) and out of pity decides to adopt Anne early in the play. In the novel, by contrast, Marilla puts Anne through a trial period (which for Anne and the reader seems painfully long); the decision that Anne may stay at Green Gables is made only in chapter eight. In the play, Anne's childhood memory is more than expository information; the memories represent a pivotal moment because through them Anne wins Marilla's heart and secures her home at Green Gables.

A more subtle yet equally significant way in which the memory structure informs the content lies in the remembering of the story as a voice of popular or cultural resonance. Specifically, most people have an awareness of Anne through the various media versions available. In using the memory structure, therefore, Ledoux invites his audience to recall *their* memories of the well-known story.[11] Along with Rachel and Ruby, audience members piece the story together through both the play and their personal recollections. However, like most adaptations, Ledoux's reconstruction of the Anne story adds yet another reading, while the audience's past memories, preconceptions, and assumptions are challenged by the new version. The emphasis on memory through theme and structure creates a visually enticing play for youths while adding another layer to the popular imaginings of Anne.

Voices

By shortening his title to *Anne*, Ledoux signals that place (Green Gables) bears less importance in his version. The voice of nature and place embraced in the novel by Anne and the narrator through the numerous natural descriptions of Avonlea is practically absent in the stage play. To emphasize the struggles and concerns of youth, Ledoux heightens the concept of binary oppositions between the adolescents, especially between Anne and Josie. These tensions exist in the novel, but as Frank Davey suggests, the '[p]otential conflicts between good and evil, arrogance and modesty, cruelty and kindness are either dissolved by Montgomery into ambiguities ... or allowed to disappear from the novel' (169). The stage play, on the other hand, emphasizes the conflicts among the young people and, according to theatre critic Leanne Wild, the confrontation scenes between Josie Pye and Anne Shirley in the Young People's Theatre production 'were immensely well received' (172) and a high point for the audience.

The truism that drama cannot exist without conflict (Price, 8) operates fully in Ledoux's play, as good–evil, beauty–ugliness, inclusion–exclusion, to name a few opposites, are highlighted to heighten dramatic tension. The outline of dramatis personae in the published text (or theatre program) of *Anne* immediately draws our attention to conflict, for Josie Pye is described as 'jealous, catty, clever, mischievous and an all-round excellent foil for Anne,' and Gilbert Blythe is 'Anne's chief competitor' (2). Josie remains faithful to her character description in that she antagonizes Anne throughout the play by teasing her about her red hair, commenting on her bad temper, or parading her nicer clothes. She also tries to get Anne into trouble during the raspberry-cordial scene, in which Ledoux includes Josie as the catalyst for Diana's overindulgence. Josie knows what is inside the bottle, so, mischievously, encourages Diana to drink several glasses, leading to a drunken scenario with Anne as the instigator. Josie's jealousy and pettiness in trying to assert her superiority and interfering in matters between Anne and Gilbert highlight Anne's virtues and community spirit: 'I've made what I would once have called a heroic effort to like her, but Josie Pye just won't be liked. And I believe I've known that since the first day we ever met' (Ledoux, 65). Anne's ability to push the thistle (as Marilla refers to Josie) into a secondary role reflects her superiority of character. This protagonist–antagonist example operates throughout the play to create a dialectical model where one character, or one side of the argument, asserts its dominance over the other.

The dialectical model operating in *Anne* limits the subversive (or dialogic) voice identified in the novel by Mary Rubio and Sheckels; for, as the Russian literary theorist Mikhail Bakhtin cautions, dialectical relations, although often mistaken for dialogical ones, are fundamentally different from them (183).[12] In addition to emphasizing dialectical relationships between characters, Ledoux's play also highlights certain moral lessons from the novel, thereby generating a didactic, unified voice that once again downplays the dialogic tendencies. In act one, scene eleven, when Marilla believes that Anne has stolen her amethyst brooch, the scene presents the hint of a moral voice. Accused of being a thief and facing a severe punishment, Anne makes up a lie and claims to have lost the brooch in the water. When Matthew points to the brooch hanging on the shawl, clarifying the mystery, Marilla wants to know why Anne told such a tale:

> ANNE: But I could tell that you would never believe me. And why should you believe me? I'm just an orphan girl and nobody knows what I could do.
> MARILLA: Forgive me, Anne. You are right. I believed you were a thief because of what I have heard said of orphans, not because of what I knew to be true about you. (51)

Not to judge people because of their social position is an ethical principle reinforced by contemporary Canadian school curricula. Since Young People's Theatre relies almost solely on local schools for its audience, its plays reflect and respect some of the education system's demands. The French neoclassical mandate that the theatre should please but, just as importantly, *instruct* through *a unified world (or voice)* thus resonates with Ledoux's project.

The promotional packages advertised Ledoux's *Anne* as a child-centred version of the story with which contemporary youths can easily sympathize (Taylor, C3). A distinctive feature reflecting the promotional material concerns the list of characters in *Anne*, which includes five adolescents and three adults.[13] The adolescent characters not only outnumber their elders but also carry the majority of the text and focus in the adaptation. Practically all of the scenes centre on the childhood joys and struggles experienced by Anne and her schoolmates as they try to negotiate their identity and place within society. Consequently, the voice of tradition and Presbyterianism established by the adult community in Montgomery's novel is diminished. As a means to centre the action on the five adolescents, Ledoux includes several children's songs and rhymes at the beginning or end of most scenes.[14] Although not a musical in the traditional sense, the play includes numerous songs, highlighting the taunting games played by adolescents in schoolyards and foregrounding the world of Anne and her peers. With the focus on the adolescents, it is the pressure of fitting in among her peers rather than among the larger society of the novel that preoccupies Anne. Ledoux accentuates contemporary social pressures for youths through the infamous hair-dyeing episode and through Anne's desire for a puffed-sleeved dress. Wanting to fit in and be accepted still resonates with contemporary youths; ironically, instead of being horrified at having green hair or wearing different clothing, a significant percentage of today's young people find their place and acceptance through their uniqueness, which they may signal with green or purple hair.

In favouring the voices and issues of youths and reducing the adult ones, Ledoux's play significantly downplays some of the deeper undertones found in Montgomery's novel. 'The only character who goes through any sort of essential transformation is Marilla,' writes Margaret Atwood in 'Revisiting Anne' and continues: '*Anne of Green Gables* is not about Anne becoming a good little girl: it is about Marilla Cuthbert becoming a good – and more complete – woman' (225). In Ledoux's adaptation, in contrast, Marilla does not go through this transformation; 'she is soft and pliable from the start,' as Wild writes, and so we lose part of 'Marilla's struggle to demonstrate love' (171). Furthermore, with only three adult characters represented, many of Anne's female adult role models from the novel – Anne's beloved teacher, Miss Stacy, Diana's Aunt Josephine, and the Sunday-school teacher, Mrs Allan – do not appear. Ledoux's adaptation noticeably lessens the significance and depth of the relationships between Anne and the adult community, an effect that, combined with the downplaying of Marilla's metamorphosis, reduces an important element found in the novel.

The differences between 'oral modes of communication' (theatre) and 'literary modes of communication' (Fiske and Hartley, 105) (novels) are numerous, yet one of the vital distinctions between them, according to Fiske and Hartley, centres on the oral mode's use of the dramatic and the literary mode's use of the narrative. When adapting a novel to the medium of theatre, reshaping the narrative voice becomes a primary concern. Although the omnipresence of the narrative voice that describes Anne's relationship with others and her surroundings lends itself well to the medium of film, it poses significant challenges for a theatre adaptation because the narrative needs somehow to be transformed into the dramatic.

Rachel and Ruby embody some of the narrator's characteristics of a 'careful stage director' (Epperly, *Fragrance* 21) in their remembering of events; however, their voices reflect a third-person perspective that lacks the ability of the narrative voice to expose and paint some of Anne's inner feelings and motivations. Therefore, the narrative sections that Ledoux retains from Montgomery's novel need to be transposed into dramatic dialogue, or, more often, physicalized through the blocking and gestures of the actors during production. Another element that the narrative voice covers with ease but that presents a challenge to the playwright is setting. To avoid the disruption of too many set changes, Ledoux must alter and reduce the number of settings and come up with a few flexible locations to dramatize his scenes.

For example, Montgomery's narrator carefully describes distinct settings for the swearing of friendship between Anne and Diana (the Barry garden in chapter twelve) and the notorious slate-breaking episode between Anne and Gilbert (in the Avonlea School in chapter fifteen). Ledoux, on the other hand, in an effort to combine different settings and cover many events in a limited time, stages both these episodes (in act one, scene twelve) in the schoolyard:

ANNE: I think your Gilbert Blythe is handsome but I think he's very bold.
   It isn't good manners to wink at a strange girl.
   She looks at Gilbert. He winks. She looks away. He crosses to her.

GILBERT: Hi there.

He offers his hand and Anne is about to take it when he pulls her braids.

GILBERT: Carrots!

ANNE: You mean, hateful boy! How dare you!

Anne cracks her slate over Gilbert's head. (57–8)

To capture the beginning of the long-lasting rivalry between Anne and Gilbert, Ledoux reduces nearly three full pages of Montgomery's narration and dialogue (*AGG* 122–5) to the cited four-line dramatic scene. What brings meaning to these few lines occurs largely in production when the director and actors physicalize the scene, bringing the full atmosphere, tone, and setting to life through visual language. A sixthgrader from Fairbank Middle School provides a description of the events of this scene after seeing the Toronto production:

> The best scene in the play is the one where Anne hits Gilbert. She didn't like how he was acting so confident, so she tried not to look at him. You could see the tension oozing in her hands and body. At first, she tried to ignore him by talking with Diana. But he kept winking at her. Then, he went behind her back and pulled her hair. She screamed. Then he called her 'Carrots' and then Anne exploded. She hit him over the head with her slate. All the others were amazed she did that, especially Gilbert. Most of the audience laughed and cheered when that happened, because they liked that she stood up for herself and they also thought it was funny and surprising that Anne was so brave to do something like that.[15]

Individual audience members may receive the scene differently, and the actors' depiction will slightly alter in each performance, but for the most part the interpretation of the director, designers, and actors remains consistent in individual productions. Nevertheless, every new production of the play reshapes (and re-imagines) Anne's journey, which may closely resemble or substantially differ from Montgomery's original narrative descriptions.

The final voice Ledoux added to the play is that of the media. Two significant events in *Anne* arrive through the newspaper. First, Marilla and Matthew find out about Anne winning the Avery scholarship through reading the Charlottetown paper (Ledoux, 6), not through a personal letter from Anne (*AGG* 309). Secondly, and more dramatically, Matthew discovers that the Abbey Bank has gone bankrupt by reading the newspaper, a piece of news that causes his death, as the stage directions describe: 'He drops the paper and staggers towards the door. The music fails' (101).[16] The voice of the media, which pervades contemporary life with its attempt to construct social meaning, has become, according to Fiske, 'an agent of social control' (*Television Culture* 152). Information within Montgomery's world was largely transferred through personal exchanges, but the progress of media communications spills into Ledoux's version, partially paralleling the experience of today's tabloid-weary audience.

The societal and technological changes that have occurred since the publication of *Anne of Green Gables* in 1908 are numerous. It is no surprise, then, that Ledoux's adaptation, written ninety years later, alters aspects of the original story. By incorporating a non-linear structure, Ledoux appeals to the sensitivities of his youth audience and at the same time foregrounds both Anne's memories and the audience's cultural memories of the story. In shifting the control of the story away from Anne and Montgomery's narrator over to Rachel and Ruby, Ledoux's memory play places the majority of the events into a remembered past. This contrasts the dominant present of the novel, which provides perceptual distance and, in effect, creates a remembered journey rather than the vicarious one a reader enjoys.

The contemporary play is a looking-glass of sorts where the audience revisits and re-remembers the story from a new perspective. Furthermore, in transposing the novel to theatre, Ledoux, out of necessity, adapted and transformed certain voices to suit the new medium, and in doing so he added a new layer to the ongoing popular imaginings of Anne. By focusing on the adolescent world, he brings out the challenges faced by youths in the story. According to Wagner, the story's 'affirmative faith in the possibility of change' (C2) shone through in the Toronto production. Finally, a play script is only a blueprint; in performance, many layers are added through setting, blocking, and characterization. Hence, what appears to be lost on the page may very well be found on the stage.

Notes

1 Ruby Gillis speaks this line in both Montgomery's novel (240) and Ledoux's play (71).

2 The letter is addressed to a Mrs Aiken and dated 4 November 1939.

3 Elaine Campbell and Mavor Moore also wrote some of the lyrics for the musical version.

4 Born and raised in Halifax, Nova Scotia, the playwright Paul Ledoux now lives in Toronto. More than thirty of his stage plays have been produced in

Canada. His most successful plays are musicals, and they include *Love Is Strange* (1984) about singer Anne Murray; the Dora and Chalmers award-winning *Fire* (1989) about brothers Jerry Lee Lewis and Jimmy Swaggart; and *The Secret Garden* (1991), adapted from the Frances Hodgson Burnett novel. Ledoux has worked as an artistic director, dramaturge, director, and designer and has won numerous awards for his work in the theatre. The commission by Young People's Theatre to adapt *Anne of Green Gables* gave Ledoux the opportunity to reminisce about his summer holidays on Prince Edward Island when he was a youth.

5 Young People's Theatre, located in downtown Toronto, has been producing professional youth theatre since 1966. Its audience consists of primary to secondary students from Toronto. *Anne* was also professionally produced at the Neptune Theatre in Halifax (November 1999), the Grand Theatre in London, Ontario (November 1999), the Blyth Festival, in Blyth, Ontario (June 2000), Alberta Theatre Projects in Calgary (November 2000), Western Canada Theatre Company in Kamloops, B.C. (November 2000), Theatre One in Nanaimo, B.C. (December 2000), and Theatre New Brunswick (November 2001).

6 Here is a selection of a few Canadian plays written in recent decades that make use of the memory device: *The Occupation of Heather Rose* (Wendy Lill), *The Glace Bay Miners' Museum* (Wendy Lill), *Memories of You* (Wendy Lill), *Play Memory* (Johanna Glass), *Of the Fields, Lately* (David French), *Lilies* (Michael Marc Bouchard), *Albertine, in Five Times* (Michel Tremblay), *Doc* (Sharon Pollock), *The Hope Slide* (Joan MacLeod).

7 See Jeanette Malkin's *Memory-Theatre and Postmodern Drama* (1999) for a book-length discussion of the memory-play genre.

8 The memory play may very well have been influenced by the various modern theatre movements during the early part of the twentieth century, especially expressionism, symbolism, and Brecht's epic theatre, all of which in their own ways revolutionized the possibilities of dramatic form and structure. These movements challenged neoclassical, well-made, and melo-dramatic play structures and opened up new possibilities of presenting a dramatic story through their effective use of sound, visual effects, and *Verfremdungseffekt*.

9 Paul Ledoux, e-mail letter, December 2000.

10 In the same electronic-mail correspondence, Ledoux mentions that Young People's Theatre was interested in seeing a real Maritime feel in their commission of *Anne*, so he incorporated a level of story telling.

11 The story is familiar to most Canadian-born people, yet it is worth noting that new immigrants, of whom there are many in cities such as Toronto,

may very well be experiencing Anne's story for the first time when seeing the Ledoux adaptation.

12 If you consider thesis and antithesis, yielding a synthesis, the dialectical process results in a unified or dominant ideology. This differs from Bakhtin's notion of dialogism, which, he argues, consists of 'a plurality of fully valid voices [coexisting] within the limits of a single work' (34).

13 For budgetary reasons, few youth theatre companies can hire more than three or four actors for any given production, and in fact, the cast of eight in *Anne* is considered a luxury by today's standards.

14 The songs also act as segues or transitions to move from scene to scene or past to present.

15 Charles Reid, a teacher at Fairbank Middle School, who took his class to see *Anne* in April 1998, provided this quotation. He asked that the student who wrote the response remain anonymous.

16 The news of the bankruptcy appears to be the cause of Matthew's death in the novel, but the news in this case comes in a letter brought by his hired man from the post office (*AGG* 314–15).

Chapter 15

Snapshot: Listening to the Music in *Anne of Green Gables: The Musical*

CARRIE MacLELLAN

Anne of Green Gables, never change
We like you just this way.
Anne of Green Gables, sweet and strange,
Stay as you are today.

— *Anne of Green Gables: The Musical*[1]

My first ticket to *Anne of Green Gables: The Musical* was a birthday gift from my parents. I was twelve and took my best friend, Laura McNeill, to see the show in the Confederation Centre of the Arts in Charlottetown (which also houses some of Montgomery's original manuscripts). Anne Shirley (then played by Glynis Ranney) was fiery, intelligent, and exuberant as she sang and danced along with Marilla, Matthew, Diana, Gilbert, and the townspeople. I remember the big puffy dresses and the neatly tailored suits, and most of all the music coming from the pit. It was the first of many visits to the Confederation Centre to watch this musical. Several years later, I enrolled in the Music Department at the University of Prince Edward Island. How does the music represent the characters' development? And how does it affect the listener? These questions now began to interest me as subjects of study, all the more because there are as yet few scholarly studies of the music, although the musical's history is well known.

The musical was commissioned by the Charlottetown Festival in 1965 and was based on the 1956 CBC television version by Don Harron and Norman Campbell. Toronto composer Norman Campbell created the music and co-composed the lyrics with Elaine Campbell (his wife and partner), Don Harron (writer of the show), and Mavor Moore (the first director of the Confederation Centre). The musical was performed on the main stage of the Confederation Centre, a modern complex near the historical Provincehouse, the centre built in 1964 to commemorate the birthday of Canadian Confederation. It is fitting, then, that the Confederation Centre has become home to the longest-running musical in Canadian history, with performances still running today. It is performed during the summer season to audiences of tourists from across Canada, and from the United States, Japan, Australia, Britain, Germany, and numerous other countries. No doubt one of its attractions is that the tunes transcend linguistic barriers, connecting Montgomery's novel musically with listeners from a myriad of cultures. This essay, then, is an invitation to listen closely to the songs and the music in *Anne of Green Gables: The Musical*.

As children, teens, and adults settle into their seats for the Sunday matinee show, they already know the story of Anne. The musical opens like a memory play, a strategy discussed earlier by George Belliveau, with the 'Anne of Green Gables' theme song sung off-stage by the full company and proclaiming that Anne is already a legend, a figure known to the townspeople and to the audience. The action begins when the theme song is interrupted by 'Great Workers for the Cause,' sung by Mrs Rachel Lynde and the townswomen, and presenting the Avonlea women in their charity drive. There is a marchlike effect to the music as the snare drum rolls, leaving an image of the community women marching through the clay roads of Avonlea on a militant campaign for donations to the sick and the poor. The music proclaims them powerful women on a mission. Immediately following 'Great Workers' comes 'Where Is Matthew Going?,' showing the townspeople busying themselves in Matthew Cuthbert's affairs in a relentless, almost irritating, driving manner reflected in the melody: Avonlea is a panoptic universe with the community's all-seeing eye overseeing all. It is unusual for Matthew to be out and about in his good suit, sing the townspeople, and with the forward-urging music, they persist in asking again: 'Where is Matthew going and why is he going there?' Throughout the show, the music suggests the enormous community pressures in Avonlea, encoding social satire.

Also in act one, 'The Facts' represents the prodding, nosey, small-town folk, as the Avonlea women – Mrs Spencer, Mrs Blewett, and Marilla – interview Anne Shirley about her history. The music plays second string to the lyrics here: Anne's story of her past. In a breathtaking musical joyride, she proceeds to create a story of being 'abducted by gypsies' and many similar picaresque adventures, thus revealing her story-telling abilities. The orchestration follows Anne's lead, musically enacting the adventures she dramatizes. There is a celebration with gypsy music and Danube waltzes with Anne dancing along. The music then returns to the townspeople's driving marchlike pattern, as they mechanically repeat, 'The facts, the facts, the facts ... the plain, simple, homely, unembroidered facts,' with Anne's playful dance poking fun at the townspeople's language of fact. In 'Did You Hear' (sung by Josie Pye and the townspeople), the town's gossiping rumour mill ('In the schoolroom split his head? I think Gilbert's good as dead') wildly inflates Anne's crimes and satirically reveals the small-town community's prejudices towards the outsider: 'She's a vixen. / She's a hussy! / She's a terror! / She's a tartar! / We don't want her kind in Avonlea!'

Although Marilla and Matthew Cuthbert are part of the townspeople ensemble, they are often featured as soloists and undergo significant transformations in the course of the musical, as we shall see. This transformation begins early in act one in a powerfully moving trio entitled 'We Clearly Requested a Boy,' sung by Anne, Marilla, and Matthew. This heart-wrenching ballad is my personal favourite. It explores the feeling of each character at the point not long after Anne has arrived. Marilla objects to keeping the orphan girl, as they had requested a boy to help Matthew with the farm chores and have no use for a girl around the house. Meanwhile, Matthew, who has already fallen in love with Anne's spirit, finds ways to justify the reasons why Anne should stay. This song works with overlapping lyrics, its musical structure suggesting the bond that these three characters share. Matthew is outdoors, Marilla at the kitchen table, and Anne upstairs – all three characters singing together. Marilla begins by singing, 'We clearly requested a boy.' And as she sings the words 'a boy,' Matthew joins in to continue the phrase: 'A boy's what we wanted, I guess.' As Matthew sings, 'I guess,' Anne overlaps with her line: 'I guess that a girl's not so bad.' This musical-continuation technique creates one of the most moving moments in the show, as Anne is about to be welcomed into the family.

What stands out in the literature must also stand out in the musical. Composed much like an operatic recitative aria, Anne's 'Apology' proclaims the drama of the conflict between Anne and Mrs Rachel Lynde following Anne's tempestuous outbreak after Mrs Lynde mocks Anne's red hair. In a recitative, the performer generally recites lyrics by chanting quickly on a given pitch and often accompanied by strings or by a harpsichord playing tremolos. In opera, a recitative helps execute thick passages of text quickly and effectively, the aria allowing the performer to 'show off' her singing in a dramatic, lyrical way. Being the 'drama queen' she is, Anne must execute this song with much breathtaking musical strength as she performs her extraordinary mock apology to Mrs Lynde. Anne's mock humbleness (she kneels to beg Mrs Lynde's forgiveness) is contradicted by the grandiose theatricality of her music and drama, the music thus supporting Anne's inadvertent mocking of the self-righteous Mrs Lynde.

Most often in musicals, the overture is the showpiece for the orchestra, but in the *Anne* musical, this honour is taken by 'Back to School,' one of the dance passages in the show for the school children. The piece opens with the popular schoolyard call in the wind instruments: 'na nana nana!' And the school returns as an important setting in act two. With the new schoolteacher, Miss Stacy, a breath of fresh air enters the Avonlea community. Musically, the school song 'Open the Window,' sung by Miss Stacy and the pupils, differs from the rest of the show's songs, just as Miss Stacy differs from the rest of the ordinary citizens of Avonlea. 'Open the Window' reflects her classroom innovations in a new jazzy style and swing beat. 'Open the window,' she sings; 'Open the Window,' the school kids echo. The jazz section uses the brass players of the Charlottetown Festival Orchestra to their fullest ability. These sounds evoke the image of a big city with bright lights far from Avonlea. Clearly, Miss Stacy represents the style and ways of someone 'from away.'

Earlier in *Making Avonlea*, Eleanor Hersey, K.L. Poe, and Ann Howey have documented the importance of motifs of friendship and romance that involve Anne Shirley with Diana Barry and Gilbert Blythe, respectively, in the novel and in the Sullivan film productions. This is not the case in the musical, however. Anne's relationships with the two, as conveyed by the musical scores assigned to them when these characters are together on stage, are less important than other themes. Gilbert's 'Wond'rin' in act one is a romantic ballad with flowing movement and grand dynamics. It imbues the relationship between Gilbert and Anne with a light-hearted and carefree atmosphere. Sung by Anne and Diana in act two, 'Kindred Spirits' has a waltzlike sway, leaving a picture of Anne and Diana prancing in a field of flowers, without a care in the world. 'Wond'rin' and 'Kindred Spirits' are both musically eclipsed by the more powerful scores exploring Anne's relationship with her new family at Green Gables.

The musical's core, then, is really about Anne's intensifying relations with Matthew and Marilla. As they develop with the story, so does the musical style representing them. For Marilla, the music changes from marchlike to the sensitive, hesitant reprise of 'The Words' towards the end of the musical. Matthew, on the other hand, is transformed from a stuttering, clumsy, insecure man in 'General Store' to the sensitive, reflective man in the final words of the theme song, 'Anne of Green Gables.' Two songs, 'The Words' and 'General Store' (both in act two) musically highlight Matthew's awkward but gentle personality: a man who wins our hearts because he is in tune with Anne's desire for puffed sleeves, where the pragmatic Marilla is not. In the song 'General Store,' Matthew intends to get a dress with puffed sleeves for Anne. The song adds much humour to the show, as the storekeeper, Lucilla, attempts over and over again to find out what it is that Matthew is looking for, for Matthew is lacking the words to make the request. She offers him everything from potatoes to pitchforks, and as the music comes to a screeching halt, all Matthew Cuthbert can say, in his shy, uncertain, awkward manner, is 'pp- ... puff ... pp-pp.' Finally, when the request is made, the music drives on in hurried, hasty fashion, representing the townspeople as they are 'scurrying about.'

'The words! The words! The words! / Why won't they come when I want them,' sings Matthew in act two, confessing to the audience his inability to communicate his love to Anne. Even as he professes his lack of words and social skills, the audience realizes how much he has grown from a lonely hermit into a sensitive social being who challenges himself to reach out to Anne. It is the beginning of the musical's emotionally most powerful developments, culminating in the scene towards the end of act two that will leave the audience in tears: the moment of Matthew's death. In the final moments of his life, he expresses his feelings for Anne in the lyrics and music of the theme song: 'Anne of Green Gables, never change.' The pathos of the elegy ('friends / must part,' Matthew sings) is intensified by the audience's realization of how much Matthew has been transformed by allowing Anne to be herself and by proclaiming himself a Kindred Spirit ('in my heart, / you are forever young,' he tells her). Matthew's rendition of the theme song is one of the few pieces to overpower 'We Clearly Requested a Boy.' What he could not put into words before (in the original exposition of 'The Words') now comes out easily in the legacy of love he leaves for Anne.

Matthew's death is followed by Marilla's reprise of what is originally Matthew's exposition of 'The Words.' Marilla's rendition of 'The Words' expresses how she cannot find the words to express her love for her brother Matthew, even after his death. This is a sensitive moment for the usually strong and stern Marilla. The music highlights this newfound sensitivity in her character: the tune in the strings is played with a hesitant tremolo, adding to the sadness and distress of this moment and suggesting that Marilla, too, has changed. Although she cannot put her feelings into words, she does realize her love for her brother and thus rediscovers her capacity for love. 'The only character who goes through any sort of essential transformation is Marilla,' writes Margaret Atwood about the novel, an interpretation that may well be influenced by her experience of watching the musical, a visit she vividly describes in her essay's opening. '*Anne of Green Gables* is not about Anne becoming a good little girl: it is about Marilla Cuthbert becoming a good – and more complete – woman' (225). That is precisely the musical message conveyed by *Anne of Green Gables: The Musical*.

The musical ends with a duet sung by Anne and Gilbert, whose resolution of their friendship suggests a blossoming relationship in the future. Musically, however, the duet is much less powerful than the emotionally charged songs of Matthew's death and Marilla's song for him,[2] suggesting a subversion of the conventional neatness of musical endings. In a lecture at the Confederation Centre in the summer of 1999, Elaine and Norman Campbell explained that the musical's popularity has endured because its message is 'love, decency, and perspicacity.' The musical has taken that message from Charlottetown to New York, through forty Japanese cities, and to London, England, where the musical was voted best new musical of 1969 by London critics. By 1999, there were twenty non-professional companies in Canada performing the musical in one year alone, as the Campbells explained. The success of the Anne musical has paved the way for other musical adaptations: *The Blue Castle*, which runs as summer theatre on Prince Edward Island; and *Emily of New Moon* (book by Richard Ozounian, music by Marek Norman), which premiered on the Main Stage of the Confederation Centre of the Arts in 1999. While *Emily* was discontinued after two seasons, Anne has finished thirty-six years and keeps going. Anne has moved on into the twenty-first century and, like its heroine, the musical has stayed 'forever young.'

Notes

I am grateful to Irene Gammel for encouraging my research and for generously providing editorial help throughout this project. This paper would not have been possible without her support.

1 All quotations in this essay are from the Norman Campbell *Anne of Green Gables Song Album* (1969) or are transcribed from the Charlottetown Festival Production, *Anne of Green Gables.* Perf. Susan Cuthbert, Elizabeth Mawson, and Peter Mews. Cond. Fen Watkin. Charlottetown Festival Orchestra. ATTIC, ACD 1225 (1984).
2 I am indebted for this point to Charlene Morton and Andrew Zinck, who presented a guest lecture, 'L.M. Montgomery,' in English 333 at the University of Prince Edward Island, in Fall 2000.

Part III

Touring Avonlea:
Landscape, Tourism, and Spin-off Products

Chapter 16

Towards a Theory of the Popular Landscape in *Anne of Green Gables*

JANICE FIAMENGO

'[J]ust as soon as I saw it I felt it was home' (*AGG* 28). With this state-ment, Anne Shirley declares her inalienable sense of belonging to Green Gables. The logic behind Anne's declaration is central to the novel: an imaginative little girl gains the right to claim a home on the strength of her longing; in the absence of right of occupancy, family connection, or economic power, the force of her love makes it hers. Shortly after the novel's publication, as if following Anne's lead, tourists began descending upon Cavendish, seeking the home that had become theirs through a parallel act of imaginative possession. Montgomery had '[taken] the reading public by storm' (Marquis, 564) – in part, by offer-ing readers a powerful myth about the possibility of belonging to the land – and this myth continues to inform her popular reception.

Part two of *Making Avonlea* focused on film and stage adaptations. Part three focuses on the proliferation of non-literary artifacts con-nected to Montgomery's novels: the tourist trips and profusion of dolls and souvenirs that have spawned a massive Montgomery industry, powered the P.E.I. economy, and fuelled bitter and protracted copy-right battles. This chapter begins these investigations by considering that *Anne of Green Gables* was popular from its first publication, going into second and third printings and attracting fans to Lovers' Lane within a year of publication (see figure 6.1). Popular culture is not something that sprang up after Montgomery's death; rather, it was the culture she negotiated from the time of her first glowing reviews and skyrocketing sales.[1] This chapter considers Montgomery's creation of a popular landscape in its historical context to account for some of its manifestations in contemporary film and merchandise.

In *National Dreams*, Daniel Francis describes his understanding of the development of national myths, many of which – including the benevolent RCMP, the heroic railway builders, and the spiritual North – were embraced by Canadians because 'they seemed to express something that we wanted to believe about ourselves' (9). Francis's understanding of the role of myth in nation building offers a starting point for understanding *Anne* as popular culture. Because his focus is myths of history, Francis does not include Avonlea in his book, but it is not an exaggeration to see Avonlea as another of the foundations of Canadian identity. What differentiates Anne as a cultural icon from the myths Francis discusses is that, unlike the RCMP, the railway, or the imperial connection, Anne's reputation remains relatively unsullied while other Canadian institutions have been unmasked to reveal, in Francis's words, a 'sorry stew of smug, racist propaganda' (70). It may be too simplistic to suggest that *Anne* is popular not for the subversion and critique that critics have recently explored but because Anne's story 'express[es] something that we wanted [and still want] to believe about ourselves' (Francis, 9); nevertheless, I will argue that *Anne*'s popularity tells us something about our contradictory desires for an authentic connection to the land.

Transforming the Real

Many writers refer to Montgomery's nature description as an obvious explanation for her popular appeal. In 'The Uses of Setting,' Marilyn Solt stresses that Montgomery's realization of place is one source of the novel's enduring popularity; but Solt is primarily interested in setting as it illuminates character and point of view rather than as a subject in its own right (57–63). Perry Nodelman notes that *Anne*, like other popular girls' fiction of the time, is set in a 'pleasant rural location' offering 'the pleasures of nature without its wild savagery' (33), but his focus is on the promise of permanent childhood endorsed by the novel. More recently, Irene Gammel has theorized Montgomery's landscapes as 'erotic spaces' ('"My Secret Garden"' 41) where girl–girl and autoerotic pleasures can be indulged (see also Gammel's chapter 8 in this collection). Gammel's perceptive readings suggest that landscape in Montgomery is much more than a pretty and vivid rendering of the real, and Gammel's discussion can be extended by considering some of its other symbolic dimensions. In *Reading the Popular*, John Fiske argues that popular texts 'need to be understood not for and by themselves but in their interrelationships with other texts and with social life, for that is how their circulation is ensured' (4). To begin to theorize the popular landscape as Fiske suggests, I consider Montgomery's representation of landscape in *Anne of Green Gables* alongside the following related texts and aspects of social life: Montgomery's own comments on the significance of place in her fiction; the popular tourist literature of Montgomery's day; and the political significance of love of land at the turn of the last century.

The truism about Montgomery's nature description is that it has immortalized Prince Edward Island. On one level, there is no arguing with this statement. However, its implication that Montgomery's reputation rests on her detailed and authentic rendering of her beloved island deserves analysis. Whether or not Montgomery's descriptions represent Prince Edward Island faithfully, geographical fidelity seems to have little to do with her popularity. In chapter 19, Jeanette Lynes notes that her Seattle students are generally uninterested in the actual place of Prince Edward Island; in her Canadian studies class, a number of students did not know where *Anne of Green Gables* was set, leading Lynes to conclude that '[t]he regional signified (P.E.I.) as a referent seemed to be of minimal importance to them.' Tourists flock to Cavendish and Charlottetown to buy Anne memorabilia, but they are happy to purchase it from shops in Banff and Niagara Falls as well; region matters less than one might think in Montgomery's representation of P.E.I. magic.

Montgomery herself has a good deal to say about the transformation of a real setting into fiction; her journals reveal that she consciously used Cavendish scenes in complex, non-mimetic ways. Reflecting on the writing of *Anne*, she notes that 'Cavendish scenery supplied the background and *Lover's Lane* figures very prominently' (*SJ* 1: 331). Although the word 'figures' might invite poststructuralist comment on the inescapable metaphoricity of language, the statement suggests a relatively smooth passage from physical to textual landscape. But matters are complicated by Montgomery's reflection that many of her 'childhood experiences and dreams were worked up into its chapters' (*SJ* 1: 331). If the temporal setting for the novel is Montgomery's childhood, then the recorded scenery is not that of present reality but of a remembered past, coloured by recollection. As Cavendish becomes Avonlea, it is subject to the ambiguities of memory.

Further comments by Montgomery emphasize imaginative reworking. Noting a favourable review of the novel's 'happiness and optimism,' Montgomery remembers her sadness while writing the book and is thankful to 'keep the shadows of my life out of my work. I would not wish to darken any other life – I want instead to be a messenger of optimism and sunshine' (*SJ* 1: 339). In transposing the review's 'happiness and optimism' into 'optimism and sunshine,' she substitutes a metaphor for the abstract noun, suggesting her tendency to find natural correlatives for human emotions. *Anne* is indeed a sunny book on both levels, and readers have noted Montgomery's preference for spring and summer scenes over winter ones, despite her affection for sparkling snow. These few references make it clear that while Cavendish scenes may have provided the impetus for Montgomery's fiction, such scenes were always deliberately crafted and creatively transformed.

The frequency with which Montgomery returns to the question of realism in her journals indicates her awareness of its complexity. On 27 January 1911, she admits to having 'used real places and speeches freely' (*SJ* 2: 38). Again, both meanings of the word 'freely' seem to apply here, in that she not only borrowed landscapes at will but also created them anew to suit her purposes, never consistently 'confin[ing] [herself] to facts' (*SJ* 2: 39). '*Lover's Lane* was of course *my* Lover's Lane' she writes (*SJ* 2: 42), the stress on the possessive pronoun suggesting at once her special affinity for its beauty and her imaginative licence to create it anew in narrative. And while the beauty of the landscape in and of itself is always important to her, what she most values is its profound effect on her thoughts and spirits, its ability to 'thrill a chord in [her] spirit' (*SJ* 3: 110). As I will demonstrate, Montgomery's emphasis on the ecstatic response of the sympathetic viewer meant that Avonlea, unlike Cavendish, became a portable landscape, one whose enchanting details could be adapted to many regions of the world, including Japan (see chapter 21).

Landscape and Tourism

Montgomery was likely aware, even before the publication of *Anne of Green Gables* in 1908, of the complex interconnections between popular literary texts and their imputed settings. In the nineteenth century, tourists flocked to the Acadian coast of Nova Scotia so romantically presented in Henry Wadsworth Longfellow's *Evangeline* (1847). The Windsor and Annapolis Railway capitalized on the literary connection as a promotional strategy, referring to the 'Land of Evangeline' in route brochures. As D.M.R. Bentley has demonstrated, a tourist boom to Canada by wealthy Americans in the late nineteenth century encouraged a number of Canadian poets to attempt to benefit from the lure of locale; Charles G.D. Roberts and William Wilfred Campbell linked poetry with tourist writing in order to reach American audiences.[2] As someone who had travelled by train during the height of the railway's promotional campaigns, Montgomery would probably have been familiar with the alliance between literature and tourism. She was quick to note that her fictional representation had changed the meaning of Cavendish. Writing in her journal about tourist interest in her home, Montgomery appears to take satisfaction in having brought fame to Lovers' Lane, commenting that, as a result of her representation, 'the name of this little remote woodland lane is known all over the world. Visitors to Cavendish ask for it and seek it out' (*SJ* 1: 357). The pilgrimage to *Anne* places had begun, and Montgomery recognized herself as its agent.

Clarence Karr has stated that '[c]oncepts of the idyllic "Garden Province" featured in tourist promotion for modern Prince Edward Island originate, to a significant degree, with Lucy Maud Montgomery and her fiction' (128). While it is undoubtedly the case that Montgomery influenced tourist literature, the reverse is also true: Montgomery's depiction of Prince Edward Island has much in common with – and may have been influenced by – tourist literature in print at the time of the writing of *Anne*. The most popular was a series of volumes edited by George Monro Grant, Canada's premier man of letters and moral nationalist, whose name alone would have guaranteed a measure of popular interest. Published in 1899, the last of the series was titled *The Easternmost Ridge of the Continent: Historical and Descriptive Sketches of the Scenery and Life in New Brunswick, Nova Scotia, Prince Edward Island, and along the Lower St. Lawrence and Saguenay.* Published in the United States, the book was lavishly illustrated with wood engravings by some of Canada's best-known artists, including the Romantic painter Lucius O'Brien, president of the Ontario Society of Artists. The Rev. R[obert] Murray, a close friend of Grant's and pastor in the Free Church of Nova Scotia, wrote the chapter on Prince Edward Island, enumerating the island's natural splendours and recommending that visitors see it in summertime to enjoy its peak of beauty. Even a superficial reading of Murray's descriptions reveals the striking parallels between his representation, designed to attract American tourists, and Montgomery's. The following is an early paragraph in the chapter:

The face of the country is gently undulating, like a sea which has sobbed itself to rest, but has some remembrance still of a far-off storm. These low-lying hills which rib the country from north to south are but the slumbering waves of that quiet sea. Everywhere you are near the salt water and can enjoy its bracing breath from straight or long-armed creek or cove, or from the great Gulf itself. Though the country is level and fertile, and free from any too obtrusive hills, it abounds in springs and streams of the purest water. Where a bubbling fountain is not near at hand, a well is sure to bring up water without the need of digging many feet from the surface. Not Ireland itself is clad in richer green than our lovely Island when summer has bestowed upon it its crown of glory. The reddish soil cropping out here and there throws into sweeter relief the tender green of meadow and lawn and rich fields which, at the right time, will wave with golden grain. In the six weeks from the middle of June till the end of July it is a paradise of verdure, bloom, foliage; no stunted growth; no blight or mildew to break the toiling farmer's heart. (Grant, 128)

As Montgomery would do a few years later in *Anne of Green Gables*, Murray personifies the landscape, describing 'the face of the country' in feminized terms. He emphasizes the picturesque qualities of Island scenes, highlighting balanced contrasts, undulating hills, and pleasing brooks while approving the absence of any 'too obtrusive hills.' The idealizing and romantic tenor of the description is evident in language emphasizing both rest (gently, rest, slumbering, quiet, sweeter, tender) and also vitality and ethereal enchantment (bracing, abounds, bubbling, lovely, crown of glory, wave, green, golden, paradise of verdure): Prince Edward Island is designed for human pleasure, both because it is adaptable to cultivation and because it encourages a restorative, aesthetic response. Stressing harmony of detail and an 'ideal of pastoral peace and seclusion' (139), the passage exemplifies the transformation of physical space into an imaginative geography. While the passage is obviously meant to persuade readers to visit Prince Edward Island, the effect of its description is also, paradoxically, to smooth over particularities of region in order to emphasize the tranquil pleasures of a popular vacation spot. In promoting the province as a tourist destination, Murray was concerned not with its particularities but rather with its generic identity as a pastoral garden island.

Montgomery employs very similar imagery in descriptions of the Island. In July 1904, she declares Cavendish 'one of the prettiest spots on earth' and lists its features: 'Everything is so green and fresh, the ripe but not over-ripe luxuriance of midsummer without as yet a hint of decay. And beyond the green fields and slopes was the blue girdle of the gulf, forever moaning on its shining shore' (*SJ* 1: 296). This passage is paralleled by the passage in *Anne* when we learn that from her bedroom window Anne can see 'away down over green, low-sloping fields ... a sparkling blue glimpse of sea' (*AGG* 39). In the journal entry's emphasis on greenness and freshness, on the perfection of the season, on the attractiveness of green hills sloping down to blue sea, and on the gentle melancholy of the sea's 'moan,' the passage personifies the landscape to suggest a harmonious beauty that freshens and calms the spirit. Montgomery's tendency to idealize her garden isle suggests that she wrote with an eye to American audiences, careful that an over-reliance on a particular locale did not prevent distant readers from identifying with her setting. My point here is not that *Anne* is merely tourist literature, but rather that a shared discourse of revitalization and repose contributes to the popular appeal of both kinds of writing.

That Montgomery's landscape description is highly portable is proved by her descriptions of Ontario, which reveal the same interests, emotional responses, and habits of language familiar from the *Anne* books. From first to last, Montgomery's primary focus is the magical spell exerted by nature. Speaking of her Cavendish front orchard in the winter of 1905, she notes that 'the very trees are coated with snow until it is like some fairy court of marble seen in a splendid dream' (*SJ* 1: 303). Years later, travelling through the Muskoka country in July of 1922, now a married mother of two, Montgomery still finds herself carried away by a sense of magic as '[t]he continuous panorama of lake and river and island made [her] think of Stevenson's lines: Where all the ways on every hand / Lead onwards into fairyland' (*SJ* 3: 63). In January 1923, Montgomery stresses her special relationship with the world at dusk, reporting 'a dear bit of a walk all by myself tonight – in a soft white twilight under a young moon. The night was all my own and it was very kind to me. I bowed me down to my ancient gods' (*SJ* 3: 109). A few weeks later, Montgomery again finds in the beauty of the woods the solace and sustenance that her troubled domestic life and constrained social position could not afford her. On a dreary evening of visiting with Ewan, she has a moment of transcendence:

When we started I felt dreadfully depressed and down-hearted. But as we drove on through the woods my spirits rose. It was a strange weird night – cloudy but with a moon behind the clouds – snowing softly and wetly but quite calm. We drove through woods and swamps where the trees were covered with white and looked like great ranks of spectres standing in sorrowful enchantment. There was something in the eerie beauty of the landscape that thrilled a chord in my spirit and my being responded to the music. So that, in spite of Ewan's gloomy silence and the monotonous evening with a family so dull that they make others dull sandwiched between our drives, I felt oddly happy and delighted, with a secret inner happiness and delight – as of a 'fountain sealed' somewhere deep in my soul where no drop of poison from the outward universe could distil. (*SJ* 3: 110)

In emphasizing how the 'strange weird[ness]' of the night draws her out of herself and grants 'a secret inner happiness,' this passage picks up on themes of enchantment and communion developed in the fiction. The parallels here with passages from *Anne* suggest that Montgomery was far less interested in capturing the distinctiveness of Prince Edward Island than in conveying joyful affinity with the natural world. As Epperly notes, '[w]hat characterizes all the descriptions is their humanness, their invitation to participate in a kind of communion' (28). Distilling Romantic thought in an accessible language, Montgomery created a transregional magic.

Belonging to the Land

I suggested earlier that *Anne*'s enduring popularity was owing not to its subversive appeal but to the comforting myth of belonging offered in its pages: *Anne* promises that one can name a place into one's possession. But perhaps Anne's confident belonging ('[I]t's a million times nicer to be Anne of Green Gables than Anne of nowhere in particular, isn't it?' [*AGG* 69], she asks herself in front of the mirror) *is* linked to subversion: one of the key images from the novel is the pleasurable spectacle of a little orphan girl, ugly, unwanted, and destitute, boldly asserting her imaginative connection with and linguistic command of her environment. Faced with the prospect of spending a night alone at Bright Water train station, she thinks how 'lovely' it would be 'to sleep in a wild cherry-tree all white with bloom in the moonshine' (19). In her first weeks at Green Gables, this 'outspoken morsel of neglected humanity' (93) finds in trees, flowers, and streams a substitute family claimed in the absence of parents or other blood relatives. She names the landscape into her power, lovingly but authoritatively, launching a direct and ongoing challenge to the powers of Avonlea, for whom the material world is defined by its use-value, a thing to be made productive rather than loved, as is evident in Rachel Lynde's sour reflection that '[t]rees aren't much company' (*AGG* 9). For Montgomery, who had always chafed under her helplessness to save the trees she loved from her Uncle John Macneill's axe, Anne's statement of ownership is ambiguously defiant; it cannot affect the material conditions of the little girl's existence, but it is a powerful symbol of resistance none the less.

In the passage from popular novel to popular consumer merchandise, love of place has become ever more abstract, thoroughly detached from the specific region of Prince Edward Island; *Anne* becomes, as Lynes points out, 'a floating signifier' of simple connectedness and rural pleasures. The vast majority of *Anne* stationery, plates, giftwrap, mousepads, postcards, books, woodcuts, jigsaw puzzles, lollipops, watercolours, clocks, wallhangings, birdhouses, and plaques depict the Green Gables house, disconnected from its particular environment and signifying an intense love of home not dependent on region or nation. Many of the products licensed by the Anne of Green Gables Licensing Authority are designed to evoke the special relationship to nature depicted in *Anne*: wildflower seed packages, natural organic potting soil, and a leaf and flower press are connected to *Anne* only implicitly, signifying the reverence for gardens associated with a novel in which all of nature seems an enchanted park. The portability of this relationship to nature is revealed by the existence of *Anne* imagery in a location such as Robertsonville, Quebec, where one can purchase maple syrup products carrying a licensed *Anne* image.

The appeal of Avonlea as a cultural myth is based not only on its evocation of a portable landscape but also on its delineation of a portable past time when authentic relationships with the land were possible. As Aspasia Kotsopoulos has argued, Avonlea exists as a malleable 'before' time whose meanings can be interpreted by individual readers, creating "a nostalgic, sanitized vision of pastness' (101) that makes the novel particularly suited to adaptations within popular culture. Lynes makes a related argument in this volume, explaining that the commodification of Avonlea into consumer merchandise exploits a feminized version of the past as a time of family and community values. For modern consumers frightened by the horrors of climate change, ozone depletion, deforestation, and mass extinctions of species, the illusion of authentic relationship is powerful indeed.

Another kind of nostalgia in *Anne of Green Gables* just as central to its appeal is the longing for a prelapsarian world of perfect concord between language and nature, what Susan Stewart calls 'a genesis where lived and mediated experience are one' (23). In the opening scene of Anne and Matthew driving through the Avenue, we appreciate Anne not only because she recognizes the beauty of the landscape, but because she claims authority to capture its beauty in language. 'When I don't like the name of a place or a person I always imagine a new one and always think of them so' (26), she declares, with the buoyant assertiveness of the poet. The right name 'gives [her] a thrill' (27) because of the perfect match between the phrase and its referent. She never fears for a moment that language will fail her or that her conception will not do justice to the perfect beauty surrounding her; neither does reality fail her conception, for Anne finds in the White Way of Delight a place so perfect it could not be improved upon by imagination. Other critics have noted her Adamic qualities, the way her language makes things happen; but most striking is the perfect fidelity between Anne's conception and the thing itself. Through Anne, readers take delight in the harmony between language and world even as we recognize it as an illusion. The double impulse in this nostalgia – the longing for what we know to be unattainable – gives *Anne* its special sweetness and appeal.

The Politics of the Popular Landscape

According to Clarence Karr, national affiliation has not had a major impact on readers and fans of *Anne*. Reviews outside of Canada frequently failed to distinguish the novel as Canadian; South African, Australian, and Swedish readers have often understood the novel within a general North American context. Yet for Canadian readers, as Owen Edwards and Jennifer H. Litster point out, the national setting is emphasized by Marilla's desire to adopt a 'born Canadian' orphan (*AGG* 12). Therefore, it is tempting to speculate about the political importance for Canadian readers of Anne's determination to assert imaginative ownership of the land. At the turn of the century, Canadian political and cultural commentators debated the question of Canada's national and political existence. Literary critics stressed the need for a national literature to enable Canadians to imaginatively possess their homeland. As Carole Gerson demonstrates, they were 'acutely aware of the power of creative literature to valorize a place'

(36) and worried that Canada did not provide settings with suitably rich associations. Immigrant writers were distressed at the poverty of the language to describe Canadian places, which were too often designated by prosaic names such as *'Nine mile'* or *'Salmon River'* (quoted in Gerson, 38). In such a context, Anne's insistence on romantic names implicitly celebrates Canada as a place worthy of poetic language.

Canadian texts of the nineteenth century (Montgomery herself read Susanna Moodie's *Roughing It* [1852] and marvelled at Moodie's heroic struggles against homesickness and difficult terrain) tended to record the disjunction between settler expectations and the reality of Canada's vast and unyielding landscape. Montgomery's *Anne*, by contrast, asserts the effortlessness and harmony of the English and Scots integration into their new land. As Susan Glickman points out, representations of landscape are always political in settler societies where different cultures and histories come into conflict: landscape description always presents a kind of land claim, a statement of title (23). On returning to Prince Edward Island for a long-overdue visit, Montgomery wrote in her journal: 'I *belong* here. It is mine – I am its own' (*SJ* 3: 136). Her story of an outsider who comes to a place and makes it hers purely through her love and the power of her language must have resonated strongly with many Canadian readers in the early years of the twentieth century.

It might seem far-fetched to argue that *Anne* played a political role in defining Canada, and one must be cautious not to carry the argument too far. Yet Adrienne Clarkson surely speaks for many in her claim that Montgomery 'gave [her] a profound understanding of what Canada is' (ix). When I was a child growing up in Vancouver, my lasting impression of *Anne* was its ability to make Prince Edward Island – and Canada, by extension – seem a familiar and *familial* place, with trees and hills as beloved as blood relations. Prompting me to identify myself as Janice of Emerald Firs, *Anne* convinced me of the connection between Romantic imagery and poetic ownership of place. I never imagined that English-Canadian belonging and ownership were predicated on the dispossession and erasure of Aboriginal (and, in Montgomery's case, French) inhabitants of Canadian territory, but at some level *Anne of Green Gables* is about entering a territory that is not your own and taking possession of it, to paraphrase Edward Said in *Culture and Imperialism* (7). Like the mapmakers before her, Anne is discoverer, explorer, and namer, the one who becomes 'acquainted with every tree and shrub about the place' (*AGG* 70) in order to contain each one through her exuberantly imperialist language. That her possession of Avonlea is innocent and bloodless is precisely the point: don't we all long for such innocent power? By extension, Avonlea commodities and Anne memorabilia allow consumers to participate in this myth by purchasing artifacts of that innocent power.

Anne's intense love for the trees, brooks, and valleys around Green Gables – her certainty that she could name them into relationship with her, depicts the possibility of knowing a place through creative naming and loving cultivation. In suggesting that Prince Edward Island needs only to be sympathetically tended rather than arduously possessed, *Anne* might be said to assure settlers of their right to the soul of the land; certainly, the novel and its consumer images have helped to propagate the widely held notion of the Canadian as someone 'who lives with nature and is considerate of others' (201), which is how Yoshiko Akamatsu describes Japanese understandings of *Anne*'s message. We know now that this notion has covered over Canada's violent colonial past and contributed to what a number of postcolonial critics have termed a 'historical amnesia' (Boire, 3) about the relationship between Anglo-Celtic settler society and earlier Native and French inhabitants. Following from such erasure, Montgomery's Prince Edward Island is uncontested territory: there is no mention of a history in which Micmac and French inhabitants exchanged furs, goods, and alcohol, and no memory of the expulsion of the Acadians from Port La Joie (Charlottetown) in 1758 or the determined governmental eradication of Micmac people from the island.[3] In the present context of land-claims struggles by Native peoples, *Anne* asserts a kind of counter-claim of 'inherent' right. With the collapse of the civilizing mission and racial superiority as justifications for colonialism, sheer love of the land – a sense of belonging rooted in centuries of loving cultivation of the natural world – may remain the only claim that non-Native Canadians can assert, and thus perhaps *Anne* endures as a cultural myth because of the complex political and emotional needs it addresses. At the same time, the emphasis on innocent belonging is flexible enough for film and television adaptations to shape Montgomery's narratives to fit modern sensibilities. Christopher Gittings's chapter in this volume explains that the *Emily of New Moon* television series introduces a Micmac boy, Little Fox, into a reworked narrative in order to update Montgomery and rehabilitate her 'as a consumable national icon embracing French-Canadian and First Nations' differences.' Montgomery's a-local insistence on the loving cultivation of a parklike natural world enables such radical accommodation.

Reflecting on what she hoped would be her last *Anne* novel, Montgomery commented: '[t]hat will end *Anne* – and properly. For she belongs to the green, untroubled pastures and still waters of the world before the war' (*SJ* 2: 309). In this reference, Cavendish springs free of particular place and time to become a metaphor for pre-war innocence. As the history of *Anne*'s popularity and commodification reveals, the myth of Avonlea depends, to a large extent, on its detachable landscape. Like the popular descriptions of tourist destinations in Montgomery's own day, it is both the *one* place and no place at all, offering a green world of comfort and reassurance whose placid surface belies the tensions of contested territory.

Notes

1 For a discussion of Montgomery's prominent place on Canadian best-seller lists, see Mary Vipond, who finds that Montgomery made the top-ten list of the *Bookseller and Stationer*, a prominent trade magazine, in 1909, 1910, 1915, 1917, and 1918. Vipond concludes that sufficient numbers of adult readers must have been captivated by Montgomery's domestic fiction to enable her to rival 'adult' writers such as Mrs Humphrey Ward, Stephen Leacock, and Gilbert Parker (105).

2 When Roberts wrote his section on 'New Brunswick' for *Picturesque Canada* (1882), he included quotations from a number of poets and quoted his own 'To Fredericton in May-Time,' thus forging 'an alliance ... between poetry, patriotism, and tourism' (Bentley, 83). William Wilfred Campbell filled *The Canadian Lake Region* (1910) with his own poetry in an elaborate 'exercise in self-promotion' (Bentley, 92).

3 Admittedly, after the expulsion of the Acadian population in 1758 and the arrival of Scots, English, and Irish immigrants, Prince Edward Island's population was 'the most homogeneous in Canada, with people from the British Isles comprising a large majority' (Hornby, xiii). Yet there were significant black, Micmac, and French communities in the province. For a historical study of the development and demise of the black community of Prince Edward Island, see Jim Hornby's *Black Islanders* (1991).

Chapter 17

Mass Marketing, Popular Culture, and the Canadian Celebrity Author

E. HOLLY PIKE

Within a very short time of the publication of *Anne of Green Gables*, the identification of the fictional Avonlea with Cavendish and L.M. Montgomery's connection to the village were widely known. In 1909, Montgomery noted in her journal that because of her description of Lovers' Lane in *Anne of Green Gables*, 'the name of this little remote woodland lane is known all over the world. Visitors to Cavendish ask for it and seek it out' (*SJ* 1: 357). Undoubtedly, this identification was facilitated by the 'photo and personal sketch' requested by L.C. Page for 'inquisitive editors' (*SJ* 1: 339). By 1917, Montgomery's published account of her career in the magazine *Everywoman's World* had made the identification of certain 'Avonlea' locations with Cavendish ones a matter of public record. It is not surprising, therefore, that by 1928, Montgomery's friends and relatives were 'overrun' with tourists who 'carry off everything they can lay their hands on as souvenirs' (*SJ* 3: 378), and that in 1927 the poet and writer Florence Livesay (the mother of Dorothy Livesay) had found plenty of Cavendish residents willing to talk about their relationships with Montgomery (*SJ* 3: 358).

Montgomery was a 'Canadian celebrity [who] at home and abroad carefully cultivated her public image for her country and era' (Gammel and Epperly, 'L.M. Montgomery' 3). The immediate celebrity of Montgomery and Cavendish after the publication of *Anne of Green Gables*, I argue, was the result of a number of factors, some serendipitous and some deliberate. It was, perhaps, coincidental that *Anne of Green Gables* was published just after a period of intense promotion of Prince Edward Island as a tourist destination (MacEachern, 16), but the two main factors – the publicity surrounding Montgomery's home in

Prince Edward Island and the creation of a suitable authorial persona to market the books – were a deliberate choice of Montgomery's publishers based on the demands of mass marketing. In a culture in which writers are celebrities, as the American cultural critic John G. Cawelti argues, the writer 'gives us an interpretation of his work by telling us about himself, his hopes, his background, or his literary intentions. Or by his own actions, he provides us with grounds for a more intense and immediate response to his work' ('Writer as Celebrity' 173). Therefore, the clearer the picture the public has of a writer, the more opportunity there is for intense interest in the work. When the connection between work and celebrity is effective, interest in an author can reach an almost religious intensity. The interest in Montgomery created by her works, her celebrity, and her identification with a specific locale can be compared in intensity only to the cultlike manifestations around a writer such as William Shakespeare, probably the greatest literary celebrity of all time.

High Art versus Popular Culture

It is often assumed that work produced for the mass market and treated as a commodity does not have artistic merit. However, as the American philosopher and literary critic Richard Shustermann points out, 'history itself clearly shows that the popular entertainment of one culture (e.g. Greek or even Elizabethan drama) can become the high classics of a subsequent age. Indeed, even within the very same cultural period, a given work can function either as popular or as high art depending on how it is interpreted and appropriated by its public' (169). Likewise, in his analysis of Shakespeare in American culture in *Highbrow/Lowbrow: The Emergence of Cultural Hierarchy in America*, the American cultural critic Lawrence W. Levine emphatically demonstrates that popular entertainment does not have to be of 'low' aesthetic quality (chapter 1). In 1913, in a book titled *The Publisher*, the American publisher Robert Sterling Yard distinguishes between the sort of book that seeks the market and the sort that the market finds. Some novels, he says, are 'literature' and are therefore destined to succeed no matter what the current market or what sales techniques are used in their production. However, he argues, whereas the literary novel will succeed over time, gradually building up a readership over a number of years, those novels that are tailored to the market and sold through judicious marketing will have big sales in the first year or two and dwindle rapidly after that (85–6). Therefore, when a book that is, in Yard's terms, 'literature' is marketed as if it were merely a 'novel,' the public reaction to the work should show both of the commercial effects he describes, a large initial sale and ongoing, increasing interest. Without implying any endorsement of this view of the difference between 'literature' and mere 'novels,' it is worth noting that the sales of Montgomery's novels followed the latter pattern, as can be seen in the unpublished record she kept of her sales (Montgomery, 'Book Sales Record Book').

Yard also suggests that the author must make his or her work responsive to market demands, saying that the author's role is to accept sales 'as so many phenomena naturally resultant from a complicated, incalculable, and always different combination of human and commercial causes, and make such study as is possible of the elements with the purpose of producing, so far as possible, the same or more fortunate combinations with succeeding books' (45–6). It is certainly possible that the degree of popularity and commercial success Montgomery's books achieved may be at least partly attributed to their formulaic elements. The first sequel, as the Canadian literary scholar Carole Gerson points out, was produced at Page's request before publication of *Anne of Green Gables* because of 'current practices in market publishing,' producing books as commodities rather than works of art ('Dragged at Anne's Chariot Wheels' 54–5). However, the continual demand from readers for sequels shows that Montgomery's readers counted on having a certain kind of experience when reading one of her books – that is, having created a successful work with *Anne of Green Gables*, Montgomery was expected to keep using the formula she had developed.

In *Adventure, Mystery, and Romance* (1977), John G. Cawelti explores the elements of formulaic fiction that create its popularity, and while he does not deal with girls' books specifically, his general comments about formula fiction apply to Montgomery's case. 'Audiences find satisfaction and a basic emotional security in a familiar form,' he writes, and continues: 'in addition, the audience's past experience with a formula gives it a sense of what to expect in new individual examples, thereby increasing its capacity for understanding and enjoying the details of a work' (9). Arguing that the primary goals of formula literature are escape and entertainment (13), Cawelti states that the 'artistry' of formula fiction is in the author's ability 'to plunge us into a believable kind of excitement while, at the same time, confirming our confidence that in the formulaic world things always work out as we want them to' (16). The literary devices used to achieve this, he argues, are 'suspense, identification, and the creating of a slightly removed, imaginary world' (17). While suspense is not a dominant feature of Montgomery's works, the other two devices are central, identification with the heroine being the feature most likely to attract young readers, and the escape to a slightly removed world being more attractive to older readers. Cawelti cites Robert Warshow, who argues that the success of formulaic work requires that '[o]riginality is to be welcomed only in the degree that it intensifies the expected experience without fundamentally altering it' (quoted in Cawelti, *Adventure* 9). It may be argued that it is the degree of originality and the excellence of her execution that set Montgomery apart from other writers of similar type and created her celebrity. It is worth noting that the same may be said of Shakespeare, who used formulas common in his time, even borrowing from contemporary sources, and repeated formulaic elements and even phrases in his works, but did so in more original and innovative ways than most of his contemporaries did.

Let us briefly consider William Shakespeare as celebrity author, the subject of intensive cultural studies. Shakespeare's celebrity status is registered in his presence in school and university curricula, in the creation of 'Stratford' Shakespearean festivals in three countries, and in the thousands of visitors to these festivals annually. In 'Cult and Criticism: Ritual in the European Reception of Shakespeare,' the Hungarian literary historian Peter Davidhazi even proposes that Shakespeare's celebrity status borders on a cult. 'The attitude characteristic of cults is unconditional reverence, a commitment so total and devoted, so final and absolute that it precludes every conceivable criticism of its object,' he writes, and continues: 'Their ritual may include pilgrimages to sacred places, relic worship, the celebration of sacred times, and all sorts of communal festivities permeated by transcendental symbolism. Their use of language is marked by a preference for such glorifying statements that [*sic*] can be neither verified nor falsified because they are not amenable to any kind of empirical testing whatsoever' (31).

Similarly, the British literary and cultural historian F.E. Halliday shows the development of the Shakespeare cult over the period from Shakespeare's death to the nineteenth century, when it was fully formed. First, Shakespeare was a producer of popular culture. Graham Holderness, a British Shakespeare scholar, argues that Elizabethan drama's modern equivalent is television, a collective cultural experience creating interaction rather than isolation ('Boxing' 176–7). According to Holderness, the products of Elizabethan theatre could be art or formulaic mass entertainment, much like novels in the nineteenth century and after.[1] Second, much of the popularization of Shakespeare's works was carried on by others, for their own benefit.[2] In altered forms, Shakespeare's plays were so popular that, by the end of the seventeenth century, Thomas Betterton found it worthwhile to visit Stratford to find out what he could about Shakespeare from the locals, starting the circulation of the traditional stories about Shakespeare's life (Halliday, 41–3). The provision of sites for worship and pilgrimage by Stratfordians went hand in hand with increasing popularity, the two feeding off each other.[3] Finally, the cult launched a commercial aspect that exists independently of firsthand knowledge of the works or life and generates revenues for a wide variety of people from a broad range of the population.

As figures of literary celebrity, Shakespeare and Montgomery show remarkably similar career patterns. Some of the same elements identified for Shakespeare as celebrity author also apply to Montgomery and *Anne of Green Gables*. Montgomery wrote a popular culture genre, the girls' book, thereby, like Shakespeare, failing to meet contemporary 'artistic' or 'academic' standards, but appealing to a broad audience. The popularization of her work was largely for the profit of others, specifically her publisher, who set her writing a sequel before the first novel was in print (*SJ* 1: 331), refused to renegotiate her royalties despite her huge success (*SJ* 2: 171), and was sole beneficiary of movie rights (*SJ* 2: 358, 373). Davidhazi's description of the cult author, I propose, also applies to some aspects of L.M. Montgomery and *Anne of Green Gables*: the attitude of reverence for the work and sense of specialness of the character; ritual visits to the sites associated with the author and character and the creation of festivals and events; and the language used in discussions of the writer and her work, seen in titles such as *The Sacred Sites of L.M. Montgomery*. While, as with Stratford, the first 'pilgrimages' to Cavendish arose spontaneously, it did not take long for local people to capitalize on the phenomenon and start trying to attract visitors, eventually leading to an independent industry. As well, the quest for relics and information led people to acquire items of dubious provenance, as Montgomery records on 29 October 1927 with regard to the article on Cavendish published by the poet and writer Florence Livesay in the *Toronto Star* (*SJ* 3: 358). Again, on 28 September 1928, she records that a lady had 'carried off a fat bulbous iron pot which Uncle John had over there at the well, boiling pigs' potatoes!' (*SJ* 3: 378). Montgomery also records the Cavendish gossip that her old home may have been torn down to end its nuisance to her uncle in its role as a tourist attraction (*SJ* 3: 378), an echo of what happened to Shakespeare's New Place.

Just as Shakespeare's celebrity authorship relied on a particular version of the Shakespeare biography,[4] interest in Montgomery was based at least partly on the version of her life publicized during her career. Practically from the moment *Anne of Green Gables* was accepted for publication, a public persona was manufactured to suit the author of a series of girls' stories, and that persona became part of what created her celebrity. In *Intimate Strangers: The Culture of Celebrity* (1986), the American cultural critic Richard Schickel refers to the 'basic human need to give some sort of psychological substance ... to make some more active connection with' the providers of popular culture (49). While Schickel is referring to the public demand for information about the silent film actors of the early part of the twentieth century, a demand which led to various legends that had more to do with actors' screen personas than with their actual lives, it is significant that this was happening just at the time that Montgomery was becoming famous. Furthermore, Avonlea, the scenery described in pastoral and romantic terms in the novels, and Cavendish, as the acknowledged original of Avonlea, became sites of an idealized past, like Shakespeare's Stratford (Holderness, 'Bardolatry' 6). These 'pure, unimpeded images of an idealised historical past' ('Bardolatry' 6) are much like those associated with the timeless, eroticized, and commercialized presentation of Avonlea described by Janice Fiamengo, Irene Gammel, Jeanette Lynes, and Tara Nogler in *Making Avonlea*.

Marketing the Author and the Work

Montgomery's publisher operated with heavy advertising, as Montgomery mentions in a letter to Ephraim Weber: 'The Page Co. published an account of [the drunken Orangemen accosting the publisher] in a dozen different papers from Boston to California. They have also set out posters and booklets galore' (*Green Gables Letters* 74). In March 1909, Montgomery mentions Page's request for a new publicity photo, which he said it was 'urgent and important' to get before the 'American public' (*SJ* 1: 348). The urgent need, of course, was to begin to create the persona of the author, which, as the Canadian literary critic

Norman Feltes states with regard to Marie Corelli's *The Sorrows of Satan*, is part of the 'commodity-text' (124). That is, the marketing of books as commodities (already in the 1890s) included the author as part of the commodity, to be shaped to the public taste, just as the book was. 'In a market society where the writer is dependent on the sales of his work, the temptation to let one's person become an advertisement for one's work is great,' notes Cawelti ('Writer as Celebrity' 164). Montgomery was aware of the disparity between the marketing persona and herself, and saw that the persona was an idealization. On 26 May 1924, she comments: 'Judging from the letters I get, my readers, at least the young and romantic portion, seem to imagine that I never do anything, except sit, beautifully arrayed, at a desk and "create" "Annes" and "Emilys"!' (*SJ* 3: 185).

Today we may glean important insight into the marketing of Montgomery as a celebrity author by examining her unpublished scrapbooks held at the University of Guelph Archives. Montgomery kept an invaluable record of the journalistic articles, reviews, and promotional materials, inserting them into several volumes of scrapbooks.[5] Clippings in her unpublished scrapbooks advertise both the booklet about her put out by Page (*Record* Fort Worth, 30 August 1925) and her own account of her life in *Everywoman's World*. The development of a Montgomery persona is clearest in clippings that refer to people's conceptions of the author rather than actual knowledge. One from the *Star* (around 1911) expresses the writer's idea that Montgomery is like Anne; an unidentified review of *Rainbow Valley* states that 'Anne is a real person, fashioned (it is my surmise) in the image of her creator and her family is a real live bunch of Canadians'; and another (Gwendoline P. Clark in *The Free Press*) dreams that Montgomery has five daughters (two sets of twins) and 'hennaed, and 'marcelled' hair and laments that her 'ideal of the author of "Anne of Green Gables" had been so rudely shattered' (USB X25 MS A003).

Some writers, meeting Montgomery in person, describe her in terms that reinforce the expectations created by her works. For instance, an interview with Montgomery by A.V. Brown (source unknown, *ca* 1931), titled 'Anne of Green Gables at Home,' repeatedly uses phrases from Montgomery's works to describe her life, as well as quoting from the works. Here, the manse is described as an 'ideal house of dreams,' the cleanliness of the house is said to be such that not even Marilla Cuthbert or Rachel Lynde would have found fault, and the author recalls Anne's liniment-flavoured cake while at supper with Montgomery. Montgomery's personal appearance is also linked to her work, her current appearance being compared with the younger picture in Garvin's *Canadian Poets*, and her clothing is described as 'good and up-to-date,' which the author finds out of character with 'genius.' An article of about 1920, 'The Author of Anne,' similarly supports the picture of Montgomery as an essentially domestic woman, taking care of her family and house in the manner of her characters; it ends, 'She is just about what you would expect the author of Anne to be' (USB 2: X25 MS A002). Furthermore, an account of Montgomery's address to the Woman's Canadian Club states that 'she is, as one would imagine, sweet, natural, and the possessor of that charm of "motherliness"' (USB 2: X25 MS A002). The emphasis in these articles is on the identification of Montgomery with her characters and the fictional world, satisfying audience conceptions of the artist in a way similar to that Holderness describes for the myth of Shakespeare's boyhood.

The publicity material she collected and preserved in her scrapbooks documents that the advertising surrounding Montgomery consistently focused on the pastoral aspects of her work and life, her dainty physical appearance, and her domesticity. The marketing strategy was to present her as a suitable companion and guide for the young women and girls who were her readers, just as Shakespeare had been presented differently in different times to suit various cultural functions and readerships. An article in *The Republic* (Saturday, 19 November 1910) is typical, referring to Montgomery's 'fine, pure instincts,' 'the quiet green fields and woods of her own lovely island,' the fact that *Anne of Green Gables* is in its twenty-fifth edition, the public demand for sequels, and the personal impression Montgomery creates with her 'retiring manner and untouched simplicity.' An unidentified clipping announced Montgomery's marriage as 'a romance of her own,' identifying Park Corner as 'the scene of the "lake of shining waters" made famous in "Anne of Green Gables"' and assuring the public that 'this new state of affairs is not to interfere in the least with her writing. [Her publishers] state she has practically promised a sequel to "The Story Girl" for 1912' (USB 1: X25 MS A002). This notice combines all the types of information that are part of the public 'knowledge' of celebrities: details are given about the author's private life, her life is associated with her fiction and fictional locales as if there is no distinction between the real and fictional worlds, and the continuation of her link with the public through new books is asserted. Clippings that show that she provided details of her private life – such as a photo of Chester with the title 'Son of a Popular Authoress' (USB 1: X25 MS A002), an announcement of the successful outcome of her suit against Page (USB 2: X25 MS A002), and a response in the *New York Times* (23 February 1919) to a request for information about Montgomery, giving her married name and address (USB X25 MS A003) – all encourage the public to identify with Montgomery personally and to feel that the world of her persona is their world, too.

The authorial persona is also developed through the placement of advertising and reviews, both of which can be used to direct a work towards a particular audience through the types of publications in which the advertisements and reviews appear, whether newspapers, literary journals, family magazines, or children's annuals. Although the scrapbooks cannot contain all of the advertisements of Montgomery's books, the samples contained there suggest that the advertising reinforced the conception of Montgomery and her works as escapist, pastoral, wholesome, and all written to the same formula. An advertisement for *The Golden Road* describes it as 'A volume of delight by the author of *Anne of Green Gables* etc.' and quotes the foreword, framing the quotation in arch language: 'In which 'tis proven that "Life was a Rose-lipped comrade with purple flowers dripping from her fingers."' A large advertisement for *Rilla of Ingleside* (1921) with the top caption 'By the author of *Anne of Green Gables*' also refers to the book as a 'wholesome romance' and advertises the attractive appearance of the book itself ('striking jacket in color,' 'frontispiece in color') (USB X25 MS A003). A large advertisement for *Rainbow Valley* (1919) appeals to the nationalism of postwar readers by stating that Montgomery shows 'everyday life in a typical Canadian community,' as well as making the usual references to humour, beauty, and romance that emphasize to the reader the familiarity of the world depicted (USB X25 MS A003).

Other types of promotion reinforced the image of Montgomery's personal connection with her audience. One was a Canada-wide essay contest in which entrants were to write a five-hundred-word essay on 'Why I like *Emily of New Moon*,' the prize being an autographed copy of the book, a personal tie between author and reader (USB X25 MS A003). Many publicity photos showed Montgomery writing, since this was her connection to the public. Montgomery must have at least participated in, if not initiated, some of the publicity herself. Her willingness to share information about herself shows that she had accepted and actively shaped her role as a celebrity. This is confirmed by an item whose placement in the scrapbook suggests a date of around 1930, stating that 'L.M. Montgomery, the world famed Island novelist' gave large pictures of herself to schools in Cavendish and North Rustico, asserting her importance to her birthplace and her awareness of her status as both local hero and cultural figure (USB 2: X25 MS A002).

The Shrine

Part of the reason Montgomery was a local heroine by 1930 was the boost her fame had given to tourism in the Cavendish area. For instance, the review of *Anne of Green Gables* in *The Spectator* (13 March 1909) states that 'no better advertisement of the charm of its landscape could be devised than the admirable descriptions of its sylvan glories which lend decorative relief to the narrative' and that 'she makes us fall in love with [the] surroundings.' The publication could not have been better timed, since, as the Canadian historian Alan Andrew MacEachern points out, in 1906 the provincial government felt tourism was important enough to the economy to justify a five-hundred-dollar grant to the Prince Edward Island Development and Tourist Association ('Discovering' 16). According to MacEachern, the province was attractive to the seven thousand American tourists who visited in 1899 (8) because of the scenery and the 'old world' atmosphere, so different from that of American cities (10–11). Similarly, the reviews of Montgomery's books refer to the Prince Edward Island setting frequently, almost invariably mentioning it in terms of its beauty, tranquillity, and 'otherness' – a place of retreat, quiet, and old-fashioned values, as in the travel writings that MacEachern cites. This removal of the setting from the everyday world is also one of the attractions of formula fiction that Cawelti mentions, and the way it is stressed in the reviews and articles is instrumental in creating the strong local association necessary for the development of the pilgrimage. From the marketing point of view, Norman Feltes identifies interest in 'local, yet foreign' settings as a feature of best sellers of the 1890s, and this might be an equal factor with tourist marketing in the interest in Prince Edward Island generated by Montgomery's work a decade later (118).

The *Spectator* review is not the only one to draw attention to the connection. For instance, a review of *The Story Girl* in *The Republic* asks, 'We wonder if she realizes what she is doing for [the island]. We fully expect to see Prince Edward Island a favorite summer resort for American travelers, just because of her presence and her stories' (USB X25 MS A003). Another clipping, from its placement in the scrapbook probably from around 1917, notes that Montgomery has drawn 'the attention of the reading world to her home in "The Garden of the Gulf" and has awakened a kindly interest in, and a sympathy for its secluded people' (USB X25 MS A003). Again emphasizing the pastoral seclusion of the island, a clipping of a letter to the 'Nancy Durham' column claims that 'the entire island teems with romance' (USB X25 MS A003). Early in the second of the red scrapbooks (which starts in 1913), an article claims that Montgomery's 'charming stories have done so much to make her native Province known throughout the English-speaking world. Her books are so full of the invigorating wholesomeness of God's great and beautiful out-of-doors that no one can read these idylls of the country-side, where the high and better things have gripped the heart, without receiving some impulse to live a life of sweet simplicity and loving ser-vice.' This unidentified clipping ties together the same elements of removal from the real world and wholesomeness that are part of the sacralization of Montgomery and her works.

Many reviews state the fact of Montgomery's influence on tourism without claiming that the qualities of the place or people are special in themselves. A review of *Magic for Marigold* (1929) refers to *Anne of Green Gables* as having made Prince Edward Island 'the most popular summer resort in Canada,' and an earlier clipping states that the Anne books 'have made [Montgomery's] native district, Cavendish, the Mecca for tourists visiting the province' (USB X25 MS A003). Another unidentified clipping of around 1921 states that 'Every summer visitors drive to Cavendish, and question the people of that section regarding the scenes pictured in the works of L.M. Montgomery' (USB X25 MS A003), while an account of Prince Edward Island day at the Canadian National Exhibition notes that Montgomery's 'many delightful wholesome stories of "Anne of Green Gables" with their P.E.I. setting, have made both her and her province famous' (USB 2: X25 MS A002). Very early, the sites started to become famous for being tourist sites, even to those who had little firsthand knowledge of them from the books, a sure indicator of Montgomery's and Anne's entrance into the status of pop culture icon. Frank Yeigh's 'Motoring in the Island Prov-ince' (*ca* 1923), for instance, refers to the 'Anne-of-Green-Gables coun-try,' as does an account of a motor tour completed by visitors from the Canadian Federation of Teachers (USB 2: X25 MS A002). This clipping also mentions a luncheon served by the 'Avonlea Women's Institute,' showing the adoption of the fictional name by the real-life community, no doubt to strengthen the existing associations. The Canadian folklor-ist Diane Tye's pioneering research on tourism in Cavendish confirms that the fictional world was the initial lure for tourists, and that there-fore the original development of Green Gables aimed at satisfying reader expectations (124).

Montgomery called some fan response 'worship' (*SJ* 2: 232) and noted that her old home had become a 'literary shrine' (*SJ* 3: 141). An address given by Mr W.A. Stewart to the St James' Literary Society around 1926 also used religious language in describing the commer-cialization of the Cavendish area. He pointed out that 'scenes of popu-lar works and the native places of distinguished authors become shrines to be visited by the readers from all parts of the world. This is so with Burns' admirers. This is so with Sir Walter Scott's admirers ... Why should it not be so with Lucy Maud Montgomery's admirers? Why do we not seek to popularize Prince Edward Island in its associ-ation with the "Anne of Green Gables" series of novels?' The next heading of the article is 'An Island Literary Shrine,' and in that section Stewart refers to the 'pilgrims' who come to see the sights associated with *Anne of Green Gables* and suggests that the preservation of the 'historic spot' Green Gables would not only attract visitors but also encourage literary aspirations in the youth of Prince Edward Island (USB 2: X25 MS A002). A clipping from the Charlottetown newspaper *The Guardian* from around 1928 states: 'More tourists have visited the scenes of L.M. Montgomery's novels this year than ever before and the prospects are that there will be an ever increasing number of visi-tors.' As a result, it noted that signs to the sites were needed and that the sites had to be protected from 'people who do not appreciate the value of literary associations as a commercial asset' (USB 2: X25 MS A002). A commentary on this article uses the same language, with the apparent assumption that the actual scenes of the novel are there to be visited, as is suggested by the remark that 'Avonlea could, with a little enterprise, be converted into a shrine which thousands of tourists would visit, where they could purchase souvenirs, photographs of the author, photographs of an "Anne Shirly [*sic*]" of the school, of Mat-thew, the Minister's wife and a hundred different scenes, as real as any of those which have immortalized the shrines in Scotland and England' (USB 2: X25 MS A002). It is interesting to note that Mont-gomery herself took every opportunity she had to visit literary sites, both on her first trip to Boston (*SJ* 2: 32) and on her honeymoon in Great Britain (*SJ* 2: 69–77), and collected postcards at the various 'shrines.' Interestingly, while visiting Abbotsford in Scotland on her honeymoon, Montgomery was disappointed by the crowd of sightse-ers, and wondered 'if Scott would have liked this – to see his home overrun by a horde of curious sight seers. I am sure I would not' (*SJ* 2: 71).

Finally, Montgomery may not have actually seen hordes of tourists at Cavendish, but she must have sensed it was coming. In a letter to Ephraim Weber dated 18 June 1937, she discussed the formation of the National Park at Cavendish, on 'farms selected for the site because of my books.' While she was glad that the farms would be preserved, she also noted: 'I hated the thought of all those lovely old lanes and woods-encircled fields where I roved for years being desecrated – flung open to the public. It seemed *sacrilege*. They will never – can never be the same to me again' (179). Sites that had been sacred to her personally were being made commercially available for general worship and being marketed as shrines, preserving a piece of her past as well as a fictional world, and maintaining the link established between her, her characters, and an idealized version of Prince Edward Island.

Montgomery's ambivalence about the creation of the National Park – the simultaneous preservation and desecration of the past – seems inevitable given the opposing forces that ultimately led to its formation. Early in her career she distinguished between her '"pot-boiling" stuff' and 'something that *is* good – a fit and proper incarnation of the art I worship' (*SJ* 1: 279), but except in writing poetry, she was not able to maintain that distinction once the pattern of the Anne books had been established. Ultimately, by choosing to participate in the commodity marketing of her books, Montgomery created the conditions that gave her fictional world an independent, commercial existence. The development of an authorial persona to suit the public conception of a writer of girls' books and the publication of the correspondence between 'real' and 'fictional' locations somewhat distanced from the stresses of modern life created a unified concept of place, author, and works, the package needed to focus public interest. With the founding of the National Park, interest became independent of firsthand knowledge of Montgomery's works, and for many tourists the causation is now reversed. Instead of coming to Prince Edward Island because of their love of the Anne books or their interest in Montgomery, they come because of the existence of the site, and there they are introduced to the fictional world and its creator.

Notes

1 As Halliday describes it, Shakespeare's work was not free from criticism in

its time, some of the criticism being directed at its lack of high-art credentials. For instance, critics complained that Shakespeare's plays ignored the so-called unities and mixed tragedy and comedy incongruously, presumably to appeal to the uneducated elements of the audience (Davidhazi, 41).

2 The biggest boost to the development of the cult came from David Garrick's 1769 'Jubilee,' which used performance and pageantry to celebrate Shakespeare's life and works and, not incidentally, to promote Garrick's career as the foremost Shakespearean actor of the revised texts (Halliday, ch 5). The success of the jubilee also depended on the eagerness of the people of Stratford to cash in on their famous compatriot. By the middle of the nineteenth century, Stratford was actively seeking to preserve and promote its connection to Shakespeare (Halliday, chs 8, 10).

3 By the mid-eighteenth century Shakespeare's house and a mulberry tree he had supposedly planted were tourist attractions, but in 1756 the owner, tired of tourists asking to see it, had the tree cut down. It was bought and used in the production of an almost infinite series of relics (Holderness, 'Bardolatry' 3).

4 Graham Holderness argues that the popular, undocumented stories about Shakespeare's youth are part of the myth of the 'cultural hero,' who after a misspent youth is banished from his place of birth and about whose parentage there is a mystery ('Bardolatry' 11). This myth creates an engaging personality for a historical figure about whom very little is known, a personality that suits the taste of the public and fits their conception of the conditions necessary for the production of the works, including a 'neat, tidy, innocent world' (6).

5 In the following I rely extensively on sources contained in the unpublished scrapbooks in the University of Guelph Libraries. Where the scrapbooks include the date and place of publication I have cited them, but where such information is not included, I have tried to place items according to internal and contextual evidence. The scrapbooks are cited as USB (= Unpublished Scrapbooks) followed by the archival number. More specifically, I cite from two red scrapbooks: volume 1, ca 1910–13, USB 1: X25 MS A002; and volume 2, ca 1913–26, USB 2: X25 MS A002. Both volumes contain a wide range of items, from press clippings to programs of performances, not all of them relating to Montgomery's work. The scrapbook of reviews (ca 1911–36, USB X25 MS A003) contains primarily reviews and advertisements of Montgomery's works, many of them provided by a clipping service. I am grateful to the Estate of L.M. Montgomery and to the University of Guelph for access to the scrapbooks and for permission to quote from them.

Chapter 18

Through the Eyes of Memory: L.M. Montgomery's Cavendish

JAMES DE JONGE

'I am hoping that I shall be allowed to go to Prince Edward Island for I must see Green Gables before I return home.' So wrote the British prime minister, Stanley Baldwin, to L.M. Montgomery in 1927 and added: 'Not that I wouldn't be at home at Green Gables!!' (quoted in *SJ* 3: 342). Following the publication of *Anne of Green Gables* (1908), Montgomery's imaginative heroines and literary 'portraits' of the Island landscape became cultural symbols recognized internationally. What began as a modest flow of visitors during her lifetime eventually developed into a major tourist industry that now forms a key element of the provincial economy. Over the years, many Island sites have become places of pilgrimage for tourists, including the sites of the schoolhouses where Montgomery taught during the 1890s (at Bideford, Belmont, and Lower Bedeque), her well-preserved birthplace in New London, and the nearby homes of her paternal grandfather (Senator Donald Montgomery) and her maternal aunt (Annie Macneill Campbell) at Park Corner on the north shore.

Cavendish is the centre of 'Anne-Land,' as this part of the north shore is dubbed in Prince Edward Island tourist brochures. Set among rolling farm fields and wooded areas at the intersection of two county roads near the north shore, Cavendish was a 'typical' Island community, with a church, cemetery, and school, and a post office operated by her grandparents out of their farm home. For most of her first thirty-seven years, from 1876 to 1911, Montgomery lived in Cavendish at her grandparents' farm. As a writer, she transformed the community into the fictitious village of Avonlea, a place that came to hold special meaning for thousands of travellers worldwide. Today, visitors to Cavendish can still appreciate the places that reveal the formative influences on Montgomery's childhood, consequential events in her life, and a key productive period in her career as a writer. Of particular interest is the landscape that encompasses the ruins of the author's former Cavendish home; as well as the Cavendish Cemetery, the Cavendish United Church, the site of the former Cavendish school, and the natural areas known as the 'Haunted Wood' and 'Lovers' Lane' (see figure 6.1) The vibrantly bustling tourist heart of this landscape is Green Gables farmstead – a site renowned as the primary setting for her first novel.

This chapter encourages a broad appreciation of the historic values of these landscapes. My holistic 'cultural landscape' approach focuses on the 'whole' as well as the 'parts,' and reveals the linkages between landscape elements, as well as showing how the blending of natural areas and cultural resources has enhanced the character of this special place.[1] The cultural landscape of Montgomery's Cavendish is neither pristine nor static. The tourist overlay is particularly evident at Green Gables where, during the 1940s and 1950s, park officials 'transformed' the farmhouse and its surroundings, primarily in response to consumer demand and the public's desire to experience Montgomery's fictional world, rather than the historical reality of Cavendish. In recent decades, especially after the publication of the author's journals in the 1980s, visitors to the community have found more opportunities to learn about Montgomery herself. The 'recovery' in the 1980s of the ruins of the author's childhood home from the dense undergrowth and Parks Canada's redevelopment of Green Gables in the 1990s have enhanced visitors' understanding and appreciation of Montgomery as an individual. Excerpts from her private journals are displayed on interpretive panels at both sites, and information about her life in Cavendish is conveyed through brochures and other presentation media. These combined efforts have helped to enliven this landscape and to reveal the life and career of a great Canadian author.

Over the years, the Government of Canada has officially recognized the contributions of L.M. Montgomery in several ways, Shortly after her death in 1942, she was designated a person of national historic significance on the recommendation of the Historic Sites and Monuments Board of Canada, and was memorialized in 1948 by a cairn and plaque at Green Gables. Parks Canada has long administered the Green Gables site as a special heritage place within Prince Edward Island National Park in order to communicate Montgomery's national significance to the public.² Green Gables's prime location within the national park made it an obvious choice for the plaque and cairn, although, unlike the Leaskdale Manse in Ontario, Green Gables is not an official national historic site. (In 1996–7, at the request of its owners, Leaskdale Manse in Ontario was evaluated and designated a national historic site, as the place where Montgomery wrote eleven of the twenty-two books that were published during her lifetime, as well as several of her now-published journals.) Through the federal government's program of national historical commemoration, Montgomery has received a level of recognition that few Canadians achieve.³

Green Gables and the National Park

> I have woven a good deal of reality into my books. Cavendish is to a great extent Avonlea ... Green Gables was drawn from David Macneill's House, now Mr. Webb's – though not so much the house itself as the situation and scenery, and the truth of my description of it is attested by the fact that everybody has recognized it. (SJ 2: 38)

Today, the house that became synonymous with Montgomery's heroine Anne Shirley is among Canada's best-known literary landmarks. Green Gables was the farmhouse of Margaret and David Macneill – a sister and brother who were cousins of Montgomery's grandfather. Their farm, first settled in 1831, was situated to the west of Montgomery's home, beyond the Cavendish school, the cemetery, and the forested area she later called the 'Haunted Wood' in *Anne of Green Gables*. Like the site of Montgomery's former Cavendish home, Green Gables has been transformed dramatically from its early-twentieth-century appearance. In the Cavendish landscape, the two sites can be considered 'complementary opposites,' one intimately associated with Maud's real world and the other best known as the setting for her *alter ego*, Anne. Whereas the childhood home is preserved in a ruinous state with modest interpretation, Green Gables is the product of an intensive program of development involving the 're-creation' of former site components intended to portray the setting of Montgomery's novel. While both sites retain vestiges of the former agricultural landscape, they are a testimony to the impact of tourism and heritage development in Cavendish.

Beginning in her childhood years, Montgomery frequently visited Green Gables, which by the 1880s consisted of a modest, frame, storey-

and-a-half farmhouse with a smaller kitchen addition. North of the farmhouse were a large barn, woodshed, and granary arranged in an informal courtyard. In her journals, Montgomery mentions little about her elderly relatives who lived there. However, from an early age she notes repeatedly her profound attachment to the path that extended south from their farmhouse and descended gently to a wooded trail and the trout-filled stream that two bridges crossed (*SJ* 1: 381). As a child, she called it 'Lovers' Lane,' a place she visited often throughout her life to enjoy the natural surroundings. In a typical May 1905 entry, she noted: 'I escaped to Lover's Lane as soon as I could. I hadn't been able to get to it since December until May 5th. It was like a new birth to find myself in it once more – I don't know what I'm ever going to do without that lane in heaven!' (*SJ* 1: 307). Again in August 1909, she recorded: 'This evening I spent in Lover's Lane. How beautiful it was – green and alluring and beckoning!' (*SJ* 1: 357).

After she moved to Ontario in 1911, Montgomery returned to Green Gables often and stayed with her good friends Myrtle Macneill (a granddaughter by adoption of David and Margaret Macneill) and her husband, Ernest Webb, who had taken over the running of the farm in 1906. Montgomery's attachment to this place did not wane with the passage of time, and she continued to draw inspiration from its natural beauty. During her visits back to the Island into the 1920s and 1930s, the Green Gables farmhouse became her 'headquarters' and 'second home' (*My Dear Mr. M.* 182), and assumed a new importance as a place that permitted her to remain in touch with the community.

In *Anne of Green Gables*, Montgomery used the Green Gables house loosely as a model, changing the rooms and the vegetation around the property and portraying the farmyard as a more appealing place than it was in reality. She later recalled:

> Although I had the Webb place in mind I did not confine myself to the facts at all. There are, I think, willows in the yard but there are no 'Lombardies,' such as *Anne* heard talking in their sleep. Those were transplanted from the estates of my castle in Spain. And it was by no means as tidy as I pictured *Green Gables* – at least, before the Webbs came there. Quite the reverse in fact, David's yard was notoriously *untidy.* It was a local saying that if you wanted to see what the world looked like on the morning after the flood you should go into David's barnyard on a rainy day! They had a good cherry orchard but no apple orchard. However, I can easily create an apple orchard when I need one! (*SJ* 2: 39)

The overlay of tourism that now dominates Green Gables is the result of changes that began during the early decades of the twentieth century. Cavendish residents gradually catered to summer tourists. By 1922, Ernest and Myrtle Webb were taking guests into Green Gables. During a visit in 1929, Montgomery noticed that, at the entrance lane to the Webbs' place, the provincial government had recently erected signboards – one to 'Avonlea Beach' and the other to 'Green Gables.' She recorded: 'It seems of no use to protest that it is not "Green Gables" – that Green Gables was a purely imaginary place. Tourists by the hundred come here and Myrtle turns an honest penny selling picture postals of Lover's Lane etc. etc. while no one will ever believe that Cavendish Pond is not "The Lake of Shining Waters"' (*SJ* 4: 9).

The pace of development escalated after the federal government acquired Green Gables in 1936 as part of its plans to establish Prince Edward Island National Park as a seaside resort along the north shore. While the National Parks Branch recognized the growing iconic value of Green Gables, the site took a subordinate role in the grand recreational schemes for the new park. The farm property became the site of a golf course, a type of facility introduced into several national parks during the 1930s, and one that required the demolition of the outbuildings and agricultural landscape. Only the famous farmhouse was spared, and it only narrowly escaped becoming the clubhouse for the new golf course. Instead, park officials constructed a new building nearby, and by 1950 Green Gables was formally opened to the public as a museum/tea room and furnished with the help of the local Women's Institute to re-create the fictitious home of Anne Shirley.[4]

Attracting about 200,000 visitors from Canada, the United States, Japan, Europe, and Australia each year,[5] Green Gables has since evolved to become one of Canada's best-known heritage sites. The overlay of tourism established in the 1940s and 1950s has left a strong imprint on this site. Perhaps most striking is the long tradition of depicting Green Gables as the imaginary 1890s farmhouse portrayed in the novel, even though the layout of the interior does not conform precisely with the fictional accounts. The current colour scheme of white-painted clapboard and striking green gables is also a long-standing tradition based in part on the vague and varying descriptions of the house in the novel and on popular interpretations from the mid-twentieth century. Drawing upon the details and situations in the novel, Parks Canada has carefully decorated and furnished the kitchen, parlour, and dining-room to represent the 1890s period. The bedrooms formerly used by the Macneills and the Webbs are portrayed as the bedrooms of Anne and Marilla, while Matthew is given his own special place beside the kitchen.

In the past decade, Parks Canada has tempered this long-established interpretive approach inside the house by focusing more attention on the real life and career of the author through audio-visual presentations and exhibits in the new visitor reception centre. The 1990s site redevelopment also included the construction of 'farm outbuildings' inspired by the original ones that existed on the farm until the 1930s. Parks Canada has also pushed the boundaries of the golf course back to reclaim some of the property's former agricultural character. As well, interpretive walking trails highlighting Montgomery's love of nature can be found in the wooded area to the rear of the property where Lovers' Lane is located and in the Haunted Wood to the east. These areas retain much of the natural serenity that was so important to the author personally, although the wooded tract associated with Lovers' Lane has been reduced to a narrow ribbon hemmed in by the golf course.

With its meticulously furnished rooms and crisply painted exterior, the Green Gables farmhouse remains the focal point of the site. It is the quintessential locale for the tourist's Kodak moment that commemorates the traveller's journey to Anne Land for the personal album (figure 18.1). Even though Green Gables is unremarkable for its architectural qualities, and served only loosely as a model for the setting of Montgomery's famous book, her admirers have long attached significance to the house as a literary shrine, a concept discussed by Holly Pike in chapter 17. Clearly, it is the place best known and appreciated by millions worldwide for its connections with Anne and her creator. There will probably always be some confusion among visitors. Who actually lived at Green Gables – ordinary Cavendish residents, L.M. Montgomery herself, or the imaginary redheaded girl and her caring guardians?[6]

Montgomery's Cavendish Home

[T]he incidents and environment of my childhood ... had a marked influence on the development of my literary gift. A different environment would have given it a different bias. Were it not for those Cavendish years, I do not think *Anne of Green Gables* would ever have been written. (*Alpine Path* 52)

18.1   Green Gables, Cavendish, 2001. Photograph by J. Paul Boudreau.

A key element of Montgomery's Cavendish landscape is the forty-acre farmstead of her maternal grandparents, Alexander and Lucy (Woolner) Macneill. They raised L.M. Montgomery from before the age of two, after her mother died of tuberculosis in 1876 and her father departed for Saskatchewan to start a new life. The farmhouse, probably built around the mid-nineteenth century, faced west towards present-day Route 13 and had at its rear a barn, a hen-house, a granary, and other support buildings. To the north, a grove of trees sheltered and screened the property from the winds and storms of the north shore, while the farmstead's fields extended several kilometres to the south.

Today, while only the foundations of the farmhouse and traces of the outbuildings survive, this place helps visitors to understand the former agricultural landscape of Cavendish, a community once characterized by narrow farm properties laid out along either side of Route 6. Overall, the site now has a parklike setting enhanced by several mature trees and discrete interpretive panels containing excerpts from Montgomery's journals and letters. The site is especially meaningful for visitors who are familiar with her published journals and letters. These sources reveal how the Cavendish years influenced Montgomery's formative development as an individual and a writer. Consider the following 1905 letter to her friend G.B. MacMillan in which she reveals the circumstances of the childhood and early adult years she spent with her grandparents:

> In material respects they were good and kind to me and I am sincerely grateful to them. But in many respects they were unwise in their treatment of me, I think in all unprejudiced judgment. I was shut out from all social life, even such as this small country settlement could offer, and debarred from the companionship of other children and – in early youth – other young people. I had *no* companionship except that of books and solitary rambles in woods and fields. This drove me in on myself and early forced me to construct for myself a world of fancy and imagination very different indeed from the world in which I lived, moved and had my outward being. (*My Dear Mr. M.* 15–16)

From an early age, Montgomery kept a private journal and acquired an interest in the 'world of nature and the world of books.' These became her 'two great refuges and consolations' (*SJ* 1: 301) and remained so throughout her life. Feeling that her private world and the real world 'clashed hopelessly and irreconcilably,' she 'learned to keep them apart so that the former might remain for me unspoiled' (*My Dear Mr. M.* 16). She became deeply attached to the natural surroundings on the farmstead and to the community of Cavendish, from which she rarely ventured during her youth except for occasional visits to Charlottetown and to the homes of her maternal aunt and paternal grandfather at Park Corner.[7]

For the thirteen years following her grandfather's death in 1898, Montgomery stayed in Cavendish, where she dutifully cared for and worried about her aging grandmother, helping to manage the home and the post office. She continued to find solace in her natural surroundings and in her world of books. Her bedroom on the second floor offered a beautiful vista over the fields to the south. Here she passed much of her time and developed her skills as a writer, initially by writing poems and short stories for publication in magazines. According to her journals, Montgomery was also troubled by the often strained relations with her Uncle John. He owned the adjacent farm to the east and stood to inherit the Cavendish farm of her grandparents when her grandmother passed away. Montgomery and her grandmother were permitted to live in the home while her grandmother was alive, though Maud suspected at times that her uncle was anxious to take over the property.[8]

It was in this atmosphere of uncertainty that Montgomery conceived and wrote her first and most famous novel, *Anne of Green Gables*, in 1905. Montgomery acknowledged that many of her 'own childhood experiences and dreams were worked up into its chapters' (*SJ* 1: 331), but she kept the unhappy aspects of her own life out of the book. Anne succeeded where her creator had failed in transforming the lives of her old-fashioned guardians. Anne's view of Green Gables as a place of retreat, and her concern for Marilla after the death of Matthew, probably echoed Montgomery's real-life anxieties. Just as her *alter ego*, Anne Shirley, gave up her scholarship to return to Green Gables, Montgomery sacrificed her own immediate future to return to Cavendish and look after her grandmother in 1898 (*SJ* 2: x; Ross, 'Readers' 25). Here, she also wrote her sequel, *Anne of Avonlea*, and two other novels – *Kilmeny of the Orchard*, and *The Story Girl*, the latter inspired in part by the setting and situations drawn from the homes of her maternal aunt and paternal grandfather at Park Corner. At Cavendish she also began her journals, which document this important formative and early productive period of her life. And despite the stresses and constraints associated with her Cavendish years, Montgomery was deeply saddened to leave here. In the years that followed, her private journals recorded a deep longing for the farmstead and its surroundings.

After her marriage and departure from Cavendish in 1911, the farmstead witnessed dramatic changes.[9] It had long been in a deteriorated state because her Uncle John had not maintained the property and, according to Montgomery, had 'been cutting the trees down recklessly for firewood ever since grandfather's death' (*SJ* 2: 37). During visits back to the Island in 1915 and 1918, she went to see the now-vacant home, both times noting the ongoing physical decay of the farm buildings, the overgrown vegetation on the property, and her still intense attachment to the site (*SJ* 2: 168–9, 254). She recorded her pain upon hearing about its demolition in 1920 (*SJ* 2: 376), and could not bear even to look at the site in 1923 when she again visited the Island. During that visit, she remarked that many people were indignant at her uncle for tearing down 'the only "literary shrine" the Province possessed,' although she herself was 'well content that it should be torn down. It would not please me to think of it being overrun by hordes of curious tourists and carried off piecemeal' (*SJ* 3: 141). Montgomery visited the site again briefly in 1927 and expressed her shock over the disappearance of the outbuildings and many mature trees and over the relentless advance of new shrubs, trees, and undergrowth on the property. She confessed: 'If I had been set down there without knowing where I was I really doubt if I should have recognized the place at all' (*SJ* 3: 347). Writing from the manse at Norval, Ontario, in September 1928, she noted:

> My poor relatives on the Island must often wish I had never put pen to paper. The joke of it is, Uncle John's in Cavendish are likewise overrun by people who know nothing of the estrangement between us and take it for granted that Uncle John and his family must be among my intimate friends ... Everyone in Cavendish says that Uncle John tore the old home down because he was jealous of the crowds who went there to see it. But I think it was quite as much because of the very considerable nuisance of it. Whatever his reason, demolishing the house did not help any. They still go to see the spot itself – that desolate overgrown spot. And they carry off everything they can lay their hands on as souvenirs! (*SJ* 3: 378)

Into the late 1920s, the homestead site remained a place of pilgrimage for fans of L.M. Montgomery, even though the property was receding into a natural state and had not been marked or developed as a tourist attraction. In 1929, Montgomery was amused to learn of one local resident's 'crazy scheme to *rebuild* the house, exactly as it was.' She noted: 'I am *glad* the old house has gone. It can never be degraded to the uses of a tea-room. It is mine – mine. I can see every room and line of it, every picture, every stick of furniture ...' (*SJ* 4: 11).

With the passage of time, however, the site of her Cavendish home gradually faded into obscurity as a literary landmark, while nearby Green Gables grew as a tourist attraction with the development of Prince Edward Island National Park in the 1930s and 1940s. An interesting point to consider is that, had the homestead survived, it might have retained its evolving role as a literary shrine to Montgomery, perhaps even supplanting Green Gables. Instead, the ruins gradually disappeared into the landscape and were forgotten. The farmstead's current appearance is the result of an important initiative begun in the 1980s by the current owners – John Macneill (a grandson of John Franklin Macneill, Montgomery's uncle) and his wife, Jennie. Inspired by Montgomery's published journals, they appreciated how important and 'sacred' this spot had been to her during her childhood and early adult years. Over a period of several years, they developed the site as a heritage attraction by carefully removing much of the thick vegetation and preserving the older trees and remnants of the front orchard. They uncovered the well, excavated the foundation walls of the house, and constructed a modestly scaled frame building near the rear of the site to serve as a reception centre and bookstore.

Despite the loss of the farmstead buildings, the site today still evokes an appreciation of Montgomery's time here. In its ruinous state, the site has lost much of its character as a farmstead, but other qualities have come to the fore. Indeed, the site derives its essential values as a ruin. As several writers on heritage sites have noted, ruins provide a unique experience for visitors by vividly depicting the passage of time and encouraging reflection on an earlier period.[10] Ruins can reveal a powerful story, and they can challenge assumptions that the integrity and significance of heritage sites require the survival of intact buildings. Visitors to Montgomery's Cavendish home are often struck by the evocative mood created by these modest remains imprinted on the landscape. The ruins blend effectively with the mature trees and with the rolling fields to the south that remain in agricultural use and add to the site's peaceful, secluded atmosphere. Montgomery cherished the vista of farm fields from the south-facing window of her upstairs bedroom, and she also went for regular morning walks through the fields as a source of inspiration before sitting to write (*SJ* 1: 338).[11]

The remnants of the farmstead, especially, provide insight into Montgomery's adult years here. They remind us that the ultimate destruction of her Cavendish home was the conclusion, or perhaps the epilogue, of a real-life drama in Montgomery's life. Following her return to Cavendish in 1898 to look after her grandmother, Montgomery anticipated and then witnessed the homestead's gradual decline, which she came to see as inevitable. With the aid of the journals, the surviving traces of her home provide a link to this uncertain period after 1900, especially her preoccupation with the health of her grandmother, her own future prospects, and the circumstances in which she conjured up the compelling story of Anne.

The Cavendish home site is enriched not only by the interplay of the ruins, the natural setting, and Montgomery's journals, but also by its surroundings. Indeed, one could argue that this broader landscape is central to an appreciation of the author's early life and career. The Macneills have enhanced the links between their site and its broader Cavendish context by maintaining several walking paths. To the north of the Cavendish homestead, they have re-established the informal pathway leading to the Presbyterian (now United) church that faces out onto Route 6. Montgomery attended this church (which replaced the former one, demolished in 1899, inside the Cavendish Cemetery), and served as organist and choir director from 1903 to 1911. The attractive, white-clapboarded building is associated with a consequential event in her life, for it was here that Maud met Ewan Macdonald, who served as Presbyterian minister in Cavendish from 1903 to 1906. Their relationship eventually led to marriage and their departure from the Island in 1911. Though Montgomery confessed in her journals that she was not in love with Ewan, her lonely life in Cavendish at the time, her desire to have a family, and the limited alternatives available were all factors in her decision to accept his proposal of marriage (*SJ* 1: 320–3; 2: 206).[12]

The Macneills have also maintained a walking path along the original laneway leading west from the homestead site to Route 13. Immediately on the opposite (west) side of Route 13 at this point is the site of the former schoolhouse that Montgomery attended as a child and that inspired the setting for the Avonlea schoolhouse in *Anne of Green Gables*. A walking trail (maintained by Parks Canada) from the schoolhouse site leads through the partially wooded lot she crossed frequently and that became the 'Haunted Wood' in *Anne of Green Gables*. Immediately north of the schoolhouse site is the Cavendish Cemetery, a place Montgomery also visited often and where she and her husband are interred not far from the graves of her mother and maternal grandparents (figure 15.9). She purchased the plots during a visit to the Island in 1923, so that when her time came, she could 'lie among my kindred in the old spot I love so much better than any other spot on earth. As a minister's wife I shall not likely live long enough in any one place to make me feel that I want to be buried there ... Here only can I rest at last – here it is fitting I should be buried' (*SJ* 3: 138). The cemetery speaks both to her lineage and to her special attachment to Cavendish. It has expanded southward since the time of Montgomery and continues to evoke the contemplative atmosphere that made it one of her favourite places to visit during her daily walks.

The final element of this broader landscape is Green Gables, which is probably unique among sites administered by Parks Canada. The farmhouse and its setting have been reshaped not to 're-create' historical reality, but to reflect an imaginary setting drawn from Montgomery's fiction. Parks Canada has long portrayed the house as the imagined world of Anne rather than the ordinary home of Cavendish residents who once lived there. After half a century, this interpretive 'tradition' may have acquired historical significance in its own right. A common thread in the recent development of the Cavendish home site and Green Gables is the emphasis on interpreting the life and career of L.M. Montgomery, rather than her fictional world – a shift influenced in part by the publication of her extensive journals.

The evolution of the Cavendish landscape should also serve as a lesson for owners of heritage sites in general. In developing Green Gables in the 1930s and 1940s, park officials nearly 'threw out the baby with the bath water' by responding to the recreational interests of tourists rather than carefully assessing and taking into account the site's broader heritage values beyond the obvious iconic value of the house. Green Gables and the community of Cavendish possessed other tangible and intangible qualities that were cherished by the author and by local residents. To appreciate the Cavendish landscape, one must accept, as Montgomery did, that it remains important even in its altered form. During a visit to the Island in 1918, Montgomery gazed over the community 'not only with physical eyes, seeing material beauty, but with the eyes of memory which saw all that in the past had filled it with charm for me.' Even then, physical change to the landscape did not diminish her love for the places in Cavendish, including her childhood home, which she later described (in 1927) as 'sacred to me even in its ruin and degradation' (*SJ* 3: 342). Today, with the aid of the author's published journals, visitors can still view this landscape through the 'eyes of memory' and discover the special meaning that these distinct but related places held for Montgomery.

In the years to come, admirers of L.M. Montgomery will have more opportunities to see the places that were the setting of her real life. For example, the administrators of Leaskdale Manse National Historic Site in Ontario are developing plans for the preservation and presentation of the house that was the centre of the author's world between 1911 and 1926. As in Cavendish, Montgomery's journals reveal much about her accomplishments there as an author and also provide deep insights into her personal life as a wife and mother.[13] Meanwhile, the well-established Montgomery sites on Prince Edward Island will continue to respond to the often competing demands of heritage preservation and public presentation. Perhaps nowhere are these pressures more evident than in Cavendish. The evolving tourist imprint on Montgomery's Cavendish landscape is echoed in the surrounding area, where commercial establishments, including restaurants, motels, trailer parks, and amusement centres, have also left a vivid impression on the community, and one that is not always sympathetic to its heritage character. The preservation of the Cavendish landscape that inspired Montgomery will depend upon a broad and ongoing recognition of this area as a special place.

Notes

1 This paper builds upon the existing body of research on L.M. Montgomery tourist sites on Prince Edward Island: Squire, 'Ways of Seeing'; Fawcett and Cormack, 'Guarding Authenticity'; Rootland, *Anne's World*; and Hamilton and Frei, *Finding Anne on Prince Edward Island*.

2 Decisions to commemorate places, people, and events of national historic significance are made by the Minister of Canadian Heritage on the advice of the Historic Sites and Monuments Board of Canada (HSMBC), which is composed of representatives from each province and territory. Most of the sites evaluated by the HSMBC each year are proposed by members of the general public, and in principle the board recommends commemoration only with the support of property owners.

3 The commemoration of Leaskdale Manse inspired several owners of L.M. Montgomery heritage sites on Prince Edward Island to express an interest in having their properties considered for designation as national historic sites. This article is based largely upon the research I undertook in 1998–9 to assist the HSMBC in its deliberations on the historic significance of the principal Island sites associated with Montgomery, a process that has not yet been completed. It also reflects my broader interest, as a historian working for the National Historic Sites Directorate of Parks Canada, in investigating sites related to the lives and accomplishments of nationally significant individuals, such as the famous inventor Alexander Graham Bell and the poet/performer Emily Pauline Johnson.

4 On the development of Green Gables and Prince Edward Island National Park see: Lothian, *A Brief History of Canada's National Parks* (105–6); Horne 'Green Gables House'; MacEachern, 'The Greening of Green Gables' (27); Squire, 'L.M. Montgomery's Prince Edward Island' (136–45); and Ricketts, 'Cultural Selection.'

5 Green Gables received 216,273 visitors in 1998, 208,941 in 1999, and 191,036 in 2000 (statistics provided by Doug Heaney, Parks Canada).

6 It is interesting to note that in 1952 the HSMBC recommended that a

'painted wooden sign or scroll' be placed in the Green Gables house because many visitors mistakenly believed that L.M. Montgomery was born and raised there. The sign was reportedly installed in 1954. The approved text read: 'This house, and many points of interest in the surrounding National Park, commemorate the romantic childhood of Anne of Green Gables, heroine of a series of novels written by Lucy Maud Montgomery (Macdonald). Nearby, on the lawn, is the monument erected in 1948 by the Government of Canada on the recommendation of the Historic Sites and Monuments Board of Canada in honour of the authoress. Miss Montgomery's own birthplace was at Clifton Corner, New London, about 8 miles from this spot.' (HSMBC, Minutes, May 1952, 6; May 1953, 2; HSMBC Agenda Paper 1962–10)

7 In her early adult years, Montgomery moved away temporarily, in 1890–1, to Prince Albert, Saskatchewan, to live with her father, and again in 1893–4 to earn a teaching certificate at Prince of Wales College in Charlottetown. Over the next four years, she taught briefly at three Island schools (Bideford, 1894–5; Belmont, 1896–7, and Lower Bedeque, 1897–8) and studied English literature for a term at Dalhousie University (1895–6), returning to Cavendish after the end of the school terms.

8 In 1905, Montgomery referred to herself as the 'stumbling block' in her uncle's 'scheme of ousting grandmother from her home.' Montgomery noted: 'It will, of course, hurt me deeply to leave this old home which I have always loved so passionately even in years when I have been far from happy in it. But I have known, ever since grandfather's death, that the time would come when I would have to leave it, and the reality can scarcely be much worse than the long anticipation has been' (SJ 1: 310).

9 Following her grandmother's death in 1911, Montgomery married the Reverend Ewan Macdonald, to whom she had been secretly engaged since 1906. They left the Island to start a new life in Leaskdale, Ontario, where Ewan Macdonald had accepted a position as minister of the local Presbyterian church.

10 On the heritage significance of ruins, see Harbison, *The Built, the Unbuilt and the Unbuildable* (99–106), and Lowenthal, *The Past Is a Foreign Country* (163–76).

11 For an incisive look at the importance Montgomery attached to her room, see Higgins, 'Snapshot Portraits.'

12 Of interest as well is 'Green Gables Post Office,' situated beside the church and operated by Canada Post. It is an old frame farm building that was relocated here because of its resemblance to Montgomery's Cavendish home. In the post office, visitors can see a partial 're-creation' of the former

post office from Montgomery's Cavendish home, as well as exhibits on her career and on the development of postal communications on the Island.

13 There are other Ontario sites associated with Montgomery: the manse at Norval, where she and her family lived from 1926 until her husband's forced retirement in 1935; Montgomery's Toronto home near the Humber River, which she appropriately named 'Journey's End,' where she lived from 1935 until her death in 1942; and the tourist home at Bala in the Muskoka Lake district, where she and her family vacationed in 1922. Its setting inspired her first adult novel, *The Blue Castle*.

Chapter 19

Consumable Avonlea: The Commodification of the Green Gables Mythology

JEANETTE LYNES

The literary legacy of L.M. Montgomery has moved in two directions. On the one hand, largely because of the efforts of feminist scholars, Montgomery's work has become a legitimate subject of study in the academy (see Gerson's overview in chapter 1). On the other hand, Montgomery's legacy exerts a strong presence in the realm of popular culture – a realm that encompasses tourism, entertainment, and consumable artifacts, the topic of part three of *Making Avonlea*. The consumable articulation of the Green Gables mythology is of an intensely aestheticized, sentimentalized, and intertextual nature.

This chapter attempts to mediate between these two areas by premising itself on what Chandra Mukerji and Michael Schudson, in *Rethinking Popular Culture* (1991), identify as 'the legitimation of contemporary popular culture as a subject for study in universities and a subject of inquiry for serious scholars' (3). As early as 1961, Leo Lowenthal suggested that literary art and 'market-oriented commodities' (xii) may not occupy as separate realms as we might think (xii). The movement of popular culture studies from 'an academic backwater' to 'a swift intellectual [interdisciplinary] river' (Mukerji and Schudson, 1) might resonate for anyone who has worked in the areas of women's literature, children's literature, 'ethnic minority writing' (Gunew, 53), or even Canadian literature. As with popular culture studies, these areas have had to struggle for legitimation within the academy. In a 1987 article in *Signal*, Lissa Paul observed that '[b]oth women's literature and children's literature are devalued and regarded as marginal or peripheral by the literary and educational communities,' although she noted, too, that '[f]eminist critics are beginning to change that' (149). Canadian literature, too, has had to struggle for legitimation in English departments where curricula were typically built up around the British tradition.

Since the marginalization of women's writing, children's literature, and Canadian literature within the academy has been, I want to suggest cautiously, partially overcome, I bring up the above points not out of defensiveness but rather to posit a space of rich intersection between the comprehensive entity known as 'popular culture' and one of Canada's best-known woman writers and children's authors, L.M. Montgomery. Although I suspect that the study of popular culture expressions of Montgomery's work has few new insights to offer on the work itself, I believe it nevertheless articulates, in meaningful ways, messages about desire in contemporary consumer culture. The discussion that follows does not pretend to decode all these messages; it offers only a starting point and, as such, excludes a considerable amount – the televised and theatrical adaptations of Montgomery, for example – in order to examine several strategies used in marketing the Green Gables mythology within the larger context of consumer society.

Popular culture is not static. It refers, Mukerji and Schudson tell us, 'to the beliefs and practices, and the objects through which they are organized, that are widely shared among a population' (3). Dominic Strinati's description of popular culture as 'a range of artifacts and social processes' (xvii) is similar. Presumably, these beliefs, practices, and processes do not remain constant, but undergo transformations and revisions. That is why, for example, Stanley Turner's cover design for the 1937 McClelland and Stewart edition of Montgomery's *Jane of Lantern Hill* looks dated to us now, a period piece, an artifact. In their popular culture manifestations, Montgomery's heroines continue to be revised in ways that harmonize with their respective societal contexts. The Megan Followsian Anne on the Green Gables Store Internet site could have just stepped out of a Laura Ashley store. Her image embodies paradox, being a collision of past and present, stasis and the flux of fashion. In terms of the 'social processes' referred to by Strinati, the Japanese wedding ceremonies held on Prince Edward Island probably represent an example of popular culture as 'social process,' as would the tourist pilgrimages to Cavendish discussed earlier by Holly Pike and James De Jonge (chapters 17 and 18; see also figure 18.1).

John Fiske contends that 'popular culture is shot through with contradictions' (*Understanding Popular Culture* 105). One contradictory aspect of the Avonlea mythology is that it is at once regional –

grounded in a specific locale – and highly mobile or portable. For example, during a recent stroll through an upscale Seattle neighbourhood, I discovered a bed and breakfast called Green Gables. The Canadiana souvenirs in airport shops throughout Canada sometimes include Anne memorabilia. Shops in Banff, Alberta, sell Anne dolls, no doubt aware of the attachment Japanese tourists might have for these products. Anne smiles out from the licence plates of P.E.I. cars moving down the road. Even for those who never leave their armchairs, Avonlea has exerted its presence through the *Road to Avonlea* television series. And now, Internet surfers, with a few clicks of their mice, can spend Christmas with Anne, or order Green Gables products from sites such as the Anne of Green Gables Store or the Canadian Living Marketplace. Anne has entered the virtual market-place; if you can't go to her, she'll come to you – provided you can afford a modem hook-up.

Avonlea, it seems, is everywhere. At least, it seems to have become a floating signifier. Perhaps the recent Internet marketing of Anne has helped 'de-regionalize' her, pushing her into more of a virtual than a regional space, and in this sense has decontextualized her (notwithstanding the regionally specific name of the website, 'peionline'). Not all of my Canadian Studies students in Seattle knew where the novel *Anne of Green Gables* was set, even though they were all quite familiar with Montgomery and had read her novels as children.[1] They were also aware of the popular mythology predicated on her work, including the *Road to Avonlea* television series. The regional signified as a referent (Prince Edward Island) seemed to be of minimal importance to them.

The varying degrees of indifference, on the part of my students, towards the importance of place in *Anne of Green Gables* suggests to me that the commodifiers of the Avonlea mythology allow for, indeed, engineer as part of their marketing tactics, a certain amount of slippage. It is clearly in the interests of those who manufacture Avonlea products to expand their thematic range, and thus their profit range, as much as possible. In the course of this expansion, Avonlea products can become diluted, to say the least. For example, the Cavendish Shopping Centre in Prince Edward Island sells a video called *The Witches of Avonlea* priced at seventeen dollars. Another way of accounting for such slippage or dilution is to follow John Fiske's notion that popular culture is intertextual (*Understanding Popular Culture*, 124), that its meanings 'circulate intertextually' through 'primary texts (the original cultural commodities) ... secondary texts that refer to them directly (advertisements, press stories ...), and tertiary texts that are in constant process in everyday life (conversation, the ways of wearing jeans ... window shopping ...)' (124). What Fiske refers to as 'tertiary texts' seem to carry with them an element of mimicry; window shopping mimics shopping. Wearing jeans mimics some rustic concept of America (individuality within conformity?). What the commodified Green Gables mythology might be seen to be mimicking will be discussed below.

The commodification of Avonlea exploits all three levels of textual meaning in popular culture as defined by Fiske. The textual categories, however, may overlap more than Fiske's original delineation of them when we consider consumable Avonlea. The production of Anne books on CD-ROM reflects a reconstitution of primary texts, for example – a kind of at-once primary and secondary text. Avonlea spin-off products such as aprons, bibs, and preserves, which are now for sale in the virtual Green Gables Store as well as the original one, exemplify tertiary texts. The Internet store is itself a tertiary text, in a sense. Perhaps tourism, too, the middle-class ritual of the family vacation, is a kind of tertiary text, carried out in everyday life and mimicking a familial ideal.

Countrification and 'Residual Culture'

One explanation for the considerable success of Green Gables artifacts may be their built-in intertextuality, the interface of Green Gables products with the broader consumer movement of countrification or rural élitism. This movement is reflected, in part, through the phenomenon of the country store and country living – a phenomenon that is, of course, quite urban in conception. Most 'country stores' are in, or within driving distance of, urban centres. In other words, Green Gables merchandising is framed by a broader milieu of consumer fantasy fostered and disseminated through store merchandise, catalogues, and magazines such as *Country Living*, *Martha Stewart Living*, *Victoria Magazine*, the Eddie Bauer home collection, the Ralph Lauren home collection, Laura Ashley, La Cache, Crabtree and Evelyn, and, to some extent (although with a more rugged spin), L.L. Bean. This does not even take into account all the clones of the above. What these consumer outlets share is an upper-end price range and a decorative extravagance; these products are primarily for urbanites who are comfortable in their material surroundings and likely employed in some fairly lucrative profession. They are products for people with homes, which sets these consumers at a considerable thematic distance, if not a diametrically opposed position, from the homeless little girl in her plain dress waiting to be rescued at Bright River Station. Why is it that every culture seems to desire its opposite? Fiske's notion of the contradictory articulations of popular culture is highly appropriate when applied to the commodification of Avonlea.

The Anne of Green Gables Store and Avonlea Traditions Inc.

By inserting their products, through visual associations, within a broader movement of rural élitism, Avonlea producers are really marketing what Raymond Williams calls a 'residual culture' that promotes 'experiences, meanings and values, which cannot be verified or cannot be expressed in terms of the dominant culture [but] which are nevertheless lived and practised on the basis of the residue – cultural as well as social – of some previous social formation' ('Base and Superstructure' 415). To illustrate a 'residual culture,' Williams uses the example of the 'very significant popularity,' in Britain, 'of certain notions derived from a rural past' (415). Williams emphasizes the point that although 'a residual culture is usually at some distance from the effective dominant culture ... it may get incorporated into it' (415–16). British tourism's appropriation of Kenneth Grahame's pastoral world of *The Wind in the Willows* to promote travel to the English countryside seems to exemplify Williams's notion of 'residual culture.' In North America, the recent phenomenon of the 'country store' – the consumer category in which Charlottetown's Anne of Green Gables Store belongs – would also seem to exemplify 'residual culture,' harking back as it does to an earlier time. Some 'country stores' are actually situated in upscale urban malls, a location that clearly denotes their participation in dominant consumer culture. What the Green Gables Store and other 'country stores' are mimicking is the past – a sentimentalized, feminized version of it.

When I entered the Anne of Green Gables Store in Charlottetown for the first time in November 1997,[2] I experienced a sense of *déjà vu*, a strong feeling that I had been in such a store before. This *déjà vu*, I believe, had less to do with the Montgomery novels I had read and the worlds depicted therein than it did with a deliberate intertextuality the Anne Store has established with the country-store genre. Owned by Henderson and Cudmore, the Anne of Green Gables Store is located on the main level of a handsome red-brick building at the corner of Richmond and Queen in Charlottetown – as the Charlottetown Festival calendar for 1997 tells us, 'next to Confederation Centre.' There is a great deal of associative marketing going on; obviously, the idea is to combine a show with the purchase of some memories. The setting and design of the store – with its simulated handwritten sign – achieve a high degree of visual appeal. The store's rich green exterior wood trim and overall presentation are not unlike those of the Laura Ashley chain of retail outlets.

The intent of the Anne Store owners seems to be to have it both ways: to project the image of an entirely unique place (there is, as far as I know, only one Anne of Green Gables Store) and to insert the store into the larger text of countrification. Countrification, in turn, with its vaguely folkloric aspirations and its emphasis on 'authentic' hand-crafted productions and naïve art (much of which, paradoxically, is mass-produced) harks back to some nebulous 'folk' era that is, according to Ian McKay, 'part of a much bigger movement of aesthetic colonization of the country by the city' (9). The Anne Store seems to have created a ripple effect (and more intertextuality) in Charlottetown's downtown area; 'authentic' wood carvings and country crafts are sold in a number of nearby stores and galleries. 'The Two Sisters' store nearby, for example, resembles the Anne Store in design. Its advertisement in the 1997 'official guide to Charlottetown' is printed in English and Japanese, the 'Sisters,' specializing in 'country and Victorian crafts and gifts' as well as 'nostalgic treasures from Anne's land,' and it clearly has the Anne Store clientele in mind. Reflecting its dependence upon tourists, the Anne Store is open from the beginning of May to the end of December. I visited it in November 1997, around five p.m., and it was full of shoppers.

The Anne Store is decidedly not a bookstore; it is, as signs on either side of the front door tell us, a 'gift emporium' and a place of 'fond memories.' The 'Anne merchandise' is supplemented by the kind of products one would find in any country store: wooden figurines, pewter frames, jewellery, maple syrup, pottery made by local potters. No doubt this supplementation helps contextualize the Anne Store within the country-store genre. All products are displayed, for the most part, in appealing, carefully designed spaces. The store's interior is predominantly glass and wood, including hardwood floors, creating, for the most part, a feeling of warmth. Muzak-type music was playing. Surprisingly few books were for sale: the store featured only a couple of modest-sized bookshelves, and these were not prominently displayed. The books included recipe books, paperback copies of most of Montgomery's books, a small group of critical works on Montgomery, and a few first-edition 'collector' books. The book *Your Guide to Finding Anne*, a small, spiral-bound book published by Ragweed Press, sold for $12. Videotapes of *The Road to Avonlea* series and the 'officially authorized' CD-ROM of *Anne of Green Gables* were more prominently displayed than the books. The video *My Island Home* (presumably containing biographical information on Montgomery) sold for $30. The CD-ROM 'interactive storybook' was priced at $34.99. The majority of the store's merchandise fell into the 'secondary' and 'tertiary' groups, to recall Fiske's categories, and a good deal of it could be classified as pure ephemera.

The store's products specifically based on Anne could be classified into hard-core and soft-core merchandise. Much of the latter is not particularly closely related to the Anne books; items such as the lupine fridge magnets, key chains containing some Atlantic motif, sun-catchers, or maple syrup may, rather, make some broader regional allusion. The stock also included soap, body lotion, and cologne, products that do not make any direct reference to Anne but refer to the kind of country-store merchandise sold in Crabtree and Evelyn stores. Other ephemeral items were tangentially related to Anne by virtue of containing some kind of Anne-ish logo. These products do not have ephemeral prices, though. A wristwatch with a silhouette of Anne's profile on its face costs $54.99. On the lower end of the price spectrum, Anne buttons, calendars, mouse pads, and Green Gables tea and preserves were for sale. Clearly, the store endeavours to make shopping a sensory experience; there are colognes and preserves for sampling. A 250 mL jar of preserves with a Green Gables label was $5.99. The store also offered Green Gables address books, stationery, and diaries, among the few objects which relate to writing. Anne of Green Gables posters sold for $20. T-shirts featuring various Green Gables images were approximately the same price, although children's sizes cost less. Jigsaw puzzles with Green Gables images and press-out activity books were at the lower end of the price spectrum (under $20).

The store's hard-core 'Anne' merchandise consists of dolls and plates. These items have higher prices and greater claims to authenticity. There is something of a contest for authenticity among these products, the dolls in particular. Anne dolls come with various claims of specialness or authenticity. A 'special edition' porcelain doll sells for

$29.99, and the tag claims that these 'special' dolls are produced by the Green Gables Store and sold 'in limited quantities.' The Canadian Living Marketplace link of the Green Gables Store Internet site sells 'A Canadian Heroine,' an Anne doll created 'by New Brunswick artist Catherine Karnes Munn.' This doll, too, comes with a 'certificate of authenticity,' and claims to be produced in a 'limited edition of 1,000.' The Munn doll costs $69.99. Some dolls sold in the store (and, presumably, in other stores) are trademarks of Avonlea Traditions Inc. These dolls, too, claim to be authentic.

The company Avonlea Traditions Inc. epitomizes the commodification of the Montgomery legacy. Located in Newmarket, Ontario, Avonlea Traditions is owned by Kathryn Gallagher Morton, who was touted in *Chatelaine* as a leading-edge businesswoman and 'character builder.' As *Chatelaine* tells us, 'Avonlea Traditions produces more than 100 products ranging from dolls to fridge magnets. Manufactured by small firms and independent craftspeople, items sell mainly through upscale gift shops to preserve Anne's homespun image. The formula seems to be working: 1994 sales of $1.3 million made Avonlea one of Profit Magazine's 100 fastest growing companies' ('Avonlea Traditions' 44). Gallagher Morton is tapping into the mail-order market as well, and consumers can receive an Anne of Green Gables Catalogue for three dollars. The Chatelaine piece mentions as well Gallagher Morton's hundred-thousand-dollar legal battle against 'unauthorized products' and the conflict that arose when 'Prince Edward Island claimed the rights to Anne.' The fact that she was prepared to go to those lengths reflects her recognition of the profit potential of Avonlea products.

The territorial competition for 'authorized,' 'authentic' Anne products resonates more broadly with the emphasis on trademarking in the toy industry. Every child wants a real Tickle-Me-Elmo, not a knock-off: a real Barbie, not a pretender. The most fully realized expression of trademark marketing is surely that of Disney products: Lion Kings, Little Mermaids, Mickey Mouse images, and so on. The potential for cloning seems to be greater with less well-established products. The recent phenomenon of 'Beanie Babies' serves as an example; the 'real' or original Beanie Babies were trademarked by Ty, Inc., of Oakbrook, Illinois, but a rash of Beanie clones quickly appeared. This may be because Beanies are relatively easier to make than, say, convincing-looking Barbie dolls. The Beanies are also more diverse, whereas Barbie presents a more singular and static image (despite her alleged 'updates').

What are we to make of the competing claims of authenticity with respect to Anne dolls, given that dolls made in different places all claim to be 'authentic'? One dictionary definition of 'authentic' is 'of undisputed origin.' In other words, the doll must come from a recognizable source; but a source only becomes recognizable through repetition, and repetition comes about through mass production. Disney products exemplify this notion of 'authenticity'; we can recognize 'authentic' Disney products because we have seen them so frequently. Also, because their trademarks are stamped on them in some visible way, we know that product is 'of undisputed origin,' thus an original Disney product. Gallagher Morton of Avonlea Traditions Inc. no doubt hopes that her products will become so familiar, recognizable, and pervasive in the market-place that any competing claims for 'authentic' Anne products will not get very far. Although successful, her products have not yet reached that stage; that is why there is still contestation and ambiguity around Anne products in a way that there is not around Disney products. The corporatization of authenticity does not admit difference, otherness, or multiplicity of origin. What does our desire to buy 'authentic' products really signify? – our desire for recognizability or familiarity, perhaps, or a single, reductive origin we can trace , or consumer status, since products calling themselves 'authentic' tend to be among the more expensive ones. A visit to the FAO Swartz Toy store, any toy store, or even the Anne of Green Gables Store, readily reveals this.

Will the 'Real' Anne Please Stand Up?

There is as yet no definitive Anne image enshrined in a doll. Anne's dollified image is still in the cloning phase; there is, as we have seen, the Catherine Munn Anne doll, the Gallagher Morton (Avonlea Traditions) Anne doll, the Anne dolls produced by the Green Gables Store, and other unspecified dolls that do not seem to come from anywhere in particular and do not come with 'certificates of authentication.' In the Green Gables Store, a few dolls are made in Prince Edward Island but come with no 'certificate' of authentication; is the consumer to assume that these products are inauthentic? There are even a few (not prominently displayed) obviously homemade Anne dolls and other Anne ornaments made out of sea shells. These items are, if anything, closest to being 'real' and 'authentic' since they are handcrafted, yet, ironically, they have little consumer appeal placed next to the glossy posters and perfect-looking porcelain dolls. In this sense, the store represents a site of confusing overlap between technological, industrial culture (e.g., Avonlea Traditions Inc.) and the culture of the 'folk' (locally handmade artifacts), although the latter is to a considerable degree marginalized within the store. The slick, intertextual marketing tactics evidenced in the Anne Store and in the battle for 'authenticity' with respect to the definitive Anne image have managed to all but reverse the original meaning of 'authenticity,' which now seems to be closer to something corporate, Disneyfied.

The Anne Store, then, is a site of tensions between competing claims of authenticity as well as between homemade artifacts and mass-produced ones with homespun pretensions. The store owners count on the late-twentieth-century consumer's ability to accommodate contradictions. The ideal consumer, from a marketing perspective, will find little amiss in seeing a CD-ROM or computer mouse pad in an old-fashioned country store, or a ninety-dollar doll based on a literary character who was a penniless orphan.

Iconography for Sale

In the 1996 *Chatelaine* article cited above, Kathryn Gallagher Morton of Avonlea Traditions Inc. constructs the enduring appeal of Anne in terms of a nationalist iconography; 'as long as there are Mounties and beavers,' she says, 'there'll be Anne.' To what extent is identification as a national symbol really the key to Anne's (or Morton's) success in the market-place? What symbols, really, are for sale, in the Avonlea mythology?

An examination of products for sale in the Green Gables Store reveals that some images from Montgomery's books are privileged over others, and that an iconography, or set of salable symbols, has built up around this privileged set of images. We can recognize these images as privileged by virtue of their repetition. The plates and postcards underscore symbols that are not necessarily nationalistic. Many ceramic plates depict the house, Green Gables, a privileged element in the iconography. The on-line Anne of Green Gables Store sells a ceramic Green Gables replica for $39.99. It also sells a 'limited edition collector's plate' for $39.99. The image on the plate is Anne in her Megan Follows incarnation, standing in front of Green Gables. She has a book in her hand, and although the title is obscured, the image carries with it a curious self-reflexivity if we imagine that the character has stepped out of the book in which she was created. Among the eight-inch ceramic plates the Charlottetown store sells, Anne is featured on one apologizing to Mrs Lynde; on another, smashing the slate over Gilbert's head – images of subordination and rebellion, but also images that exhibit what a female whose vanity is insulted will do.

One of the most pervasive symbolic images for sale depicts Anne waiting at Bright River Station in the novel's second chapter (see figure 14.1). This is the scene depicted on the posters, and on a postcard manufactured by Avonlea Traditions Inc. It is interesting that this is such a popular image, since it depicts the young heroine at her most vulnerable and passive, a victim of circumstance. It depicts her as homeless, a migrant figure, someone on the margins of society who is not yet accepted. As a symbol, it delineates someone who has 'no place' – the placeless female at Bright River, Grand Central Station, Whitcross, wherever. It is an image that allows comfortable middle-class consumers to romanticize the margins, the plight of the outsider who must wait to be rescued. Perhaps buying the plate or card with that image on it represents in some way a symbolic act of rescue.

The most privileged consumable images of Anne depict her at her most childlike: helpless, impetuous, governed by her emotions. It is not only a countrified, sentimentalized, and feminized past that is being marketed; it is the cult of childhood as well. A more innocent time. A more traditional construction of gender. The preponderance of dolls (see figure 20.1) in the Green Gables market-place enshrines the female child as perhaps the key commodity of the Avonlea mythology. Dolls symbolically reinforce the valuing of female identity as decorative, echoing mass media's tendency 'to reproduce traditional sex roles' that position women as 'subordinate, passive, submissive and marginal, performing a limited number of secondary and uninteresting tasks confined to their sexuality, their emotions and their domesticity' (Strinati, 184).

Dolls must also, in some way, empower their owner. Every child is larger than his or her doll, owns his or her doll, bends the doll to his or her will. What is for sale in the Avonlea mythology is at once power and submissiveness; access to the world of the outsider from a position of comfort; participation in a quaint 'residual' culture. The articulation of the Avonlea mythology in popular culture is fraught with meanings that are, often enough, contradictory. In this way, the popular culture texts predicated on *Anne of Green Gables* resonate with popular culture texts at large: as Fiske puts it, 'full of gaps, contradictions, and inadequacies' (*Understanding Popular Culture* 126).

However flawed, these popular culture texts (for those who can afford them) allow the possibility of letting other worlds into our lives. They may even serve to take us back to the primary texts – in this case, Montgomery's novels. The acquisition of a ceramic replica of Green Gables or its heroine reflects our own desire for the iconography of a green world, childhood, and innocence, all bound up with our desire for things knowable (we know Anne's story ends happily), and for control and possession. Consumable Avonlea embodies innocence and experience. Consumable Avonlea embraces both art and life; in the poster of Anne waiting at Bright River station displayed in some child's bedroom Anne will wait forever, suspended between past and future, like the child-owner of the bedroom herself, waiting for her future to begin.

Notes

I am grateful to *CCL: Canadian Children's Literature / Littérature canadienne pour la jeunesse* for permission to reprint 'Consumable Avonlea: The Commodification of the Green Gables Mythology' which originally appeared in *CCL* 91/92. 24.3/4 (Fall/winter 1998): 7–21.

1 In the spring session, 1998, I designed a course called 'Green Gables and After: Women Writers of Atlantic Canada,' which I taught in the Canadian Studies program, University of Washington, Seattle. Canadian students may have responded differently to the distinctly Canadian regional setting of *Anne of Green Gables*.
2 Prices and merchandise may have changed slightly since then.

Chapter 20

Snapshot: Making Anne and Emily Dolls

TARA MacPHAIL

My sister, Anne MacPhail, is a professional doll-maker on Prince Edward Island. For her and many other craftswomen, making porcelain dolls is a labour of love (figure 20.1). Like an artist, she signs each doll with her name and dates it. On Prince Edward Island, the popularity of L.M. Montgomery's *Anne of Green Gables* has created an entire industry, as noted by Jeanette Lynes in the preceding chapter. On entering any craft store in Charlottetown or across the Island, the visitor will find a cornucopia of Anne and Emily dolls varying in look and size, in price and quality. In addition to Anne, there are Diana Barry and, more recently, the black-haired Emily Byrd Starr, whose popularity has been rising in the wake of the television series *Emily of New Moon*.

Professional doll-makers challenge themselves to capture Anne's fiery spirit in original designs that do not always conform to all the details of the novels. In the novel, Anne Shirley has red hair, green eyes, and a skinny figure. Freckles are liberally spread all over her face. The ordinary observer, says the narrator in *Anne of Green Gables*, sees this: 'A child of about eleven, garbed in a very short, very tight, very ugly dress of yellowish gray wincey. She wore a faded brown sailor hat and beneath the hat, extending down her back, were two braids of very thick, decidedly red hair. Her face was small, white and thin, also much freckled; her mouth was large and so were her eyes, that looked green in some lights and moods and gray in others' (*AGG* 18). This is a poor little girl, not a conventionally attractive damsel. Yet tourists strolling through P.E.I. stores will be hard pressed to find a doll that wears a short, tight, ugly, wincey dress and a faded sailor's hat. Nor

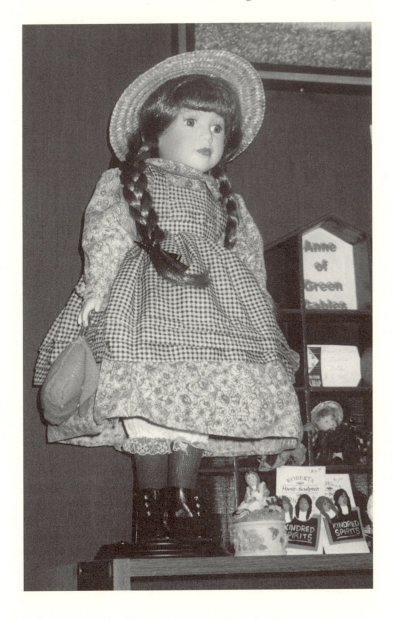

20.1   Handmade 'Anne' doll by Island doll-maker Florence MacDougall, Confederation Centre of the Arts Giftstore, 2001. Photograph by J. Paul Boudreau.

are purchasers interested in this type of realistic authenticity. Most Anne dolls offered for sale in the stores wear a green dress with an apron on top, the green alluding to *Green* Gables.

Like Anne, Emily Byrd Starr presents a challenge for doll-makers in that she is not conventionally beautiful. Yet she presents a striking visual contrast with Anne 'in her large, purplish-grey eyes with their very long lashes and black brows, in her high, white forehead – too high for beauty – in the delicate modeling of her pale oval face and sensitive mouth, in the little ears that were pointed just a wee bit to show that she was kin to tribes of elfland' (*ENM* 13). Perhaps overwhelmed by the challenge, some doll-makers make their Emilys with 'grand' dresses, with the result that Emily sometimes looks like Diana Barry, Anne Shirley's bosom friend. 'Most Emily dolls I have seen look as though they are five or so years old,' says Anne MacPhail, who defends her own creation. 'Our doll, I think, looks more like the age she should look; and she does not look like Diana.'[1] The former House of International Dolls in DeSable, P.E.I., produced one of the first Emily dolls, modelling it on Ben Stahl's cover illustration of the McClelland and Stewart 1992 edition of *Emily of New Moon*. In this picture, Emily wears a white dress with a purplish-blue petticoat, echoing the colour of the eyes as described by Montgomery; the white sleeves and collar of the dress are visible; this doll's black hair is braided with red bows at the end of each braid.

It takes a full week to produce a porcelain Anne or Emily doll with a cloth body, that is, working on one doll exclusively. Anne MacPhail moves us through the intricate steps of the process. She begins by pouring the moulds with porcelain slip, a claylike mud substance. This produces the 'greenware,' which is removed from the mould and is left to dry. She cleans the greenware of all the seams left by the moulds, using fine brushes and scalpels to smooth out bumps or scratches on the surface of the greenware. This process usually takes a full day, provided all goes well. Breakage happens quite often, either because the porcelain is too thin or because the piece is accidentally dropped or bumped. When that happens, the process has to start all over again. Once the head section is cleaned, the doll is signed: my sister's signature reads 'Anne of Argyle Shore.' After the signing, the greenware is fired in a kiln. Once baked, it has become porcelain, and it is time to paint the face. This time-intensive process requires artistic talent and a steady hand. After a second firing, the eyes are set in, usually with a plaster-like compound.

While the greenware is undergoing the transition into porcelain, Anne starts making the clothes. Again, it takes a full day of fussy precision work to produce the undergarments, the dress, and the apron in miniature sizes to fit the doll. To assemble the cloth body, she stuffs the body firmly with cotton batting, sews the body together at the top, and glues the arms to the cotton body. She attaches the head to the shoulder plate and sews the entire unit onto the body: the doll begins to look finished. To create the pate that rounds out the head, styrofoam balls are cut in half and shaped like the back of a head. Then the glorious red wig is glued in place, the hair is braided and arranged, and the doll is dressed. A new Anne has come to life at the end of a full week's work.

The perceptive observer may notice that there are only seven freckles on the nose of Anne MacPhail's Anne doll, although, according to the novel, she is covered in freckles. So why only seven? 'It seemed to be the most reasonable number for us to use,' she explains. 'It was also a number that could be spread evenly, three freckles on either side of the nose, and one on the bridge of the nose. We also thought it looked the best when we were coming up with our Anne doll.' Most Anne dolls in stores today have freckles only on the cheeks.

In the preceding chapter, Lynes noted the higher prices on Anne dolls with greater claims to authenticity, prompting this excellent question: 'What are we to make of the competing claims of authenticity with respect to Anne dolls, given that dolls made in different places all claim to be "authentic"?'(17). There is fierce competition among dollmakers about whose dolls best capture the spirit of Anne; and it takes an expert to ascertain degrees of quality in a handmade doll. But the majority of the Anne dolls sold are mass-produced, many of them imported from China and other countries and sold by the hundreds during the summer tourist season on the Island, as well as being retailed across Canada. After working as a summer student in a P.E.I. museum and gift store that made and sold its own Anne dolls, I witnessed at first hand that the imported, mass-produced dolls outsold the hand-made ones by far. This was for at least two reasons: the imported dolls gave a reasonable and always attractive depiction of Anne; and they were affordable, costing from ten to twenty-five dollars. Contrast that to the price of a hand-made doll, which ranges from fifty to two-hundred-and-fifty dollars. Still, the motto holds that you get what you pay for. Professional doll-makers are quick to point to the shortcomings of mass-manufactured dolls: the body is sometimes bent when it arrives at the store; the head is often glued to the body instead of being securely fastened to a shoulder plate and sewn onto the cloth body; the body may lose its firmness and become soft. And the list goes on.

The expert collector, therefore, checks for a number of items before purchasing a doll. First, in the case of a porcelain doll, collectors ensure that there are no bubbles or scratches on the surface of the porcelain, for impairments suggest that the doll was improperly or hastily made. If the doll's body is made of cloth and is stuffed with a cotton batting, the collector ensures the firmness of the body. If the body is not firm at the time of purchase, the body will sag and the doll will lose its ability to stand straight. To the collector, therefore, the structure of the doll is almost as important as its appearance. Collectors also check behind the ears, at the base of the neck, and perhaps even a little under the wig, where the doll-maker has applied her signature. The lack of a signature signifies that the doll is manufactured rather than handcrafted, and thus is less valuable. A signed doll is handmade, whereas a doll that has a stamp or some other form of insignia on either the back of the neck or behind an ear is more likely mass produced.

Intent on controlling the aggressive commodification of Montgomery, the Anne of Green Gables Licensing Authority on Prince Edward Island (established in 1994) has created the following guidelines to which Anne dolls and other Anne products must adhere:[2]

1. They must be appropriate to the image of Anne (or other characters, e.g., Diana Barry, Marilla, Matthew, or places, e.g., Green Gables house) as depicted by L.M. Montgomery;
2. They must be of high quality and meet standards specified by the Anne Authority; and
3. They must be appropriate to the use or purpose for which they were intended. (Anne of Green Gables Licensing Authority, 3)

The person seeking a licence fills out an application form, pays a fifty-dollar fee, and submits a sample product. The 'Anne Authority' evaluates the product and makes a decision. This is, as the 'Anne Authority' sees it, a way of ensuring some quality control of the products linked to Montgomery's name. Still, Anne products continue to be sold that are not licensed, including mass-produced dolls imported from other countries. Other products are licensed that not all Montgomery readers will find tasteful or appropriate.

Dolls continue to be made in private homes across the Island – for many, a proud tradition. Anne MacPhail, for one, is thrilled that her work is travelling around the world, with Japanese, American, Australian and European tourists falling in love with her vision of Anne and Emily. Lynes writes that the 'most privileged consumable images of Anne depict her at her most childlike: helpless, impetuous, governed by her emotions.' Yet when I look through the assortment of my sister's dolls, and through the myriad porcelain characters offered in stores, I also see many other representations – of the seriousness of Anne, the overachiever, and of Emily, the driven young girl as a poet. As carriers of gender-specific codes, Anne and Emily always present the antithesis to the sexualized and utopian-bodied Barbie dolls. But this does not make them any less complex. Anne and Emily dolls are steeped in a more ordinary world of girl culture and encourage their owners to be just that: proud and independent girls.

Notes

1 This and all other quotations are based on my interview with Anne MacPhail, 15 February 2001.
2 The Anne of Green Gables Licensing Authority on Prince Edward Island consists of a board of members representing Montgomery's heirs and the Province of Prince Edward Island. Part of the mandate of the 'Anne Authority' is to safeguard the integrity of L.M. Montgomery's image and of the Anne images as they appear on commercial and other products.

Chapter 21

Snapshot: My Life as Anne in Japan

TARA NOGLER

As a shy yet excitable redhead growing up on Prince Edward Island, I vividly recall my first viewing of the musical production at age four, an experience marked by my parents' frantic attempts to keep me in my seat. *Anne of Green Gables* was one of the first novels I read. At age thirteen, I was hired by a company named 'Anne and I on P.E.I.' to play the red-haired Anne Shirley during the summer tourist season in Cavendish. Playacting Anne, I attended birthday parties and weekend picnics and was interviewed on radio to promote the company. I had my picture taken with tourists, many of them Japanese. Even with the language barrier, my introduction to the Japanese love of Anne was memorable. I vividly recall a young Japanese woman clinging to my body, crying and sobbing uncontrollably: at thirteen, a powerful if somewhat disconcerting experience.

In April 1996, by then a university student, I noticed a classified advertisement in Charlottetown's *The Guardian* newspaper:

Employment opportunity:

Applications are being accepted for employment as 'Theme Park Hosts' with Canadian World in Ashibetsu, Japan. Successful Candidates will portray Anne, Diana, Gilbert and Miss Stacy. Acting experience required.

Even though I no longer harboured illusions of grandeur concerning my acting ability, I took my cue from my encouraging mother and made the call to Charlottetown's City Hall.

Three weeks later, I was on a plane bound for Sapporo, the capital city of Hokkaido, the north-eastern island of Japan. Much like Anne Shirley upon her arrival at Bright River Station, I was transported to a different world, one that would be my adoptive home for little more than six months. The intense shock of the time change after an eighteen-hour trip, combined with my apparent deafness in one ear (a result of the shift in altitude), lack of sleep, water, and nutrition, not to mention the language barrier, all combined to produce what must have seemed a countenance of stunned semi-catatosis. My anxiety was somewhat allayed by my good-humoured translator/guide/boss, Hiromi Fukada, who slipped in a CD with 'The Vapors.' To the tune of 'I Think I'm Turning Japanese,' we departed from Sapporo's Narita Airport.

On the drive to Ashibetsu City, we stopped at the local Seven-Eleven for my first moment of local culture. While the layout was much like that of North-American convenience stores, there was a mid-sized water tank with live octopus, squid, and other sea urchins. One refrigerated aisle was lined with rice balls, of a variety of shapes and sizes, labelled in one of the four Japanese alphabets. Another section was devoted to snack foods – different combinations of rice crackers, dried and smoked seafood, and trail mixes with mini-dried fish mixed in with peanuts, raisins, and coconut. The walls surrounding the store were lined with a plethora of refrigerated drinks, many of which, as I later learned, were iced teas, coffees, and high-powered sports drinks with names such as 'Pocari Sweat.' The stop produced the desired effect: I had my glimpse of Japanese junk-food culture.

Our destination was Canadian World in Hokkaido, one of many theme parks in Japan dedicated to cultural and national figures. Presenting Canada through a nineteenth-century lens, Canadian World had opened its gates in 1991.[1] Upon entering the park, guests received a 'Canadian' passport, which mapped out the park's terrain and in which they could collect stamps from each of the 'countries.' The theme park spanned one hundred acres, each of the six areas labelled as a 'country.' Avonlea spanned the largest area and served as the main attraction of Canadian World, housing an exact replica of Green Gables. The house was built using the blueprints of the original located in Cavendish, P.E.I.; even the kitchen utensils were placed strategically to reflect the original. Across the way was Diana Barry's house, where guests could rent period clothing and have their pictures taken posing with Anne amid the natural scenery. It was not uncommon to see Japanese women enter sporting long, lacy, and extravagant dresses with petticoats, even in the heat of summer, bearing everything from parasols to Anne dolls. Behind Diana's house was the Haunted Wood, where guests could take a long hike, and Lovers' Lane, which led up to Terra Nova, a large chalet that housed a gift shop, an art gallery, a large collection of antique organs and other musical instruments, and a traditional English-style tea-room. Across a field of sunflowers was Orwell School, where Miss Stacy – or myself, on her days off – conducted hourly basic English lessons.

My life as Anne Shirley (figure 21.1) involved greeting guests, conducting tours, posing for photographs with tourists and for promotional and advertising shoots, doing interviews for various television shows, and performing skits from *Anne of Green Gables*. My average daily schedule looked like this:

6–7:00 a.m.	Wake up and prepare for work.
7:30 a.m.	Catch Canadian World bus at Maple Heights, Kamiashibetsu.
8:00 a.m.	Arrive at Canadian World 'Parliament' (main office).
8:00–8:25 a.m.	Get into costume, prepare make-up, braid hair, etc.
8:25 a.m.	Attend staff meeting with three big bosses and office staff. Greetings, prayers, and debriefing session on the day's events.
8:45 a.m.	Walk to the front gates of Canadian World with four fellow Canadian actors.
9–10:00 a.m.	Greet guests entering the park; pose for pictures, etc.
10:00 a.m.	Walk from front gate through Bright River Station, past clock tower, to Avonlea and Green Gables.
11:30 a.m.	Have lunch.
12:20 p.m.	Walk to Terrase Dufferin to make appearance and attend the lunchtime performance shows; once or twice a week, do weekly performance or skit of scenes from the play.
12:50 p.m.	With Miss Stacy and Diana, take bus to Orwell Schoolhouse for 1:00 p.m. English conversation lessons.
2:00 p.m.	Leave Orwell School and return to Green Gables or Colts to converse with guests.
2:30 p.m.	Go to Mrs Lynde's Restaurant for 'Teatime with Anne,' to socialize with guests and discuss Canada and Island life and culture.

21.1 Anne (Tara Nogler) and Diana in Canadian World, Hokkaido, Japan, 1996. Private photograph.

3:00 p.m.	Return to Green Gables for pictures, pictures, and more ...
4:45 p.m.	Return to main entrance to bid farewell to guests.
6:00 p.m.	Return to Parliament (main office) and change.
6:20 p.m.	Take bus back to Kamiashibetsu.
6:45–7:00 p.m.	Arrive home.

While this schedule made up my regular daily routine, there was some room for spontaneity.[2] To guests, I was 'Akage no An chan,' literally translated, 'Anne of Red Hair child.' As Anne, I went wherever my 'Anne spirit' took me. That meant trekking over to Diana Barry's house, where guests paid to dress up in nineteenth-century period clothing, complete with 'Anne' paraphernalia: parasols, wigs, hats, and make-up. As Anne, I ran down to Terrase Dufferin, a strip of restaurants and cafés styled after Old Quebec, featuring 'Canadian' cuisine and gift shops on the bank of 'The Lake of Shining Waters,' in front of which buskers and performers displayed their talents to an eager audience. Still as Anne, I also enjoyed horseback riding, picnicking, or canoeing in the Lake of Shining Waters on quiet days. Sometimes I was able to steal away to the First Aid Station for a lunchtime nap.

During the busy months of June to August, we routinely welcomed up to two thousand Japanese guests per day, including five to ten tour buses with high school girls or Anne clubs from across Japan. As the only 'Anne' working in the park, I was in high demand. Along with four other Canadians who played Diana, Miss Stacy, and other characters from the novel, I felt an experience akin to the 'Mickey Mouse' phenomenon in the United States. As Anne, I was the star of the show, for visitors did not always remember the other characters in the novel, many having been exposed to the film versions or to *Animé*, a popular, condensed pocketbook version of the story.[3]

Within its beautiful nature setting, the park served as site for various Canadian rituals, most notably the Western wedding. Surrounded by immaculate gardens, there was a church in which many Japanese couples had Christian weddings performed after their traditional Shinto wedding. Many young women devoted to Canadian culture saw the Christian wedding as an act designed to bring good luck or good fortune. This practice of the double wedding, a recent trend, seemed more common with couples from Honshu, the most densely populated central island of Japan. Similarly, Anne was most popular in the biggest cities such as Tokyo and Osaka, as city dwellers are drawn to Anne's longing for innocence, simplicity, and beauty in nature. In this way, the appeal of Hokkaido was obvious: natural beauty, scenery, and serenity were marketed as avidly as Anne Shirley herself. Historians and literary scholars, including Douglas Baldwin in 'L.M. Montgomery's *Anne of Green Gables*: The Japanese Connection' and Yoshiko Akamatsu in 'Japanese Readings of *Anne of Green Gables*,' have documented that this desire for nature and innocence explains aspects of Anne's appeal to the Japanese. Canadian life amid beautiful natural scenery and surrounded by mountains (reminiscent of the Canadian West) provided an ideal setting. Not only was the climate similar to Canada's, Hokkaido being subject to climatic extremes and unpredictable weather, but there was little boundary between the park itself and the surrounding wildlife, with foxes and rabbits wandering freely in the park.

The natural setting of Canadian World was not only part of the park's allure; it also became, like the many Anne products in the gift shops, a marketable product. From bags of lavender bearing the title, 'Anne's Lavender Dreams' to dried and pressed flowers and squash from the Craft Village botanical and vegetable gardens, some of the best-selling products came from nature and were used to sell an image of Canada to the Japanese consumer. The products ranged from Anne beanbag dolls to Anne wines and beers, Anne-shaped chocolates, cookies, and candy, and T-shirts bearing the mysterious misprint *Anne of Green Gavole*. When I was touring Osaka, we went to a 'Canadian Bakery' that was selling 'Anne cakies,' a sweet white donut with red bean paste in the middle. Part of our work involved preparing, organizing, and packaging various products to be sold at gift shops in the park and, on a larger scale, at shops in various urban centres. Some of my most vivid memories involve afternoons spent at Green Gables, with friends and fellow workers, separating and packaging bundles of lavender, clover, chives, and other natural products while guests passed through and took our pictures.[4]

In my Anne costume I was a cultural ambassador for Prince Edward Island, but also a promoter of products. Besides my work at the theme park, my position required my participation on many promotional tours and trips across Japan. On my travels, I visited Osaka, Tokyo, Kobe, Asahikawa, and Obihiro. These trips involved non-stop activity. For example, on a five-day trip to Osaka, we spent each day meeting with newspaper and magazine companies (fourteen in one day), appearing on television talk and game shows and at cultural events and department stores, and signing autographs. On these tours, I did television promotions and photography shoots to promote Canadian World and commercial Japanese products, attended business meetings with various company officials (major tourist and commercial companies), and handed out promotional flyers. As Anne, I was constantly in the public eye.

The Japanese fascination with cultural authenticity extended beyond the material trappings of Green Gables and its household products to us as Canadians – foreigners and representatives of Canadian culture. One incident in particular encapsulates for me this pursuit of authenticity, when a television crew for a Tokyo talk show came to do a profile of Canadian World. The hosts were two women in their twenties with cutesy, bright-coloured attire, short skirts, pigtails, and high-heeled boots. I had a short interview with one of the hosts and then gave a tour of the house. While the sight of Anne's room evoked sighs and great enthusiasm, a good portion of the tour was spent in the kitchen where the two hosts fawned over each and every item, from meat grinder to washboard, spoon to broom, wood-stove to wrought-iron pots. Everything was 'authentic' in the words of the hosts!

In the afternoons, Mrs Lynde's Restaurant provided the setting for 'Teatime with Anne,' a period reserved for socializing, during which the guests had an opportunity to test their recently learned English phrases and ask me questions about my life in Canada.[5] While I was asked the typical questions ('What does P.E.I. look like?' 'How many kindred spirits do you have?'), I was also frequently asked questions that seemed odd to me (though commonplace and acceptable to many guests): 'Is that your real hair?' 'What's your blood type?' 'How many teeth do you have?' 'What colour is the roof of your mouth?' 'How many toes do you have?' (The list goes on.) As Anne, I had my hair examined, my skin touched and gawked at, my breasts touched, and my nose tweaked on a daily basis. When I greeted guests, their typical first reaction would involve excited exclamations of *kawaii* ('cute'), followed by *Shashin?* ('May I take a picture?'). While I was often the exotic object of the visitor's gaze, I was also looking in on Japanese culture. The obsession with cuteness and the perfect body image – even more pervasive than in North America – remains a forceful memory. It seemed that Anne's biggest fans were the teenage girls and women in their early twenties who embodied sweetness with their ponytails, short skirts, high-heeled shoes, and 'Hello Kitty' backpacks.

In 'my life as Anne,' certain incidents and experiences stand out. While my promotional tours across Japan gave me insight into Japa-nese pop and traditional culture, I also visited a live volcano and the hot springs that are reputed to be ancient forms of therapy in Japan and are abundant in the mountains of Hokkaido. Yet my most pro-found human experience occurred on my visit to Kobe. In 1995, an earthquake had killed nearly 6,000 people and left more than 300,000 homeless; in May 1996, when I visited, people were still picking up the broken pieces of devastation. On the edge of central Kobe, set along a land-filled port, were tents and shelters, temporary housing for the vic-tims of the earthquake. During our stay, we spent a day at an orphan-age with children whose parents had been killed in the earthquake. Many of the younger children had never heard of Anne, while others knew her only through the *Animé* cartoon that was popular at the time. Whether or not they knew Anne or the story, however, these children embraced us literally with open arms. I left that orphanage feeling a mixture of sadness, frustration, compassion, yet also of hope and gratitude for the light that shone in their eyes. While I certainly cannot fathom the very real sense of loss and isolation these children must have felt, I could not help but draw connections to Montgomery herself, orphaned as a child, whose adult work weaves the thematic threads of orphans who attempt to forge identities and homes in foreign communities.

I met people who shared their love for L.M. Montgomery and Anne Shirley, as well as sharing their homes and traditions, taking me inside their rich cultures. In Osaka, I visited numerous ancient Shinto and Buddhist shrines and participated in a traditional Japanese tea ceremony, complete with the kimono and obi, conducted by a Shinto priestess. Japan provided for me a stage for exploring my identity and culture. Just as Anne's fictional character negotiates personal spaces of identity in a new home, so did I, and I will always remember the sound of Japanese girls calling out, 'Hello An Chan,' as I walked by in my Anne costume, an exotic attraction in Hokkaido's Avonlea.

Notes

1 The park shut down in 1998 when it was bought out by the City of Ashibetsu. It is now run as a government amusement park. I later learned that Japan housed such theme parks as German World, Spanish World, Dutch World, and American World, among others.

2 Traditional Japanese (Obon, Candle Art, and Cherry Blossom) festivals and celebrations often commanded special celebrations in the park.

3 The renowned Japanese animator-director team of Hayao Miyazaki and Isao Takahata collaborated on the original *animé* screen adaptation of *Akage no An* (1979), while Miyazaki illustrated and produced several picture-book classics, including *Akage no An* (*Anne of Green Gables*), vols 1–5, videocassettes (1992) and *'Akage No An': Tokuma Anime Ehon* (*'Anne of Green Gables': Tokuma Animé Picturebook*) (1996), abbreviated and illustrated versions of *Anne of Green Gables* for children. For a detailed discussion, see Timothy Craig, *Japan Pop!*

4 At one point, we had small bushels of lavender and chives hanging from the ceiling across the whole first floor of Green Gables. Also, during the weeks

preceding Halloween, we carved and painted pumpkins, which were sold at the main entrance to the park.

5 Commercial culture played upon this obsession with North American culture, using popular English words and phrases to sell products. It was not uncommon, for example, in a department store, to see a large stock of clothing items with words such as 'happy,' 'beautiful,' 'I Love You' printed on them in a variety of colours and textures. Popular cultural icons ranged, at the time, from Michael Jackson to Elvis Presley to The Carpenters.

Chapter 22

Taishu Bunka and Anne Clubs in Japan

DANIÈLE ALLARD

In 1997, I began graduate studies in comparative literature at the Université de Sherbrooke in Quebec. My project was to investigate the reception of Hanako Muraoka's renowned translation of *Anne of Green Gables* (*Akage no An*, 1952). The following year, thanks to a scholarship granted by the Japanese government, I left for Osaka, Japan, where I first spent six months studying Japanese and then enrolled as a research student for a year at Nara Women's University. It was during that year that I became immersed in Japanese culture – its festivals and traditions – and became acquainted with Anne clubs, which are the focus of this chapter.

The most unusual encounter I had with Anne clubs was accidental. It happened at the *Awa Odori*, a spectacular summer dance festival; I had been invited to participate in one of the parades. Women generally wear light, colourful kimonos and a peculiar hat associated with the event, while men put on a *happi* coat (Japanese festival vest), shorts, and a bandanna. A woman was kindly and expertly helping me don the traditional wear, and we began to chat. 'What are you doing in Japan?' she asked me. 'I am interested in red-haired Anne,' I replied. 'Are you *really*?' she exclaimed enthusiastically and added: 'I love Anne myself! In fact, I belong to a group called "Anne's Group."' The woman I had thus met was none other than Mrs Noriko Seo, a pharmacist and the editor of the newsletter and publications of Anne's Group, a club inspired by L.M. Montgomery's heroine. Noriko Seo was an important contact.

Anne of Green Gables is intensely popular in Japan. After the publication of Muraoka's first translation in 1952, Anne immediately won the hearts of many Japanese, and her popularity has steadily grown since (e.g., Katsura, 'Red-Haired Anne' 58–61; Akamatsu, 'Japanese Readings' 201–12). Now, five decades later, not only is *Anne of Green Gables* a widely read novel in translation, but Anne herself is a vastly popular figure in comic books, television animation, and movies. Throughout the country, reflections of Anne can also be found in various commercial ventures and in educational contexts: there are Anne-related books, pastry shops, cafés, and home-furnishing boutiques, Avonlea-type inns, and institutions using her name, such as a nurses' training school called 'The School of Green Gables.' As Tara Nogler reported (in chapter 21), until 1998 there was even a replica of Avonlea in northern Japan, in a theme park called Canadian World, where the visitor could meet Anne, Matthew, Marilla, and other Green Gables characters as impersonated by Canadians from Prince Edward Island.

In exploring the Anne clubs as a popular culture phenomenon, I begin with the concept of popular culture itself. In North America and Europe, popular culture has come to the forefront as a specific field of research in the latter half of this century, especially the last twenty years. One of its current concerns calls for a dismantling of the 'sacred frontiers' existing between high culture and mass culture, an enterprise in which this collection on L.M. Montgomery participates. These frontiers, however, do not exist to the same degree in Japan. An intriguing discovery was that 'popular culture' does not have an equivalent expression in the Japanese language. *Taishu bunka*, the most frequent translation, is closer in meaning to 'mass culture.' Professor Hidetoshi Kato,[1] a leading expert on Japanese *taishu bunka*, who is also familiar with Western culture, explains in his *Handbook of Japanese Popular Culture*:[2] 'Why the American sense of "popular culture" is not applicable in the Japanese context is an interesting intellectual and cultural question. In the first place, the term *taishu*, which originates in the Buddhist tradition, has an egalitarian meaning where there is no distinction between "elite" and "mass," "literate" and "non-literate," and so on ...' (xviii).

Kato further situates Japanese *taishu bunka* in historical perspective, explaining that *taishu bunka* ripened during Japan's period of isolation, approximately between 1612 and 1868. During this time, peace prevailed for two and a half centuries and society devoted itself to various cultural enterprises. There were nominal class distinctions, but nevertheless *taishu bunka*, ranging from the tea ceremony to kabuki theatre, thrived: culture could be enjoyed by all. Japan also had a literacy rate that was among the highest in the world at that time, estimated at 45 to 50 per cent. Western missionaries visiting Japan in the eighteenth century stated in awe that 'in Japan, even a peasant is a poet.' Given these facts, Kato considers that Japan was an egalitarian society in several respects.

Taishu bunka, in the past and today, is actually *the* culture shared by every single Japanese individual. It may even be acting as a social cement, diminishing what gaps there are between the upper and the lower middle class, between the university educated and high school graduates, and perhaps even between male and female. The tea ceremony, flower arranging, sumo, martial arts, baseball, and popular singers are shared by millions, regardless of social status and level of education. Kato explains that, before the isolation period, the samurai exchanged poetry with their opponents before fighting and were certainly expected to have literary taste. Following the disarmament of the population proclaimed at the end of sixteenth century, the samurai, who as a consequence became more civilian bureaucrats than fighters, invested highly in institutions of higher education. Because of their leadership position, they also had to be educated in various disciplines so as to maintain a healthy economy. In their leisure time, they indulged in a variety of artistic activities, including the tea ceremony, music, and drama. The merchant and farmer class also made efforts to remain highly literate and versed in the arts, and the ideal was for a successful merchant to retire early and relish these arts and literature. Merchants were also the patrons of artists, of which many are famous today. As for the farmers, although they had little money, they had to be literate since the responsibility for keeping records of the village fell upon them. They may not have been patrons of artists, but they offered hospitality to artists and travelling men of letters in exchange for artworks or formal learning. Moreover, education was available to farmers through Buddhist temples.

Parallel to this development, arts that were sacred became secular. Such was the case for kabuki theatre, sumo wrestling, and specific forms of storytelling – forms originally dedicated to deities. Popular fiction also appeared in the eighteenth century and, because of Japan's high literacy rate, there quickly was a 'mass audience' to receive it. Historians claim that one of the best-selling authors of the time (Takizawa Bakin) was in fact the first author in the world to earn his living solely through his writing activities.

Contemporary Japanese have followed the path of their ancestors. In

The Japanese Today (1988), Edwin Reischauer states that Japan's population is most likely the best educated in the world, especially in terms of a solid general education (190). He corroborates information provided by Kato in relation to 'mass culture' in Japan, namely with regard to its pervasiveness across classes and to the lack of a 'high culture' reserved for an élite. 'Culture, of course has various levels, from mass customs at the bottom to the most sophisticated fine arts at the top, but even these horizontal layers are not very pronounced in Japan ... and surprisingly high levels of artistic appreciation and etiquette reach down to the virtual bottom of society ... in a way that is rare elsewhere in the world' (216–17).

The existence of Anne clubs in Japan, therefore, needs to be considered within this specific Japanese cultural context. Anne is an integral element of Japanese *taishu bunka* – as are other Western icons[3] – and Anne clubs are one of the many ways in which this becomes apparent. In trying to understand why Anne clubs exist, we need to consider the specific cultural factors that come into play. Learning English is a priority for many Japanese, as is becoming familiar with the Western lifestyle. The Anne series and other L.M. Montgomery novels provide an important means of access to Western society (see, for example, Akamatsu, 210; Stoffman, 57) and, combined with the wide variety of Japanese publications pertaining to Anne's everyday life, the novels inspire many Japanese, women especially, to cross the threshold of this door to the West. Albeit a fictional character, Anne is also often perceived as charismatic and having an endearing personality. She is admired for her optimism, perseverance in the face of hardship, diligence, imagination, and orientation towards family, as well as for the affection she holds for and receives from those around her. In addition, Prince Edward Island and various sites described in the novels are fully accessible today in much of their pristine state, and the Japanese can afford the trip, if only for a short time.

Most importantly, Japanese society is a group-oriented society.[4] The Japanese carry out activities in groups to a far greater degree than in the West, and clubs of all kinds abound. Anne clubs are indeed original, yet they are also part of the fabric of Japanese culture, and the Japanese fascination with Anne, I propose, needs to be understood within that context. It is not possible to have an exact idea of how many such clubs exist, because clubs in general are often local, of a small scale, and not always active in recruiting new members or making themselves widely known. The frequency with which they meet and the level of members' involvement also vary greatly. In addition, there are clubs that temporarily focus on activities related to Anne within a broader range of goals and activities, and this makes precise tabulation of Anne clubs even more difficult.

As the appendix to this chapter shows, my study is based on a selection of eleven Anne clubs in Japan. Among them are the oldest and most important clubs in terms of numbers and renown: The Anne Clan (1973), Buttercups (1981), Anne Academy (1989), the Japan P.E.I. Society (1992), Lupins (1992), the L.M. Montgomery Land Trust – Japan Branch (1999). These, in addition to smaller clubs, were referred to me while I was in Japan or have been written about in scholarly articles, in the press, or on the World Wide Web, as being active and accessible or publicly recruiting members.[5] The appendix provides a good representation of Anne clubs in Japan, although some clubs do not necessarily fall within my working definition of a small club that meets regularly. All groups that accorded priority to Anne and Montgomery were included.

People from all walks of life join together in Anne clubs: housewives, students, models, professional writers, teachers, scholars, engineers, and business people. Activities vary greatly, and for this reason the clubs often differ substantially from one another. Some could also be thought of as fan clubs, although it is important to note that the negative stereotypes often applied to fandom in North America – cultivation of worthless knowledge, brainless consumerism, intellectual immaturity, inability to separate fantasy from reality (Jenkins, 10) – do not necessarily apply to Japanese clubs. 'To be a fan is to exemplify cultural values of loyalty and dedication, service to one's public superior, and empathetic support' explains Christine Yano, who has studied fandom in relation to the Japanese music industry (Yano, 336). Ultimately, the position of fan is culturally affirmed and lauded in Japan.

Many of these Anne fans, then, hope to emulate aspects of Anne's personality. They also use the story as a reference book for learning about Western culture. In other words, as Yoshiko Akamatsu has explained, *Anne of Green Gables* is used as a guidebook for life, on both a spiritual and a practical level (209–10). The novel was published in Japan shortly after the Second World War, and it came as a ray of sunlight to many trying to cope in a devastated country, and especially to young girls. Here was an optimistic orphan who fought to overcome difficulties and won the love of the adults surrounding her.[6] Those who loved Anne then often continued to do so later in life, and many adult women today find comfort in reading over favourite passages of the novel in times of personal turmoil (see Yokokawa 'The Forty Years,' 39–40; Stoffman, 57).

In numerous conversations, club members have underscored their desire to integrate some of Anne's values into their lives. Indeed, the Anne Clan (*An o Shiru Ichizoku*), one of the largest clubs, with one hundred members and almost a thirty-year history, has made this an area of focus for the group. The Anne Clan's leader and founder, Mrs Kazue Kenmotsu, explains that the Anne series is like 'the special passport to enter the fantasy world from the real world.' Thus she has suggested that members keep a daily diary in which poetic moments that Anne might appreciate are recorded. If there is nothing special to chronicle on a given day, then favourite quotations from the series should be written down. Members of the Anne Clan, and perhaps of the other clubs as well, share Mrs Kenmotsu's views of emulating some of Anne's personal values. They also share an interest in exposing themselves to practical aspects of Western culture.

That all the Anne clubs have open windows onto Western culture is reflected in club activities, which include travelling abroad, preserving the Montgomery heritage, investing in arts and crafts, and learning English. The Japan P.E.I. Society, for instance, prides itself on providing up-to-date information on Prince Edward Island and L.M. Montgomery through publications, contributions to the press, and the Internet. There is also an English-language Web page with an electronic question-and-answer forum and useful links to many other informative websites.[7] This organization is even recognized by Visitor's Information in Prince Edward Island.

The increase in Japanese tourism to Prince Edward Island is likely related to the 1979–80 telecast of the animated series *Red-Haired Anne*, which ran on prime-time television for a full year. The island's scenery is beautifully reproduced in the series, as the Japanese crew is said to have gone to Canada in preparation for production (Akamatsu, 210). The nineteen-eighties also witnessed the appearance of books featuring superb photography of Prince Edward Island to complement the growing number of books related to Anne's lifestyle, including cookbooks and handicraft and home entertainment books. Visual images of the island as a wondrous nature haven may have paved the way for Japanese tourists, including men who were not originally interested in Montgomery's work. In other cases, clubs were created following a trip to Prince Edward Island. The experience of visiting an island whose beauty often exceeds expectations and where one can fully experience Montgomery's world and that of her beloved heroines seems to have been a catalyst for the setting up of clubs.

The Japanese are making a concerted effort to help preserve this world, not just for ecological reasons but because genuine sites of pilgrimage are at stake. To this end, a branch of P.E.I.'s L.M. Montgomery Land Trust was recently established. The objective is to protect a portion of the northern shore of Prince Edward Island – the setting of the Anne series – in the hope of maintaining it as natural landscape or agricultural land. In addition, L.M. Montgomery heritage locations in Canada are receiving monetary donations from Japan, towards which Buttercups club members have been especially generous. Just a few examples of this generosity include donations of $3,000 (in 1988) towards the renovation of the Lower Bedeque Schoolhouse; $1,700 (in 1996) towards the restoration of the Leaskdale Manse; and a contribution to the restoration of Green Gables in Cavendish after the 1998 fire.

In Japan, one of the ways in which Anne clubs have chosen to learn about the Western lifestyle is through the study of an important variety of arts and crafts. These include making quilts, dolls, and clothing, developing a flair for Western cuisine, teatime, flower arranging, maintaining a garden Anne would relish, and much more. The learning involved sometimes allows for interesting insights. Mrs Kenmotsu, leader of the Anne Clan, studied quilt making and became very impressed with Mrs Lynde. Mrs Lynde was a 'notable housewife,' who was highly invested in Avonlea institutions, kept a sharp eye on the community's goings-on, and was able to knit sixteen 'cotton warp' quilts in addition to all this activity (*AGG* 7–8). Mrs Kenmotsu states that 'to accomplish activities that appear in the Anne series makes me aware of how great a woman Mrs Lynde is, she who creates many quilts amid her busy housework.'

The Hot Heart Anne Room, a different club altogether, concentrates exclusively on arts, crafts, and Western culture. Members are all familiar with the world of Anne, but they do not engage in other activities besides craft making. Other clubs feature experts and amateurs on specific arts and crafts reminiscent of Anne's lifestyle, but these generally remain personal activities. The works produced can be impressive. Visitors to Prince Edward Island may have seen the beautiful replica of Green Gables made of confectioner's sugar that was donated to the province after it was exhibited by Lupins club members in a commercial Anne fair in Osaka in 1992.

Anne also provides motivation for students to improve their English. Japanese university students have the option of getting involved in a wide variety of clubs on campus, one of them being the 'English Society' or a variant thereof. At different points in time in different institutions, Anne can feature prominently in these clubs' activities. For example, during the academic year 1999–2000, a section of the English Society of Nara Women's University became intensively involved in Anne as they put together an abridged stage production of the musical. They practised five days a week for months. I was indirectly involved, and there was no doubt that enthusiasm for Anne and her world fuelled the huge amount of energy expended on this project. At Toyama University in 1999, an Anne Club was formed by a group of Japanese and Canadian students. The guiding principles were as follows:

1. Let's get lovely – the heart of Anne's world! For example: an imagination that makes the world wide, and the heart feel joy sensitively, bear sadness and try to grow to dream.
2. Let's converse in living English (using) the power of imagination (and) courage (just like Anne).
3. Let's promote cultural exchange between Japan and Canada. ('Fans' 5)

The Anne Academy, a club located in southern Japan, consists of both a network of members and an English conversation school. The network, mainly a forum for those interested in Prince Edward Island, has gathered more than one thousand members over the years. The English conversation school is an institution for part-time study of English. An average of seventy students of all ages and from all walks of life attend yearly, and emphasis on Anne within the curriculum varies according to student interest. In 1993, a full-time educational institute for women of all ages, called Anne Shirley Jogakkou, was established as part of the Anne Academy. It focused on the study of English and Anne-related topics. It closed after one year because students had difficulties maintaining the full-time schedule. Although most clubs have travelled to Prince Edward Island, this particular one has organized tours to the Island two to three times a year for several years in a row. Currently, they organize one trip per year.

After the Second World War, Japan became one of the world's leading countries. As such, relations with and understanding of other countries, particularly Western ones, have taken on significant importance. 'Internationalization' is inscribed within *taishu bunka* as a priority. As a foreigner living and working for a year as an English teacher in rural Japan before starting my doctoral studies, I had to get used to the idea of being a part-time ambassador for Canada and of being constantly invited to join in 'international' activities.

Interestingly, contact with the West has motivated the creation of clubs seriously involved in researching Montgomery's world from a literary point of view; examples are the Montgomery Research Club and Buttercups. Founders created these after returning from a memorable trip to Prince Edward Island. These two clubs, in addition to the Anne Clan, have produced an impressive amount of serious research. The Montgomery Research Club investigates the work and world of writers of children's literature through conferences, participation in special events, and trips related to the author or novel being studied. The topics investigated include 'Anne's charm,' 'Comparing heroines in the Montgomery/Muraoka series,' 'A look at the plants in the series,' 'On imagination,' 'On cooking,' 'Anne, Marilla, and Matthew,' and 'Comparing Japanese translations of Montgomery' (Nakamura, 147). Of the close to thirty Japanese translations of *Anne* currently available, Mrs Hanako Muraoka's translations of the Anne series are by far the most widely read. Consequently, they are also the ones that have been the most investigated by the various clubs.

Through the years, the Anne Clan has acquired in-depth knowledge of Montgomery/Muraoka's world, and research is a main priority. A book called *Anne's Birthday Book* was published in 1984. In addition, one of Mrs Kenmotsu's personal projects in 1988 was to create a poetry book entitled *The Eighty Pearls of Anne*, a work gathering various descriptions and impressions of Anne as seen from the point of view of eighty different characters in the series. This was to commemorate the very first publication of *Anne of Green Gables* eighty years before (Kenmotsu). In 2000, the Anne Clan was researching the Emily series. An annual newsletter and collection of poems are published and regular meetings take place.

Another seriously invested club is Buttercups.[8] Buttercups created an English Web page, maintained by Mrs Yuka Kajihara of the Osborne Collection of Children's Books, in the Toronto Public Library. Buttercups publishes a bimonthly newsletter, to which I have subscribed, a regular 'Who's Who?' of members, and publications containing letters and contributions from members, information relating to Montgomery's world, and academic articles and essays; 10 per cent of members are professional writers and scholars. Reading circles and local activities are conducted in Tokyo and in the different branch offices. In June 2000, the Tokyo reading circle explored *Anne of Ingleside*, and in July the Nagoya branch analysed *The Blue Castle*. Attending a reading circle in November 1999 on *Jane of Lantern Hill*, I was very impressed with the group's professionalism. Interaction with Buttercups allowed me to see how members stay up to date on the latest Montgomery information, both abroad and in Japan. The extensive social network (150 members), the ties maintained with Canada, the social and formal gatherings, and the publications all combine to produce this result.

In 1997, a new Anne comic-book series was published, and each of the five books contained an afterword written by a different Buttercups member, one of these being Montgomery scholar Yoshiko Akamatsu. In 2000, Buttercups launched an electronic mailing list on the Internet to promote mutual friendship and exchange of ideas. It is currently restricted in access, yet it may be interesting eventually to compare this list with the Montgomery discussion lists examined by Alice van der Klei in chapter 23.

The Anne Clan and the Anne Academy have what we could call private L.M. Montgomery/Muraoka museums, replete with wonderful memorabilia related to Montgomery's world and providing access to a library. Many club members also have their own private collections, and dolls or figurines are often awarded places of honour in the home. In fact, possession of memorabilia seems important to Japanese Anne fans, and I believe further research in this respect would lead to valuable insights regarding the popularity of Anne in Japan.

Akamatsu notes that 'the feminist approach to reading *Anne of Green Gables* is not especially popular in Japan' (210).[9] In contrast, Yuko Katsura states that 'the feministic approach to the literature is now getting strong in Japan' ('Reception' 42), and Ochiai recalls that in the seventies she gladly welcomed feminism in patriarchal Japan: 'Reading works again with the eyes of a feminist critic, there are new discoveries to be made, which is one of the charms of the Anne series' (41). Indeed, the existence of Anne's Group – the only club whose main objective is to foster equality between men and women – clearly shows that feminist readings of the novel are being performed. The club's name was suggested by Mrs Akemi Murakami, a club member and a children's author. The club's logo features a drawing of Anne (figure 22.1).

22.1   Anne's Group logo, Tokushima, Japan, 2000. Photograph courtesy of Noriko Seo.

Although this group does not research L.M. Montgomery's world *per se*, members are familiar with it, and a spirit of Anne seems to animate them. Here are excerpts of letters written in English that I have received from Mrs Noriko Seo, editor of the group's publication *Anne's News*:

> Anne is very popular in Japan. Our leader likes her very much. And so do we. The way of Anne's life is positive and this encourages us. She always tries to overcome any trouble, and women's discrimination. Japan's society is men's society still now. The right of women is not equal to that of men. We would like to improve Japan's society. We learned women should have rights and power like men in Canada. Anne is the symbol of powerful women, too.

Mrs Matsufuji of the Anne Academy also states that 'Anne is just a wonderful person for us Japanese because women feel trapped. She can do anything, which is what we want to do' (quoted in Trillin, 220). Moreover, in a personal interview, Mrs Yasuko Yaoi, sixty years old, explained to me that Anne opened windows on how life could be different for a woman. Anne's mere existence filled her with hope, especially for future generations. 'Nobody may tell you this overtly,' she added, 'but I'm telling you that many women my age thought this inside.' These women introduced their daughters to Anne. The subversive Montgomery who camouflaged a subtle agenda of empowerment within the traditional romance genre has not been lost in translation.

Anne of Green Gables immediately became a smashing success following its publication fifty years ago in Japan. Anne is now a widely known figure throughout the country. She is fully integrated into Japanese *taishu bunka* and, given the nature of *taishu bunka*, she belongs to neither 'high' nor 'low' culture. Anne clubs are one manifestation of her obvious presence in Japan, and club members take pride in belonging and contributing to their respective associations. Clubs imply the creation of Anne-related communities. Montgomery's nature descriptions have also touched a very sensitive chord in many Japanese readers (cf Baldwin, 127–8), and Anne's awe of the Snow Queen, the cherry tree she could see from her bedroom window at Green Gables, is not difficult to imagine for people who have long appreciated the exquisite blossoms spring brings. Furthermore, commercial Anne fairs and public events featuring Anne and Montgomery take place fairly regularly in Japan. Buttercups was associated with a major commercial Anne exhibit in a Tokyo department store (Sogo) in 1983 and Lupins with one in Osaka in 1992 (Hankyu). The Lupins club actually puts on one public event every year in the Kansai area, which includes the cities of Osaka, Kobe, and Kyoto. In March 2000, I attended a combined Lupins/Land Trust event at which L.M. Montgomery's granddaughter, Ms Luella Veijlainen, was the guest of honour.

Japan has learned much about Canada through Anne. I applauded Prime Minister Chrétien when he publicly acknowledged this fact in Tokyo in September 1999 by awarding Mrs Muraoka, through her two granddaughters, Eri and Mie Muraoka, a certificate of distinction in a grand ceremony celebrating seventy years of Canada–Japan relations (figure 22.2). In this new millennium, it may now be Canada's turn to learn more about Japan. Will Anne of Red Hair be one of the guides along the journey?

22.2   Team Canada Gala with (left to right) Eri Muraoka, Danièle Allard, P.E.I. Premier Patrick Binns, and Mie Muraoka, Tokyo, Japan, September 1999. Private photograph.

Appendix

Anne Clubs in Japan

The following information is based on data obtained from club representatives in June 2000. It does not show fluctuations in number of members or activities over the years. Clubs are listed in chronological order of founding.

The Anne Clan (An o Shiru Ichizoku) (1973): 100 members; Saitama prefecture. Leader and founder: Mrs Kazue Kenmotsu. Activities: Literary research, publications, and newsletter; arts, crafts, and Western lifestyle; Anne as a philosophical guide.

Buttercups (1981): 150 members; Tokyo, with branch offices. Leader: Mrs Kahoru Kishikawa. Activities: Literary research, publications, and newsletter; preservation of Canadian heritage; presence on the Internet; fairs and events.

Anne Academy (1989): Current network of 300 members, 70 students in the English school; Fukuoka prefecture. Leader and founder: Mrs Kiyomi Matsufuji. Activities: Study of English; yearly trips to Canada.

Montgomery Research Club (1991): 17 members; Nagano prefecture. Accessed through Koma Shoten bookstore. Activities: Literary research (this club is not currently focusing on L.M. Montgomery, but their research work is available upon request).

The Japan P.E.I. Society (1992): Tokyo. Founders: Mr Akira Hotai and Mr Masaru Onuma. Acitivities: Dissemination of general and specific information regarding Prince Edward Island and L.M. Montgomery and her works; presence on the Internet.

Lupins (1992): 35 members; Osaka. Leader and founder: Ms Aoi Nozawa. Activities: Fairs and events; newsletter related to Canada and Montgomery.

Hot Heart Anne Room (1993): 6 members; Kanagawa prefecture. Leader: Mrs Keiko Nakamura. Activities: arts and crafts.

Anne's Group (An no Kai) (1997): 16 members; Tokushima prefecture. Leader and founder: Mrs Harumi Motoki. Activities: Activities and publications related to female empowerment.

L.M. Montgomery Land Trust – Japan Branch (1999): 50 members; Osaka (Lupins and Land Trust members largely overlap). Leader: Ms Aoi Nozawa. Activities: Preservation of Canadian heritage.

Nara Women's University – Toyama University (1999–2000): 12 members; Nara and Nagano prefectures. Activities: Study of English.

Notes

I would like to thank the government of Japan for a scholarship that enabled me to research and write this study, and all who generously provided help and feedback with this chapter including Winfried Slemerling and Yoshiko Fujita.
1 In the 1950s, Professor Kato was a Rockefeller Fellow at both Harvard University and the University of Chicago. In the course of his career, he has often represented the Japanese government in international conferences and has conducted field work in Japan, Canada, England, the United States, New Zealand, and the South Pacific Islands (Kato, 27; Powers and Kato, 348).
2 In *Handbook of Japanese Popular Culture*, a book written in English, Kato actu-

ally uses 'popular culture' rather than *taishu bunka* in his writing, after he has explained that *taishu bunka* does not have an accurate English equivalent. For the purpose of this article, I have chosen to use the Japanese expression in order to maintain the sense that *taishu bunka* is specific to Japan.

3 As Calvin Trillin states: 'Of course, it is well known that the Japanese are regularly gripped with intense enthusiasm for any number of things that Westerners think of as distinctly non-Japanese – fifties doo-wop or bluejeans or Peter Rabbit.' He mentions the Japanese infatuation with Audrey Hepburn (213).

4 See Reischauer's chapter 13, 'The Group.'

5 I am indebted to Mrs Yuka Kajihara of the Osborne Collection of Children's Books, Toronto Public Library, for drawing my attention to the Toyama University Club and introducing me to members of Buttercups.

6 This point has been made before; see Akamatsu, 207; Baldwin, 127; and Katsura 'Reception' 43.

7 The address is *www.lares.dti.ne.jp/~pei-club/english.htm.*

8 Mrs Kajihara has kindly provided information on Buttercups and has translated some of the Japanese quotations. She has also corroborated information regarding some of the other clubs. See *www.yukazine.com* for the Buttercups English-language home page.

9 See also Stoffman, 'Anne in Japanese Popular Culture': 'in the country of her birth Anne is a model of female self-respect and assertiveness, a feminist before her time. But this reading is rejected in Japan' (56). In contrast, Fawcett states: 'Montgomery's characters and plots reconfirm rather than question traditional definitions of the role of Japanese society' (quoted in Trillin, 220).

Chapter 23

Avonlea in Cyberspace, Or an Invitation to a Hyperreal Tea Party

ALICE VAN DER KLEI

'... Oh, Marilla, can I use the rosebud spray tea-set? ... I can just imagine myself sitting down at the head of the table and pouring out the tea,' said Anne, shutting her eyes ecstatically.

– Montgomery, *Anne of Green Gables* (135)

I pour myself a cup of tea, sit down at my desk, turn on the computer, hook on to the Internet, and begin to read my e-mail messages with a warm sense of anticipation. *Voilà*: I am in the hyperreal world of Avonlea. Numerous users of the electronic highways go through these rituals at least twice a day as they enter their e-mail lists. Those signed up to any of the many discussion lists will find their mailboxes flooded with friendly, connecting, and often emotionally charged messages. There is the immediate intimacy of friends here, as Kindred Spirits share their love of Anne and Emily, pictures, and their reader responses to Montgomery's fiction and the films of her books. They also share their personal stories, tales about their pets, and their ecstasies and tragedies – e-mail narratives soliciting understanding and friendly support.

There are myriad electronic discussion lists, many of them informal and unmoderated, with members from all walks of life following the discussion threads that often take us far away from the Montgomery focus. There is the Avonlea Village Mailing List, founded in May 1998, with currently 245 members; members discuss the *Road to Avonlea* series itself, but also welcome any tangential discussion (or TAN, in hyperspace lingo) and 'flights of fancy,' as the welcoming page tells the visiting guest (*http://homepages.infoseek.com/~avonlea_village*). There is the Emily of New Moon Mailing List, founded in September 1998, currently with 60 members. There is the Kindred Spirits List, founded April 1998, currently with 83 members. And there is the Kindred Spirits List at the University of Prince Edward Island, launched in 1994, currently with 466 members (based on Web page information on 27 March 2001, *kind_spirits@upei.ca*). All the lists invite their guests to an international conversation, with members from Canada, the United States, Britain, Germany, Finland, Sweden, Japan, New Zealand, Australia, and so on. The only list with severely limited membership access is the L.M. Montgomery List, moderated at the University of Toronto, its Web page beginning, in fact, with a disclaimer that it is not intended for 'students and casual researchers.' Perhaps it was in response to the chattiness of the other lists, where a sense of non-scholarly intimacy and privacy dominates in chats that often revolve around everyday occurrences, that the L.M. Montgomery List was conceived as a home for the 'discussion of scholarly and academic topics.' Indeed, so determined was the L.M. Montgomery List to keep the chatters out of its exclusive club that it limited membership to those who have published scholarly articles. No hyperrealist tea parties here!

My discussion, then, focuses on the lists with open memberships where, in addition to updates about the movies and threads about Montgomery-related research projects, the Montgomery aficionado may receive a message like this:

> Kindred teas are another popular activity in Kindredland. Tea, you ask? Well, okay, so we generally don't truly have tea, but we just like the sound of it. There have been many such get-togethers of kindreds in various parts of the United States and Canada and many members will try to meet on Prince Edward Island to hold on to what makes Avonlea just the way Lucy Maud Montgomery described it by using the term 'Kindred spirits' to define the bond of friendship between people of similar interests. (*http://webpages.marshall.edu./~irby1/kindred.html*)

These twenty-first-century electronic pen pals like to dream about dresses with puffed sleeves and indulge in sweet childhood memories. It is interesting to note that *Victoria Magazine* in the United States regularly features an advertisement for the *Kindred Spirits* magazine. Yet such Victorian-style fantasies and tea invitations are only seemingly anachronistic: they are sent out by many young members hungry for traditions and thirsting for intimacy and meaningful connection. And they take charge in building community.

In their posts, pen pals copy Montgomery's style and, like Anne, identify themselves by noting a belonging to a specific place. They sign their posts with their name, often followed by that of an imaginary place, such as Autumn Hill, Whispering Sands, Fir Grove, Pansy Palace, Big Smoke, Grasshopper Falls, Turtle Bay, High Winds, Treasuryland, Shaken Pine, Crystal of the Valley, Red Barns, or even Windom Gables or Gray Gables. Despite these flights of fancy, the last two letters of their e-mail addresses often give away their real-life location (ca = Canada; de = Germany; se = Sweden; jp = Japan, and so on). Reading this myriad of e-mails from different corners of the globe, we marvel at this urge of Montgomery fans to sip a cup of virtual tea while slipping on an Anne T-shirt or straw hat and thus changing identities. Chatting on the Net with other 'connected Kindred Spirits' in a Virtual Reading Room makes like-minded people come together and allows them to talk and live the hyperreality of their favourite fictional world. This is 'Anne of Cyber Gables,' a new space that clearly would not be possible without the relentless transformation of the world into a globally networked and computer-literate universe. In this technologically advanced globe, the craving for a hyperreal Green Gables space makes these faithful Montgomery readers communicate with each other and come back for more.

The story of Anne in cyberspace has only begun to be told by cultural-studies scholars. This field of research is still in its infancy. In a 1998 article entitled 'Montgomery's Island in the Net: Metaphor and Community on the Kindred Spirits E-mail,' Jason Nolan, Jeff Lawrence, and Yuka Kajihara use as their case study the Kindred Spirits List (launched in 1994) to distinguish three stages of formation of the e-mail community. They write: 'Whereas original members were primarily wedded to discussions focussing directly on Montgomery's works and life, interest shifted to [...] what became known as TANs or tangential discussions of personal issues. Members talked about shows they watched, personal events, triumphs, tragedies, and discussed tea parties and other kindredly activities' (66). This community is vibrantly alive, as these authors emphasize: 'The goal is often to construct a meaningful social and virtual environment that reflects or reconstructs a literary environment and then communicate in real time as if you were a character in a living novel' (Nolan et al., 67). Impersonating a character in a novel or enacting a fictional plot may be what many participants desire, but they also desire more. In addition to their search for community, I argue, they long for something *beyond reality.*

The electronic mailers are enjoying an odyssey in *hyperreality,* a term coined by the Italian theorist Umberto Eco. In his landmark collection of essays, *Travels in Hyperreality* (1986), Eco comments upon fake worlds, such as wax museums and Disneyland, in the American cultural landscape, where visitors are given a reproduction of a famous person or a fake work of art so real and powerful that visitors no longer feel any need or desire to see the original. Hyperreality, according to Eco, connects the fake and the genuine. Similarly, the French philosopher Jean Baudrillard, commenting on simulacra and simulations in postmodern work, argues that modern consumer society is often out of touch with the real. The electronic media use the hyperreal to replace and reproduce the lost realm of the real. In the proliferation of simulated worlds, the hyperreal space opened up by the Internet presents a vast range of communication options in which only our imagination limits our abilities. From Baudrillard's perspective, distance disappears into immediacy, and presence becomes a state of simultaneity where we can save the principle of reality by regenerating our imagination and creating our own reality (*Simulacres et Simulations* 10).

Translating traditional reading-room activities into an on-line environment, Montgomery fans become involved in Internet communities. In cyberspace, the participants actively create an emotionally charged space. By finding people with similar interests, they claim the electronic space to generate a powerful, nostalgic sense of home and feeling of homecoming for themselves. They use the fictional world as their springboard, a world they transform in the here and now of their computer screen and their daily interaction. Whereas in Baudrillard's dystopian interpretation of the media there is no room for communication, the many Montgomery-inspired lists have developed into very busy and cosy towns that lead lives of their own by thriving on both fiction and reality.

In this hyperreal world, then, what exactly is the connection with the original text that sparked the community? The 'original' comprises both the books and the spin-off films, for it is the films that have sparked many of the lists. Bringing *Anne of Green Gables* to life in cyberspace is not primarily prompted by a desire to remember a folkloric past. It is often prompted by the desire to revive an emotionally charged childhood and adolescent reading or viewing experience, the source of memories so vivid that they may be recalled in the reader's

23.1   Betsy Jones (third from the left) has invited 'kindreds' from Florida and Oklahoma to a tea party in Dallas, Texas, 1999. Photograph courtesy of Betsy Jones.

imagination at a later stage of life in a new space. Alongside the commercial websites, there are numerous personal Web pages hosted by fans dedicated to the promotion of their favourite author and fictional characters, as well as the e-mail correspondences dedicated to L.M. Montgomery, through all of which electronic letter writers seek to recreate a feeling, an idea, and an imaginary world. Judging by the number of messages received daily, it is the intensity and loyalty of these pen pals that allow this hyperrealistic world to live.

Pouring the Tea

What begins in the hyperreal space of quotidian e-mail threads often eventually prompts the list members to leave their computers for face-to-face gatherings in tea houses (figure 23.1). These 'Kindred Teas' take the form sometimes of semi-formal teas, sometimes of casual lunches. Calls for tea parties regularly flash on my computer screen; they are organized in my home city of Montreal, Canada; in Texas, U.S.A.; and even in Sydney, Australia. After the tea party, Montgomery fans come back to their virtual diary and report the events to other list members who do not live in the area and so could not attend. They nevertheless form a community, each member assuming citizenship in a large virtual village, the simulated literary space and cyberspace. Take Betsy Jones's post for instance:

Date: Mon, 26 Mar 2001 14:25:04 -0400 (AST)
Sender: kind_spirits@upei.ca
To: Multiple recipients of list <kind_spirits@upei.ca>
Subject: KS Dallas tea report

ANNE'S BIRTHDAY PARTY TEA REPORT
Seven of us met for tea last Saturday at the Simple Pleasures Tea Room in Grapevine, Texas, which is one of the many cities in the Dallas/Fort Worth metroplex area. It was a rainy, blustery day outside but warm and inviting inside the tea room – I know I had a lovely time!

Attending were myself, Christy Danger, Melissa Prycer, Barbara of the Bluebonnets, Carolyn Mitchem, Kathleen Boaz and Barbara, a friend of Kathleen. We enjoyed tea, orange-almond scones (with lemon curd or raspberry jam and Devonshire cream), blueberry mini muffins, three finger sandwiches (curried chicken, tuna and vegetable) and then topped that off with Texas brownies and bread pudding with caramel sauce. Yummy!

After tea, we exchanged Anne's birthday gifts. Each person was asked to bring something Anne-related (and with the Anne quote when possible) for exchange. It was such fun to see what each person came up with – what a creative bunch we have! The gifts included the following:

A potted lavender plant and lavender candle (for Miss Lavender, of course!)
A blank book journal with Susan Branch's lovely watercolor illustrations, including a green gabled house, and tea stickers
A miniature herbarium with seeds ... I only remember that there were forget-me-not seeds but there were several varieties and it looked like such fun!
A tea set including a 2 cup tea pot, mug, teas, cookies, etc.
A pair of miniature pictures of Victorian tea pots
An ice cream bowl, recipe for homemade ice cream and an AGG pencil
A slate with carrots gracing each corner and 'Kindred Spirits are not as scarce as I once thought' written in chalk.

It was a lovely day and we've decided to make this an annual event. Hope to see more of you next year!
All the best, Betsy in Dallas

These meetings are thus archived in an attempt to translate hyperreality into reality. Indeed, the practice instils collective memory, reinforcing social cohesion by an emotional belonging to the group.

Another list member replies to another tea party with this thread highlighting her sense of virtual community:

Date: Tue, 27 Mar 2001 02:59:02 -0400 (AST)
Sender: kind_spirits@upei.ca
To: Multiple recipients of list <kind_spirits@upei.ca>
Subject: No Tea For Me

I am here in Virginia, and mourning the fact that there aren't any kindred teas in my area. Being a poor college student limits my travel, so I can't pop up to Canada or anything :-) I hope that you continue to have them and to have a wonderful time! keep the stories coming! It's nice to know that the kindred spirit is still alive and well!
Meg of Silver Maples

On the Internet, L.M. Montgomery fans have made a new path that leads to the imaginary Avonlea. By reading and writing together while sipping virtual and real tea, the pen pals on electronic mailing lists transcend the boundaries of regions and culture, as they come together in order to discuss, as they put it, 'kindredly stuff.' They are reminiscing and recycling information that creates a collective memory for those who enjoy writing about the books by L.M. Montgomery and Prince Edward Island. These correspondences are often reading comments as if they were participating in a kind of book club, with a book of the month to read. But the stories also include personal biographies and birthday wishes.

Kindred identity is just the most recent of many permutations of Montgomery's legacy. As Anne Shirley says: 'Kindred spirits are not so scarce as I used to think. It's splendid to find out there are so many of them in the world' (AGG 174). This quotation often recurs in Kindred Spirits electronic posts. The motto is apt. And so is Anne's fantasized tea party in the epigraph, as she 'imagine[s] [her]self sitting down at the head of the table and pouring out the tea,' an apt metaphor for the tea-sipping Montgomery fan on the Internet. For the twenty-first-century Kindred Spirit, the imagining and re-imagining of Green Gables space often happens in front of a computer screen, a new space of preserving and of permutating the fictional world of L.M. Montgomery.

Epilogue: A Letter from Germany

BEATE NOCK

From L.M. Montgomery in cyberspace, this epilogue returns us to old-style epis-tolary art. In a personal letter, Beate Nock describes her discovery of Montgomery as an adult in her hometown of Altensteig in the Black Forest in Germany. I first met Beate Nock in August 1999 in the airport in Reykjavik, Iceland, when our planes were delayed for many hours; in follow-up correspondence, she told me that she was reading Montgomery. So intimate and poetic were her reflections that I encouraged her to write more, as I was interested in learning more about her German and European perspective on Montgomery. She sent me a fifteen-page letter, which made for such interesting reading that I decided to excerpt and translate it for this epilogue.

Altensteig, 11 March 2001

Dear Irene,

I finally want to write out my thoughts about 'Anne.' On a rainy Sun-day like today, which is supposed to put an end to this winter that never was, I find a few moments' time.

I am now reading *Anne's House of Dreams* and still marvel today at the circuitous routes through which these beautiful narratives have finally reached me. When I first travelled to the eastern coast of Can-ada, now almost two years ago, I knew very little about the Maritimes. I was drawn to P.E.I., whereas Peter, my husband, preferred New Brunswick. In some of the brochures, I had seen a few photos of P.E.I. which spoke to me – that was all. The first few days we spent in Nova Scotia in a lonely and rugged environment. I was not unhappy to leave it, enjoying the ferry ride and the first impressions of P.E.I. The Island

E1   Beate Nock, Altensteig, 2001. Private photograph.

was like a ray of sunshine that felt good. (In retrospect I think that
Anne must have felt this way after her difficult and hard time in Nova
Scotia.)

It was beautiful to drive along the large fields, past gentle hills and
compact forests, and again and again spotting the colourful barns
which spread like blossoms on a green summer meadow across the
Island. I absorbed the lovely landscape on our drive to Charlottetown.
I was surprised by Charlottetown's cultural and historical flair, which
reminded me of home in Altensteig (figure E.1): I had finally arrived!
The beautiful northern towns and the sea made this feeling of *Heimat*
even more complete. I was a little surprised, though, to see how much
Cavendish was geared towards tourism, as there was no escaping the
omnipresent signs of 'Anne of Green Gables' and 'Avonlea' at every
street corner. This was my first connection with Anne and, unfortunately, my aversion about such 'commodification' was stronger than
my curiosity. I felt overpowered by it and preferred to spend my time
in nature, at the seashore, swimming and always fascinated by the

colours of the evening sky. In short, I absorbed the beauty of the Island with all my senses, and Anne walked past me unrecognized.

Today, of course, I regret my perhaps overly hasty conclusion that commodification had rendered Anne less valuable or even worthless. For Anne is too meaningful, too deep, and too much a solid part of this Island. And she is more: she embodies the sensuality of the Island. I did not travel to the Island to trace her steps, and did not leave inspired by her existence to learn more about her. Instead I chose a third path to meet her. It was over coffee at my home in Altensteig; with me were Heather, a friend from New Zealand, and Marcy, from New York. Heather told us about L.M. Montgomery and said she had wonderful videos based on the novels. Whereupon Marcy said that she had purchased the entire set of Anne volumes in Japan (she had worked there for a year) and had brought them with her to Altensteig; she was happy to lend them to me. Anne thus had to travel around the hemisphere in order to meet me! Yet I appreciated her all the more. From the first page on, she captivated and fascinated me, drawing me into her orbit of feeling. I was sure I had found the best way to meet her. I already had a first-hand conception of the Island (albeit a limited one), of the people, the houses, nature. Through her thoughts P.E.I. came alive again. She gives a voice to the beauty of the island, express-ing that beauty in brilliantly imaginative verbal imagery that awak-ened in me (and probably in other readers) a profound longing: *Sehnsucht* to do as she does. That is, in the modern reader she touched the quality that so affected the fictional characters of Green Gables a hundred years ago: the ability to express her feelings, to translate them into words and into *deeds*, and thereby make them come alive in the reader's senses and soul. (Probably also the reason why Japanese women are so drawn to her, as this ability remains uncultivated in Japanese education.)

With Anne, the personification of Life itself moves into Green Gables. Green is the colour of the new beginning, a symbol for birth. For Matthew, she is a positive experience with the female sex which he has so carefully avoided all his life; for Marilla, she is a mirror, a paral-lel life. Through Anne, Marilla recognizes the mistakes she has made in her life, her inability to express feelings, her false pride. Living-through-Anne (*sie mit-er-lebte Anne*), Marilla achieves a peace of soul, filling the empty spaces of her hungry life. Anne enters Green Gables like a fresh spring wind that sweeps through the spaces of an old building and fills the rooms with life in a myriad of forms: flowers, blossoming twigs, laughter, and joy. It is a spring wind that drives the musty scents out of the closets. She blows away the old idea that life has to be hard and has to be met with a fierceness, an attitude that inevitably leads to hardness against oneself and to bitterness. Anne shows that everybody has the capacity for happiness and the right to love. She senses love in all beautiful things; she has an open eye and heart for the sunshine that transforms the surface of water into a thousand stars; and she sees even the tiniest blossom that moves towards the sun with the first ray of spring; and yes, through this very ability to experience the world through her senses – happiness always comes to her.

There was a change in Anne, though, that I noticed in particular in *Anne's House of Dreams*. There intruded a feeling of resignation, of giving up, yes, even something like bitterness. And I could not help but notice my sense of disappointment that she – the carrier of female-centred values within her patriarchally defined context – seemed to give up. Surely we cannot see the death of her baby, a girl, as symbolic for the fact that such female-centred values had to fail during her time. (O. Edwards and J. Litster read this issue from a political perspective as reflecting the madness of the First World War.) [...] I see Anne's life at Four Winds Harbour as a significant departure. Montgomery's nature symbolism – the rough sea, the fog, the roaring seashore – bombards Anne literally with the roughness of life that is also reflected in the fate of Leslie Moore. And yet, female-centred values resurface in this book, most notably with Miss Cordelia.

I hope that Anne will be able to maintain her lightheartedness, her curiosity, openness, ingenuousness, and her ability to give of herself. I hope that she will be able to preserve in herself the female-centred values which she embodies with so much freshness and which are so often dismissed as merely feminine values. Even today, women often assimilate male values in order to survive in the world of men instead of enriching themselves through their own values. Anne, I hope, will remain true to herself.

And now I want to close, dear Irene, and hope that I could inspire you with my thoughts. Of course, these written thoughts express only a fraction of what I would like to express but I would like to talk with you more about L.M. Montgomery ...

Yours, Beate.

Translated from the German by Irene Gammel.

Works Cited

I. L.M. Montgomery's Published Work

Akin to Anne: Tales of Other Orphans. Ed. Rea Wilmshurst. Toronto: McClelland and Stewart, 1988.

Along the Shore: Tales by the Sea. Ed. Rea Wilmshurst. Toronto: McClelland and Stewart, 1989.

The Alpine Path: The Story of My Career, 1917. Markham, ON: Fitzhenry and Whiteside, 1997.

Among the Shadows: Tales from the Darker Side. Ed. Rea Wilmshurst. Toronto: McClelland and Stewart, 1990.

Anne of Avonlea. 1909. Toronto: McClelland–Bantam, 1992.

Anne of Green Gables. 1908. Toronto: McClelland and Stewart, 1992.

Anne of Ingleside. 1939. Toronto: McClelland–Bantam, 1983.

Anne of the Island. 1915. Toronto: McClelland–Bantam, 1992.

Anne of Windy Poplars. 1936. Toronto: McClelland–Bantam, 1992.

Anne's House of Dreams. 1917. Toronto: McClelland–Bantam, 1992.

The Annotated Anne of Green Gables. Ed. Wendy E. Barry, Margaret Anne Doody, Mary E. Doody Jones. New York: Oxford UP, 1997.

The Blue Castle. 1926. Toronto: McClelland–Bantam, 1988.

Chronicles of Avonlea. 1912. Toronto: McClelland–Bantam, 1987.

Emily Climbs. 1925. Toronto: McClelland and Stewart, 1989.

Emily of New Moon. 1923. Toronto: McClelland and Stewart, 1989.

Emily's Quest. 1927. Toronto: McClelland and Stewart, 1989.

The Green Gables Letters: From L.M. Montgomery to Ephraim Weber, 1905–1909. Ed. Wilfrid Eggleston. Toronto: Ryerson, 1960.

L.M. Montgomery's Ephraim Weber: Letters 1916–1941. Ed. Paul Gerard Tiessen and Hildi Froese Tiessen. Waterloo, ON: MLR Editions, 1999.

My Dear Mr. M.: Letters to G.B. MacMillan from L.M. Montgomery. Ed. Francis W.P. Bolger and Elizabeth R. Epperly. Toronto: Oxford UP, 1992.

Rilla of Ingleside. 1920. Toronto: McClelland–Bantam, 1992.

The Road to Yesterday. Toronto: McGraw-Hill Ryerson, 1974.

The Selected Journals of L.M. Montgomery. Vol. 1. *1889–1910.* Ed. Mary Rubio and Elizabeth Waterston. Toronto: Oxford UP, 1985.

The Selected Journals of L.M. Montgomery. Vol. 2. *1910–1921.* Ed. Mary Rubio and Elizabeth Waterston. Toronto: Oxford UP, 1987.

The Selected Journals of L.M. Montgomery. Vol. 3. *1921–1929.* Ed. Mary Rubio and Elizabeth Waterston. Toronto: Oxford UP, 1992.

The Selected Journals of L.M. Montgomery. Vol. 4. *1929–1935.* Ed. Mary Rubio and Elizabeth Waterston. Toronto: Oxford UP, 1998.

II. L.M. Montgomery's Unpublished Work

'Book Sales Record Book.' L.M. Montgomery Collection, University of Guelph. X21 MS A098042.

Unpublished Scrapbooks. Confederation Centre Art Gallery and Museum. Charlottetown, Prince Edward Island. *CM67.5.11; CM67.5.12; CM67.5.14; CM67.5.15; CM67.5.18; CM67.5.24.*

Unpublished Scrapbooks. L.M. Montgomery Papers, U of Guelph Archives. XZ5 MS A002.

Unpublished Scrapbooks, 2 vols with red covers: vol. 1, *ca* 1910–13; vol. 2, *ca.* 1913–26. L.M. Montgomery Collection, U of Guelph. X25 MS A002.

Unpublished Scrapbooks, 1 vol. containing reviews, *ca* 1911–36. L.M. Montgomery Collection, U of Guelph. X25 MS A003.

III. Adaptations: Film, Television, Drama, Musical, Animation

Akage no An (*Anne of Green Gables*). TV Series. Dir. Isao Takahata. Nippon Animation, Fuji Television Network Inc., 1979.

Akage no An (*Anne of Green Gables*). TV Series Laserdiscs. 13 vols. Bandai Visual. March 1986–June 1988.

Anne of Green Gables. Dir. Kevin Sullivan. Writ. Kevin Sullivan and Joe Wiesenfeld. Sullivan Films. 1985.

Anne of Green Gables: The Continuing Story. Writ. Kevin Sullivan and Laurie Pearson. Dir. Stefan Scaini. Sullivan Films. 2000.

Anne of Green Gables: The Sequel. Writ. and dir. Kevin Sullivan. Sullivan Films. 1987.

Campbell, Elaine, Norman Campbell, Don Harron, and Mavor Moore. *Anne of Green Gables: The Musical.* 1970. New York and Toronto: Samuel French, 1972.

Campbell, Norman. *Anne of Green Gables: Song Album.* New York: Chappell, 1969.

Charlottetown Festival Production. *Anne of Green Gables.* Perf. Susan Cuthbert, Elizabeth Mawson, and Peter Mews. Cond. Fen Watkin. Charlottetown Festival Orchestra. ATTIC, ACD 1225, 1984.

Emily of New Moon. 'Falling Angels.' Canadian Broadcasting Corporation. 22 Feb. 1998.

Emily of New Moon. 'Paradise Lost.' Canadian Broadcasting Corporation. 1 Feb. 1998.

Igarashi, Yumiko. *Akage no An* (*Anne of Green Gables*). Tokyo: Kumon Shuppan, 1997–8. (A series of 3 animated videos)

– *An no aijo* (*Anne of the Island*). Tokyo: Kumon Shuppan, 1998. (Translation of *Anne of the Island* with colour illustrations)

Ledoux, Paul. *Anne.* Toronto: Playwrights Canada Press, 1999.

Miyazaki, Hayao, and Isao Takahata, Dir. *Akage no An* (*Anne of Green Gables*). Newtype Illustrated Collection. Illust. Tokyo: Kadokawa Shoten, 1992. (Colour picturebook from animated Anne TV show)

– '*Akage No An*': *Tokuma Anime Ehon* ('*Anne of Green Gables*': *Tokuma Anime Picturebook*). Tokyo: Tokuma Shoten, 1996. (Hard-cover animated storybook)

– *Akage no An* (*Anne of Green Gables*). World Masterpiece Theater TV Series. Nippon Animation: Fuji Television Network Inc., 1979. (Animated 100-min. movie adaptatation)

– *Akage no An* (*Anne of Green Gables*), vols. 1–5. Videocassettes. Tokyo: Shinchosha, 1992. (Colour animated re-released video series)

– 'Anime Bukku (Book): "Akage no An."' (Anne of Green Gables), vols. 1–5. Shinchosha, 1992.

– 'Tokuma Anime Ehon: "Akage No An"' (Tokuma Anime Picturebook: 'Anne of Green Gables'). Tokuma Shoten, 1996.

Road to Avonlea. Episode I.1/1: 'The Journey Begins.' Dir. Paul Shapiro. Writ. Heather Conkie. Sullivan Films/CBC/Disney, 1990. Videocassette. *Road to Avonlea, Volume 1.* Astral Communications, 1990.

Road to Avonlea. Episode I.4/4: 'The Materializing of Duncan.' Dir. Don McBrearty. Writ. Heather Conkie. Sullivan Films/CBC/Disney, 1990. Videocassette. *Road to Avonlea: Secrets and True Love.* Sullivan Releasing, 1996.

Road to Avonlea. Episode I.7/7: 'Conversions.' Dir. Stuart Gillard. Writ. Patricia

Watson. Sullivan Films/CBC/Disney, 1990. Videocassette. *Road to Avonlea, Volume 5*. Astral Communications, 1990.

Road to Avonlea. Episode II.2/25: Dir. Don McBrearty. Writ. Suzette Couture. Sullivan Films/CBC/Disney, 1991. Videocassette. *Road to Avonlea: Misfits and Miracles*. Sullivan Releasing, 1996.

Road to Avonlea. Episode VI.4/69: 'Comings and Goings.' Dir. Eleanore Lindo. Writ. Deborah Nathan. Sullivan Entertainment/CBC/Disney, 1994. CBC broadcast, 5 Feb. 1995.

Sullivan, Kevin, and Laurie Pearson. *Anne of Green Gables: The Continuing Story*. Screenplay, 2000.

Tales from Avonlea, Volume 1: The Journey Begins. Dir. Paul Shapiro and Dick Benner. Writ. Heather Conkie and Suzette Couture. Sullivan Films/CBC/Disney, 1990. Videocassette. Walt Disney Home Video, 1993.

IV. Illustrated Book Covers and Visual Art

Emily Och Hennes Vänner dust jacket. Swedish translation of *Emily of New Moon*. Np: Gleerups, 1956.

Emily van de Nieuwe Maan dust jacket. Dutch translation of *Emily of New Moon*. Haarlem: H.D. Tjeenk, 1924.

Emily's Eerzucht dust jacket. Dutch translation of *Emily's Quest*. Haarlem: H.D. Tjeenk, 1928.

Kirk, M[aria] L[ouise]. *Emily Climbs* cover illustration. Toronto: McClelland and Stewart, 1925.

– *Emily of New Moon* cover illustration. Toronto: McClelland and Stewart, 1923.

– *Emily's Quest* cover illustration. Toronto: McClelland and Stewart, 1927.

Laurell, Eva. *Emily Pa Egna Vägar* dust jacket. Swedish translation of *Emily Climbs*. Np: Gleerups, 1957.

Rutherford, Erica. *L.M. Montgomery*. 1997. Watercolour painting. 10 in. × 24 in. Charlottetown, Private Collection.

Turner, Stanley Francis. *Emily Climbs* dust jacket. Cavendish edition. Toronto: McClelland and Stewart, 1939.

V.   L.M. Montgomery and Popular Culture: Secondary Sources

Adams, Oscar Fay. *Post Laureate Idylls*. Boston: Lothrop, 1886.

Åhmansson, Gabriella. *A Life and Its Mirrors: A Feminist Reading of L.M. Montgomery's Fiction*. Vol. 1. Uppsala, Sweden: Almquist and Wiksell International, 1991.

– 'Textual/Sexual Space in *The Blue Castle:* Valancy Sterling's "Room of Her Own."' *Harvesting Thistles.* Ed. Rubio. 146–54.

Akamatsu, Yoshiko. 'Japanese Readings of *Anne of Green Gables.*' *L.M. Montgomery and Canadian Culture.* Ed. Gammel and Epperly. 201–12.

Alcott, Louisa May. *Little Women.* 1868. Ed. Elaine Showalter. New York: Penguin, 1989.

Allard, Danièle. Interview with Yasuko Yaoi. Mar. 2000.

Anne of Green Gables Store website. http://www.peionline.com/anne/other4.htm (2000).

'An no Yumei Duku shika Sutori- Raifu o Motomete.' *Polka* 6 (1992): 10–14.

Anderson, Benedict. *Imagined Communities: Reflections on the Origin and Spread of Nationalism.* London: Verso, 1983.

'Anne of Green Gables Controversy.' *Edmonton Journal* 2 June 2000: A19.

'Anne of Green Gables Licensing Authority.' *The Official Website of Prince Edward Island, Canada. http://www.gov.pe.ca/anne/license.php3* (Nov. 2000).

Anonymous. 'Why Did They Have to Differ so Radically from L.M.M.'s Work?' Rev. of *Anne of Green Gables: The Sequel.* Dir. Kevin Sullivan. 8 Nov. 1998. *The Internet Movie Database. http://us.imdb.com* (20 Dec. 2000).

'Anti-academic Rant.' Letter to the editor. *Globe and Mail* 6 June 2000: A18.

Arnold, Matthew. 'Tristram and Iseult.' *Empedocles on Etna and Other Poems.* London: B. Fellowes, 1852.

Atherton, Tony. 'CBC, CTV Shows Suffer Huge Viewer Declines.' *Ottawa Citizen* 30 Apr. 1998: A1, A3.

– 'Kevin Sullivan Veers from Road to Avonlea.' *Montreal Gazette* 7 Jan. 1996: F2.

Atwood, Margaret. 'Reflection Piece – Revisiting Anne.' *L.M. Montgomery and Canadian Culture.* Ed. Gammel and Epperly. 222–6.

– *Survival: A Thematic Guide to Canadian Literature.* Toronto: Anansi, 1972.

Austen, Jane. *Love and Freindship [sic].* 1790. Ed. Juliet McMaster et al. Edmonton: Juvenilia Press, 1995.

'Avonlea Traditions Inc: Character Builder: Kathryn Gallagher Morton.' *Chatelaine* 69. 4 (Apr. 1996): 44.

Bakhtin, Mikhail. *Problems of Dostoevsky's Poetics.* Trans. and ed. Caryl Emerson. Minneapolis: U of Minnesota P, 1984.

Balázs, Béla. *Theory of the Film: Character and Growth of a New Art.* Trans. Edith Bone. London: Dennis Dobson, 1952

Baldwin, Douglas. 'L.M. Montgomery's *Anne of Green Gables*: The Japanese Connection.' *Journal of Canadian Studies* 28.3 (1993): 123–33.

Balibar, Etienne. 'The Nation Form: History and Ideology.' *Race, Nation, Class:*

Ambiguous Identities. Ed. Etienne Balibar and Immanuel Wallerstein. London: Verso, 1991. 86–106.

Baudrillard, Jean. *Simulacres et Simulations*. Paris: Galilee, 1981.

Bawden, Jim. '*Anne of Green Gables: The Sequel*.' Rev. of *Anne of Green Gables: The Sequel* Dir. Kevin Sullivan. *Toronto Star* 5 Dec. 1987: F1, F12.

– 'Women Cop Top Emmys.' *Toronto Star* 22 Sept. 1986: D1.

Bell, Elizabeth, Lynda Haas, and Laura Sells, ed. and intro. *From Mouse to Mermaid: The Politics of Film, Gender, and Culture*. Bloomington: Indiana UP, 1995. 1–17.

The Bend in the Road: An Invitation to the World and Work of L.M. Montgomery. CD-ROM. Charlottetown: L.M. Montgomery Institute, 2000.

Benjamin, Walter. 'The Task of the Translator.' *Illuminations*. Trans. Harry Zohn. 1955. New York: Schocken Books, 1969.

Bentley, D.M.R. 'Charles G.D. Roberts and William Wilfred Campbell as Canadian Tour Guides.' *Journal of Canadian Studies* 32.2 (Summer 1997): 79–99.

Berg, Temma F. '*Anne of Green Gables*: A Girl's Reading.' *Children's Literature Association Quarterly* 13.3 (Fall 1988): 124–8.

Berger, Carl. 'The True North Strong and Free.' *Nationalism in Canada*. Ed. Peter Russell. Toronto: McGraw-Hill 1966.

Bertens, Hans. *The Idea of the Postmodern*. London and New York: Routledge, 1995.

Bhabha, Homi K. 'DissemiNation: Time, Narrative and the Margins of the Modern Nation.' *Nation and Narration*. Ed. Homi K. Bhabha. London: Routledge, 1990. 291–322.

Blakey, Bob. 'P.E.I.'s Spirited Redhead Returns.' Rev. of *Anne of Green Gables: The Sequel*. Dir. Kevin Sullivan. *Calgary Herald* 2 Dec. 1987: D1.

Bloch, Mark. 'Japan's Anime Earns U.S. Fans.' *ABC NewsWorld* 15 Apr. 1997.

Bloom, Harold. *Shakespeare: The Invention of the Human*. New York: Riverhead Books, 1998.

Bluestone, George. *Novels into Film: The Metamorphosis of Fiction into Cinema*. 1957. Berkeley: U of California P, 1968.

Boire, Gary. 'Canadian (Tw)ink: Surviving the Whiteouts.' *Essays on Canadian Writing* 35 (Winter 1987): 1–16.

'Books of the Century: One Hundred Years of Globe Reviews.' *Globe and Mail* 27 Nov. 1999: D16–17.

Boone, Mike. '*Anne of Green Gables* Big Winner at Geminis.' *Montreal Gazette* 5 Dec. 1986: D1.

– 'Follow Road to Avonlea for Good Family Viewing.' *Montreal Gazette* 2 Dec. 1990: F2.

- 'Road to Avonlea Series Takes Viewers Back to Anne-land.' *Montreal Gazette* 7 Jan. 1990: F1.
Bourdieu, Pierre. *Distinction: A Social Critique of the Judgement of Taste*. Cambridge, MA: Harvard UP, 1984.
- *Language and Symbolic Power*. Ed. John B. Thompson. Trans. Gino Raymond and Matthew Adamson. Cambridge, MA: Harvard UP, 1991.
- *The Field of Cultural Production*. Ed. and trans. Randal Johnson. New York: Columbia UP, 1993.
Boyum, Jay Gould. *Double Exposure: Fiction into Film*. New York: Universe, 1985.
Brennan, Patricia. 'Disney Offers "Green Gables" Sequel.' *Washington Post* 17 May 1987: Y5.
Brogan, Daniel. 'Megan Follows Grows Up with "Anne" Role.' *Chicago Tribune* 19 May 1987: 5: 5.
Brontë, Charlotte. *Jane Eyre*. 1847. Ed. Jane Jack and Margaret Smith. Oxford: Clarendon Press, 1969.
Brooymans, Hanneke. 'Did Our Anne of Green Gables Nurture Gay Fantasies? Or Has a Professor Had Too Many Sips of Marilla's Cordial?' *Edmonton Journal* 26 May 2000: A3.
Brown, E.K. 'The Problem of a Canadian Literature.' *Responses and Evaluations: Essays on Canada*. Ed. David Staines. Toronto: McClelland and Stewart, 1977. 1–23.
Buckley, Jerome Hamilton. *Seasons of Youth: The Bildungsroman from Dickens to Golding*. Cambridge, MA: Harvard UP, 1974.
Buss, Helen. 'Decoding L.M. Montgomery's Journals / Encoding a Critical Practice for Women's Private Literature.' *Essays on Canadian Writing* 54 (1992): 80–99.
'Buttercups.' *Kaiho* 21 (1996).
Campbell, Marie C. 'Lucy Maud Montgomery.' *Children's Books and Their Authors*. Ed. Anita Silvey. New York: Houghton, 1995. 466.
- 'Wedding Bells and Death Knells: The Writer as Bride in the Emily Trilogy.' *Harvesting Thistles*. Ed. Rubio. 137–45.
Campbell, Murray. 'The Week.' *Globe and Mail* 3 June 2001: A10.
Campbell, William Wilfred. *The Beauty, History, Romance and Mystery of the Canadian Lake Region*. Toronto: Musson, 1910.
Cawelti, John G. *Adventure, Mystery, and Romance: Formula Stories as Art and Popular Culture*. Chicago: U of Chicago P, 1976.
- 'The Writer as Celebrity: Some Aspects of American Literature as Popular Culture.' *Studies in American Fiction* 5 (1977): 161–74.

Chambers, D. Laurance. 'Tennysoniana.' *Modern Language Notes* 18.8 (Dec. 1903): 227–33.

Cixous, Hélène. 'The Laugh of the Medusa.' Trans. Keith Cohen and Paula Cohen. *Signs: Journal of Women in Culture and Society* 1.4 (1976): 875–93.

Clarkson, Adrienne. 'Foreword.' *L.M. Montgomery and Canadian Culture*. Ed. Gammel and Epperly. ix–xii.

Collins, Richard. *Culture, Communication and National Identity: The Case of Canadian Television*. Toronto: U of Toronto P, 1990.

Cooper, James Fenimore. *The Last of the Mohicans*. 1826. Illust. N.C. Wyeth. New York: Charles Scribner's Sons, 1947.

Coulbourn, John. 'Redhead Bleached.' *Toronto Sun* 8 Apr. 1998: 52.

Craig, Timothy J., ed. *Japan Pop! Inside the World of Japanese Popular Culture*. Armonk, NY: M.E. Sharpe, 2000.

Cuff, John Haslett. 'Slick *Anne* Sequel Takes No Chances with Success.' Rev. of *Anne of Green Gables: The Sequel*. Dir. Kevin Sullivan. *Globe and Mail* 5 Dec. 1987: C5.

Currie, Dawn H. *Girl Talk: Adolescent Magazines and Their Readers*. Toronto: U of Toronto P, 1999.

Davey, Frank. 'The Hard-Won Power of Canadian Womanhood: Reading *Anne of Green Gables* Today.' *L.M. Montgomery and Canadian Culture*. Ed. Gammel and Epperly. 163–82.

Davidhazi, Peter. 'Cult and Criticism: Ritual in the European Reception of Shakespeare.' *Literature and Its Cults: An Anthropological Approach*. Ed. Peter Davidhazi and Judit Karafiath. Budapest: Argumentum, 1994. 29–45.

Davidson, Lars. 'On the Road to Avonlea ... the Island Footage.' *Atlantic Advocate* Mar. 1991: 9– 10.

Deacon, W.A. *Poteen: A Pot-Pourri of Canadian Essays*. Ottawa: Graphic, 1926.

Deakin, Basil. '*Anne* "Quite Irresistible."' Rev. of *Anne of Green Gables*. Dir. Kevin Sullivan. *Halifax Chronicle-Herald* 30 Nov. 1985: 44.

Dickens, Charles. *Dombey and Son*. 1847–8. Ed. Peter Fairclough. Harmondsworth: Penguin Books, 1979.

Dilthey, Wilhelm. *Introduction to the Human Sciences*. Ed. and intro. Rudolf Makkreel and Frithjof Rodi. Princeton, NJ: Princeton UP, 1989.

Donovan, Josephine. *New England Local Color Literature: A Women's Tradition*. New York: Frederick Ungar, 1983.

Doody, Margaret Anne. 'Introduction.' Montgomery, *The Annotated Anne of Green Gables*. Ed. Barry et al. 9–34.

Doucet, Jane. 'New Moon Rising.' *Elm Street* Nov.–Dec. 1997: 22–30.

Drain, Susan. 'Community and the Individual in Anne of Green Gables: The

Meaning of Belonging.' *Children's Literature Association Quarterly* 11.1 (1986): 15–19.

– '"Too Much Love-Making": *Anne of Green Gables* on Television.' *The Lion and the Unicorn: A Critical Journal of Children's Literature* 11.2 (1987): 63–72.

Drew, Lorna. 'The Emily Connection: Ann Radcliffe, L.M. Montgomery and "The Female Gothic."' *CCL: Canadian Children's Literature/Littérature canadienne pour la jeunesse* 77 (1995): 19–32.

Dufort, Lynn. 'Sharon Pollock Talks about Her New Work.' *Foothills* 2.2 (1986): 3–5.

Eco, Umberto. 'Towards a Semiotic Inquiry into the TV Message.' *Working Papers in Cultural Studies* 3 (Autumn 1972): 103–21.

– *Travels in Hyperreality: Essays*. San Diego: HBJ Publishers, 1986.

Edwards, Owen Dudley. 'L.M. Montgomery's *Rilla of Ingleside*: Intention, Inclusion, Implosion.' *Harvesting Thistles*. Ed. Rubio. 126–36.

Edwards, Owen Dudley, and Jennifer H. Litster. 'The End of Canadian Innocence: L.M. Montgomery and the First World War.' *L.M. Montgomery and Canadian Culture*. Ed. Gammel and Epperly. 30–46.

Eliot, George. *The Mill on the Floss*. 1860. Ed. A.S. Byatt. Harmondsworth: Penguin, 1979.

Elsaesser, Thomas. 'Tales of Sound and Fury: Observations on the Family Melodrama.' *Film Theory and Criticism: Introductory Readings*. 1974. New York: Oxford UP, 1992. 512–35.

Epperly, Elizabeth R. 'Approaching the Montgomery Manuscripts.' *Harvesting Thistles*. Ed. Rubio. 74–83.

– *The Fragrance of Sweet-Grass: L.M. Montgomery's Heroines and the Pursuit of Romance*. Toronto: U of Toronto P, 1992.

Everett-Green, Robert. 'Glenn Gould, Growth Industry.' *Globe and Mail* 18 Sept. 1999: C5.

Faludi, Susan. *Backlash: The Undeclared War against American Women*. New York: Crown, 1991.

'Family Hour.' *TV Guide* 9 Sept. 1989: 11.

'Fans of Anne (of Green Gables) in Japan Start Their Own "Anne Club."' *Kindred Spirits* (Autumn 1999): 5.

Fawcett, Clare, and Patricia Cormack. 'Guarding Authenticity: L.M. Montgomery Tourist Sites.' *Annals of Tourism Research* 28.3 (2001): 686–704.

Feltes, Norman. *Literary Capital and the Late Victorian Novel*. Madison: U of Wisconsin P, 1993.

Ferns, W. Paterson. 'Co-production.' *Making It: The Business of Film and Television Production in Canada*. Ed. Barbara Hehner and Andra Sheffer. Toronto: Doubleday Canada, 1995. 253–71.

Fisher, Jennifer. 'Life after Anne.' *TV Guide* 6 Jan. 1990: 16–17.

Fiske, John. *Reading the Popular*. London: Routledge, 1991.

– *Television Culture*. London: Routledge, 1987.

– *Understanding Popular Culture*. London: Routledge, 1989.

Fiske, John, and John Hartley. *Reading Television*. London and New York: Methuen, 1988.

Fitzgerald, F. Scott. 'Bernice Bobs Her Hair.' 1920. *The Stories of F. Scott Fitzgerald*. Ed. Malcolm Cowley. New York: Charles Scribner's Sons, 1954. 39–60.

Flaherty, David H., and Frank E. Manning, ed. *The Beaver Bites Back: American Popular Culture in Canada*. Montreal and Kingston: McGill-Queen's UP, 1993.

Flynn, Richard. 'Imitation Oz: The Sequel as Commodity.' *The Lion and the Unicorn* 20.1 (1996): 121–36.

Foster, Shirley, and Judy Simons. '*Anne of Green Gables*.' In *What Katy Read: Feminist Re-readings of 'Classic Stories' for Girls*. Iowa City: U of Iowa P, 1995.

Francis, Daniel. *National Dreams: Myth, Memory, and Canadian History*. Vancouver: Arsenal Pulp P, 1997.

Freire, Paulo. *Pedagogy of the Oppressed*. Trans. Myra Bergman Ramos. New York: Herder and Herder, 1970.

Frever, Trinna S. 'Vaguely Familiar: Cinematic Intertextuality in Kevin Sullivan's *Anne of Avonlea*.' *CCL: Canadian Children's Literature/Littérature canadienne pour la jeunesse* 91/92. 24.3/4 (Fall/Winter 1998): 36–52.

Frow, John. *Cultural Studies and Cultural Value*. Oxford: Oxford UP, 1995.

Fulford, Robert. 'Anne's Secret Quality Keeps Her Coming Back.' Rev. of *Anne of Green Gables: The Sequel*. Dir. Kevin Sullivan. *Toronto Star* 5 Dec. 1987: F1.

Fuller, Danielle. Rev. of *L.M. Montgomery and Canadian Culture. ARIEL: A Review of International English* 31.3 (July 2000): 180–4.

Gammel, Irene, ed. and intro. *Confessional Politics: Women's Sexual Self-Representations in Life Writing and Popular Media*. Carbondale: Southern Illinois UP, 1999.

– '"My Secret Garden": Dis/Pleasure in L.M. Montgomery and F.P. Grove.' *English Studies in Canada* 25 (1999): 39–65.

– 'The Visual and Performative Diaries of L.M. Montgomery, the Baroness Elsa, and Elvira Bach.' *Interfaces: Visualizing and Performing Women's Lives*. Ed. Sidonie Smith and Julia Watson. Ann Arbor: Michigan UP, 2002.

Gammel, Irene, and Elizabeth Epperly, eds. *L.M. Montgomery and Canadian Culture*. Toronto: U of Toronto P, 1999.

– 'L.M. Montgomery and the Shaping of Canadian Culture.' *L.M. Montgomery and Canadian Culture*. Ed. Gammel and Epperly. 3–13.

Gay, Carol. '"Kindred Spirits" All: Green Gables Revisited.' *Children's Literature Association Quarterly* 11.1 (1986): 9–12.

Gerson, Carole. '"Dragged at Anne's Chariot Wheels": The Triangle of Author, Publisher, and Fictional Character.' *L.M. Montgomery and Canadian Culture.* Ed. Gammel and Epperly. 49–63.

– '"Fitted to Earn Her Own Living": Figures of the New Woman in the Writing of L.M. Montgomery.' *Children's Voices in Atlantic Literature and Culture: Essays on Childhood.* Ed. Hilary Thompson. Guelph, ON: Canadian Children's P, 1995. 24–34.

– *A Purer Taste: The Writing and Reading of Fiction in English in Nineteenth-Century Canada.* Toronto: U of Toronto P, 1989.

Gianetti, Louis. *Understanding Movies.* 6th ed. Englewood Cliffs, NJ: Prentice-Hall, 1993.

Gilbert, Sandra, and Susan Gubar. *The Madwoman in the Attic: The Woman Writer and the Nineteenth-Century Literary Imagination.* New Haven: Yale UP, 1979.

Gillispie, Julaine. 'American Film Adaptations of *The Secret Garden*: Reflections of Sociological and Historical Change.' *The Lion and the Unicorn* 20.1 (1996): 132–52.

Giroux, Henry A. 'Memory and Pedagogy in the "Wonderful World of Disney": Beyond the Politics of Innocence.' *From Mouse to Mermaid.* Ed. Bell, Haas, and Sells. 43–61.

Gitter, Elisabeth G. 'The Power of Women's Hair in the Victorian Imagination.' *PMLA* 99.5 (Oct. 1984): 936–54.

Gittings, Christopher. Telephone interview with Linda Jackson. 7 May 1998.

– Telephone interview with Marlene Matthews. 3 Nov. 1997.

Gledhill, Christine. 'Melodrama.' *The Cinema Book.* Ed. Pam Cook. London: British Film Institute, 1985.

– 'The Melodramatic Field: An Investigation.' *Home Is Where the Heart Is: Studies in Melodrama and the Woman's Film.* Ed. Christine Gledhill. London: British Film Institute, 1987. 5–39.

Glickman, Susan. *The Picturesque and the Sublime: A Poetics of the Canadian Landscape.* Montreal and Kingston: McGill-Queen's UP, 1998.

Grant, George Monro, ed. *The Easternmost Ridge of the Continent. Historical and Descriptive Sketch of the Scenery and Life in New Brunswick, Nova Scotia, and Prince Edward Island.* Chicago: Alexander Belford, 1899.

– *Picturesque Canada: The Country as It Was and Is.* 3 vols. Toronto: Belden Bros., 1882.

Gray, J.M. 'Images from Malory in the Lady of Shalott.' *Tennyson Research Bulletin* 2.5 (Nov. 1976): 210–11.

Greenhill, Pauline. *True Poetry: Traditional and Popular Verse in Ontario.* Montreal and Kingston: McGill-Queen's UP, 1989.

Greenhill, Ralph, and Andrew Birrell. *Canadian Photography: 1839–1920*. Toronto: Coach House P, 1979.

'The Greening of an Old Favourite.' *Atlantic Books Today* 27 (Winter 1999): 10.

Grescoe, Paul. *The Merchants of Venus: Inside Harlequin and the Empire of Romance*. Vancouver: Raincoast, 1996

Griffith, James. *Adaptations as Imitations: Films from Novels*. Newark: U of Delaware P, 1997.

Groen, Rick. '*Anne*'s a Winner of Hearts.' Rev. of *Anne of Green Gables*. Dir. Kevin Sullivan. *Globe and Mail* 30 Nov. 1985: D1.

Gruneau, Richard, and David Whitson. *Hockey Night in Canada: Sports, Identity, and Cultural Politics*. Toronto: Garamond, 1993.

Gubar, Marah. '"Where Is the Boy?" The Pleasures of Postponement in the *Anne of Green Gables* Series.' *The Lion and the Unicorn* 25.1 (2001): 47–69.

Gunew, Sneja. *Framing Marginality: Multicultural Literary Studies*. Australia: Melbourne UP, 1994.

Gwyn, Sandra. 'The Emily Effect.' *Elm Street* (Nov.–Dec. 1997): 71–80.

Halliday, F.E. *The Cult of Shakespeare*. London: Gerald Duckworth, 1957.

Hamilton, Kathleen, and Sibyl Frei. *Finding Anne on Prince Edward Island*. Charlottetown: Ragweed Press, 1991.

Harbison, Robert. *The Built, the Unbuilt and the Unbuildable: In Pursuit of Architectural Meaning*. Cambridge, MA: MIT P, 1994.

Hardy, Thomas. *The Woodlanders*. 1887. Ed. Ian Gregor. Harmondsworth: Penguin, 1987.

Hartmann, Sadakichi. *The Valiant Knights of Daguerre: Selected Critical Essays on Photography and Profiles of Photographic Pioneers*. Ed. Harry W. Lawton, George Knox, and Wistaria Hartmann Linton. Berkeley: U of California P, 1978.

Hassett, Constance W., and James Richardson. 'Looking at Elaine: Keats, Tennyson, and the Directions of the Poetic Gaze.' *Arthurian Women: A Casebook*. Ed. Thelma S. Fenster. New York: Garland, 1996. 287–303.

Hayward, Susan. 'Melodrama.' *Key Concepts in Cinema Studies*. London and New York: Routledge, 1996.

Hearne, Betsy. 'Disney Revisited, Or, Jiminy Cricket, It's Musty Down Here!' *Horn Book Magazine* 73.2 (1997): 137–46.

Henry, O. 'The Gift of the Magi.' *The Complete Works of O. Henry*. New York: Garden City Publishing, 1937. 8–12.

Higgins, Laura. 'Snapshot Portraits: Finding L.M. Montgomery in her "Dear Den."' *Harvesting Thistles*. Ed. Rubio. 101–12.

Higson, Andrew. 'Re-presenting the National Past: Nostalgia and Pastiche in the Heritage Film.' *Fires Were Started: British Genres and Thatcherism*. Ed. Lester Friedman. Minneapolis: U of Minnesota P, 1993. 109–29.

Holderness, Graham. 'Bardolatry; or, The Cultural Materialist's Guide to Stratford-upon-Avon.' *The Shakespeare Myth*. Ed. Graham Holderness. Manchester: Manchester UP, 1988. 2–15.

– 'Boxing the Bard: Shakespeare and Television.' *The Shakespeare Myth*. Ed. Graham Holderness. Manchester: Manchester UP, 1988. 173–89.

Hornby, Jim. *Black Islanders: Prince Edward Island's Historical Black Community*. Charlottetown: Institute of Island Studies, 1991.

Horne, Fred. 'Green Gables House Report.' *Manuscript Report Series No. 352*. Ottawa: Parks Canada, 1979.

'How Green Were Anne's Gables?' Editorial. *Globe and Mail* 3 June 2000: A14.

Hubler, Angela E.'Can Anne Shirley Help "Revive Ophelia"? Listening to Girl Readers.' *Delinquents and Debutantes*. Ed. Inness. 266–84.

Hutcheon, Linda, and Marion Richmond, eds. *Other Solitudes: Canadian Multicultural Fictions*. Toronto: Oxford UP, 1990.

Inness, Sherrie A., ed. *Delinquents and Debutantes: Twentieth-Century American Girls' Cultures*. New York and London: New York UP, 1998.

– ed. *Nancy Drew and Company: Gender, Culture, and Girls' Series*. Bowling Green: Bowling Green State UP, 1997.

'Is Anne of Green Gables Really from Sunnybrook Farm?' *National Post* 10 Apr. 1999: A1.

Jenkins, Henry. *Textual Poachers: Television Fans and Participatory Culture*. New York: Routledge, 1992.

Johnson, Brian D., Barbara MacAndrew, and Ann Shortnell. 'Anne of Green Gables Grows Up.' *Maclean's* 7 Dec. 1987: 46–50.

Joseph, Gerard. *Tennysonian Love: The Strange Diagonal*. Minneapolis: U of Minnesota P, 1969.

Kamikawa, Terry. *Akage no An no Seikatsu Jiten* (*A Dictionary of Red-haired Anne's Daily Life: A Guide to the Good Old Days*). Tokyo: Koudansya, 1997.

Karr, Clarence. *Authors and Audiences: Popular Canadian Fiction in the Early Twentieth Century*. Montreal: McGill-Queen's UP, 2000.

Kato, Hidetoshi, ed. and trans. *Japanese Popular Culture*. 1959. Westport, CT: Greenwood P, 1973.

Katsura, Yuko. 'The Reception of *Anne of Green Gables* and Its Popularity in Japan.' *Okayama Prefectural College Faculty of Design Bulletin* 2.1 (1995): 39–44.

– 'Red-haired Anne in Japan.' *CCL: Canadian Children's Literature/Littérature canadienne pour la jeunesse* 34 (1984): 58–61.

Kearney, Mark, and Randy Ray. *The Great Canadian Book of Lists*. Toronto: Dundurn, 1999.

Kenmotsu, Kazue, 'An o Shiru Ichizoku Shusai.' *Polka* 2 (1991).

King, Susan. 'Returning to "Green Gables": It's Not "90210."' *Los Angeles Times* 22 July 2000: F6.

Knelman, Martin. 'Mickey on the Road to Avonlea.' *Financial Post Magazine* (Mar. 1996): 22+.

Kotsopoulos, Aspasia. 'Our Avonlea: Imagining Community in an Imaginary Past.' *Pop Can: Popular Culture in Canada*. Ed. Van Luven and Walton. 98–105.

Kress, Gunther, and Theo van Leeuwen. *Reading Images*. Victoria: Deakin UP, 1990.

Labbe, Jacqueline M. 'Cultivating One's Understanding: The Female Romantic Garden.' *Women's Writing* 4.1 (1997): 39–56.

Lavater, John C. *Essays on Physiognomy*. Trans. Thomas Holcroft. London: Ward Lock. n.d.

– 'Regarding *Anne*.' E-mail letter to George Belliveau. 21 Dec. 2000.

Ledoux, Trish, and Doug Ranney. *The Complete Anime Guide*. Issaquah, WA: Tiger Mountain Press, 1995.

Levine, Lawrence W. *Highbrow/Lowbrow: The Emergence of Cultural Hierarchy in America*. Cambridge, MA: Harvard UP, 1988.

Lindenberger, Herbert. *On Wordsworth's Prelude*. Princeton: Princeton UP, 1963.

Litt, Paul. *The Muses, The Masses, and the Massey Commission*. Toronto: U of Toronto P, 1992.

Logan, John D., and Donald G. French. *Highways of Canadian Literature*. Toronto: McClelland, 1924.

Longfellow, Henry Wadsworth. *Evangeline, A Tale of Acadie*. Boston: William D. Ticknor, 1847.

Lord, Barbara. Letter 'Read the Books.' *Globe and Mail* 4 Apr. 1998: D7.

Lothian, W.F. *A Brief History of Canada's National Parks*. Ottawa: Environment Canada, 1987.

Lowenthal, David. *The Past Is a Foreign Country*. Cambridge: Cambridge UP, 1986.

Lowenthal, Leo. *Literature, Popular Culture, and Society*. Englewood Cliffs, NJ: Prentice-Hall, 1961.

McCabe, Kevin, and Alexandra Heilbron, ed. *The Lucy Maud Montgomery Album*. Toronto: Fitzhenry and Whiteside, 1999.

McCallum, Robyn. 'The Present Reshaping the Past Reshaping the Present: Film Versions of *Little Women*.' *The Lion and the Unicorn* 24.1 (2000): 81–96.

McCarthy, Helen. *Anime! A Beginner's Guide to Japanese Animation*. London: Titan Books, 1993.

MacEachern, Alan Andrew. 'Discovering an Island: Travel Writers and Tourism on Prince Edward Island.' *Island Magazine* 29 (Spring/Summer 1991): 8–16.

– 'The Greening of Green Gables: Establishing Prince Edward Island National Park.' *Island Magazine* 45 (1999): 22–31.

McFarlane, Brian. *Novel to Film: In Introduction to the Theory of Adaptation.* Oxford: Clarendon, 1996.

MacFarlane, David. 'Cheap Seats.' *Globe and Mail*, 5 June 2000: R2.

Macfee, Holly. 'Drawing Out the Innocent.' *Disney Channel Magazine* (Mar./Apr. 1990): 18–22.

McGillis, Roderick. '*Anne*: The Book from the Film.' *CCL: Canadian Children's Literature/Littérature canadienne pour la jeunesse* 55 (1989): 73–5.

McHugh, Fiona. *The Anne of Green Gables Storybook.* Scarborough, ON: Firefly Books, 1987.

Mackay, Gillian. 'Bringing a Classic to the Screen.' *Maclean's* 2 Dec. 1985: 78.

McKay, Ian. *The Quest of the Folk: Antimodernism and Cultural Selection in Twentieth-Century Nova Scotia.* Montreal and Kingston: McGill-Queen's UP, 1994.

McLaren, Angus. *Our Own Master Race: Eugenics in Canada, 1885–1945.* Toronto: McClelland and Stewart, 1990.

MacLeod, Don. 'An Interview with Steven Temple – Collecting English-Canadian Literature: Boom or Bust?' *Canadian Notes and Queries* 56 (1999): 4–11.

MacLulich, T.D. 'L.M. Montgomery's Portraits of the Artist: Realism, Idealism, and the Domestic Imagination.' *English Studies in Canada* 11.4 (December 1985): 459–73.

MacMechan, Archibald. *Headwaters of Canadian Literature.* 1924. Rpt. Toronto: McClelland and Stewart (New Canadian Library), 1974.

MacPhail, Tara. Interview with Anne MacPhail. 27 Nov. 2000.

McRobbie, Angela. *Feminism and Youth Culture.* Basingstoke: Macmillan, 2000.

Malkin, Jeanette. *Memory-Theatre and Postmodern Drama.* Ann Arbor: U of Michigan P, 1999.

Malory, Sir Thomas. *The Works of Sir Thomas Malory.* Ed. Eugene Vinaver. Oxford: Clarendon, 1947.

'Many Called – But Few Chosen.' *Canadian Author and Bookman* 24.2 (June 1948): 34–42.

Marquis, Thomas Guthrie. 'English-Canadian Literature.' *Literature of Canada: Poetry and Prose in Reprint.* Ed. Douglas Lockhead. Toronto: U of Toronto P, 1973. 493–589.

Marsh, Jan, and Pamela Gerrish Nunn. *Pre-Raphaelite Women Artists.* Catalogue for the Exhibition at Manchester City Art Gallery, 1998. New York: Thames and Hudson, 1999.

Martens, Doreen. 'With Superb Cast, *Anne*'s a Joy.' Rev. of *Anne of Green Gables*. Dir. Kevin Sullivan. *Winnipeg Free Press* 30 Nov. 1985: 18.

Mason, M.S. 'Anne of Green Gables Marches Off to War.' *Christian Science Monitor* 21 July 2000: 17.

Menzies, Ian. 'The Moral of the Rose: L.M. Montgomery's Emily.' *CCL: Canadian Children's Literature/Littérature canadienne pour la jeunesse* 65 (1992): 48–61.

Miller, Judith. 'The Writer-as-a-Young-Woman and Her Family: Montgomery's Emily.' *New Quarterly* 7.1–2 (1987): 301–19.

Moers, Ellen. *Literary Women*. Garden City, NY: Anchor Books/Doubleday, 1977.

Morris, Pam. *Literature and Feminism: An Introduction*. Oxford: Blackwell, 1993.

Morris, William. *The Defence of Guenevere and Other Poems*. London: Bell and Daldy, 1858.

Mukerji, Chandra, and Michael Schudson. *Rethinking Popular Culture: Contemporary Perspectives in Cultural Studies*. Berkeley and Los Angeles: U of California P, 1991.

Munro, Alice. 'Afterword.' Montgomery, *Emily of New Moon*. 357–61.

Murphy, Rex. 'Lord T'underin' Jaysus, Anne Dealt Crack and Voted NDP.' *Globe and Mail* 2 June 2000: A11

Musselwhite, Bill. 'CBC's Version of *Anne* Would Please the Author.' Rev. of *Anne of Green Gables*. Dir. Kevin Sullivan. *Calgary Herald* 1 Dec. 1985: F1.

Nakamura, Keiko. 'Akage no An no Sekai he.' *Polka: Gakken Mook* (1993): 144–51.

Nash, Knowlton. *Cue the Elephant!: Backstage Tales at the CBC*. Toronto: McClelland and Stewart, 1996.

Nelson, Joyce. 'Kevin Sullivan's *Anne of Green Gables*.' *Cinema Canada* 126 (Jan. 1986): 35–6.

– 'When Books Become Grist for the Media Mill.' *Cinema Canada* 126 (Jan. 1986): 37.

Nicholls, Stephen. 'Road to Avonlea Benched for Hockey.' *Montreal Gazette* 27 Feb. 1990: F1.

Nin, Anaïs. *Fire, From a Journal of Love: The Unexpurgated Diary of Anaïs Nin, 1934–1937*. New York: Harcourt Brace, 1995.

Noble, John. 'Doll.' *The World Book Encyclopedia*. Vol. 5. Chicago: World Book, 1987.

Nodelman, Perry. 'Progressive Utopia: Or, How to Grow Up without Growing Up.' *Such a Simple Little Tale*. Ed. Reimer. 29–38.

Nolan Jason, Jeff Lawrence, and Yuka Kajihara. 'Montgomery's Island in the Net: Metaphor and Community on the Kindred Spirits E-mail List.' *CCL: Canadian Children's Literature/Littérature canadienne pour la jeunesse* 91/2 24:3/4 (Fall/Winter 1998): 64–77.

Nolen, Stephanie. 'Avonlea all Astir.' *Globe and Mail* 31 May 2000: A1, A7.

Ong, Walter. *Orality and Literacy: The Technologizing of the Word*. London: Routledge, 1982.

Pacey, Desmond. *Creative Writing in Canada*. 1952. Toronto: McGraw-Hill Ryerson, 1961.

Paul, Lissa. '"Enigmatic Variations": What Feminist Theory Knows about Children's Literature.' *Children's Literature: The Development of Criticism*. Ed. Peter Hunt. London: Routledge, 1990. 148–65.

Peacock, Thomas Love. *The Misfortunes of Elphin*. London: Thomas Hookham, 1829.

Perkins, David, ed. *English Romantic Writers*. 2nd ed. Fort Worth: Harcourt, Brace, and Company, 1995.

– *Is Literary History Possible?* Baltimore: Johns Hopkins UP, 1992.

Pevere, Geoff, and Greig Dymond. *Mondo Canuck: A Canadian Pop Culture Odyssey*. Scarborough, ON: Prentice Hall, 1996.

Pike, Holly. '(Re)Producing Canadian Literature: L.M. Montgomery's Emily Novels.' *L.M. Montgomery and Canadian Culture*. Ed. Gammel and Epperly. 64–76.

Poe, K.L. 'The Whole of the Moon: L.M. Montgomery's *Anne of Green Gables* Series.' *Nancy Drew and Company*. Ed. Inness. 15–35.

Postman, Neil. *The Disappearance of Childhood*. New York: Delacorte Press, 1982.

Powers, Richard Gid, and Hidetoshi Kato, eds. *Handbook of Japanese Popular Culture*. Westport, CT: Greenwood Press, 1989.

Price, Thomas. *Dramatic Structure and Meaning in Theatrical Productions*. San Francisco: Edwin Mellen P, 1992.

Radway, Janice. *A Feeling for Books: The Book-of-the-Month Club, Literary Taste, and Middle-Class Desire*. Chapel Hill: U of North Carolina P, 1997.

– *Reading the Romance: Women, Patriarchy, and Popular Literature*. Chapel Hill: U of North Carolina P, 1984.

Reimer, Mavis, ed. *Such a Simple Little Tale: Critical Responses to L.M. Montgomery's 'Anne of Green Gables.'* Metuchen, NJ: Children's Literature Association and Scarecrow P, 1992.

Reischauer, Edwin O. *The Japanese Today*. Cambridge, MA: Belknap P of Harvard UP, 1988.

Rhodenizer, V.B. 'Who's Who in Canadian Literature,' *Canadian Bookman* (Aug. 1927): 227–8.

Rich, Adrienne. 'Compulsory Heterosexuality and Lesbian Existence.' *Adrienne Rich's Poetry and Prose*. 1980. Ed. Barbara Charlesworth Gelpi and Albert Gelpi. New York: Norton, 1993. 203–24.

Ricketts, Shannon. 'Cultural Selection and National Identity: Establishing Historic Sites in a National Framework, 1920–1939.' *The Public Historian* 18.3 (1996): 23–41.

Ricks, Christopher, ed. *The Poems of Tennyson in Three Volumes*. 2nd Ed. Berkeley: U of California P, 1987.

Robinson, Laura M. '"A Born Canadian": The Bonds of Communal Identity in *Anne of Green Gables* and *A Tangled Web*.' *L.M. Montgomery and Canadian Culture*. Ed. Gammel and Epperly. 19–30.

– 'Bosom Friends: Lesbian Desire in L.M. Montgomery's Anne Books.' Paper presented at the Congress of the Humanities and Social Sciences, University of Alberta, 25 May 2000.

– 'ACCUTE and the Media: Bosom Friends?' *ACCUTE Newsletter* June 2000: 37–9.

– '"Pruned Down and Branched Out": Embracing Contradiction in Anne of Green Gables.' *Children's Voices in Atlantic Literature and Culture: Essays on Childhood*. Ed. Hilary Thompson. Guelph, ON: Canadian Children's P, 1995. 35–43.

Rooney, Frances. *Working Light: The Wandering Life of Photographer Edith S. Watson*. Ottawa: Carleton UP, 1996.

Rootland, Nancy. *Anne's World, Maud's World: The Sacred Sites of L.M. Montgomery*. Halifax: Nimbus P, 1996.

Roper, Gordon S., Ross Beharriell, and Rupert Schieder. 'Writers of Fiction, 1880–1920.' *Literary History of Canada*. Gen. ed. Carl F. Klinck. Toronto: U of Toronto P, 1965.

Ross, Catherine Sheldrick. 'Readers Reading L.M. Montgomery.' *Harvesting Thistles*. Ed. Rubio. 23–55.

Rubin, Joan Shelley. *The Making of Middlebrow Culture*. Chapel Hill: U of North Carolina P, 1992.

Rubio, Mary Henley. '*Anne of Green Gables*.' *The Oxford Companion to Canadian Theatre*. Ed. Eugene Benson and L.W. Conolly. Toronto: Oxford UP, 1989. 24–5.

– '"A Dusting Off": An Anecdotal Account of Editing the L.M. Montgomery Journals.' *Working in Women's Archives: Researching Women's Private Literature and Archival Documents*. Ed. Helen M. Buss and Marlene Kadar. Waterloo, ON: Wilfrid Laurier UP, 2001. 51–78.

– 'L.M. Montgomery: Scottish-Presbyterian Agency in Canadian Culture.' *L.M. Montgomery and Canadian Culture*. Ed. Gammel and Epperly. 89–105.

– 'Subverting the Trite: L.M. Montgomery's "Room of Her Own."' *CCL: Canadian Children's Literature/Littérature canadienne pour la jeunesse* 65 (1992): 6–39.

Rubio, Mary Henley, ed. *Harvesting Thistles: The Textual Garden of L.M. Montgomery. Essays on Her Novels and Journals*. Guelph, ON: Canadian Children's P, 1994.

Rubio, Mary Henley, and Elizabeth Waterston. *Writing a Life: L.M. Montgomery.* Toronto: ECW P, 1995.

Said, Edward W. *Culture and Imperialism.* 1993. New York: Vintage, 1994.

St Germain, Pat. 'Queen Anne.' *Winnipeg Sun.* 5 March 2000. On-line.

Salamon, Julie. 'Anne Faces a Messy World Far from Green Gables.' *New York Times* 22 July 2000: B7, B15.

Sayers, Dorothy L. *Strong Poison.* 1930. London: New English Library, 1977.

Schickel, Richard. *Intimate Strangers: The Culture of Celebrity.* New York: Fromm International, 1986.

Scott MacLeod, Anne. 'American Girlhood in the Nineteenth Century: Caddie Woodlawn's Sisters,' in *American Childhood: Essays on Children's Literature of the Nineteenth and Twentieth Centuries.* Athens, GA: U of Georgia P, 1994. 3–29.

Scott, Sir Walter. *Anne of Geierstein. 1829. The Waverley Novels: Centenary Edition. Vol. 23.* Edinburgh: Adam and Charles Black, 1887.

– *Ivanhoe. 1819. The Waverley Novels: Centenary Edition. Vol. 9.* Edinburgh: Adam and Charles Black, 1886.

– *The Pirate. 1821. The Waverley Novels: Centenary Edition. Vol. 13.* Edinburgh: Adam and Charles Black, 1886.

– *Waverley. 1814. The Waverley Novels: Centenary Edition. Vol. 1.* Edinburgh: Adam and Charles Black, 1886.

'Sequel to *Anne of Green Gables* to Be Seen First on US Pay-TV.' *Vancouver Sun* 14 Feb. 1987: H7.

Shales, Tom. '"Avonlea": More from the Able "Gables" Group.' *Washington Post* 19 May 1987: C3.

Shaw, Ted. 'Return to Avonlea.' *Montreal Gazette* 9 Jan. 1994: F1.

Sheckels, Theodore F. 'Anne in Hollywood: The Americanization of a Canadian Icon.' *L.M. Montgomery and Canadian Culture.* Ed. Gammel and Epperly. 183–91.

Shelley, Mary. *Frankenstein, or, The Modern Prometheus.* 2nd ed. 1831. New York: Oxford UP, 1969.

Shields, Carol. 'Loving Lucy.' *Globe and Mail* 3 Oct. 1998: D 18.

– *The Stone Diaries.* Toronto and New York: Random House, 1993.

Shires, Linda M. 'Rereading Tennyson's Gender Politics.' *Victorian Sages and Cultural Discourse: Renegotiating Gender and Power.* Ed. Thais E. Morgan. New Brunswick, NJ, and London: Rutgers UP, 1990. 46–65, 273–6.

Shustermann, Richard. *Pragmatist Aesthetics: Living Beauty, Rethinking Art.* Oxford: Blackwell, 1992.

Simpson, Arthur L., Jr. 'Elaine the Unfair, Elaine the Unlovable: The Socially Destructive Artist/Woman in Idylls of the King.' *Modern Philology* 89.3 (Feb. 1992): 341–62.

Singard, Neil. *Filming Literature: The Art of Screen Adaptation*. London: Croom Helm, 1986.

Skidmore, Colleen. '"All That Is Interesting in the Canada's": William Notman's Maple Box Portfolio of Stereographic Views, 1860.' *Journal of Canadian Studies* 32.4 (1997–8): 69–90.

Smith, Stephen. 'Forty Great Works of Canadian Fiction.' *Quill and Quire* (July 1999): Front cover, 21–3.

Snitow, Ann Barr. 'Mass Market Romance: Pornography for Women Is Different.' *Powers of Desire: The Politics of Sexuality*. Ed. Ann Snitow, Christine Stansell, and Sharon Thompson. New York: Monthly Review P, 1983. 245–63.

Solt, Marilyn. 'The Uses of Setting in *Anne of Green Gables*.' *Such a Simple Little Tale*. Ed. Reimer. 57–63.

Sontag, Susan. *On Photography*. New York: Farrar, Straus and Giroux, 1977.

Spears, Tom. '"Outrageously Sexual" Anne Was a Lesbian, Scholar Insists.' *Ottawa Citizen* 25 May 2000: A3.

Squire, Sheila J. 'L.M. Montgomery's Prince Edward Island: A Study of Literary Landscapes and Tourist Development.' MA thesis, Carleton U, 1998.

– 'Ways of Seeing, Ways of Being: Literature, Place, and Tourism in L.M. Montgomery's Prince Edward Island.' *A Few Acres of Snow: Literary and Artistic Images of Canada*. Ed. Paul Simpson-Housley and Glen Norcliffe. Toronto and Oxford: Dundurn Press, 1992. 137–47.

Staines, David. 'King Arthur in Victorian Fiction.' *The Worlds of Victorian Fiction*. Ed. Jerome H. Buckley. Cambridge, MA: Harvard UP, 1975.

Stevenson, Deborah. 'Sentiment and Significance: The Impossibility of Recovery in the Children's Literature Canon or, The Drowning of *The Water-Babies*.' *The Lion and the Unicorn* 21.1 (1997): 112–30.

Stewart, Susan. *On Longing: Narratives of the Miniature, the Gigantic, the Souvenir, the Collection*. Durham, NC: Duke UP, 1985.

Stoffman, Judy. 'Anne in Japanese Popular Culture.' *CCL: Canadian Children's Literature/Littérature canadienne pour la jeunesse* 91/92. 24.3/4 (Fall/Winter 1998): 53–63.

Strachan, Alex. 'CBC Pulls Plug on Popular Children's Drama.' *Vancouver Sun* 13 Jan. 1996: B11.

Strinati, Dominic. *An Introduction to Theories of Popular Culture*. London: Routledge, 1995.

Strom Collins, Carolyn, and Christina Wyss Eriksson. *The Anne of Green Gables Treasury*. New York: Viking, 1991.

Sullivan, Kevin. Telephone interview with Eleanor Hersey. 23 Nov. 2000.

Sullivan, Paul. 'Same-Sex Marriage: The Good, the Bad and the Pious.' *Globe and Mail* 1 June 2000: A15.

Sullivan Entertainment. '*Road to Avonlea* Returns for Its Sixth Season.' Press release. Toronto: 1995.

Swinburne, Algernon Charles. *Tristram of Lyonesse and Other Poems*. London: Chatto and Windus, 1882.

Taylor, Kate. 'Anne of Green Gables Story Made Fresh with Adaptation.' *Globe and Mail* 9 Apr. 1998: C3.

Tennyson, Alfred, Lord. 'Lancelot and Elaine.' *Idylls of the King*. Ed. J.M. Gray. London: Penguin, 1983. 168–205.

– 'The Lady of Shalott.' *The Poems of Tennyson in Three Volumes*. 2nd ed. Ed. Christopher Ricks. Berkeley: U of California P, 1987. 387–95.

Terry, Clifford. '"Anne" Sequel Charms but Shows Its Age, Too.' *Chicago Tribune* 19 May 1987: 5: 5.

Tertius (pseud.) 'Subjects and Objects.' *Globe and Mail* 2 June 2000: R2.

Textual Studies in Canada 12 (1999) (issue dedicated to topic of hockey).

Thacker, Deborah. 'Feminine Language and the Politics of Children's Literature.' *The Lion and the Unicorn* 25.1 (2001): 3–16.

Thackeray, William Makepeace. *The Rose and the Ring*. 1855. *Christmas Books: The Biographical Edition of the Works of William Makepeace Thackeray*. Vol. 9. London: Smith, Elder, 1898.

Tompkins, Jane. *Sensational Designs: The Cultural Work of American Fiction, 1790–1860*. New York: Oxford UP, 1985.

Trillin, Calvin. 'Anne of Red Hair: What Do the Japanese See in *Anne of Green Gables*?' *L.M. Montgomery and Canadian Culture*. Ed. Gammel and Epperly. 213–21.

Turim, Maureen. *Flashbacks in Film: Memory and History*. New York: Routledge, 1989.

Turner, Margaret E. '"I mean to try, as far as in me lies, to paint my life and deeds truthfully": Autobiographical Process in L.M. Montgomery's Journals.' *Harvesting Thistles*. Ed. Rubio. 93–100.

Twain, Mark. *A Connecticut Yankee in King Arthur's Court*. New York and London: Harper, 1889.

Tye, Diane. 'Multiple Meanings Called Cavendish: The Interaction of Tourism with Traditional Culture.' *Journal of Canadian Studies* 29.1 (Spring 1994): 122–34.

'US Critics Rave over *Anne of Green Gables* Sequel.' Rev. of *Anne of Green Gables: The Sequel*. Dir. Kevin Sullivan. *Montreal Gazette* 26 May 1987: D10.

Van Luven, Lynne, and Priscilla Walton, ed. and intro. *Pop Can: Popular Culture in Canada*. Scarborough, ON: Prentice Hall Allyn and Bacon Canada, 1999.

Vipond, Mary. 'Best Sellers in English Canada, 1899–1918: An Overview.' *Journal of Canadian Fiction* 24 (1979): 96–119.

Wagner, Geoffrey. *The Novel and the Cinema*. Rutherford: Fairleigh Dickinson UP, 1995.

Wagner, Vit. 'Anne Perfect for Theatre's Blues.' *Toronto Star* 8 Apr. 1998: C2.

Walker, Barbara G. *The Woman's Encyclopedia of Myths and Secrets*. New York: Harper and Row, 1983.

Warner, Marina. *From the Beast to the Blonde: On Fairy Tales and Their Tellers*. London: Vintage, 1995.

Warren, Joyce. 'Introduction: Canons and Canon Fodder.' *The (Other) American Traditions: Nineteenth-Century Women Writers*. Ed. Joyce W. Warren. New Brunswick, NJ: Rutgers UP, 1993.

Weiss-Town, Janet. 'Sexism Down on the Farm? *Anne of Green Gables*.' *Children's Literature Association Quarterly* 11.1 (Spring 1986): 9–12.

White, Hayden. 'Historical Pluralism.' *Critical Inquiry* 12.3 (Spring 1986): 480–93.

Wiggins, Genevieve. *L.M. Montgomery*. New York: Twayne, 1992.

Wild, Leanne. 'A New "Anne" on the YPT Stage.' *CCL: Canadian Children's Literature/ Littérature canadienne pour la jeunesse* 91/92 24.3/4 (Fall/Winter 1998): 169–72.

Williams, Raymond. 'Base and Superstructure in Marxist Cultural Theory.' *Rethinking Popular Culture*. Ed. Mukerji and Schudson. 407–23.

– *Culture*. London: Fontana, 1981.

Williams, Tennessee. *The Glass Menagerie*. 1949 reprint. London: Heinemann Educational Books, 1988.

Wilmshurst, Rea. 'L.M. Montgomery's Use of Quotations and Allusions in the "Anne" Books.' *CCL: Canadian Children's Literature/Littérature canadienne pour la jeunesse* 56 (1989): 15–45.

Wirten, Eva Hemmungs. *Global Infatuation: Explorations in Transnational Publishing and Texts*. Uppsala: University of Uppsala, 1998.

Wittig, Monique. 'One Is Not Born a Woman.' *Feminist Frameworks: Alternative Theoretical Accounts of the Relations between Men and Women*. Ed. Alison M. Jagger and Paula S. Rothenberg. New York: McGraw-Hill, 1984. 148–52.

Yano, Christine. 'Charisma's Realm: Fandom in Japan.' *Ethnology* 36.4 (1997): 335–49.

Yard, Robert Sterling. *The Publisher*. Boston: Houghton Mifflin, 1913.

Yokokawa, Sumiko. 'The Forty Years of *Anne of Green Gables* in Japan.' *Teaching and Learning Literature with Children and Young Adults* (March/April 1996): 39–43.

– *'Akage No An' No Chousen*. Tokyo: Takarajimasha, 1994.

York, Geoffrey. 'On Iranian TV, Avonlea Rules.' *Globe and Mail* 4 Mar. 2000: A1+.

Zerbisias, Antonia. 'Happiness on the Road to Avonlea.' *Toronto Star* 7 Jan. 1990: C1.

Contributors

Danièle Allard has studied at Nara Women's University (1999–2000) and at the Osaka University of Foreign Languages (1998) in Japan. Her doctoral dissertation in comparative Canadian literature at the Université de Sherbrooke examined the Japanese reception of Hanako Muraoka's translation of *Anne of Green Gables*.

George Belliveau is an assistant professor of education at the University of Prince Edward Island. He has completed a doctoral dissertation on Canadian playwright Sharon Pollock's use of the memory play. A 1999 recipient of the Plant Award for a promising young scholar in Canadian drama, he has worked as an actor, director, and playwright, as well as writing theatre reviews.

Cecily Devereux teaches English-Canadian literature of the late nineteenth and early twentieth centuries at the University of Alberta. Her publications on L.M. Montgomery, Sara Jeannette Duncan, Nellie McClung, and Isabella Valancy Crawford have appeared in *Women's Studies International Forum* (1999), *Victorian Poetry* (1998), *Essays on Canadian Writing* (1998), *Victorian Review* (2000), and *CCL: Canadian Children's Literature/Littérature canadienne pour la jeunesse* (2001).

Elizabeth R. Epperly is a professor of English, founding chair of the L.M. Montgomery Institute, and a member of its advisory committee at the University of Prince Edward Island. She is the author of *The Fragrance of Sweet-Grass: L.M. Montgomery's Heroines and the Pursuit of Romance* (1992), editor of *My Dear Mr. M.* (with F.W.P. Bolger, 1980,

1992) and *L.M. Montgomery and Canadian Culture* (with I. Gammel, 1999), and creative team member for CD-ROM *The Bend in the Road: An Invitation to the World and Work of L.M. Montgomery* (2000). She has curated three exhibitions on Montgomery's work for the Confederation Centre Art Gallery and Museum, including *The Visual Imagination of Lucy Maud Montgomery* (1999).

Janice Fiamengo is an assistant professor of English at the University of Saskatchewan with a special interest in early-Canadian women writers. She is researching the socially oriented literature of Agnes Maule Machar, Flora MacDonald Denison, Marshall Saunders, and Nellie McClung and has published essays on McClung, Sara Jeannette Duncan, and Charlotte Yonge.

Irene Gammel teaches modern literature and culture at the University of Prince Edward Island. In addition to authoring many articles and chapters on issues of gender and sexuality, she is the author of *Baroness Elsa: Gender, Dada, and Everyday Modernity, A Cultural Biography* (2002) and *Sexualizing Power in Naturalism: Theodore Dreiser and Frederick Philip Grove* (1994); editor of *L.M. Montgomery and Canadian Culture* (with E. Epperly, 1999) and *Confessional Politics: Women's Sexual Self Representations in Life Writing and Popular Media* (1999). She is the past president of the Canadian Comparative Literature Association.

Carole Gerson is a professor of English at Simon Fraser University. Her extensive publications on early Canadian women writers include co-authorship of a major study of Pauline Johnson, *Paddling Her Own Canoe: Times and Texts of E. Pauline Johnson (Tekahionwake).* Currently a member of the editorial team for the History of the Book in Canada, she has written many articles that examine the social and historical contexts of Montgomery's fiction and publishing history.

Christopher Gittings teaches twentieth-century Canadian literatures and films at the University of Alberta. In addition to articles on cultural translation, gender, and popular culture, he is the author of *Canadian National Cinema(s): Ideology, Difference and Representation* (2002) and editor of *Imperialism and Gender: Constructions of Masculinity* (1996). He is the past director of the Centre for Canadian Studies at the University of Birmingham, U.K.

Eleanor Hersey is writing a doctoral dissertation on television film adaptations of novels by L.M. Montgomery, Willa Cather, and Edith Wharton at the University of Iowa. She has published articles in *The Journal of Popular Film and Television, Legacy: A Journal of American Women Writers,* and *Studies in Popular Culture.*

Ann F. Howey teaches English literature at the University of Alberta. She is the author of *Rewriting the Women of Camelot: Feminism and Arthurian Popular Fiction* (2001) and of scholarly articles on Arthurian popular fiction in *Extrapolation* and *Arthuriana.*

James De Jonge is a historian and architectural historian for Parks Canada. His chapter is adapted from reports he prepared for the Historic Sites and Monuments Board of Canada to assist in evaluating heritage sites on Prince Edward Island associated with L.M. Montgomery. He has published articles on the architectural heritage of the Royal Canadian Mounted Police and on Canadian medical history.

Alice van der Klei is completing a doctoral dissertation on hypertext and literature at the Université de Montréal. A graduate of the University of Amsterdam, she serves on the boards of the Canadian Comparative Literature Association and the Canadian Association for the Advancement of Netherlandic Studies.

Benjamin Lefebvre is a graduate student in English at the University of Guelph and co-moderator of the LMM-L Electronic List and has published articles in *CCL: Canadian Children's Literature/Littérature canadienne pour la jeunesse, Journal of Religion and Culture,* and *The Lucy Maud Montgomery Album* (1999).

Jeanette Lynes is an associate professor of English at St Francis Xavier University in Nova Scotia. She is the author of the poetry collection *A Woman Alone on the Atikokan Highway* (1999) and editor of *Words Out There: Women Poets in Atlantic Canada* (1999). Her poems are forthcoming in *Canadian Dimension, Grain,* and *The New Delta Review.*

Carrie MacLellan is a music student at the University of Prince Edward Island, specializing in music history.

Juliet McMaster is University Professor of English at the University of

Alberta. Specializing in the eighteenth- and nineteenth-century British novel, and in children's literature, she is the author of many articles and books on Thackeray, Austen, Trollope, and Dickens, and co-editor, with Bruce Stovel, of *Jane Austen's Business* and, with Edward Copeland, of *The Cambridge Companion to Jane Austen*. A fellow of the Royal Society of Canada and winner of the Molson Prize, she is also the founder and general editor of the Juvenilia Press.

Andrea McKenzie is a lecturer in writing and humanistic studies at the Massachusetts Institute of Technology. Her doctoral dissertation, 'Witnesses to War' (1999), examined the archival First World War correspondence of Vera Brittain. She has contributed a chapter on Montgomery to *Windows and Words: A Look at Canadian Children's Literature* (forthcoming).

Tara MacPhail studies English and psychology at the University of Prince Edward Island. She lives on the Argyle Shore and has a passion for Anne and Emily dolls.

Beate Nock has a degree in jewellery design and lives in Altensteig, Baden-Württemberg, Germany. Along with her interests in art and L.M. Montgomery, she is an avid letter writer.

Tara Nogler holds a Master's degree in English literature from McMaster University.

E. Holly Pike is an associate professor of English at Sir Wilfred Grenfell College, Corner Brook, Newfoundland. She is the author of *Family and Society in the Works of Elizabeth Gaskell* and has previously published on Montgomery in *Harvesting Thistles: The Textual Garden of L.M. Montgomery* (1994) and *L.M. Montgomery and Canadian Culture* (1999).

K.L. Poe is a doctoral student in English literature at Loyola University, Chicago, specializing in gender studies, culture studies, and young adult fiction for girls. Her work on Montgomery has appeared in *Nancy Drew and Company: Culture, Gender, and Girls' Series* (1997).

Margaret Steffler teaches Canadian literature at Trent University. She is book review editor for the *Journal of Canadian Studies*, author of 'The Canadian Romantic Child' in *CCL: Canadian Children's Literature/*

Littérature canadienne pour la jeunesse, and is researching Canadian women's life writing.

Brenda R. Weber's doctoral dissertation is titled, 'Writing the Woman Writing: The Ethos of Authorship in the Anglo-American Literary Marketplace, 1850–1900.' She teaches in the Honors Program at the University of Kentucky.